QP 363.3 b585 2008 4

D0722003

Blindness and Brain Plasticity in Navigation and Object Perception

TITLES OF RELATED INTEREST

Touch and Blindness: Psychology and Neuroscience
by Morton A. Heller (ed.) and Soledad Ballesteros (ed.)

Psychophysics of Reading in Normal and Low Vision
by Gordon E. Legge

Gaze-Following: Its Development and Significance
by Ross Flom (ed.), Kang Lee (ed.) and Darwin Muir (ed.)

Studies in Perception and Action VIII: Thirteenth International Conference
on Perception and Action
by Harry Heft and Kerry L. Marsh (ed.)

International Handbook of Cross-Cultural Neuropsychology
by B. P. Uzzell (ed.), Marcel O. Ponton (ed.) and Alfredo Ardila (ed.)

Measurement and Representation of Sensations
by Hans Colonius (ed.) and Ehtibar N. Dzhafarov (ed.)

Psychophysics Beyond Sensation: Laws and Invariants of Human Cognition
by Christian Kaernbach (ed.), Erich Schröger (ed.), Hermann Müller (ed.)

Plasticity in the Central Nervous System: Learning and Memory
*by James L. McGaugh (ed.), Federico Bermúdez-Rattoni (ed.),
Roberto A. Prado-Alcalá (ed.)*

Brain Plasticity and Behavior
by Bryan Kolb

Blindness and Brain Plasticity in Navigation and Object Perception

EDITED BY

John J. Rieser

Daniel H. Ashmead

Ford F. Ebner

Anne L. Corn

Lawrence Erlbaum Associates
Taylor & Francis Group

New York   London

Cover design by Tomai Maridou.

Lawrence Erlbaum Associates
Taylor & Francis Group
270 Madison Avenue
New York, NY 10016

Lawrence Erlbaum Associates
Taylor & Francis Group
2 Park Square
Milton Park, Abingdon
Oxon OX14 4RN

© 2008 by Taylor & Francis Group, LLC
Lawrence Erlbaum Associates is an imprint of Taylor & Francis Group, an Informa business

Printed in the United States of America on acid-free paper
10 9 8 7 6 5 4 3 2 1

International Standard Book Number-13: 978-0-8058-6294-2 (Softcover) 978-0-8058-5551-7 (Hardcover)

No part of this book may be reprinted, reproduced, transmitted, or utilized in any form by any electronic, mechanical, or other means, now known or hereafter invented, including photocopying, microfilming, and recording, or in any information storage or retrieval system, without written permission from the publishers.

Trademark Notice: Product or corporate names may be trademarks or registered trademarks, and are used only for identification and explanation without intent to infringe.

Visit the Taylor & Francis Web site at
http://www.taylorandfrancis.com

and the LEA Web site at
http://www.erlbaum.com

Contents

v

Color Plate Figures

Preface

The idea for this volume began when we presented a symposium titled "Blindness, Brain Plasticity and Spatial Function" at the 2001 meetings of the Society for Research in Child Development. The symposium was well received, and the presenters, Dan Ashmead, Ford Ebner, David Guth, Herb Pick, and John Rieser, were enthused about exploring connections across the topics of blindness, animal models of brain plasticity, human brain imaging, cognitive science, and rehabilitation engineering.

Around that time Vanderbilt University received a gift from the Leveritt Miller family to express appreciation for their daughter's educational experience at Vanderbilt. The family generously placed few restrictions on their gift, part of which was used as the initial funding for the workshop on which this volume is based. The organizers of this volume wish to thank the Leveritt Miller family for their support.

Our discussions centered on use-oriented research, which considers how cognitive and brain processes are modified when specific functional goals are to be accomplished in the context of restricted sensory input. Of course this issue cuts across different sensory modalities, but we chose to focus on blindness because several of us have backgrounds in that area of research. In the course of these conversations, the idea for a workshop was born.

Our next step was to solicit funding from the National Eye Institute (NEI) of the National Institutes of Health. A scientific workshop application was submitted by John Rieser, Daniel Ashmead, Ford Ebner, and Anne Corn. NEI approved the proposal (Grant U13 EY1 5005), and we benefited from guidance by the reviewers and the enthusiastic support of our program officer, Dr. Michael Oberdorfer. Additional financial support was provided by Vanderbilt University (Vanderbilt Kennedy Center for Research on Human Development; Vanderbilt Vision Research Center; Vanderbilt Center for Integrative & Cognitive Neuroscience) and Western Michigan University (Department of Blindness and Low Vision Studies). Other Vanderbilt departments that lent material support were Hearing & Speech Science; Ophthalmology and Visual Sciences; Psychology, Psychology & Human Development; and Special Education.

The workshop was held from March 11–14, 2004, at the Scarritt Bennett Center in Nashville, Tennessee. All authors whose chapters appear here made formal presentations at the workshop. Also making significant contributions through their organized discussions at the conference were Jane Erin, Michael May, Joseph Lappin, and Kay Ferrell. We express our appreciation to these participants for the uniformly high quality of their presentations, and for productive and constructive discussions. Also in attendance at the workshop were a number of graduate students, postdoctoral fellows, and representatives from several professional organizations associated with blindness, all of whom participated actively in formal and informal discussions.

We thank various individuals who have provided critical administrative support. Linda Dupré coordinated our NEI grant application. Gale Fox and Carol Wiley handled all travel arrangements and countless logistical details for lodging, meeting rooms, and social functions. Jan Rosemergy helped to coordinate the overall administrative effort, and handled publicity materials through her assistant, Stephanie Comer Newton. Nancy Huffman kept track of the budget and paid our bills. David Salisbury provided local press coverage for the workshop. Tony Maupin handled photography chores. Robert Wall Emerson coordinated all of the audiovisual tasks, including computer displays and a video record of all presentations. Kelly Lusk assisted with audiovisual services and provided Braille copies of speakers' materials. Finally, Dona Tapp served in an indispensable role as the managing editor of the volume. She made us think more clearly about the book that we wanted to create, edited chapters with the educated nonspecialist reader in mind, and cheerfully handled communications with authors.

We wish to acknowledge that there is considerable diversity in the preferred terminology for referring to blindness and other sensory losses. In this edited volume we have not imposed a uniform set of terms, instead allowing chapter authors to make their own choices. Neither the editors nor the chapter authors intend any disrespect by the terminology used. We are pleased that the authors have worked so hard to illuminate the central theme of the conference.

Blindness and Brain Plasticity in Navigation and Object Perception

I
INTRODUCTION

1

Theory and Issues in Research on Blindness and Brain Plasticity

John J. Rieser

The content of this volume is focused on perceiving, learning, and remembering about objects and environments when exploring them without vision by locomoting, touching, and listening. It is about how perception, knowledge, and action come to be coupled together in the absence of vision.

Some people who are blind or have severely impaired vision are highly effective at navigating and show high levels of skill in getting from place to place. Some are highly effective at recognizing and manipulating objects and show high levels of skill in daily life, with tools for thought (such as computer keyboards, maps, dictionaries) and tools for action (such as those used in the factory, school, and home). And some are highly effective at understanding and imagining the spatial and temporal relationships that define the areas of science and mathematics. Examples of individuals achieving high levels of effectiveness are apparent in many areas, including participation in athletics (Ponchillia, Strause, & Ponchillia, 2002), spatial orientation (Loomis, Klatzky, Golledge, Ciccinelli, & Pellegrino, 1993), and musical performance (Rauschecker & Korte, 1993). But some individuals are not highly effective. The chapters in this volume are focused on some of the causes that might underlie differences in effective spatial functioning among individuals with severely impaired vision and are aimed at developing implications for future research, education, and rehabilitation.

The content is organized around three main issues—cortical remapping, sensory substitution, and development of individual differences. The chapters were written by scientists from the brain, cognitive, developmental, and rehabilitative sciences. Each author worked to understand the skillful and not-so-skillful levels of perception, learning, and action that can be associated with blindness and visual impairment. One major goal of this volume is to integrate findings from basic research within the brain sciences with research in the cognitive and developmental sciences. The purpose is to examine the implications of findings of the brain sciences showing plasticity with findings from the cognitive and developmental sciences showing cognitive limitations, individual differences, and developmental differences. We hope the resulting discussions are useful in identifying where further research is needed and inspiring people to focus on the problems. A second major goal is to integrate the basic findings and theory from the brain and cognitive and developmental sciences with techniques and theory of the educational and rehabilitative sciences for persons with severe visual impairment. The individual chapter authors were not invited to end by listing recommendations for new methods of rehabilitation. Instead they were invited to write about their own areas of research, believing that the collection will inspire new research and technologies aimed at rehabilitation.

The purpose of this introductory chapter is to describe how the coeditors set the stage for the chapter writers and in this way provide an overview of the central disciplines and main themes of the chapters in the volume.

USE-ORIENTED RESEARCH AND THE INTERDISCIPLINARY AND MULTIDISCIPLINARY NATURE OF THE WORKS

Research orientations can be classified in many ways; for example, basic research, applied research, and mission-oriented research. A defining theme of this collection is use-oriented research. By use-oriented we mean research using scientific methods to understand how the mind and brain work, in the context of a set of practical problems. Stokes (1997) wrote about use-oriented research and focused on Louis Pasteur's research—which resulted in the technique of pasteurization of milk and led to the new field of bacteriology. This volume is focused on how mind and brain accomplish skillful navigation and object perception without vision, while focusing on the practicalities of intervention.

The issues and questions examined here originate from six professional and scientific groups, namely, animal models and brain science, human cognitive neuroscience, cognitive sciences (emphasizing perceptual, cognitive, and developmental psychology), engineering; blind education and rehabilitation, and advocacy. Many of the chapter authors participate actively in two or more of these scientific/professional groups. Findings from scientists working at three of the disciplinary intersections are featured here. One finding consists of recent research from animal models and human brain imaging and suggests that the occipital cortex of people with vision impaired from birth is recruited in nonvisual processing to a greater degree than in sighted people who wear blindfolds. A second finding consists of demonstrations that nonvisual information can, in some cases, substitute neatly for visual information in the control of some tasks. And the third finding consists of demonstrations that visual input relatively early in life may facilitate the development of some types of nonvisual spatial functioning stemming from auditory, tactual, and motor input.

BRAIN IMAGINING STUDIES DEMONSTRATING THE EXPERIENCE-DEPENDENT PLASTICITY OF THE OCCIPITAL CORTEX FOR PROCESSING TACTUAL AND AUDITORY INFORMATION

Brain imaging studies during the last 10 to 20 years have shown differences in the degree to which the occipital cortex of persons with congenitally impaired vision participates in nonvisual processing compared to the occipital cortex of blindfolded sighted persons.

For processing tactual and haptic stimuli such as reading Braille or identifying raised line Roman letter this has been shown via the use of positron emission tomography, functional magnetic resonance imagery, and transmagnetic ressonance and evoked potentials (Burton et al., 2002; Cohen et al., 1997; Melzer et al., 2001; Pascual-Leone, Wassermann, Sadato, & Hallett, 1995; Roeder, Rosler, & Neville, 2001; among others). The same methods have been used to demonstrate this for processing auditory information for spatial localization, pattern recognition, and language comprehension (Rauschecker & Korte, 1993; Roeder, Roesler, & Neville, 2000).

This body of empirical work makes it clear that the occipital cortex of people born with severely impaired vision is participating in the processing of nonvisually explored spatial inputs from touch and from audition to a greater or different degree than in sighted persons who are blindfolded. Little is known about the possible brain plasticity of persons who lost their vision after infancy or early childhood. Little is known about the possible plasticity of persons who had severe but partial losses of vision involving, for example, only their visual fields, as in the case of macular degeneration or advanced glaucoma, or their acuity and contrast sensitivity, as in the case of congenital cataracts. And finally, virtually nothing is known about the implications of such plasticity for gaining high levels of skill at spatial functioning. A major goal of this volume is to discuss what is and is not yet known, what needs to be known, and the possible implications for spatial functioning and sensory substitution.

SENSORY SUBSTITUTION AND SPATIAL FUNCTIONING

The concept of sensory substitution is that information about objects and the environment that is usually provided by one sensory modality can be supplied by other modalities. This is a fundamental basis of education and rehabilitation designed for learners who are blind or have severe visual impairment, and it is clear that touch, hearing, and motor exploration can provide information about objects and environments that many people typically glean via vision (Blasch, Wiener, & Welsh, 1997). For example, hearing can supply information that is used to steer locomotion around walls (Ashmead et al., 1998), and hearing is used as an aid to dynamic spatial orientation when people walk in unfamiliar surroundings (Easton & Bentzen, 1999). Recent quantitative research is specifying the acoustic frequencies that specify the locations of objects and the sensitivities of listeners with impaired vision to them (Ashmead, Davis, & Northington, 1995).

When people locomote, it is important for them to keep up to date on their spatial orientation, that is, the changing network of self-to-object distances and directions. When walking with vision or with severely impaired vision, people tend to rely on vision for orientation, but when walking without vision people navigate with good precision by integrating the distances walked and turned during the path of their walk (Loomis et al., 1993; Philbeck, Klatzky, Behrmann, Loomis, & Goodridge, 2001; Rieser & Pick, 2002; Thinus-Blanc & Gaunet, 1997). In addition, nonvisual cues can be used effectively to steer walking along straight lines, without unintended veering (Guth & LaDuke, 1995; Millar, 1999). When exploring new environments by walking, people not only keep up to date on their spatial orientation relative to different places along their path but they also learn the spatial layout of objects and other landmarks encountered along the way (Haber, Haber, Penningroth, Novak, & Radgowski, 1993; Rieser, Lockman, & Pick, 1980; Wanet-Defalque, Vanlierde, & Michaux, 2001).

Finally, active touch provides important information about the shapes of objects as well as the texture and rigidity of their materials (Lederman & Klatzky, 1997), faces (Kilgour & Lederman, 2002) and in addition is a good basis for reading Braille. Although it is clear that hearing, active touch, and active motor exploration can provide information to substitute for vision, what are not clear are what forms of information combine precision with range and ease of perceiving, and what accounts for individual differences in how efficiently different individuals learn to use the information.

DEVELOPMENTAL AND INDIVIDUAL DIFFERENCES IN SPATIAL FUNCTIONING AMONG PERSONS WITH SEVERE VISUAL IMPAIRMENT

As noted above, there is a broad range of individual differences in the spatial functioning of persons who are blind or have severe visual impairment (e.g. Barth & Foulke, 1979; Long & Hill, 1997), and some believe that the range of variation is greater among persons with severe visual impairment than among persons with normal vision (Warren, 1994). Rieser, Hill, and their colleagues found this to be the case in an unpublished study of the spatial orientation of 40 persons born without vision compared to 25 persons who lost vision later in childhood. The standard deviation of those with early loss of vision was nearly twice that of the late-onset group. Although the top 10 performers were equally divided across the two groups, the worst 15 performers were all congenitally blind.

In the case of some areas of nonvisual spatial functioning, the differences seem to follow a developmental pattern: People whose blindness or severely impaired vision occurred after a period of normal vision during childhood seem to develop better nonvisual skills than those who are born with severely impaired vision. This developmental pattern seems to apply to some spatial skills; for example, dynamic spatial orientation (Easton & Bentzen, 1999; Morrongiello, Timney, Humphrey, & Anderson, 1995; Rieser, Guth, & Hill, 1986; Rieser, Hill, & Taylor, 1992; but see also Loomis et al., 1993). However, the development of other nonvisual spatial skills such as listening to detect walls and other obstacles, may not show such a developmental pattern (Ashmead et al., 1998; Erin & Corn, 1994).

SEVEN SPECIFIC ISSUES ON WHICH THE CHAPTERS ARE FOCUSED

The chapters in this volume are aimed at answering one or more of the following specific questions involving blindness and brain plasticity:

1. Given that for people with early onset blindness the visual cortex is recruited to participate in tactile processing, what are the possible benefits of the recruitment to tactile pattern recognition and Braille reading and for object manipulation and object perception?
2. Given that for people with early onset blindness the visual cortex is recruited to participate in auditory processing, what are the possible benefits of the recruitment to auditory localization, sensitivity to auditory information for obstacles, and sensitivity to language or music?
3. To what degree does the recruitment of visual cortex to nonvisual spatial processing depend on heavy "doses" of experience using a particular nonvisual spatial skill versus to what degree is the recruitment of visual cortex a developmental phenomenon and heavily determined by the age of onset of blindness?
4. Given different tasks of daily living (for example wayfinding and spatial orientation, manipulating objects when using tools to cook, dress, or build things) and academic learning (for example reading Braille, comprehending text, understanding scientific concepts), for which of them does nonvisual information seem to substitute effectively and result in satisfactory learning and for which does sensory substitution seem to fall short?

5. Congenital and early onset blindness are associated with a larger range of individual differences in spatial skill than blindness acquired later in life and may be associated with a lower mean level of performance. Whereas the top-performing individuals with congenital blindness match the top-performing late-blinded and blindfolded sighted individuals, there are many more low-performing individuals among the congenitally blind. These individual differences among congenitally blind people cut across different etiologies of blindness. Can they be associated with different sensory substitution strategies or cognitive strategies? Can they be associated to different patterns of participation of the visual cortex in non-visual spatial processing?

6. What do we already know about experience-dependent brain plasticity that can be applied to steer educational and rehabilitation interventions? What are the critical questions that need to be answered?

7. What do we already know about sensory substitution and spatial functioning and how can emerging technologies be used to steer educational and rehabilitation interventions? What are the critical questions that need to be answered?

CONCLUSIONS: THREE MAJOR ISSUES AND RELATED QUESTIONS TO KEEP IN MIND WHILE READING THIS VOLUME

Brain Plasticity—Cortical Remapping of Sensory, Sensorimotor, and Cognitive Functioning as a Function of Blindness

- What is the evidence that cortical remapping occurs in general?
- What is the evidence that the occipital cortex is remapped for people who are blind?
- How long-lived is the remapping? Are there developmental constraints on the remapping?
- What is the effect of the remapping on spatial functioning?
- What are the implications of the remapping for educational and rehabilitative strategies?

Developmental and Individual Differences in Cognitive Function and Learning

- What is the evidence that early visual experience either matters or does not matter for skill in navigating environments and manipulating objects?

- Is the range of individual differences in spatial functioning broader among people with congenital blindness and congenital severe visual impairment than among people with later-onset blindness or visual impairment?
- How might cortical remapping influence individual differences in spatial functioning among people who are blind or severely visually impaired?
- How might alternative sensory substitution strategies influence individual differences in spatial functioning among people who are blind or have severely impaired vision?
- Do different types of severely impaired blindness (for example, severe loss of acuity and contrast sensitivity versus severe visual field loss) have different effects on different spatial skills?

Sensory Integration and Sensory Substitution

- "What" can substitute for "what" when perceiving and learning about objects?
- "What" can substitute for "what" when perceiving and learning about environments?
- "What" can substitute for "what" for detecting obstacles and for maintaining orientation when exploring new places?
- Does development constrain sensory substitution? Does early- or late-onset blindness influence the usefulness of nonvisual information?

We co-editors of this volume find these issues intellectually exciting, scientifically fruitful, and embedded in varieties of networks aimed at sets of overlapping goals. We hope for the same for the readers of this volume.

REFERENCES

Ashmead, D. H., Davis, D., & Northington, A. (1995). Contribution of listeners' approaching motion to auditory distance perception. *Journal of Experimental Psychology: Human Perception and Performance, 21*, 239–56.

Ashmead, D. H., Wall, R. S., Eaton, S. B., Ebinger, K. A., Snook-Hill, M-M, Guth, D. A., & Yang, X. (1998). Echolocation reconsidered: Using spatial variations in the ambient sound field to guide locomotion. *Journal of Visual Impairment and Blindness, 92,* 615–32.

Barth, J. L., & Foulke, E. (1979). Preview: A neglected variable in orientation and mobility. *Journal of Visual Impairment and Blindness, 73,* 41–48.

Blasch, B., Wiener, W., & Welsh, R. (1997). Introduction. In B. Blasch, W. Wiener & R. Welsh (Eds.), *Foundations of orientation and mobility* (2nd ed., pp. 1–6). New York: American Foundation for the Blind.

Burton, H., Snyder, A. Z., Conturo, T. E., Akbukak, E., Ollinger, J. M., & Raichle, M. E. (2002). Adaptive changes in early and late blind: An fMRI study of Braille reading. *Journal of Neurophysiology, 87,* 589–607.

Cohen, L. G., Celnik, P., Pascual-Leone, A., Corwell, B., Faiz, L., Dambrosia, J., et al. (1997). Functional relevance of cross-modal plasticity in blind humans. *Nature, 389,* 180–83.

Easton, R. D., & Bentzen, B. L. (1999). The effect of extended acoustic training on spatial updating in adults who are congenitally blind. *Journal of Visual Impairment and Blindness, 93,* 405–15.

Erin, J. N., & Corn, A. L. (1994). A survey of children's first understanding of being visually impaired. *Journal of Visual Impairment and Blindness, 88,* 132–39.

Guth, D., & LaDuke, R. (1995). Veering by blind pedestrians: Individual differences and their implications for instruction. *Journal of Visual Impairment and Blindness, 89,* 28–37.

Haber, L., Haber, R. N., Penningroth, S., Novak, K., & Radgowski, H. (1993). Comparison of nine methods of indicating the direction to objects: Data from blind adults. *Perception, 221,* 35–47.

Kilgour, A. R., & Lederman, S. (2002). Face recognition by hand. *Perception & Psychophysics, 64,* 339–352.

Lederman, S. J., & Klatzky, R. L. (1997). Relative availability of surface and object properties during early haptic processing. *Journal of Experimental Psychology: Human Perception and Performance, 23,* 1–28.

Loomis, J. M., Klatzky, R. L., Golledge, R. G., Ciccinelli, J. G., & Pellegrino, J. W. (1993). Non-visual navigation by blind and sighted: Assessment of path integration ability. *Journal of Experimental Psychology: General, 122,* 73–91.

Long, R., & Hill, E. (1997). Establishing and maintaining orientation for mobility. In B. Blasch, W. Wiener, & R. Welsh (Eds.), *Foundations of orientation and mobility* (2nd ed., pp. 39–59). New York: American Foundation for the Blind.

Meltzer, P., Morgan, V. L., Pickens, D. R., Price, R. R., Wall, R. S., & Ebner, F. F. (2001). Cortical activation during Braille reading is influenced by early visual experience in subjects with severe visual disability: A correlational fMRI study. *Human Brain Mapping, 14,* 186–95.

Millar, S. (1999). Veering re-visited: Noise and posture cues in walking without sight. *Perception, 28,* 765–80.

Morrongiello, B. A., Timney, B., Humphrey, G. K., & Anderson, S. (1995). Spatial knowledge in blind and sighted children. *Journal of Experimental Child Psychology, 59,* 211–33.

Pascual-Leone, A., Wassermann, E. M., Sadato, N., & Hallett, M. (1995). The role of reading activity on the modulation of motor cortical outputs to the reading hand in Braille readers. *Annals of Neurology, 38,* 910–15.

Philbeck, J. W., Klatzky, R. L., Behrmann, M., Loomis, J. M., & Goodridge, J. (2001). Active control of locomotion facilitates non-visual navigation. *Journal of Experimental Psychology: Human Perception and Performance, 27,* 141–53.

Ponchillia, P. E., Strause, B., & Ponchillia, S. V. (2002). Athletes with visual impairments: Attributes and sports participation. *Journal of Visual Impairment and Blindness, 96,* 267–72.

Rauschecker, J. P., & Korte, M. (1993). Auditory compensation for early blindness in cat cerebral cortex. *Journal of Neuroscience, 13,* 4538–48.

Rieser, J. J., Guth, D. A., & Hill, E. W. (1986). Sensitivity to perspective structure while walking without vision. *Perception, 15,* 173–88.

Rieser, J. J., Hill, E. W., & Taylor, C. R. (1992). Visual experience, visual field size, and the development of non-visual sensitivity to the spatial structure of outdoor neighborhoods explored by walking. *Journal of Experimental Psychology: General, 121,* 210–21.

Rieser, J. J., & Pick, H. L. (2002). Perceiving locomotion and locomoting to perceive. In W. Prinz & B. Hommel (Eds.). *Attention and performance XIX: Common mechanisms in perception and action.* Oxford University Press, 177–193

Rieser, J. J., Lockman, J. J., & Pick, H. L., Jr. (1980). The role of visual experience in knowledge of spatial layout. *Perception and Psychophysics, 28,* 185–190.

Roeder, B., Rosler, F., & Neville, H. J. (2001). Auditory memory in congenitally blind adults: A behavioral-electrophysiological investigation. *Cognitive Brain Research, 11,* 289–303.

Roeder, B., Rosler, F., & Neville, H. J. (2000). Event-related potentials during auditory language processing in congenitally blind and sighted people. *Neuropsychologia, 38,* 1482–1502.

Stokes, D. E. (1997). *Pasteur's quadrant: Basic science and technological innovation.* Washington, DC: Brookings Institution Press.

Thinus-Blanc, C. & Gaunet, F. (1997). Representation of space in blind persons: Vision as a spatial sense? *Psychological Bulletin, 131,* 20–42.

Wanet-Defalque, M.-C., Vanlierde, A., & Michaux, G. (2001). Mental representation of spaces and objects in a historic site: Influence of visual impairment. *Journal of Visual Impairment and Blindness, 95,* 172–75.

Warren, D. H. (1994). *Blindness and children: An individual differences approach.* Cambridge, UK: Cambridge University Press.

2

History of Research on Blindness and Brain Plasticity

Herbert I. Pick

Suppose a Man born blind, and now adult, and taught by his touch to distinguish between a Cube and a Sphere of the same metal, and nighly of the same big-
ness, so as to tell, when he felt one and t'other, which is the Cube, which the
Sphere. Suppose then the Cube and Sphere placed on a Table, and the Blind
Man to be made to see. Qaere, Whether by his sight before he touch'd them, he
could now distinguish, and tell, which is the Globe, which the Cube? (Molyneaux, 1688; Locke, 1690/1978, II, p. 76; see also Eilan, 1993)

Issues of blindness, plasticity, and spatial function have a long history in philosophy, physiology, and psychology. It is not clear where to begin in trying to
introduce the topic. Rather arbitrarily, I begin with the renaissance philosophers. A major idea, pointing out similarities between touch and vision, can be
traced at least as far back as Descartes' *Dioptrics* in 1635. He argued that distance was perceptible by means of a natural geometry based on angles of the
wrists holding two rods. The angles of the wrists and the distances between the
two hands gave a basis for estimating the distance of intersection of the rods.
Similarly, binocular vision can support distance perception of a fixated object
by registering the angles of convergence of the two eyes along with the interocular distance.

Berkeley (1709/1897) elaborated this basic idea in a particular direction in
his *New Theory of Vision*. He noted that an object's distance could not be perceived directly because the same point in the eye would be stimulated by
objects at different distances. Therefore, if we perceive distance visually, it
must be on the basis of previous nonvisual experience. Cues like the amount of
strain of our eye muscles indicate different distances because they were associated with having to reach or walk different distances when particular strains

were present in the past. Such an associationist view is captured in a more recent saying, "touch teaches vision."

Berkeley took this view one step further in considering the opening quotation of this chapter. The quotation is from a letter to John Locke by his frequently referred to friend, George Molyneux. Berkeley was consistent in his position, concluding that, to the extent that touch teaches vision, a blind man with restored sight would not immediately be able to recognize visually objects that he already knew tactually. It should be noted that this conclusion goes beyond the issue of distance perception and includes shape perception as well. It should be noted also that Berkeley was drawing a conclusion from a thought experiment. He was not providing evidence from blind persons with restored vision. However, centuries later and relatively recently, relevant evidence did become available. Hebb (1949) summarized cases of blind persons who had restored sight by virtue of cataract removal. This report was followed by Gregory's report of such a case study (Gregory & Wallace, 1963) and other similar reports. The results of these reports seem to suggest problems with depth perception and, except for Gregory, problems with shape perception as well. Definitive interpretation of the data from these studies is difficult because the time and extent of vision loss wasn't always clear nor was the precision and extent of the pre- and postoperative tests. Further light is shed on this intriguing idea in the current volume by discussions of "MM" (see Fine, chapter 8).

WHAT DOES THE POSSIBLE RESTORATION OF VISION HAVE TO DO WITH BLINDNESS AND PLASTICITY?

Implicit in the idea of touch teaching vision is the concept of intermodal transfer between sense modalities. How might this work? Let's assume that Berkeley's answer to the Molyneux question was correct. The blind man who could identify a sphere and cube haptically was unable to do so visually when his sight was restored. However, let's further assume that he could distinguish between the sphere and the cube; he could tell they were different, he just didn't know which was which. Then he simply needs to learn by association which one of the visual stimuli is the tactual sphere and which the cube. This is a very *specific* association. Intermodal transfer in the case of Descartes' triangulation is slightly more complex. Distance perception based on the arm/wrist angles plus intermanual distance transfers to distance perception based on binocular convergence angles plus interocular distance. This is a *dimensional* relationship, not a specific one. The situation may be even more complex if the haptic triangulation procedure transfers to visual motion parallax. For example, the visual distance of an object is perceived on the basis of the change in visual direction in relation to how far the eye has moved. In this case, intermodal transfer would be more systemic than a single dimension and possibly would generalize across wide ranges of distance and depth. The basic issue here is the degree of specificity of intermodal transfer, ranging from object specific to systemic. This issue of degree of specificity has been elaborated in relation to distance perception but could be developed in relation to shape perception on the basis of general properties or dimensions of shape such as curvature/straightness and parallelity/convergence (e.g., see Biederman, 1987).

In the case of the possibility of intermodal transfer of bimanual to binocular convergence, the dimensions in the two modalities are formally similar. This formal similarity may make it relatively easy for there to be intermodal transfer from touch to vision. However, it is possible to have dimensional correspondence between two sense modalities when there is not such formal correspondence. An example of this is the Sonicguide, a binaural sensory aid devised by Kay (1974) to provide spatial information for the blind. Ultrasonic sound is emitted from a helmet and is reflected back from nearby objects. The echo is converted into a binaural audible signal in which amplitude differences to the two ears specify the direction of the object reflecting the sound (as in usual auditory localization) and sound frequency specifies its distance. The higher the frequency, the farther away is the object reflecting the sound. The functional relation between acoustic frequency and distance is not formally similar to any haptic or visual cue for distance—disregarding the Doppler effect, which is quite a different phenomenon. And in fact, that functional relationship is not any kind of ecological valid relationship for which we might have evolved sensitivity. Evidence suggests that people can use frequency variation to perceive the distance of objects. If so, the functional relationship would have to have been learned as an arbitrary correspondence between touch and audition. (See Humphrey and Humphrey, 1985, for a thorough review of developmental research using this sensory aid.)

An alternative theoretical perspective to that of touch teaching vision and its implication of *intermodal* transfer for conceiving of how different sense modalities carry the same perceptual information is that of *amodal* information. For many perceptual events, the same information is present in different sense modalities. Perhaps a clear example of this occurs with object unity. The visual event of a single object (e.g., a marble) dropping onto a surface is clearly that of one object. This may be contrasted with the visual event of a set of multiple marbles dropping. Similarly, the same events presented auditorily are clearly distinguished as single versus many marbles dropping. The same information is detected, in one case visually and in the other auditorily. It has been shown that even young infants are sensitive to the correspondence between the same such events in the visual and auditory sense modalities (Bahrick, 1988).

Relevant to spatial function and blindness was the introduction of a sensory substitution system by Bach-y-Rita and his colleagues (White, Saunders, Scadden, Bach-y-Rita, & Collins, 1970). This system converted a visual image to a tactual one. A TV camera controlled manually by a blind or blindfolded observer registered a visual scene that was converted to a tactual pattern by an array of vibrators strapped to the observer's back. So, for example, if the camera were pointed toward some shape, say a square, the observer's back would be stimulated by a square pattern of vibrators. With relatively little training, both blind and blindfolded sighted observers were able to recognize several different shapes and objects as they guided the camera. Of particular interest were the results for distance perception of a few observers. In visual perception, an expanding optical image is compelling information for the approach of an object. One blind observer suddenly experienced this size–distance relationship when the vibrator display on the back expanded in size as an object was moved slowly toward the camera. In a few other cases, observers ducked when the vibrator display suddenly expanded in size when the zoom lens on the camera was inadvertently moved. Here again, it may not be surprising that shape recognition occurred in both sense modalities because the information for shape is formally similar in both vision and touch and fits well with an amodal perspective. It is somewhat surprising that tactual pattern expansion provides the same information for an approaching object as optical expansion. However, it suggests that sensory arrays identified as objects, whether visual or tactual, specify approach if they are expanding.

The philosophical origins of the plasticity in the associationist perspective started as noted above, with Locke and Berkeley. It continued to be a strong orientation as the formal disciplines of physiology and psychology evolved. In a slightly modified and generalized form it was manifest in the ideas of the great physiologist/physicist/psychologist Helmholtz. It was a strong part of the theoretical orientation of early psychologists Wundt and Titchener and is easily identifiable in relatively recent research and writings (e.g., Leibowitz, 1973).

A somewhat different plasticity theme also evolved and can be traced back to Helmholtz. This is adaptation to a perceptual rearrangement. Helmholtz (Southall, 1925) described a situation in which the visual field is shifted laterally by means of prisms placed in front of the eyes. A person attempting to reach for a viewed object without the benefit of visual feedback will miss, depending on the strength of the prisms. The error decreases gradually as a function of experience with this optical rearrangement. Helmholtz's interest in this kind of experiment was motivated by trying to explain perception (or judgment) of direction of gaze.

This rearrangement paradigm was used subsequently to investigate the functional significance of the retinal image being inverted. This fact had been known since the time of Kepler and Descartes. Philosophers and early psychologists reasoned that this posed a problem as to whether we had to learn to see the world right side up. Suppose the retinal image could be righted. If adults were able to adjust to this change, it was reasoned, we must have had to learn to perceive the world as right side up in the first place. With such motivation in mind, Stratton (1897) carried out the first experiments. By means of an optical device, he rotated an observer's retinal image by 180°. This resulted in an inversion plus a left-right reversal of the retinal image. This device was worn for eight days. Eye–hand coordination and other perceptual-motor actions, markedly disturbed initially, improved and were relatively normal by the end of this period. The *subjective* perception of the world being upright was quite problematic even at the end of the eight days.

In the subsequent 50 years, variations of Stratton's experiments were carried out, including exposing participants to purely right-left reversals or purely up-down inversions of the visual field. In general, similar results were obtained, that is, major perceptual-motor adjustment to the rearrangement but somewhat sketchy and at best partial adjustment to the subjective perceptual aspects of the rearrangement. One of the most impressive of these subsequent studies was that of Kohler (1964), who had a participant wear an inverting optical device for 37 days. More and more objects were reported as appearing to be right side up, but it is not completely clear what that meant. Nevertheless, perceptual motor activities, even skiing, were carried out quite normally. (See Harris, 1965; Smith & Smith, 1962; Welch, 1978, for extensive reviews of this work.)

The faulty logic of the initial motivation persisted almost until the time of Kohler's research (e.g., Ewert, 1930; Snyder & Pronko, 1952). Certainly the orientation of the image on the retina has no necessary connection with the orientation in which we perceive the world. Furthermore, whether adults might or might not adjust to a rearrangement has no necessary implication as to the original status of the phenomenon. Although the original motivation for research on inverted and reversed retinal images was misguided, the investigations provide some intriguing evidence for plasticity in the perceptual and perceptual-motor systems.

With Kohler's experiments, research on this particular problem wound down, but research on Helmholtz's original lateral shifting of the visual field experienced a rebirth of interest. A major instigator of this was Richard Held and his colleagues (e.g., Held & Hein, 1958, 1963). Held demonstrated again the kind of adjustment that Helmholtz had described and provided evidence that such adaptation only occurred when the optical device, in his case prisms, produced a mismatch between expected feedback of an efferent signal (motor command) and the actual feedback (re-afferance). This theoretical position elicited a lively controversy. There was considerable agreement on the fact that adjustment or adaptation occurred but disagreement on the exact nature of the adaptation and on the conditions necessary to produce it. One example is adaptation of eye–hand coordination, in which one view was that the *felt* position of the hand had changed while another view was that there was a new calibration of hand–eye coordination. In another example, focused on the conditions necessary for adaptation, one view held that active movements were necessary, while another view held that any information about the discrepancy in hand–eye coordination would suffice.

Of more direct relevance to blindness was analogous research on perceptual-motor rearrangement involving the auditory system. Similar to shifting the visual field by means of a prism, the direction of the auditory field can be shifted by means of a so-called pseudophone. This device consists of a pair of microphones that can be separated by varying distances and used effectively to manipulate the interaural distance of the sounds input to the listener's ears. The auditory stimulation received by each microphone is input to one of the two ears. Mounted on an observer's head, the axis between the two microphones can be rotated to any desired angle. This produces a systematic direction change in all auditory stimulation. Freedman (1968) developed a sophisticated form of such a pseudophone. Sound localizations of an observer outfitted with this sort of device is initially at the apparent positions of the sound sources rather than at their true positions. After some exposure to relatively small rotations of the axis of the pseudophone observers will adapt and localize sounds correctly. Such a result has been found for observers sitting in the dark who move their hand back and forth while holding a sound source. Again, this type of experiment demonstrates plasticity in the calibration of the auditory-motor system.

The areas of plasticity noted in this historical overview have been very selective. A large domain of perceptual learning has not been covered. See, for example, Gibson (1969). A very interesting comparative physiological domain of recombination experiments by Weiss (1941) has not even been mentioned. Nevertheless, a number of issues have been highlighted that might well be kept in mind as we consider contemporary approaches to blindness, plasticity, and spatial function.

One is the level of function under consideration. Plasticity may occur at a purely sensory level or it may occur at a highly complex cognitive level or at various places in between. So if one is interested in the practical problem of spatial functioning in blind persons, one can consider how auditory sensitivity might have changed in a psychophysical sense, how echo location might have improved, how attention might have changed to take advantage of various traffic sounds, and how conceptualization of spatial layout might have changed.

Another issue is the degree to which plasticity from specific experiences generalizes to entire sensorimotor systems. If one learns a particular skill, to what extent is that change general over a whole domain? If one learns to read Braille, to what extent does that improve all tactual or haptic perception? At least what is the range of generalization?

How does the higher-order information that we can process through one sense modality lend itself to processing through other sense modalities?

These and other general questions should be kept in mind as we exploit our modern approaches to plasticity. In thinking historically about our field, one is impressed with how little application of the research seemed to be in the minds of the investigators. This volume represents a change in that direction.

REFERENCES

Bahrick, L. E. (1988). Intermodal learning in infancy: Learning on the basis of two kinds of invariant relations in audible and visible events. *Child Development, 59,* 197–209.

Berkeley, G. (1709/1897). An essay towards a new theory of vision. In G. Sampson (Ed.), *The works of George Berkeley.* London: Georg Bell and Sons.

Biederman, I. (1987). Recognition-by-components: A theory of human image understanding. *Psychological Review, 94,* 115–17.

Eilan, N. (1993). Introduction: Spatial presentation in the sensory modalities. In N. Eilan, R. McCarthy, & B. Brewer, *Spatial representation.* Oxford, UK: Blackwell.

Ewert, P. H. (1930). A study of the effect of inverted retinal stimulation upon spatially coordinated behavior. *Genetic Psychology Monographs, 7,* 177–363.

Freedman, S. J. (1968). Perceptual compensation and learning. In S. J. Freedman (Ed.), *Neuropsychology of spatially oriented behavior.* Homewood, IL: Dorsey.

Gibson, E. J. (1969). *Principles of perceptual learning and development.* Eastorwalk, CT: Appleton-Century-Crofts.

Gregory, R. L., & Wallace, J. G. (1963). Recovery from early blindness: A case study. *Experimental Psychology Society Monograph, 2.*

Harris, C. S. (1965). Perceptual adaptation to inverted, reversed, and displaced vision. *Psychological Review, 72,* 419–44.

Hebb, D. O. (1949). *The organization of behavior.* New York: Wiley.

Held, R., & Hein, A. V. (1958). Adaptation of disarranged hand-eye coordination contingent upon reafferent stimuluation. *Perceptual & Motor Skills, 8,* 87–90.

Held, R., & Hein, A. (1963). Movement-produced stimulation in the development of visually guided behavior. *Journal of Comparative and Physiological Psychology, 56,* 872–76.

Humphrey, G. K., & Humphrey, D. E. (1985). The use of binaural sensory aids by blind infants and children: Theoretical and applied issues. In F. J. Morrison, C. J. Lord, & D. P. Keating (Eds.) *Applied developmental psychology.* Vol 2. (pp. 59–97).

Kay, L. (1974). A sonar aid to enhance spatial perception of the blind: Engineering design and evaluation. *The Radio and Electronic Engineer, 44,* 605–27.

Kohler, I. (1964). Formation and transformation of the perceptual world. *Psychological Issues, 3,* 1–173.

Leibowitz, H. W., & Harvey, L. O. (1973). Perception. *Annual Review of Psychology,* 207–40.

Locke, J. (1690/1978). *An essay concerning human understanding.* A. S. Pringle-Pattison (Ed.) Atlantic Highlands, NJ: Humanities Press.

Molyneaux, W. (1688). Letter to John Locke, 7 July, in *The correspondence of John Locke,* E. S. de Beer (Ed.), Oxford, UK: Clarendon Press, 1978, Vol. 3, no. 1064.

Smith, K. U., & Smith, W. K. (1962). *Perception and motion.* Philadelphia: Saunders.

Snyder, F. W., & Pronko, N. H. (1952). *Vision with spatial inversion.* Oxford, UK: Mccormich-Armstrong.

Southall, J. P. C. (1925). *Helmholtz's Treatise on physiological optics* Vol. III (pp. 246–47). New York: Dover Publications.

Stratton, G. M. (1897). Vision without inversion of the retinal image. *Psychological Review, 4,* 463–81.

Weiss, P. (1941). Self-differentiation of the basic patterns of coordination. *Comparative Psychology Monographs, 17,* No. 4.

Welch, R. B. (1978). *Perceptual modification: Adapting to altered sensory environments.* New York: Academic Press.

White, B. W., Saunders, F. A., Scadden, L., Bach-y-Rita, P., & Collins, C. C. (1970). Seeing with the skin. *Perception and Psychophysics, 7,* 23–27.

II

EXPERIENCE-DEPENDENT RECRUITMENT OF VISUAL CORTEX FOR NONVISUAL LEARNING AND DEVELOPMENT

3

The Plastic Human Brain in Blind Individuals: The Cause of Disability and the Opportunity for Rehabilitation

Lofti B. Merabet, Naomi Bass Pitskel, Amir Amedi, and Alvaro Pascual-Leone

The brain of blind individuals is different than that of sighted individuals. Loss of vision induces changes to adapt to the modification in afferent inputs and efferent demands to the brain, and reflect shifts in information processing. Dynamic shifts in the strength of preexisting connections across distributed neural networks, changes in task-related cortico–cortical and cortico–subcortical coherence, and modifications of the mapping between behavior and neural activity take place in response to changes in afferent input or efferent demand. Such changes are rapid and ongoing, and even temporary loss of vision due to blindfolding induces such changes in the human brain. Prolonged loss of vision, particularly early blindness, can induce the establishment of new connections through dendritic growth and arborization.

Some of these plastic changes promote adaptation to blindness and result in behavioral gains for visually deprived and blind individuals. However, plastic changes harbor the danger that the evolving pattern of neural activation may in itself lead to abnormal behavior. They may limit aspects of rehabilitation and may make blind individuals poor candidates for procedures aimed at restoring vision. The challenge is to learn enough about the mechanisms of plasticity to be able to guide them, suppressing changes that may lead to undesirable behaviors while accelerating or enhancing those that result in a behavioral benefit for the subject or patient.

Neurostimulation, including noninvasive brain stimulation techniques, provides an opportunity to modulate brain plasticity in a controlled and specific manner. Cross-modal sensory processing may serve as a means to exploit existing compensatory strategies following sensory deprivation. Such interventions may serve as a novel rehabilitative strategy for augmented vision following visual sensory deprivation.

AN INTRINSICALLY PLASTIC NERVOUS SYSTEM

Plasticity is not an occasional state of the nervous system. Instead, we conceive of plasticity as an intrinsic property of the nervous system retained throughout the lifespan and as the normal ongoing state of the human nervous system. Therefore, it is not possible to understand normal psychological function or the manifestations or consequences of sensory loss without invoking the concept of brain plasticity.

A full, coherent account of any sensory or cognitive theory has to build into its framework the fact that the nervous system, and particularly the brain, undergoes continuous changes in response to modifications in its input afferents and output targets. The nervous system might then be viewed as a continuously changing structure of which plasticity is an integral property and the obligatory consequence of each sensory input, motor act, association, reward signal, action plan, or awareness.

In this framework, notions such as psychological processes as distinct from organic-based functions or dysfunctions cease to be informative. Behavior will lead to changes in brain circuitry, just as changes in brain circuitry will lead to behavioral modifications.

Ultimately, depending on the circumstances, neural plasticity can confer no perceptible change in the behavioral output of the brain, manifest changes demonstrated only under special testing conditions, or even lead to compensatory behaviors. Plasticity is thus an ongoing process that can not only lead to symptoms of disease but can also offer the opportunity to adapt to deficits and overcome dysfunctions. The changes that follow blindness serve as an excellent example for all these aforementioned principles. Because of plasticity, the brain of blind individuals is different than that of the sighted. However, it is also because of plasticity that we have the opportunity to develop novel rehabilitative strategies for subjects with impaired vision.

Plasticity might be studied at multiple different levels, from neural systems to molecules. In this chapter, we will focus on the level of neural systems and will argue that the brain is organized in dynamically shifting neuronal networks as they provide a most energy efficient, spatially compact, and precise means to process input signals and generate responses (for review see Pascual-Leone,

Amedi, Fregni, & Merabet, 2005). We propose that nodes within networks act as operators that contribute a given computation independent of the input (for discussion of the notion of a "meta-modal brain," see Pascual-Leone & Hamilton, 2001). Inputs shift depending on the integration of a region in a distributed neural network, and the layered and reticular structure of the cortex with rich re-afferent loops provides the substrate for rapid modulation of the engaged network nodes. In this conceptualization, plasticity represents a highly efficient way to utilize the brain's limited resources. It might in fact be argued that the high degree of plasticity at the neural network level is a most beneficial adaptation to the resistance to plastic change at the cellular level. Individual neurons are highly complex, and exquisitely optimized cellular elements, and their capacity of change and plastic modification is necessarily very limited. Integration of highly stable and nonplastic cellular elements into dynamically changing, intrinsically plastic neural networks assures functional stability while providing a substrate for rapid adaptation to shifting demands.

We thus consider that the representation of brain function is best conceptualized by the notion of distributed neural networks, a series of assemblies of neurons that might be widely dispersed anatomically but are structurally interconnected and can be functionally integrated to serve a specific behavioral role. Such notions of dedicated but multifocal networks, which can shift dynamically depending on demands for a given behavioral output, provide a current resolution to the long-standing dispute between localizationists and equipotential theorists. Function comes to be identified with a certain pattern of activation of specific, spatially-distributed but interconnected neuronal assemblies in a specific time window and temporal order. In such distributed networks, specific nodes may be critical for a given behavioral outcome. Knowledge of such instances is clinically useful to explain findings in patients and localize their lesions, but it provides an oversimplified conceptualization of brain–behavior relations. In the case of blindness, we may be better served realizing that behavior is not so much the result of sensory deprivation but rather the consequence of how the rest of the brain is capable of sustaining function following loss of vision. The challenge is to understand enough about the involved mechanisms to be able to promote adaptive changes and suppress maladaptive ones, ultimately optimizing outcomes for a given individual.

PLASTICITY AND GENETICS

Neural plasticity may be thought of as "evolution's invention" to enable the nervous system to escape the restrictions of its own genome (and its highly specialized cellular specification) and thus adapt to environmental pressures, physiologic changes, and experiences. The relation between brain activity and structure on the one hand, and brain function on the other, is not one to one but is in itself variable. Neurons may be highly stable and nonplastic cellular structures, but they are engaged in dynamically changing, intrinsically plastic neural networks. As long as an output pathway to manifest the behavior is preserved (even if following injury alternate pathways need to be unmasked or facilitated), changes in the activity across a distributed neural network may be able to establish new patterns of brain activation and sustain function. Such plastic processes may follow two distinct steps: unmasking existing connections possibly followed by establishment of new ones including integration of new neural structures and neurons (Pascual-Leone et al., 2005). The former is very rapid and represents the range of core aspects of normal physiology (e.g., the role of cross-modal interactions in visual perception). Following the loss of vision, rapid changes take place initially and may account for such phenomena as those seen in sighted subjects during complete, temporary blindfolding as well as phantom vision and other transient experiences in recently blind subjects. With time, slowly over months and years of sustained visual deprivation, establishment of new connections can give rise to unexpected capacities (e.g., superior verbal memory in blind individuals).

Therefore, the scope of possible plastic changes is determined initially by existing connections, which are the result of genetically controlled neural development and thus different across individuals. Genetically controlled aspects of brain development define neuronal elements and initial patterns of connectivity. Subsequently, afferent input, efferent demand, contextual and environmental changes, and brain activity in general shape neural network structures and brain-behavior relations by mechanisms of plasticity. Given the initial, genetically determined, individually different brain substrate, the same events will result in diverse consequences as plastic brain mechanisms act upon individually distinct neural substrates. Furthermore, genetic factors may regulate and define the range of plastic changes and their magnitude, stability, and chronometry.

The conceptualization of a genetically determined starting point and subsequent environmentally and behaviorally driven plastic changes is reminiscent of the debate over the relative roles of "nature versus nurture," which remains unresolved in many fields of study, from childhood education to animal behavior or neurodegenerative disorders. Genetic factors may be thought of as laying the foundation on which environmental agents exert their influence. Although certain environmental factors alone (regardless of genetic factors) and certain genetic factors alone (regardless of environmental influences) may explain some behaviors and disease states, most of the time the interaction of both genetic and environmental factors will be required. A consequence of such formulation is the notion that human behavior and the manifestations of human disease are ultimately heavily defined by brain plasticity, and that an intervention to guide behavior or treat pathological symptomatology might be more immediate in its behavioral repercussions and thus more effective if aimed at modulating plasticity, than if intent on addressing underlying genetic predispositions. The challenge we face is to learn enough about the mechanisms of plasticity and the mapping relations between brain activity and behavior to be able to guide it, suppressing changes that may lead to undesirable behaviors while accelerating or enhancing those that result in a behavioral benefit for the subject or patient.

THE OCCIPITAL CORTEX AND NEUROPLASTICITY IN BLIND INDIVIDUALS

The core principles of neural function and the fundamental nature of plasticity obviously apply within the context of visual loss and occipital cortical function. We live in a society that relies heavily on vision. Therefore, blind individuals have to make striking adjustments to their loss of sight to interact effectively with their environment. One may thus imagine that blind individuals need to develop superior abilities in the use of their remaining senses (compensatory hypothesis). However, blindness could also be the cause for maladjustments (general-loss hypothesis). For example, the loss of sight could be detrimental to sensory perception/spatial information processing mediated by the remaining senses because of our strong reliance on vision for the acquisition and construction of spatial and form representations. Against the general-loss hypothesis is evidence that blind individuals show normal and often superior skills in tasks implicating touch and hearing as compared with the average sighted population (Doucet et al., 2005; Gougoux et al., 2004; Gougoux, Zatorre, Lassonde, Voss, & Lepore, 2005; Hollins & Kelley, 1988; Lessard, Lepore, Poirier, Villemagne, & Lassonde, 1999; Rauschecker, 1995; Van Boven, Hamilton, Kauffmann, Keenan, & Pascual-Leone, 2000; Voss et al., 2004). Growing experimental evidence suggests that in blind individuals, brain areas commonly associated with the processing of visual information are recruited in a compensatory cross-modal manner that may account for these superior nonvisual capabilities (Merabet, Maquire, et al., 2004; Merabet, Thut, et al., 2004; Pascual-Leone et al., 2005; Theoret, Merabet, & Pascual-Leone, 2004).

Phelps and colleagues (Phelps et al., 1981) followed by Wanet-Defalque and colleagues (Wanet-Defalque et al., 1988) were among the first to suggest that the occipital cortex is active in blind individuals and furthermore, that puberty may represent an important developmental milestone for this activation. Using event-related electroencephalograph (EEG) recordings, Uhl and colleagues (Uhl, Franzen, Lindinger, Lang, & Deecke, 1991, and later confirmed by a follow-up study using SPECT imaging, Uhl, Franzen, Podreka, Steiner, & Deecke, 1993) provided early support for the notion of task-related (tactile) occipital cortex activation in blind subjects. Sadato and colleagues (Sadato et al., 1998; Sadato et al., 1996) employed PET imaging and demonstrated that occipital cortex is activated in early blind subjects performing a Braille reading task (see Figure 3–1, top image). Specifically, the group observed bilateral activation in medial occipital cortex (area 17) with concomitant activity in extrastriate areas. Activation of the primary visual cortex was also evident in non-Braille tactile discrimination tasks (e.g., discrimination of angle, width, and Roman-embossed characters encoded in Braille cells), though to a

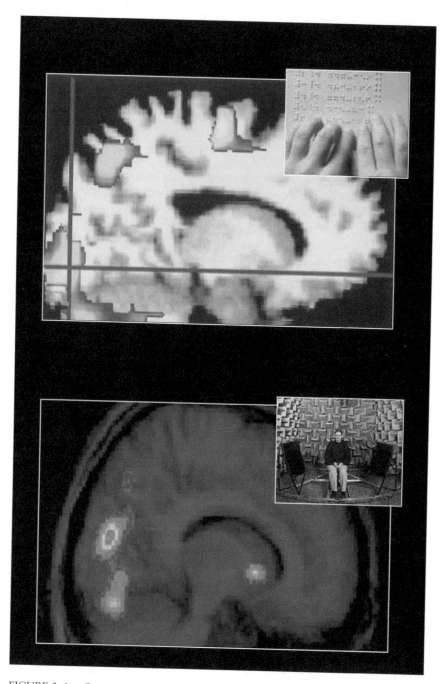

FIGURE 3–1.   Occipital activation in the early blind (identified by circle) during Braille reading (A: modified from Sadato et al., 1996) and auditory localization task (B: modified from Gougoux et al., 2005). [See Color Plate]

lesser extent. Subsequent investigators have refined and extended these early findings further, addressing the role of imagery, the differences between early- and late-blind, and the role of tactile versus verbal/linguistic aspects of the task (Amedi, Raz, Pianke, Malach, & Zohary, 2003; Buchel, Price, Frackowiak, & Friston, 1998; Burton, Snyder, Diamond, & Raichle, 2002; Melzer et al., 2001; Sadato, Okada, Honda, & Yonekura, 2002).

In parallel, similar accounts also appear to emerge regarding the recruitment of occipital visual cortical areas for the processing of auditory information. Activation of occipital cortical areas has also been demonstrated in congenitally blind subjects during tasks of auditory localization, investigated using event-related potential (ERP; Kujala, Alho, Paavielainen, Summala, & Naatanen, 1992) and positron emission tomography (PET; Weeks et al., 2000) and more recently with fMRI (Gougoux et al., 2004; Gougoux et al., 2005) (see Figure 3–1, bottom image).

Functional neuroimaging, at best, establishes an association between activity in a given region or network and task performance. Therefore, the observation of activity in visual cortical areas in blind individuals fails to prove that this activity is necessary for the sensory processing. In support of a causal link between occipital function and the ability to read Braille is the remarkable case study reported by Hamilton and colleagues (Hamilton, Keenan, Catala, & Pascual-Leone, 2000). A congenitally blind woman (from retinopathy of prematurity) was once a highly proficient Braille reader (learning Braille at the age of six and reading at a rate of 120–150 symbols per minute). Following bilateral posterior cerebral artery strokes, she was rendered unable to read Braille despite the fact that her somatosensory sensation, peripheral motor, and sensory nerve functions were all intact. Even though she was well aware of the presence of the dot elements contained in the Braille text, she was "unable to extract enough information" to determine which letters and words were written. Despite her profound inability to read, she had no difficulty in performing simple tactile discrimination tasks, such as identifying the roughness of a surface, distinguishing between different coins, or identifying her house key from a given set. However, she was not able to judge distance between Braille dots or read Braille (Hamilton et al., 2000; Merabet, Thut, et al., 2004). This serendipitous experiment of nature (and tragic event for the patient) provides strong clinical evidence that a functioning occipital cortex is needed to carry out the task of Braille reading.

In an experimental setting, Cohen and colleagues used Transcranial Magnetic Stimulation (TMS) to induce transient disruption of cortical function during a Braille identification task (Cohen et al., 1997). Identification of Braille characters or embossed Roman letters was impaired following TMS to the occipital cortex in early-onset blind subjects but not in sighted subjects (Figure 3-2-A). In blind subjects, occipital stimulation with TMS not only induced errors in Braille identification but also distorted tactile perceptions. Subjects knew that they were touching Braille symbols but were unable to

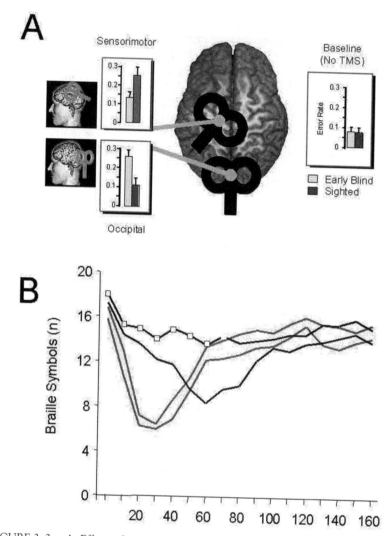

FIGURE 3–2. A: Effects of transient disruption of the contralateral somatosensory cortex or the occipital cortex by TMS on the tactile Braille reading skill in early blind subjects (light gray) and sighted controls (dark gray). The sighted controls performed a difficulty-matched task of tactile reading of embossed Roman letters (modified from Cohen et al., 1997). B: Effect of single-pulse TMS on tactile Braille character recognition in congenitally blind subjects. The TMS was delivered at different times (interstimulus interval) after presentation of the tactile stimulus to the digit pad. The graph displays the number of tactile stimuli detected (open symbols) and correctly identified (filled symbols). Disruption of somatosensory cortex lead to a decrease in the number of detected and identified letters at an interstimulus interval of 30 ms (red line). Disruption of occipital cortex lead to a decrease in the number of identified letters only at an interstimulus interval of approximately 60 ms (blue line). (Modified from Hamilton and Pascual-Leone 1998). [See Color Plate]

identify them, reporting instead that the Braille dots felt "different," "flatter," "less sharp and less well-defined." Occasionally, some subjects even reported feeling additional ("phantom") dots in the Braille cell (Cohen et al., 1997).

The functional significance of the occipital activation during Braille reading in the early-blind has been further evaluated using single-pulse TMS to obtain information about the timing (chronometry) of information processing (Pascual-Leone, Walsh, & Rothwell, 2000). A disruptive TMS pulse was delivered to the occipital or the somatosensory cortex (contralateral to the reading hand) at a variable interval after a peripheral stimulus was applied to the pad of the subject's index finger (Figure 3–2-B). In normal sighted subjects, stimuli to the occipital cortex had no effect, but TMS delivered to the somatosensory cortex approximately 20–30 ms after a tactile stimulus to a contralateral finger interfered with the detection of the peripheral somatosensory stimulus (presumably by disrupting the arrival of the thalamo-cortical volley into the primary sensory cortex (Pascual-Leone, Cohen, Brasil-Neto, Valls-Sole, & Hallett, 1994). In congenitally blind subjects, TMS to the left somatosensory cortex disrupted detection of Braille stimuli presented to their right index finger at interstimulus intervals of 20–40 ms (Hamilton & Pascual-Leone, 1998). Similar to the findings in the sighted, in some cases the subjects did not realize that a peripheral stimulus had been presented to their finger. When they did realize it, they were able to identify correctly which Braille symbol was presented. On the other hand, TMS to the striate cortex disrupted the processing of the peripheral stimuli at interstimulus intervals of 50–80 ms. Contrary to the findings after sensorimotor TMS, the subjects generally knew whether a peripheral stimulus had been presented. However, they could not discriminate which Braille symbol had been presented. These results suggest that in early-blind subjects, the somatosensory cortex appears engaged in detection, whereas the occipital cortex contributes to the perception of tactile stimuli (Hamilton & Pascual-Leone, 1998).

Recent fMRI studies in blind individuals have demonstrated occipital cortex activation (including V1) during tasks requiring auditory verb-generation and similar linguistic tasks (Amedi et al., 2003; Burton, Snyder, Diamond, et al., 2002), semantic judgment tasks (Burton, 2003), and speech processing (Roder, Stock, Bein, Neville, & Rosler, 2002). In a comparative analysis of brain activation in early- and late-blind during a verb-generation task, Burton and colleagues instructed subjects to generate covertly a verb in response to reading a noun cue presented in Braille (e.g., reading the word "cake" would generate "bake") or using auditory words. They found that occipital cortex activation (including V1) was much more prominent in early- than in late-blind subjects (Burton, 2003). Amedi et al. (2003) observed robust left-lateralized V1 activation for a verbal-memory task requiring the retrieval of abstract words from long-term memory. The striking finding of this report is that, contrary to previous studies, the observed occipital activation was demonstrated without introducing any tactile or auditory sensory input (Figure 3–3-A).

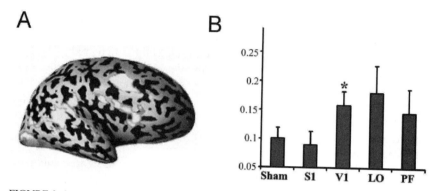

FIGURE 3–3. A: Activation of occipital cortex in the early blind during a verb-generation task versus baseline (circle identifies occipital cortex activation found in the blind group only). B: Repetitive TMS delivered over V1 increased error rates compared to somatosensory cortex (S1) or baseline (sham) stimulation. A similar trend was observed following stimulation of lateral occipital (LO) cortex. (Modified from (Amedi et al., 2004). [See Color Plate]

Notably, blind subjects showed superior verbal memory capabilities compared not only with age-matched, sighted controls but also with reported population averages (using the Wechsler verbal memory test). Furthermore, investigators found a strong positive correlation between the magnitude of V1 activation and the verbal memory capability in that the degree of activation increased with increasing word-recall ability. The functional relevance of these findings was demonstrated with repetitive TMS (rTMS). In early blind subjects, the activity in the left calcarine sulcus or left occipito-temporal cortex was disrupted using repetitive TMS. Following TMS, performance in a verb-generation task was impaired (increase in error rate, see Figure 3–3-B) (Amedi, Floel, Knecht, Zohary, & Cohen, 2004). An analysis of error types revealed that the most common error produced after rTMS was semantic (e.g., apple would lead to jump, instead of eat, one possible correct response). Phonological errors and interference with motor execution or articulation (stuttering and slurring of the responses) were rare (Amedi et al., 2004). Thus, in blind subjects, a transient virtual lesion of the left occipital cortex can interfere with high-level verbal processing and not only with the processing of tactile stimuli and Braille reading. This finding suggests that, beyond changes in connectivity across sensory systems, in early-blind the visually de-afferented occipital cortex becomes engaged in higher-order cognitive functions.

THE BRAIN OF BLIND INDIVIDUALS: DRAWING CONCLUSIONS

The above summary of findings reveals that blind individuals, particularly the early- and congenitally blind, show an organization of the brain and a cortical processing of sensory information that is substantially different from that found in the sighted (see more extensive discussions elsewhere, e.g., Merabet, Rizzo, Amedi, Somers, & Pascual-Leone, 2005, Pascual-Leone et al., 2005, Theoret et al., 2004). It is clear, for example, that the functional and structural identity of the occipital cortex may change from processing visual information to processing information related to another sensory modality or even supramodal high-level cognitive functions. However, is this a unique consequence of early blindness? The occipital cortex may inherently possess the computational machinery necessary for nonvisual information processing (Pascual-Leone & Hamilton, 2001). Under specific conditions this potential could be revealed. If so, visual deprivation may simply allow for the manifestation of the "true" potential of certain brain regions. Burton (2003) suggested the definition of two distinct mechanisms: (a) "cross-modal plasticity de novo" in response to visual deprivation, and (b) "expression of normal physiology" that is normally inhibited or masked when sight is present (Burton, 2003). As discussed above, in the context of the intrinsically plastic brain, these two mechanisms are inextricably linked. The unmasking of preexisting connections and shifts in connectivity represent rapid, early plastic changes, which can lead, if sustained and reinforced, to slower developing but more permanent structural changes with dendritic arborization, sprouting, and growth. This hypothesis can account for the magnitude of the difference in reorganization between early- and late-blind (Burton, Snyder, Conturo, et al., 2002). This hypothesis also results in the strong prediction that careful task choice and experimental design will reveal the nonvisual roles of the occipital cortex in the sighted. For example, Amedi and colleagues reported convergence of visual and tactile object recognition in the ventral visual stream in an occipito-temporal area termed the lateral occipital tactile visual area (LOtv; Amedi, Jacobson, Hendler, Malach, & Zohary, 2002; Amedi, Malach, Hendler, Peled, & Zohary, 2001). The defining feature of this region is that it is activated preferentially by object shape rather than by texture and scrambled images of the object. Similarly, TMS studies have revealed that the visual cortex of the sighted is functionally involved in tactile processing of orientation (Zangaladze, Epstein, Grafton, & Sathian, 1999) and judging of distance between Braille dots (Merabet, Thut et al., 2004). Therefore, in response to loss of visual input, we encounter a situation that is in line with our predictions and notions regarding plasticity mentioned in the introduction: in a first step, the nervous system is molded rapidly by shifts of strength in existing connections. In a second step, new structural connections are established giving rise to new capacities such as improved verbal memory through recruitment of the occipital cortex (Amedi et al., 2003), the remarkably high incidence of absolute pitch in early-blind subjects in the absence of the expected changes in planum temporal asymmetry (Hamilton, Pascual-Leone, & Schlaug, 2004), or the superior auditory localization ability of blind subjects (Gougoux et al., 2005; Lessard et al., 1999).

However, at the same time, plasticity can be the cause of pathology. For example, acutely after visual de-afferentation, just as after a focal lesion of the occipital cortex, altered cortical excitability and rapid changes in cortico-cortical connectivity frequently lead to visual hallucinations and phantom vision (Merabet, Kobayashi, Barton, & Pascual-Leone, 2003; Merabet, Maguire, et al., 2004). Such hallucinations can be suppressed by reducing cortical excitability using low frequency repetitive TMS (Merabet et al., 2003). Eventually, hallucinations tend to subside, perhaps correlating with the long-lasting, cross-modal plasticity changes and the recruitment of the occipital cortex for high-order cognitive tasks. This same plasticity, although aiding in the adaptation to blindness may pose difficult challenges in other domains such as efforts aimed at developing visual prostheses for resorting functional vision. This later concept rests upon the premise that appropriate delivery of electrical stimulation to the retina or the occipital cortex can evoke patterned sensations of light even in those who have been blind for many years (Dobelle, 2000; see also Merabet et al., 2005, for review). Nonetheless, success in developing functional visual prostheses requires an understanding of how to communicate effectively with the plastically changed, visually deprived brain to merge what is perceived visually with what is generated electrically (Merabet et al., 2005). Similarly challenging is the situation for patients who recover sight through surgical approaches (e.g., cataract removal or corneal stem-cell transplant) after long-term visual deprivation (Fine et al., 2003).

REHABILITATION STRATEGIES IN LIGHT OF PLASTICITY

In response to a growing and unmet need, efforts in bioengineering and microtechnology are pursuing the development of sensory substitution devices (SSDs) designed to augment or replace vision by exploiting the processing capabilities of intact sensory modalities (in particular, touch and hearing). Concurrently, sophisticated microelectronic devices are being developed to stimulate viable neuronal tissue in the hopes of generating functional vision artificially.

Current applications of SSD technology (e.g., walking canes and sound echo-location devices) serve as a means of "augmented vision" and have helped tremendously in increasing a blind individual's mobility and functional independence (Bach-y-Rita & Kercel, 2003). However, previous approaches lack the sophistication needed to generate truly functional sensory percepts that would allow an individual to recognize, say, a complex object within a visual scene. Furthermore, as originally conceived, these devices do not exploit the functional and behavioral advantage of integrating sensory information from multiple sensory modalities.

Within the realm of prosthetic vision, numerous groups worldwide are pursuing a variety of approaches and human clinical trials are currently underway. Considerable technical advances have been achieved; however, a key milestone has yet to be demonstrated conclusively: that an implanted microelectronic device can create truly meaningful and functional visual percepts. Arguably, the greatest impediments to future progress in prosthesis research are not technical and surgical issues but rather the development of specific strategies designed to communicate with the visually deprived brain (Merabet et al., 2005). Specifically, it has become increasingly clear that the correspondence between the pattern of electrical stimulation and the target object for which it encodes is not intuitively obvious (Rizzo, Wyatt, Loewenstein, Kelly & Shire, 2003). Thus, novel stimulation strategies are needed so functionally meaningful sensory information can be extracted and integrated from neuroprosthetic inputs (Merabet et al., 2005).

We have argued that the compensatory recruitment of the occipital cortex may represent the exploitation of intrinsic spatial and temporal processing capabilities inherent to the visual system. Furthermore, these neuroplastic changes indicate that the potential of the adult brain to "reprogram" itself might be much greater than has previously been assumed (Pascual-Leone et al., 2005)—a conclusion that has obvious important repercussions in terms of neurorehabilitation. By studying the changes that follow visual deprivation, we can begin to elucidate the conditions and constraints that underlie these functional adaptations. With this in mind, it would be logical to conclude that these same neuroplastic changes are inextricably linked to the clinical outcome and success of visual sensory substitution and neuroprosthetic devices (Pascual-Leone et al., 2005).

Case studies of surgical sight restoration following long-term visual deprivation (e.g., Fine et al., 2003; Gregory, 2004)) provide a relevant insight. Following ocular surgical procedures aimed at regaining some degree of functional vision, patients blinded for many years experience profound difficulty in a variety of visual tasks, particularly those requiring the identification and recognition of objects through sight alone. Interestingly, if patients are allowed to explore the same object through touch, they can recognize it immediately as if to register their newly acquired visual percepts with their existing senses. These accounts demonstrate that even when vision reaches the brain physiologically, visual perception remains nonetheless impaired. Thus, the simple restoration of a lost sensory input may not itself suffice in reconstituting the sense it normally provides.

There remains a considerable gap between effective SSDs and visual prosthesis device implementation and the rehabilitative challenges needed to integrate these new technologies in patients. The modest success achieved to date with human experimentation is not merely limited by the technical issues that remain to be solved but is more likely related to our ignorance regarding how to communicate with the visually deprived brain (Merabet et al., 2005). As we have discussed above, the visually deprived brain is changed due to plasticity. Therefore, any rehabilitative strategy will ultimately require an understanding of these neuroplastic mechanisms in order to predict their feasibility and evaluate their success. These concepts are also likely to extend to the development of nonvisual neuroprosthetic devices (e.g. cochlear implants and motor prosthetics) and bring hope to the people who need them.

AUGMENTED VISION

The novelty of the proposed approach is based upon the optimization of the sensory processing capabilities of both touch and hearing. Visually impaired patients can benefit from this multimodal approach regardless of the cause or time of onset of their vision loss. Once a visually impaired user becomes proficient in using combined SSD technology, the patient can transfer these adaptive skills into activities of daily living. If the patient is selected for implantation with a visual prosthesis, the same approach can serve as a pre- and postsurgical training platform to assist in developing appropriate encoding strategies for enhancing the interpretation of visual percepts generated though prosthetic vision.

The insights on the plastic changes that take place in the brain of blind individuals suggest that integrated tactile and auditory stimulation encoding for spatial and temporal attributes of objects can be used by a blind individual to generate sensory percepts that can be manipulated and interacted with. This notion leads to the principle that tactile and auditory inputs (processed within the cross-modally altered visual cortex) can be used to "remap" restored visual sensations and serve as a means of augmented vision. Furthermore, rehabilitation with a visual neuroprosthesis could be coupled with sensory-guided plasticity to maximize the "re-learning" process that is necessary to regain functional sight. Current notions in computational neuroscience suggest that sensory representations are shared by different pathways and modalities and thus are likely to share common computational mechanisms and processing strategies (Pascual-Leone & Hamilton, 2001; Riesenhuber & Poggio, 2000). Consider the case of object recognition. Clearly, there is a correspondence between how an object appears, how it sounds, and how the same object feels when it is explored through touch. We have discussed recent evidence demonstrating that there is significant overlap between cortical areas that are implicated in object recognition through different modalities. This suggests that certain cortical areas may contain more abstract features of object form rather than just simple representations of visual images (Amedi, von Kriegstein, von Atteveldt, Beauchamp, & Naumer, 2005). Given that such functional overlaps exist in blind individuals (as well as in sighted individuals), potentially, these underlying mechanisms may serve as a foundation for optimizing an approach for effective rehabilitative strategies. In particular, the possibility exists that a blind individual using a SSD-based device can manipulate concordant tactile and auditory inputs in order to translate cross-modal visual sensations into functionally meaningful sensory percepts (see Figure 3–4 for explanation and details of the approach). Furthermore, in the case of a patient implanted with a visual neuroprosthetic device, it should be possible to incorporate patient-directed feedback that iteratively alters stimulation parameters of the prosthesis based on the user's cross-modal sensory experiences.

CONCLUSIONS

We have argued that the brain is highly plastic and that plasticity represents evolution's invention to enable the nervous system to escape the restrictions of its own genome (and its highly specialized cellular specification) and adapt to

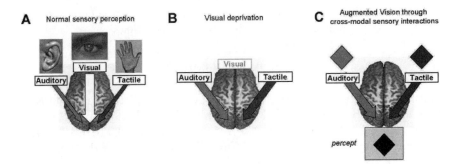

FIGURE 3–4. Summary of multimodal sensory processing and it implication to neuroplasticity and means to restore functional vision. A: Under normal conditions, the occipital cortex receives predominantly visual inputs, but perception is also highly influenced by cross-modal sensory information obtained from other sources (e.g., touch and hearing). B: Following visual deprivation, neuroplastic changes occur such that the visual cortex is recruited to process sensory information from other senses (illustrated by larger arrows for touch and hearing). This might be through the potential "unmasking" or enhancement of connections that are already present. After neuroplastic changes associated with vision loss have occurred, the visual cortex is fundamentally altered in terms of its sensory processing, so that simple reintroduction of visual input (e.g., by a visual prosthesis) is not sufficient to create meaningful vision. C: To create meaningful percepts, a visually impaired patient (using SSDs or in association with an implanted visual prosthesis) can incorporate concordant information from remaining sensory sources. In this case, the shape of the object can be determined by simultaneous exploration of tactile presented information and directionality information provided by auditory input. Training with SSDs or modifying visual input by a visual neuroprosthesis in conjunction with appropriate auditory and tactile stimulation could potentially maximize the functional significance of generated sensory percepts and regain behaviorally relevant augmented vision. (Modified from Merabet et al., 2005). [See Color Plate]

rapidly shifting and often unpredictable environmental and experiential changes. Because of this plasticity, given the profound functional consequences of loss of sight, the brain of visually impaired and blind individuals is fundamentally different from that of the sighted in many aspects. Some of these plastic changes result in crucial functional advantages for blind individuals who can localize sound sources or resolve tactile textures better than the sighted. However, plastic changes may not necessarily represent a behavioral gain for a given subject, and they represent a main mechanism for development and learning, as well as a cause of pathology and disease. In the case of blindness, a grave challenge of neural plasticity is that restoration of sight may not result in functional vision. Novel strategies are needed to guide brain plasticity and utilize cross-modal interactions to promote functional adaptation to blindness and reshape the brain of blind individuals following restoration of vision. Such strategies require a careful consideration of brain plasticity mechanisms and the modulation of brain function to guide plastic changes, enhancing those that promote behavioral gains and suppressing those that may be maladaptive and deleterious. Ultimately, such approaches need to take into consideration the different "starting points" imposed by genetic factors, and thus require individualized tailoring of the interventions.

ACKNOWLEDGMENTS

Work on this chapter was supported in part by grants from the National Institutes of Health (K24 RR018875, RO1-EY12091, R21-EY0116168, RO1-EY016559, RO1-MH069898, RO1-NS 47754, RO1-NS 20068, RO1-EB 005047) and the Harvard-Thorndike General Clinical Research Center (NCRR MO1 RR01032). Lofti Merabet is supported by a mentored career development award from the National Eye Institute (K23 EY016131-01). Amir Amedi is supported by The International Human Frontier Science Program Organization. We thank Mark Thivierge for his invaluable administrative support.

REFERENCES

Amedi., A., Floel, A., Knecht, S., Zohary, E., & Cohen, L. G. (2004). Transcranial magnetic stimulation of the occipital pole interferes with verbal processing in blind subjects. *Natural Neuroscience, 7*, 1266–70.

Amedi, A., Jacobson, G., Hendler, T., Malach, R., & Zohary, E. (2002). Convergence of visual and tactile shape processing in the human lateral occipital complex. *Cerebral Cortex, 12*, 1202–12.

Amedi, A., Malach, R., Hendler, T., Peled, S., & Zohary, E. (2001). Visuo-haptic object-related activation in the ventral visual pathway. *Natural Neuroscience, 4*, 324–30.

Amedi, A., Raz, N., Pianka, P., Malach, R., & Zohary, E. (2003). Early 'visual' cortex activation correlates with superior verbal memory performance in the blind. *Natural Neuroscience, 6*, 758–66.

Amedi, A., von Kriegstein, K., van Atteveldt, N. M., Beauchamp, M. S., & Naumer, M. J. (2005). Functional imaging of human crossmodal identification and object recognition. *Experimental Brain Research, 166*, 559–71.

Bach-y-Rita, P., & Kercel, W. (2003). Sensory substitution and the human-machine interface. *Trends in Cognitive Sciences, 7*, 541–46.

Buchel, C., Price, C., Frackowiak, R. S., & Friston, K. (1998). Different activation patterns in the visual cortex of late and congenitally blind subjects. *Brain, 121*(Pt 3), 409–19.

Burton, H. (2003). Visual cortex activity in early and late blind people. *Journal of Neuroscience, 23*, 4005–11.

Burton, H., Snyder, A. Z., Conturo, T. E., Akbudak, E., Ollinger, J. M., & Raichle, M. E. (2002). Adaptive changes in early and late blind: a fMRI study of Braille reading. *Journal of Neurophysiology, 87*, 589–607.

Burton, H., Snyder, A. Z., Diamond, J. B., & Raichle, M. E. (2002). Adaptive changes in early and late blind: a FMRI study of verb generation to heard nouns. *Journal of Neurophysiology, 88*, 3359–71.

Cohen, L.G., Celnik, P., Pascual-Leone, A., Corwell, B., Falz, L., Dambrosia, J., et al. (1997). Functional relevance of cross-modal plasticity in blind humans. *Nature, 389*, 180–83.

Dobelle, W. H. (2000). Artificial vision for the blind by connecting a television camera to the visual cortex. *ASAIO Journal, 46*, 3–9.

Doucet, M. E., Guillemot, J. P., Lassonde, M., Gagne, J. P., Leclerc, C., & Lepore, F. (2005). Blind subjects process auditory spectral cues more efficiently than sighted individuals. *Experimental Brain Research, 160*, 194–202.

Fine, I., Wade, A. R., Brewer, A. A., May, M. G., Goodman, D. F., Boynton, G. M., et al. (2003). Long-term deprivation affects visual perception and cortex. *Nature Neuroscience, 6*, 915–16.

Gougoux, F., Lepore, F., Lassonde, M., Voss, P., Zatorre, R. J., & Belin, P. (2004). Neuropsychology: Pitch discrimination in the early blind. *Nature, 430*, 309.

Gougoux, F., Zatorre, R. J., Lassonde, M., Voss, P., & Lepore, F. (2005). A functional neuroimaging study of sound localization: visual cortex activity predicts performance in early-blind individuals. *PLoS Biology, 3*, 27.

Gregory, R. (2004). The blind leading the sighted. *Nature 430:* 836.

Hamilton, R., Keenan, J. P., Catala, M., & Pascual-Leone, A. (2000). Alexia for Braille following bilateral occipital stroke in an early blind woman. *Neuroreport, 11*, 237–40.

Hamilton, R., & Pascual-Leone, A. (1998). Cortical plasticity associated with Braille learning. *Trends in Cognitive Science, 2*(5), 168–74.

Hamilton, R. H., Pascual-Leone, A., & Schlaug, G. (2004). Absolute pitch in blind musicians. *NeuroReport, 15*, 803–6.

Hollins, M., & Kelley, E. K. (1988). Spatial updating in blind and sighted people. *Perception and Psychophysics, 43*: 380–88.

Kujala, T., Alho, K., Paavilainen, P., Summala, H., & Naatanen, R. (1992). Neural plasticity in processing of sound location by the early blind: An event-related potential study. *Electroencephalography and Clinical Neurophysiology, 84*, 469–72.

Lessard, N., Lepore, F., Poirier, P., Villemagne, J., & Lassonde, M. (1999). Localization of moving sounds byhemispherectomized subjects. *Behavioural Brain Research, 104*, 37–49.

Melzer, P., Morgan, V. L., Pickens, D. R., Price, R. R., Wall, R. S., & Ebner, F. F. (2001). Cortical activation during Braille reading is influenced by early visual experience in subjects with severe visual disability: A correlational fMRI study. *Human Brain Mapping, 14*, 186–95.

Merabet, L. B., Kobayashi, M., Barton, J., & Pascual-Leone, A. (2003). Suppression of complex visual hallucinatory experiences by occipital transcranial magnetic stimulation: a case report. *Neurocase, 9,* 436–40.

Merabet, L. B., Maguire, D., Warde, A., Alterescu, K., Stickgold, R., & Pascual-Leone, A. (2004). Visual hallucinations during prolonged blindfolding in sighted subjects. *Journal of Neuroophthalmology, 24,* 109–13.

Merabet, L. B., Rizzo, J. F., Amedi, A., Somers, D. C., & Pascual-Leone, A. (2005). What blindness can tell us about seeing again: Merging neuroplasticity and neuroprostheses. *Nature Reviews Neuroscience, 6,* 71–77.

Merabet, L., Thut, G., Murray, B., Andrews, J., Hsiao, S., & Pascual-Leone, A. (2004). Feeling by sight or seeing by touch? *Neuron, 42,* 173–79.

Pascual-Leone, A., Amedi, A., Fregni, F., & Merabet, L. B. (2005). The plastic human brain cortex. *Annual Review of Neuroscience, 28,* 377–401.

Pascual-Leone, A., Cohen, L. G., Brasil-Neto, J. P., Valls-Sole, J., & Hallett, M. (1994). Differentiation of sensorimotor neuronal structures responsible for induction of motor evoked potentials, attenuation in detection of somatosensory stimuli, and induction of sensation of movement by mapping of optimal current directions. *Electroencephalography and Clinical Neurophysiology, 93,* 230–36.

Pascual-Leone, A., & Hamilton, R. (2001). The metamodal organization of the brain. *Progress in Brain Research, 134,* 427–45.

Pascual-Leone, A., Walsh, V., & Rothwell, J. (2000). Transcranial magnetic stimulation in cognitive neuroscience—virtual lesion, chronometry, and functional connectivity. *Current Opinion in Neurobiology, 10,* 232–37.

Phelps, M. E., Mazziotta, J. C., Kuhl, D. E., Nuwer, M., Packwood, J., Metter, J., et al. (1981). Tomographic mapping of human cerebral metabolism visual stimulation and deprivation. *Neurology, 31,* 517–29.

Rauschecker, J. P. (1995). Compensatory plasticity and sensory substitution in the cerebral cortex. *Trends in Neuroscience, 18,* 36–43.

Riesenhuber, M., & Poggio, T. (2000). Models of object recognition. *Natural Neuroscience, 3(Suppl.),* 1199–1204.

Rizzo, J. F., 3rd, Wyatt, J., Loewenstein, J., Kelly, S., & Shire, D. (2003). Perceptual efficacy of electrical stimulation of human retina with a microelectrode array during short-term surgical trials. *Investigative Ophthalmology and Visual Science, 44,* 5362–69.

Roder, B., Stock, O., Bien, S., Neville, H., & Rosler, F. (2002). Speech processing activates visual cortex in congenitally blind humans. *European Journal of Neuroscience, 16,* 930–36.

Sadato, N., Okada, T., Honda, M., & Yonekura, Y. (2002). Critical period for cross-modal plasticity in blind humans: A functional MRI study. *Neuroimage, 16,* 389–400.

Sadato, N., Pascual-Leone, A., Grafman, J., Deiber, M. P., Ibanez, V., & Hallett, M. (1998). Neural networks for Braille reading by the blind. *Brain, 121*(Pt 7), 1213–29.

Sadato, N., Pascual-Leone, A., Grafman, J., Ibanez, V., Deiber, M. P., et al. (1996). Activation of the primary visual cortex by Braille reading in blind subjects. *Nature, 380,* 526–28.

Theoret, H., Merabet, L., & Pascual-Leone, A. (2004). Behavioral and neuroplastic changes in the blind: Evidence for functionally relevant cross-modal interactions. *Journal of Physiology, 98,* 221–33.

Uhl, F., Franzen, P., Lindinger, G., Lang, W., & Deecke, L. (1991). On the functionality of the visually deprived occipital cortex in early blind persons. *Neuroscience Letters*, 124, 256–59.

Uhl, F., Franzen, P., Podreka, I., Steiner, M., & Deecke, L. (1993). Increased regional cerebral blood flow in inferior occipital cortex and cerebellum of early blind humans. *Neuroscience Letters*, 150, 162–64.

Van Boven, R. W., Hamilton, R. H., Kauffman, T., Keenan, J. P., & Pascual-Leone, A. (2000). Tactile spatial resolution in blind braille readers. *Neurology*, 54, 2230–36.

Voss, P., Lassonde, M., Gougoux, F., Fortin, M., Guillemot, J. P., & Lepore, F. (2004). Early- and late-onset blind individuals show supra-normal auditory abilities in far-space. *Current Biology*, 14, 1734–38.

Wanet-Defalque, M. C., Veraart, C., De Volder, A., Metz, R., Michel, C., Dooms, G., et al. (1988). High metabolic activity in the visual cortex of early blind human subjects. *Brain Research*, 446, 369–73.

Weeks, R., Horwitz, B., Aziz-Sultan, A., Tian, B., Wessinger, C. M., Cohen, L. G., et al. (2000). A positron emission tomographic study of auditory localization in the congenitally blind. *Journal of Neuroscience*, 20, 2664–72.

Zangaladze, A., Epstein, C. M., Grafton, S. T., & Sathian, K. (1999). Involvement of visual cortex in tactile discrimination of orientation. *Nature*, 401, 587–90.

4

Plasticity of Cortical Maps in Visual Deprivation

Josef P. Rauschecker

EXPERIENCE-DEPENDENT PLASTICITY OF THE CEREBRAL CORTEX

Sensory deprivation from birth leads to deleterious consequences for connectivity and function of the cerebral cortex. Beginning with the pioneering work of Wiesel and Hubel (1963, 1965), this has been especially well documented for the visual cortex. Binocular lid suture at birth, which prevents all pattern vision, renders the majority of neurons in the visual cortex either unresponsive to light or unselective to oriented contours. Loss of selectivity can be considered just as devastating as loss of responsiveness because it renders the cortical system essentially dysfunctional. These negative effects of sensory deprivation are thought to result from disuse and, consequently, lack of activation of corresponding circuits in the brain.

Increased use, on the other hand, leads to a strengthening of synaptic connections, an increase in selectivity, and an expansion of cortical tissue activated by the corresponding stimuli. This has been shown particularly well for the somatosensory cortex, where increased stimulation of particular body parts results in their expanded representation, even in adult animals (Merzenich, Recanzone, Jenkins, Allard, & Nudo, 1988; Kaas, 1991). Since the overall size of the cortical surface does not change, one has to assume that the expansion of certain body-part representations occurs at the expense of others. Thus, while the relative size of cortical representations is determined innately by the number or density of afferent fibers from the sensory periphery, the actual size of these maps is modulated constantly as a function of sensory experience.

If shifting map sizes are possible within one sensory modality, similar changes can be expected across modalities depending on relative levels of activation. Increased use of the auditory sense, for instance, should lead to an expansion of auditory cortex, possibly at the expense of lesser used areas. Similarly, deprivation of one modality, such as in early blindness or deafness, could lead to compensation of these deprivation effects by other modalities. Therefore, the increased use of nonvisual senses, such as the use of Braille reading in the blind, could lead to an expansion of these modalities in the brain, concomitant with an improvement of their behavioral abilities.

Visual Plasticity

The effects of monocular deprivation can be seen as adaptive only insofar as the circuitry changes in the visual cortex reflect the reality of the visual inputs: The eye that was occluded during a critical period ends up driving fewer neurons and innervating less cortical tissue than the open eye (Wiesel & Hubel, 1963). This physiological change is accompanied by a dramatic loss of visual acuity (amblyopia) at the behavioral level. However, apart from small improvements in hyperacuity, the experienced eye does not seem to garner any advantage from its vastly expanded control of visual cortical neurons. It seems, therefore, that the visual cortical system is already working at an optimum, and a ceiling effect prevents it from improving even further.

Clearly adaptive effects of cortical plasticity can be demonstrated in reverse-occlusion studies. If the previously deprived eye of a young kitten is opened and the previously open is now closed, the deprived eye can regain connections with the cortex, drive neurons and reestablish normal vision through the initially deprived eye (Blakemore & Van Sluyters, 1974; Hubel & Wiesel, 1970). This is only possible, however, if the previously open eye is indeed occluded, as this prevents it from defending its territory. If the previously deprived eye is simply reopened (without occluding the other eye), it cannot fully regain its normal function, as is well known from the treatment of amblyopic children. Some success of amblyopia treatment has also been shown in adult amblyopes, although it is generally agreed that this is much more limited than in young children. This has been considered as proof for the existence of a critical period for certain types of visual development in humans.

In strabismic amblyopia, which results from a deviation of the axis of one eye (or "crossed eyes"), another effect is the loss of stereoscopic vision or the ability to combine the 2-D input from both eyes to the visual cortex in order to compute 3-D vision. This loss of stereovision, however, as bad as it is, prevents an even more deleterious effect, namely the persistence of double vision (diplopia), as it would result from an erroneous combination (and lack of fusion) of the two images. Thus, to a certain extent, even the effects of strabismus can be considered adaptive. In some cases, the development of an anomalous correspondence is observed, where plastic reorganization leads to fusion between the fovea of one eye and a pseudo-fovea in the other eye, but this works only for small strabismic angles.

Other examples of adaptive plasticity in the visual system come from studies of receptive field properties in the visual cortex, such as orientation and direction selectivity. As was shown in the early days of cortical plasticity work, the distribution of both parameters can be influenced by visual experience (Blakemore & Mitchell, 1973; Hirsch & Spinelli, 1970; Tretter, Cyander, & Singer, 1975; for review see Rauschecker, 1991; Singer, 1995). However, studies disagreed about the mechanisms of how these changes are effected (Stryker, Leventhal, & Hirsch, 1978; Stryker & Sherk, 1975). Eventually, agreement was reached that Hebb-type synapses can account for modification of orientation and direction selectivity just as they can for changes in ocular dominance (Rauschecker & Singer, 1979, Rauschecker, 1981). The consequence of this rather simple mechanism, however, is that there are limits as to the extent of the changes that are possible. As has been argued before, a Hebbian mechanism could account for changes only within a neuron's existing tuning range but would not permit unlimited changes of response preference (Rauschecker, 1991). Even taking into account the broader tuning of neurons in young animals, the shaping of response preference would largely be based on a loss of responsiveness in neurons that are not adequately stimulated by the visual environment.

In conclusion, the visual deprivation literature contains only limited evidence for truly adaptive plasticity. By contrast, it tends to highlight the huge vulnerability of the young animal by an impoverished environment. The degrees of freedom kept open by the genetic apparatus, which are filled by normal visual experience during normal development, leave the system underspecified under abnormal circumstances.

Somatosensory Plasticity

An extensive literature exists also about adaptive plasticity in the somatosensory system, especially in nonhuman primates. Whereas deprivation-type studies are more difficult to accomplish in this system, a great deal of work has been performed with either peripheral lesions or stimulation/training of particular body parts (Jones & Pons, 1998; Kaas, 1991; Merzenich et al., 1988; Pons et al., 1991; Recanzone, Allard, Jenkins, & Merzenich, 1990; Recanzone, Jenkins, Hradek, & Merzenich, 1992). Many of these studies reveal an extent of plasticity not seen in other systems. Overall, they certainly speak to the enormous amount of plasticity inherent in cortical organization, mediated undoubtedly by long-range excitatory connections but also by local inhibitory circuits.

Auditory Plasticity

Some pioneering work notwithstanding (Calford, Rajan, & Irvine, 1993; Edeline & Weinberger, 1993; Rajan, Irvine, Wise, & Heil, 1993; Recanzone, Schreiner, & Merzenich, 1993; Weinberger & Diamond, 1987), the recognition that auditory cortical structure and function are highly plastic was slower to arrive than in the visual and somatosensory cortical systems. This was partly due to the relative isolation of this field and a partial resistance against the idea that the auditory system with its rather distinct peripheral mechanisms might actually be quite similar to other sensory systems at the level of the cerebral cortex. Once this realization set in, however, a flurry of recent studies confirmed that auditory cortical plasticity is just as massive as that in the visual or somatosensory system (Bao, Chang, Davis, Gobeske, & Merzenich, 2003; Beitel, Schreiner, Cheung, Wang, & Merzenich, 2003; Blake & Merzenich, 2002; Kilgard & Merzenich, 1998a, 1998b; Klinke, Kral, Heil, Tillein, & Hartmann, 1999; Zhang, Bao, & Merzenich, 2001). Parallels with other sensory systems include the use-dependence and the role of gating signals such as acetylcholine in the enhancement of cortical plasticity (Bakin & Weinberger, 1996; Cruikshank & Weinberger, 1996).

Behavioral Compensation for Early Blindness

Some of the above considerations, especially those on the role of visual deprivation, could lead to the impression that the malleability of the cerebral cortex poses more risks than benefits to the developing organism. It would be surprising, however, if cortical plasticity was in fact largely maladaptive. Perhaps brain optimization takes into account more than a single sensory system at a time. Reports that sensory deprivation in one modality leads to compensatory changes in other modalities can be found from various sources. Anecdotal accounts about the disproportionate number of blind musicians abound (Rauschecker, 2001) and have recently been substantiated (Gaab and colleagues, unpublished data). Behavioral observations of visually deprived animals demonstrate that they are highly adept at a variety of behaviors, including the localization of objects. In one of their first papers on the effects of visual deprivation, Wiesel and Hubel (1965) note: "As the lid-sutured kittens grew up, they adapted remarkably well to their blindness. They learned to move about adroitly in the large room where they were kept, and became so familiar with the objects in the room that a casual observer would hardly have guessed they could not see."

These qualitative observations were later quantified in controlled studies. Rauschecker and Kniepert (1994) trained cats to walk towards sound sources that emitted brief (40-ms) tone pips at eight different randomized azimuth positions around a centered start box. Cats that were visually deprived from birth localized sounds with significantly smaller errors, particularly in

lateral and rear positions. The same result was found for visually deprived ferrets (King & Parsons, 1999). Both results correspond extremely well with those
obtained in studies of blind humans (Rice, Feinstein, & Schusterman, 1965;
Rice, 1970; Röder et al., 1999).

CORTICAL PROCESSING OF AUDITORY SPACE

In order to consider the neural basis of improved sound localization in the
blind, it is necessary first to describe the neural systems involved in auditory
space processing.

Brainstem Processing of Auditory Space

The superior colliculus (SC) is often considered the seat of auditory spatial
perception because it contains a map of auditory space. This has been shown
in various species: owls (Knudsen & Konishi, 1978), guinea pigs (King &
Hutchings, 1987), cats (Middlebrooks & Knudsen, 1984). The SC receives
its input from the inferior colliculus (IC), in particular the "external" nuclei
of the IC, which in turn receive their input from the dorsal part of the cochlear
nuclei (DCN). The medial and lateral superior olive (MSO, LSO) are responsible for encoding interaural time and level differences (ITD and ILD), respectively. (For a more complete review of brainstem mechanisms of auditory
space processing see Irvine, 1992.)

Spatial Selectivity in Primary
and Nonprimary Auditory Cortex

Early studies have suggested a role for auditory cortex in sound localization
(Diamond, Fisher, Neff, & Yela, 1956; Heffner & Masterton, 1975; Ravizza &
Masterton, 1972). However, the first study to demonstrate unequivocally that
a lesion of primary auditory cortex (A1) causes a deficit in sound localization
was performed in cats by Jenkins and Merzenich (1984). Their findings were
confirmed in later studies using different tasks (Beitel & Kaas, 1993; Heffner
& Heffner, 1990). In these studies, A1 appeared to be the only region of auditory cortex whose ablation caused a localization deficit. However, cats have
an auditory cortical region that is hidden deep in the anterior ectosylvian sulcus (AES; Meredith & Clemo, 1989) which was later implicated in sound
localization as well (Korte & Rauschecker, 1993; Middlebrooks, Clock, Xu, &
Green, 1994; Rauschecker & Korte, 1993). It is the main source of auditory
cortical input to the SC. In addition, on the basis of cortical cooling studies,
the posterior auditory field (PAF) has also been claimed to play a role in sound
localization (Malhotra, Hall, & Lomber, 2004).

Spatial tuning of single cortical neurons in A1 was measured by a number of groups (Imig, Irons, & Samson, 1990; Rajan, Aitkin, & Irvine, 1990a; Rajan, Aitkin, & Irivine, 1990b). They all found two types of spatial tuning: single-peak and hemi-field. In single-peak neurons, the best response is found at a particular azimuth location; in hemi-field neurons, the response is largely restricted to speaker locations in the contra- or ipsi-lateral hemifield.

In rhesus monkeys, spatially tuned neurons are also found in A1, but even more of these neurons are found in the caudo-medial field (CM; Rauschecker, Tian, Pons, & Mishkin, 1997; Recanzone, 2000). When monkeys are trained in an auditory localization task, the firing rate of neurons in CM correlates more tightly with behavioral performance than that of neurons in A1, which is a strong indication that CM plays an important role in sound localization (Recanzone, Guard, Phan, & Su, 2000).

Early Parallel Processing in the Auditory Cortex

Parallel processing streams in the auditory cortex start as early as the primary-like core areas, A1 and R. Combined lesion and tracer studies (Rauschecker et al., 1997) have shown that both cortical core areas receive input from the principal relay nucleus of the auditory thalamus, the ventral nucleus of the medial geniculate (MGv). By contrast, area CM receives input only from the medial and dorsal subnuclei of the medial geniculate (MGm and MGd, respectively).

The parallel input to areas of the supratemporal plane may start even more peripherally than the thalamus. Studies of the auditory brainstem indicate that the ventral and dorsal cochlear nuclei have very different response characteristics and may subserve different functions of hearing, including auditory object and space processing, respectively (Yu & Young, 2000). Area CM, which contains large numbers of spatially tuned neurons (Rauschecker et al., 1997; Recanzone, 2000), could receive at least some of its input from the dorsal cochlear nucleus via the external nuclei of the inferior colliculus and the MGd (Rauschecker, 1997).

Spatial and Pattern Selectivity in the Lateral Auditory Belt Cortex

In order to compare the spatial selectivity of neurons in the rostral and caudal lateral belt (LB) directly in the same animals, broad-band, species-specific communication calls were presented from different locations (Tian, Reser, Durham, Kustov, & Rauschecker, 2001). To quantify the response selectivity to different monkey calls (MC), a monkey call preference index (MCPI) was calculated depending on the number of calls the neuron responds to. Subdivisions of the LB areas differed in their degree of MC selectivity. The anterolateral area (AL) had the greatest percentage of highly selective neurons (MCPI ≤ 2), followed by the middle lateral area (ML). The caudolateral area (CL) had the smallest percentage of highly MC-selective neurons. Naturally, for the most nonselective neurons (MCPI ≥ 6), the opposite was found: CL had the greatest percentage of such nonselective neurons, AL the least, with ML somewhere between those two extremes.

Spatial tuning in neurons of the LB showed the opposite areal distribution: The highest selectivity was found in CL and the lowest in AL. This has led to the hypothesis that these two areas, which lie on opposite ends of the LB along its rostro–caudal extent, form the beginning of two processing streams for the processing of auditory space and pattern information (see Figure 4–1) (Rauschecker & Tian, 2000; Tian et al., 2001). The anterior

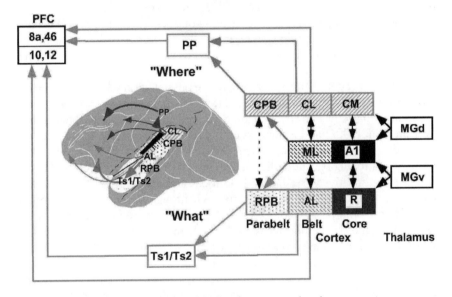

FIGURE 4–1.   Schematic diagram of dual auditory cortical pathways in primates representing auditory object/pattern ("what") processing in an antero-ventral projection and auditory space ("where") processing in a postero-dorsal projection (modified and expanded from Rauschecker, 1998, and Rauschecker & Tian, 2000). The auditory "where"-pathway is the main topic of the present chapter. Its projections are highlighted in solid lines; participating cortical areas are marked with oblique lines. The antero-ventral pathway is shown in dashed lines. Areas that are not uniquely participating in either pathway are shown in dark blocks (primary auditory cortex, A1) or stippled (middle lateral belt area, ML). Prefrontal connections of the lateral belt areas are also shown directly on a lateral view of a rhesus monkey brain (from Romanski et al., 1999). Abbreviations: MGd = medial geniculate nucleus, dorsal division; MGv = medial geniculate nucleus, ventral division; CM = caudomedial area; R = rostral area; AL = anterolateral area; CL = caudolateral area; CPB = caudal parabelt area; RPB = rostral parabelt area; TPJ = temporoparietal junction; PP = posterior parietal cortex; Ts1, Ts2 = rostral temporal areas of (Pandya & Sanides, 1973); PFC = prefrontal cortex. Brodmann areas are abbreviated with their respective numbers. [See Color Plate]

"what"-stream extends all the way to the temporal pole (Poremba et al., 2003). By contrast, the posterior "where"-stream projects to parietal cortex and dorsolateral prefrontal cortex.

Auditory Belt Projections to Parietal and Prefrontal Cortex

Prefrontal projections. Anatomical studies in rhesus monkeys have demonstrated the existence of largely separate pathways that originate in the LB and project to different target regions in the prefrontal cortex (Romanski et al., 1999), as seen in Figure 4–1. Fluorescent tracer injections into area AL produce label in ventrolateral and orbital regions of prefrontal cortex (areas 10, 12), whereas CL injections lead to labeling of dorsolateral prefrontal cortex (areas 8a, 46). The latter is known for its involvement in spatial working memory, whereas the former regions are assumed to participate in object working memory (Goldman-Rakic, 1996).

These projection patterns conform to the physiological response properties found in the study of Tian et al. (2001), which assigned superior selectivity for auditory patterns and space to areas AL and CL, respectively. The studies by Tian et al. (2001) and Romanski et al. (1999), therefore, form the cornerstones of a recent theory according to which dual processing streams in nonprimary auditory cortex underlie the perception of auditory objects and auditory space, respectively (see Figure 4–1; also Rauschecker & Tian, 2000). One pathway projecting antero-ventrally from A1 through AL and the rostral STG and STS into orbitofrontal cortex forms the main substrate for auditory pattern recognition and object identification. Indeed, an auditory domain is found in ventrolateral prefrontal cortex, in which neurons show responses to complex sounds, including animal and human vocalizations (Romanski & Goldman-Rakic, 2002). Another pathway projecting caudo-dorsally from A1 to the caudal belt (areas CM and CL) and parabelt, including the tempororietal area (Tpt) and CPB, into posterior parietal (PP) and dorsolateral prefrontal cortex is thought to be involved in auditory spatial processing.

Parietal projections. A projection from posterior STG to posterior parietal cortex in monkeys has been found independently by Lewis and Van Essen (2000). Specifically, the ventral intraparietal area (VIP) in the PP has been identified as the primary recipient of auditory input to PP. The lateral intraparietal area (LIP) has been found to contain auditory neurons as well, but only after training monkeys on auditory saccades (Mazzoni, Bracewell, Barash, & Andersen, 1996; Stricanne, Andersen, & Massoni, 1996; Andersen, 1997). Auditory activation of inferior PP has also been demonstrated in human imaging studies (Bremmer et al., 2001; Bushara et al., 1999; Weeks et al., 1999). By testing the subjects in a visual task as well as in an auditory task during the same imaging session, it was shown that PP does contain a unimodal auditory spatial representation before multisensory convergence occurs in superior parietal cortex (Bushara et al., 1999). A similar conclusion was reached on the basis of clinical and psychophysical studies by Griffiths and colleauges (Griffiths et al., 1996; Griffiths et al., 1997; Griffiths et al., 1998).

HUMAN IMAGING STUDIES OF AUDITORY SPATIAL PERCEPTION

Dual Streams in Human Auditory Cortical Processing: Patterns and Space

Various findings from human neuroimaging support the dual-stream hypothesis of auditory processing: Antero-lateral areas of the superior temporal cortex are activated by intelligible speech or speech-like sounds (Alain, Arnott, Hevenor, Graham, & Grady, 2001; Binder et al., 2000; Binder, Liebenthal, Possing, Medler, & Ward, 2004; Maeder et al., 2001; Obleser et al., 2005; Scott, Blank, Rosen, & Wise, 2000). Thus it becomes more and more obvious that behaviorally relevant auditory patterns, including speech sounds, are discriminated selectively within an anterior auditory "what"-stream and not in the *planum temporale* which is located posterior to Heschl's gyrus. Auditory areas in the planum temporale are still quite unspecific and involved in a variety of auditory functions.

Further posterior in the STG and STS are regions of the caudal belt and parabelt (projecting up dorsally into inferior posterior parietal cortex) that are specifically active during spatial tasks, such as auditory spatial discrimination or tasks involving auditory motion in space (Arnott, Binns, Grady, & Alain, 2004; Barrett & Hall, 2006; Brunetti et al., 2005; Degerman, Rinne, Salmi, Salonen, & Alho, 2006; Jääskeläinen et al., 2004; Krumbholz, Schonwiesner, Rubasmen, et al., 2005; Krumbholz, Schonwiesner, von Cramen, et al., 2005; Maeder et al., 2001; Tata & Ward, 2005a, 2005b; Zatorre, Bouffard, Ahad, & Belin, 2002; Warren, Zielinski, Green, Rauschecker, & Griffiths, 2002; Zimmer & Macaluso, 2005;).

In a meta-analysis, Arnott and collegues. (2004) reviewed evidence from auditory functional magnetic resonance imaging (fMRI) and positron emission tomography (PET) studies to determine the reliability of the auditory dual-pathway model in humans. Activation coordinates from 11 "spatial" studies (i.e., listeners made localization judgments on sounds that could occur at two or more perceptually different positions) and 27 "nonspatial" studies (i.e., listeners completed nonspatial tasks involving sounds presented from the same location) were entered into the analysis. Almost all temporal lobe activity observed during spatial tasks was confined to posterior areas. In addition, all but one of the spatial studies reported activation within the inferior parietal lobule as opposed to only 41% of the nonspatial studies. Finally, inferior frontal activity (Brodmann's areas 45 and 47) was reported in only 9% of the spatial studies but in 56% of the nonspatial studies. These results support an auditory dual-pathway model in humans in which nonspatial sound information (e.g., sound identity) is processed primarily along an antero-ventral stream whereas sound location is processed along a postero-dorsal stream (i.e. within areas posterior to primary auditory cortex).

In a PET study by Zatorre et al. (2002) posterior auditory cortex responded to sounds that varied in their spatial distribution but only when multiple complex stimuli were presented simultaneously. Consistent with other studies, these authors also found that the right inferior parietal cortex was recruited specifically in localization tasks.

An fMRI study by Krumbholz and Schonwiesner, von Cramen, and colleagues (2005) found that interaural time differences were represented along a posterior pathway comprising the planum temporale (PT) and inferior parietal lobe (IPL) of the respective contralateral hemisphere. The response was stronger and extended further into adjacent regions of the IPL when the sound was moving than when it was stationary, a finding that confirmed earlier results by Warren and colleagues (2002). In contrast to Zatorre and colleagues (2002), the study by Krumbholz, Schonwiesner, von Cramen, and colleagues (2005) found that stationary lateralized sounds did produce a significant activation increase in the PT of the respective contralateral hemisphere compared to a centrally presented sound. This discrepancy may be due to the inferior sensitivity of PET relative to fMRI, or to the fact that the spatial ranges of the sounds used by Zatorre and colleagues were centered around the midline, and thus always comprised equal parts of both hemifields. These differences suggest that Zatorre and colleagues were unable to detect the contralateral tuning that was observed in the study of Krumbholz and colleagues.

Timing differences between the two ears can be used to localize sounds in space only when the inputs to the two ears have similar spectro-temporal profiles (high binaural coherence). Zimmer and Macaluso (2005) used fMRI to investigate any modulation of auditory responses by binaural coherence. They assessed how processing of these cues depends on spatial information being task-relevant and whether brain activity correlates with subjects' localization performance. They found that activity in Heschl's gyrus increased with increasing coherence, irrespective of localization being task-relevant. Posterior auditory regions also showed increased activity for high coherence but only when sound localization was required and subjects were able to do so. Zimmer and Macaluso concluded that binaural coherence cues are processed throughout the auditory cortex but that these cues are used in posterior regions of the STG for successful auditory localization.

Tata and Ward (2005a; 2005b) used auditory evoked potentials to explore the putative auditory "where"-pathway in humans. The mismatch negativity (MMN) elicited by deviations in sound location is comprised of two temporally and anatomically distinct phases: an early phase with a generator posterior to primary auditory cortex and contralateral to the deviant stimulus, and a later phase with generators that are more frontal and bilaterally symmetric. The posterior location of the early-phase generator suggests the engagement of neurons within a posterior "where"-pathway for processing spatial auditory information (Tata & Ward, 2005b). Transient attention oriented in cue-target paradigms results in several modulations of the auditory event-related potential. Its earliest component (the Nd1) also reflects modulation of neurons posterior to primary auditory cortex within or near the temporo-parietal junction (TPJ; Tata & Ward, 2005a).

Selective attention was also used to differentiate the effects of sound location and pitch of an auditory stimulus in an fMRI study (Degerman et al., 2006). Attention to either sound feature produced activation in areas of the superior temporal cortex and in prefrontal and inferior parietal regions. However, during attention to location, these activations were located more posterior on the STG than during attention to pitch.

Finally, in a superb study combining fMRI and MEG, Brunetti and colleagues found that the processing of sound coming from different locations activates a neural circuit similar to the auditory "where" pathway described in monkeys (Brunetti et al., 2005). This system included Heschl's gyrus, the posterior STG, and the inferior parietal lobule. Their MEG analysis allowed assessment of the timing of this circuit: activation of Heschl's gyrus was observed 139 ms after the auditory stimulus, the peak latency of the source located in the posterior STG was at 156 ms, and the inferior parietal lobule and the supramarginal gyrus peaked at 162 ms. Both hemispheres were found to be involved in the processing of sounds coming from different locations, but a stronger activation was observed in the right hemisphere (Brunetti et al., 2005).

NEURAL BASIS OF IMPROVED SOUND LOCALIZATION IN THE BLIND

Neurophysiological recordings were undertaken in visually deprived cats to find the neural basis of the improved sound localization abilities in blind animals and humans. At first an involvement of the SC in the midbrain, a pivotal structure for orienting behavior, was suspected. Indeed, an increased number of neurons responsive to auditory (and somatosensory) stimuli was found (Rauschecker & Harris, 1983). Later, attention turned to the cerebral cortex: It was found on the basis of retrograde tracer experiments that the projection from visual cortex to the SC was greatly reduced, whereas that from association areas such as the anterior ectosylvian sulcus (AES) was preserved in at least the same strength as in normal animals (Rauschecker & Aschoff, unpublished data).

The AES region quickly moved into focus, as it is also the main source of auditory cortical input to the SC (Meredith & Clemo, 1989). In the AES region, visual responses of area AEV in the fundus of the AES (the probable homologue of posterior parietal cortex in primates) virtually disappeared. Neurons in this region, however, did not become unresponsive but were replaced by neurons with brisk responses to auditory and tactile stimuli. Apparently, auditory and somatosensory areas within the AES had expanded at the expense of formerly visual territory (Rauschecker & Korte, 1993).

The response properties of the expanded auditory ectosylvian area (AEA) and those of neighboring auditory fields in the AES region were homogeneous. Auditory spatial tuning (the tuning for the location of a sound source in free field) was significantly sharper in the whole AES region when compared to sighted controls. Visually deprived cats had close to 90% spatially tuned cells (with a spatial tuning ratio of better than 2:1 between best and worst location). In addition, neurons with spatial tuning ratios of 10:1 or better were more abundant in blind cats (Korte & Rauschecker, 1993). The increased number of auditory cortical neurons, together with their sharpened spatial filtering characteristics, is likely to improve the sampling density of auditory space and provide the neural basis for the improved spatial abilities of early blind cats and ferrets (Rauschecker, 1995, 2002).

TACTILE COMPENSATION FOR VISUAL DEPRIVATION

Tactile Behavior and Whisker Growth in Visually Deprived Animals

Many animal species rely heavily on their facial vibrissae for orientation during locomotion. It is thus not surprising that blind animals are found to rely on them even more strongly and seem to be quite adept at using tactile information (Cremieux, Veraart, & Wanet-Defalque, 1986; Rauschecker & Henning, 2001). Thus, crossmodal changes should also occur in the somatosensory system of visually deprived cats and rodents. Visually deprived cats grow longer and thicker facial vibrissae (Rauschecker, Tian, Korte, & Egert, 1992). The same is true for mice and rats in which both eyes were removed (binocularly enucleated) at birth.

Somatosensory Cortical Map Changes in Visually Deprived Mice

Binocularly enucleated mice also show an expansion of the whisker barrels, the neural representation of the vibrissae in the primary somatosensory cortex (Rauschecker et al., 1992). Barrels corresponding to whiskers in lateral positions show the most significant expansion, and whiskers in these same positions show the greatest hypertrophy, thus increasing the lateral range of the vibrissae as a tactile organ. Increased usage and stimulation of the whiskers seems to be the common cause of both processes, but different signals may be responsible on the two levels. Increased whisker growth could be mediated by an overabundance of local growth factors; expansion of the barrel field could follow the well-known activity-dependent processes at the cortical synaptic level.

Thus, the expansion of the whisker representation in the somatosensory cortex could simply be a use-dependent effect similar to the training effects of specific fingers (Recanzone et al., 1992). However, since the overall volume of cortex must remain constant, expansion of specific parts has to occur at the expense of other parts. In the finger-training paradigm, it is assumed that expansion of one finger representation usually occurs at the expense of that for another finger. In the case of barrel expansion after neonatal enucleation, there is evidence that the expansion happens at the expense of visual cortical regions because the overall size of the visual cortex in enucleated rhesus monkeys is reduced and contains smaller cell bodies (Rakic, 1981). Although in the latter studies enucleation was performed prenatally, there is every reason to believe that visual cortical shrinkage (concomitantly with barrel cortex expansion) will also happen after neonatal enucleation.

NEURAL MECHANISMS OF CORTICAL MAP PLASTICITY IN VISUAL DEPRIVATION AND RELEVANCE FOR HUMAN STUDIES

Compensatory Plasticity in Early Blindness

How do the changes in visually deprived animals translate into compensation of early blindness in man? Apart from behavioral studies, modern neuroimaging has contributed to a better understanding of these processes. One of the first imaging studies in the blind was performed by Veraart and colleagues, who found that visual cortex displayed cerebral blood flow that was actually higher, on average, than in sighted controls (Wanet-Defalque et al., 1988). These results were later substantiated by a number of studies from several laboratories that showed specific activation of occipital cortex in the blind by nonvisual stimuli (Arno et al., 2001; Büchel, Price, Frackowiak, & Friston, 1998; De Volder et al., 1999; Sadato et al., 1996; Weeks et al., 2000;).

The study by Sadato and colleagues (1996) was the first to demonstrate robust activation of visual cortex, including primary area V1, during Braille reading in the blind. This finding raises several interesting questions: First, does the activation of occipital areas actually contribute to Braille reading in the blind? A subsequent study in which occipital cortex was briefly inactivated by transcranial magnetic stimulation showed that it was indeed functionally involved and contributed specifically to Braille reading (Cohen et al., 1997). A single-case study of a blind subject later becoming alexic for Braille after a stroke in occipital cortex is also instructive in this context (Hamilton, Keenan, Catala, & Pascual-Leone, 2000). Cohen and colleagues (1999) later demonstrated that compensation of blindness is most effective in the early or congenitally blind, suggesting the existence of a critical period for crossmodal reorganization.

Another question pertains to the more philosophical problem of what activation of formerly visual cortex by tactile stimuli actually means perceptually. Is it simply an extension of the somatosensory cortex into occipital areas, thereby refining the sense of touch by providing it with more neurons and thus greater resolution and processing power? Or is it a substantiation of the fact that tactile stimuli can be visualized, as even sighted subjects may experience under certain circumstances (Zangaladze, Epstein, Grafton, & Sathian, 1999; Sathian & Zangaladze, 2001)? Along these lines, one might argue that visual cortex lends itself as a substitution device for tactile input, as both stimulus domains are organized into two-dimensional arrays, and a rerouting and rewiring of tactile input into visual cortex could be fairly straightforward.

If this reasoning is correct, a rewiring of auditory signals into visual cortex should be more complicated, as auditory cortex is not organized as a 2-D map of space but as a tonotopic map of stimulus frequency. It was of interest, therefore, to determine whether occipital cortex in the blind could also be activated by sounds and in which fashion. A study by Weeks et al. (2000) was designed to answer this question. Congenitally blind and sighted subjects were tested in a virtual auditory space environment (simulating quasi-free-field sound with standardized head-related transfer functions and headphones) and their relative cerebral blood flow (rCBF) was measured in a whole-head PET scanner. The task was (a) to decide whether two subsequent sounds were coming from the same or a different azimuth position in space, or (b) to move a joystick into the presumed direction. Both tasks yielded similar results:

In all subjects (sighted or blind) posterior inferior parietal cortex was activated, which provides clear evidence for an involvement of this region in auditory spatial processing. It was confirmed by independent studies that this parietal region (presumably the human analog of monkey area VIP) contains in fact a unimodal auditory area (Bushara et al., 1999; Weeks et al., 1999). It is part and parcel of the dorsal auditory processing stream (Rauschecker & Tian, 2000) and receives its input from auditory belt and parabelt cortex in the posterior superior temporal gyrus (Lewis & Van Essen, 2000). Both sighted and blind subjects also activated frontal areas, owing to the delayed matching task involving working memory, which are also part of the auditory "where" stream (Romanski et al., 1999).

In blind subjects, occipital cortex was activated in addition to the above areas. Activation zones originated in posterior parietal cortex and extended all the way into Brodmann areas 18 and 19, as determined on the basis of Talairach coordinates (Talairach & Tournoux, 1988). The expansion was most extensive in the right hemisphere, which testifies to its special involvement in spatial processes (Mesulam, 1999). Similar results of auditory activation in the occipital cortex of blind subjects were obtained using event-related potential techniques (Kujala, Alho, Paavilainen, Summala, & Näätänen, 1992; Kujala et al., 1995).

The fact that primary visual cortex (BA 17 or V1) was not or was only minimally activated supports the hypothesis put forward that V1 acts as a 2-D matrix that can receive planar information regardless of modality (visual or somatosensory but not auditory). Nevertheless, the question arises how secondary visual areas differ from this layout to make them suitable for the processing of auditory spatial information. Also, it will be interesting to perform imaging studies on blind subjects with both tactile and auditory tasks, in order to see how the two modalities share occipital cortex, possibly forming an interdigitating or "columnar" pattern.

Attempts to build prostheses for the blind based on the fact that occipital cortex is innervated by auditory input appear promising. Most devices use a transformation of visual position into frequency (Arno et al., 2001; Meijer, 1992). Complex visual patterns are transformed into complex auditory stimuli, and subjects learn to interpret them readily. In fact, many of them are cited as "seeing" a visual scene through their ears.

How does the auditory input get relayed into occipital cortex in the blind? Three principal, not mutually exclusive, possibilities exist:

1. Feedforward connections from classical auditory areas to visual cortex could exist. This possibility was raised early on by Innocenti and Clarke (1984) on the basis of their finding that young kittens display transitory connections from auditory to visual cortex. This explanation was discounted for a while because these transitory connections could not be stabilized by visual deprivation (Innocenti, personal communication). However, the hypothesis has come back in force recently when it was discovered independently by two different groups that the occipital cortex of rhesus monkeys is indeed a multimodal convergence site even in normal adult animals (Falchier, Renaud, Barone, & Kennedy, 2001; Rockland & Ojima, 2003).

2. Feedback connections from the inferior parietal lobule (IPL) could carry a stronger auditory signal in blind than in sighted individuals. This possibility is illustrated in Figure 4–2. Strong evidence for this possibility stems from interregional analysis of the PET imaging data by Weeks et al. (2000). Whereas visual cortex provides the strongest source of input to the right IPL, auditory cortex in the superior temporal region provides most of the input to the IPL in blind subjects. Thus the IPL region is dominated by auditory imput in the blind, which must be reflected in the signal carried by the back-projection from IPL to occipital cortex.

Crossmodal reassignment

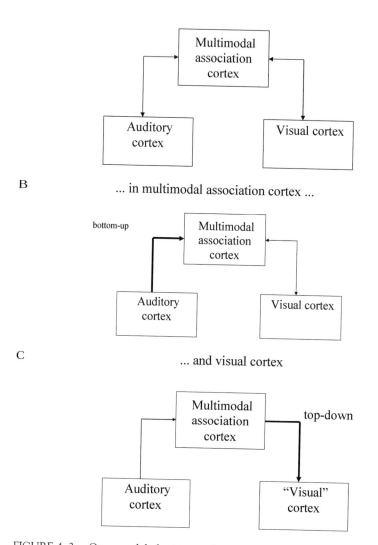

FIGURE 4–2. Cross-modal plasticity in the early blind. The reassignment of ordinarily visual areas in occipital cortex to the auditory modality is illustrated schematically. In this hypothetical scheme, multimodal association areas of the dorsal pathway, such as AEV in cats or posterior parietal cortex in humans, play a pivotal role for the reorganization: In newborns (A), parietal cortex receives input from both visual and auditory sensory regions. In visually deprived individuals (B), the visual input remains largely silent during development, so the auditory input obtains a competitive advantage and takes over large portions of posterior parietal cortex. After a period of blindness (C), "visual" occipital areas become activated by auditory input during a sound localization task. It has been shown that this nonvisual input is indeed functionally and behaviorally relevant.

3. A third possibility, which cannot be discounted, is that subcortical inputs from parts of the thalamus, such as the pulvinar or even the lateral geniculate nucleus, change their predominant modality and thus provide auditory rather than visual input to occipital cortex in the blind. Even the possibility of a newly formed projection in the blind from predominantly auditory nuclei, such as the medial geniculate nucleus, could be considered.

Due to the difficulty of performing tract-tracing studies in humans, these alternative explanatory hypotheses will have to be investigated in animal models. The surprising finding of massive auditory activation of occipital cortex in blind humans should warrant a new wave of visual deprivation studies in animals. This is one example where human imaging work has actually provided a new impetus to perform animal work, although normally the movement is in the opposite direction.

ACKNOWLEDGEMENTS

These studies were supported by grants from the National Institutes of Health, from the National Science Foundation and the Tinnitus Research Consortium. Substantial portions of text were adapted from Rauschecker (2002, 2006a, 2006b) and Rauschecker and Tian (2006).

REFERENCES

Alain, C., Arnott, S. R., Hevenor, S., Graham, S., & Grady, C. L. (2001). "What" and "where" in the human auditory system. *Proceedings of the National Academy of Sciences of the United States of America, 98*, 12301–12306.

Andersen, R. A. (1997). Multimodal integration for the representation of space in the posterior parietal cortex. *Philosophical Transactions: Biological Sciences, 352*, 1421–1428.

Arno, P., De Volder, A. G., Vanlierde, A., Wanet-Defalque, M. C., Streel, E., Robert, A., et al. (2001). Occipital activation by pattern recognition in the early blind using auditory substitution for vision. *Neuroimage, 13*, 632–645.

Arnott, S. R., Binns, M. A., Grady, C. L., & Alain, C. (2004). Assessing the auditory dual-pathway model in humans. *Neuroimage, 22*, 401–408.

Bakin, J. S., & Weinberger, N. M. (1996). Induction of a physiological memory in the cerebral cortex by stimulation of the nucleus basalis. *Proceedings of the National Academy of Science of the United States of America, 93*, 11219–11224.

Bao, S., Chang, E. F., Davis, J. D., Gobeske, K. T., & Merzenich, M. M. (2003). Progressive degradation and subsequent refinement of acoustic representations in the adult auditory cortex. *Journal of Neuroscience, 23*,10765–10775.

Barrett, D. J., & Hall, D. A. (2006). Response preferences for "what" and "where" in human non-primary auditory cortex. *Neuroimage, 32*(2), 968–977.

Beitel, R. E., & Kaas, J. H. (1993). Effects of bilateral and unilateral ablation of auditory cortex in cats on the unconditioned head orienting response to acoustic stimuli. *Journal of Neurophysiology, 70,* 351–369.

Beitel, R. E., Schreiner, C. E., Cheung, S. W., Wang, X., & Merzenich, M. M. (2003). Reward-dependent plasticity in the primary auditory cortex of adult monkeys trained to discriminate temporally modulated signals. *Proceedings of the National Academy of Sciences of the United States of America, 100,* 11070–11075.

Binder, J. R., Frost, J. A., Hammeke, T. A., Bellgowan, P. S., Springer, J. A., Kaufman, J. N., et al. (2000). Human temporal lobe activation by speech and nonspeech sounds. *Cerebral Cortex, 10,* 512–528.

Binder, J. R., Liebenthal, E., Possing, E. T., Medler, D. A., Ward, B. D. (2004). Neural correlates of sensory and decision processes in auditory object identification. *Nature Neuroscience, 7,* 295–301.

Blake, D. T., & Merzenich, M. M. (2002). Changes of AI receptive fields with sound density. *Journal of Neurophysiology, 88,* 3409–3420.

Blakemore, C., & Mitchell, D. E. (1973). Environmental modification of the visual cortex and the neural basis of learning and memory. *Nature, 241,* 467–468.

Blakemore, C., Van Sluyters, R. C. (1974). Reversal of the physiological effects of monocular deprivation in kittens: further evidence for a sensitive period. *Journal of Physiology, 237,* 195–216.

Bremmer, F., Schlack, A., Shah, N. J., Zafiris, O., Kubischik, M., Hoffmann, K., et al. (2001). Polymodal motion processing in posterior parietal and premotor cortex: a human fMRI study strongly implies equivalencies between humans and monkeys. *Neuron, 29,* 287–296.

Brunetti, M., Belardinelli, P., Caulo, M., Del Gratta, C., Della Penna, S., Ferretti, A., Lucci, G., et al. (2005). Human brain activation during passive listening to sounds from different locations: An fMRI and MEG study. *Human Brain Mapping, 26,* 251–261.

Büchel, C., Price, C., Frackowiak, R. S., & Friston, K. (1998). Different activation patterns in the visual cortex of late and congenitally blind subjects. *Brain, 121,* 409–419.

Bushara, K. O., Weeks, R. A., Ishii, K., Catalan, M.-J., Tian, B., Rauschecker, J. P., et al. (1999). Modality-specific frontal and parietal areas for auditory and visual spatial localization in humans. *Nature Neuroscience, 2,* 759–766.

Calford, M. B., Rajan, R., & Irvine, D. R. (1993). Rapid changes in the frequency tuning of neurons in cat auditory cortex resulting from pure-tone-induced temporary threshold shift. *Neuroscience, 55,* 953–964.

Cohen, L. G., Celnik, P., Pascual-Leone, A., Corwell, B., Falz, L., Dambrosia, J., et al. (1997). Functional relevance of cross-modal plasticity in blind humans. *Nature, 389,* 180–183.

Cohen, L. G., Weeks, R. A., Sadato, N., Celnik, P., Ishii, K., Hallett, M. (1999). Period of susceptibility for cross-modal plasticity in the blind. *Annals of Neurology, 45,* 451–460.

Cremieux, J., Veraart, C., & Wanet-Defalque, M. C. (1986). Effects of deprivation of vision and vibrissae on goal-directed locomotion in cats. *Experimental Brain Research, 65,* 229–234.

Cruikshank, S. J., Weinberger, N. M. (1996). Evidence for the Hebbian hypothesis in experience-dependent physiological plasticity of neocortex: A critical review. *Brain Research Review, 22,* 191–228.

Degerman, A., Rinne, T., Salmi, J., Salonen, O., & Alho, K. (2006). Selective attention to sound location or pitch studied with fMRI. *Brain Research* (in press).

De Volder, A. G., Catalan-Ahumada, M., Robert, A., Bol, A., Labar, D., Coppens, A., Michel, C., et al. (1999). Changes in occipital cortex activity in early blind humans using a sensory substitution device. *Brain Research, 826,* 128–134.

Diamond, I. T., Fisher, J. F., Neff, W. D., & Yela, M. (1956). Role of auditory cortex in discrimination requiring localization of sound in space. *Journal of Neurophysiology, 19,* 500–512.

Edeline, J. M., & Weinberger, N. M. (1993). Receptive field plasticity in the auditory cortex during frequency discrimination training: selective retuning independent of task difficulty. *Behavioral Neuroscience, 107,* 82–103.

Falchier, A., Renaud, L., Barone, P., & Kennedy, H. (2001). Extensive projections from the primary auditory cortex and polysensory area STP to peripheral area V1 in the macaque. *Society for Neuroscience Abstracts, 31,* 511–521.

Goldman-Rakic, P. S. (1996). The prefrontal landscape: implications of functional architecture for understanding human mentation and the central executive. *Philosophical Transactions: Biological Sciences, 351,* 1445–1453.

Griffiths, T. D., Rees, G., Rees, A., Green, G. G., Witton, C., Rowe, D., et al. (1998). Right parietal cortex is involved in the perception of sound movement in humans. *Nature Neurosciences, 1,* 74–79.

Griffiths, T. D., Rees, A., Witton, C., Cross, P. M., Shakir, R. A., & Green, G. G. (1997). Spatial and temporal auditory processing deficits following right hemisphere infarction. A psychophysical study. *Brain, 120,* 785–794.

Griffiths, T. D., Rees, A., Witton, C., Shakir, R. A., Henning, G. B., & Green, G. G. (1996). Evidence for a sound movement area in the human cerebral cortex. *Nature, 383,* 425–427.

Hamilton, R., Keenan, J. P., Catala, M. D., & Pascual-Leone, A. (2000). Alexia for Braille following bilateral occipital stroke in an early blind woman. *NeuroReport, 11,* 237–240.

Heffner, H. E., & Heffner, R. S. (1990). Effect of bilateral auditory cortex lesions on sound localization in Japanese macaques. *Journal of Neurophysiology, 64,* 915–931.

Heffner, H., & Masterton, B. (1975). Contribution of auditory cortex to sound localization in the monkey (Macaca mulatta). *Journal of Neurophysiology, 38,* 1340–1358.

Hirsch, H. V., & Spinelli, D. N. (1970). Visual experience modifies distribution of horizontally and vertically oriented receptive fields in cats. *Science, 168,* 869–871.

Hubel, D. H., & Wiesel, T. N. (1970). The period of susceptibility to the physiological effects of unilateral eye closure in kittens. *Journal of Physiology, 206,* 419–436.

Imig, T. J., Irons, W. A., & Samson, F. R. (1990). Single-unit selectivity to azimuthal direction and sound pressure level of noise bursts in cat high-frequency primary auditory cortex. *Journal of Neurophysiology, 63,* 1448–1466.

Innocenti, G. M., & Clarke, S. (1984). Bilateral transitory projection to visual areas from auditory cortex in kittens. *Brain Research, 14,* 143–148.

Irvine, D. R. F. (1992). Physiology of auditory brainstem pathways. In R. R. Fay & A. A. Popper, eds, *Springer Handbook of Auditory Research.* Volume 2. *The Mammalian Auditory Pathway: Neurophysiology,* pp. 153–231. Berlin: Springer-Verlag.

Jääskeläinen, I. P., Ahveninen, J., Bonmassar, G., Dale, A. M., Ilmoniemi, R. J., Levänen, S., et al. (2004). Human posterior auditory cortex gates novel sounds to consciousness. *Proceedings of the National Academy of Sciences of the United States of America, 101,* 6809–6814.

Jenkins, W. M., & Merzenich, M. M. (1984). Role of cat primary auditory cortex for sound-localization behavior. *Journal of Neurophysiology, 52,* 819–847.

Jones, E. G., & Pons, T. P. (1998). Thalamic and brainstem contributions to large-scale plasticity of primate somatosensory cortex. *Science, 282,* 1121–1125.

Kaas, J. H. (1991). Plasticity of sensory and motor maps in adult mammals. *Annual Review of Neuroscience, 14,* 137–167.

Kilgard, M. P., & Merzenich, M. M. (1998a). Cortical map reorganization enabled by nucleus basalis activity. *Science, 279,* 1714–1718.

Kilgard, M. P., & Merzenich, M. M. (1998b). Plasticity of temporal information processing in the primary auditory cortex. *Nature Neurosciences, 1,* 727–731.

King, A. J., & Hutchings, M. E. (1987). Spatial response properties of acoustically responsive neurons in the superior colliculus of the ferret: A map of auditory space. *Journal of Neurophysiology, 57,* 596–624.

King, A. J., & Parsons, C. (1999). Improved auditory spatial acuity in visually deprived ferrets. *European Journal of Neuroscience, 11,* 3945–3956.

Klinke, R., Kral, A., Heid, S., Tillein, J., & Hartmann, R. (1999). Recruitment of the auditory cortex in congenitally deaf cats by long-term electrostimulation through a cochlear implant. *Science, 285,* 1729–1733.

Knudsen, E. I., & Konishi, M. (1978). A neural map of auditory space in the owl. *Science, 200,* 795–797.

Korte, M., & Rauschecker, J. P. (1993). Auditory spatial tuning of cortical neurons is sharpened in cats with early blindness. *Journal of Neurophysiology, 70,* 1717–1721.

Krumbholz, K., Schonwiesner, M., Rubsamen, R., Zilles, K., Fink, G. R., & von Cramon, D. Y. (2005). Hierarchical processing of sound location and motion in the human brainstem and planum temporale. *European Journal of Neuroscience, 21,* 230–238.

Krumbholz, K., Schonwiesner, M., von Cramon, D. Y., Rubsamen, R., Shah, N. J., Zilles, K., et al. (2005). Representation of interaural temporal information from left and right auditory space in the human planum temporale and inferior parietal lobe. *Cereberal Cortex, 15,* 317–324.

Kujala, T., Alho, K., Paavilainen, P., Summala, H., & Näätänen, R. (1992). Neural plasticity in processing sound location by the early blind: an event-related potential study. *Electroencephalography and Clinical Neurophysiology, 84,* 469–472.

Kujala, T., Huotilainen, M., Sinkkonen, J., Ahonen, A. I., Alho, K., Hamalainen, M. S., et al. (1995). Visual cortex activation in blind humans during sound discrimination. *Neuroscience Letters, 183,* 143–146.

Lewis, J. W., & Van Essen, D. C. (2000). Corticocortical connections of visual, sensorimotor, and multimodal processing areas in the parietal lobe of the macaque monkey. *Journal of Comparitive Neurology, 428,* 112–137.

Maeder, P. P., Meuli, R. A., Adriani, M., Bellmann, A., Fornari, E., Thiran, J. P., et al. (2001). Distinct Pathways Involved in Sound Recognition and Localization: A Human fMRI Study. *Neuroimage, 14,* 802–816.

Malhotra, S., Hall, A. J., & Lomber, S. G. (2004). Cortical control of sound localization in the cat: unilateral cooling deactivation of 19 cerebral areas. *Journal of Neurophysiology, 92,* 1625–1643.

Mazzoni, P., Bracewell, R. M., Barash, S., & Andersen, R. A. (1996). Spatially tuned auditory responses in area LIP of macaques performing delayed memory saccades to acoustic targets. *Journal of Neurophysiology, 75,* 1233–1241.

Meijer, P. B. (1992). An experimental system for auditory image representations. *IEEE Transactions on Biomedical Engineering, 39,* 112–121.

Meredith, M. A., & Clemo, H. R. (1989). Auditory cortical projection from the anterior ectosylvian sulcus (Field AES). to the superior colliculus in the cat: an anatomical and electrophysiological study. *Journal of Comparative Neurology, 289,* 687–707.

Merzenich, M. M., Recanzone, G., Jenkins, W. M., Allard, T. T., & Nudo, R. J. (1988). Cortical representational plasticity. In P. Rakic, W. Singer, eds., *Neurobiology of Neocortex,* pp. 41–67. New York: Wiley.

Mesulam, M. M. (1999). Spatial attention and neglect: parietal, frontal and cingulate contributions to the mental representation and attentional targeting of salient extrapersonal events. *Philosophical Transactions: Biological Sciences, 354,* 1325–1346.

Middlebrooks, J. C., Clock, A. E., Xu, L., & Green, D. M. (1994). A panoramic code for sound location by cortical neurons. *Science, 264,* 842–844.

Middlebrooks, J. C., & Knudsen, E. I. (1984). A neural code for auditory space in the cat's superior colliculus. *Journal of Neuroscience, 4,* 2621–2634.

Obleser, J., Boecker, H., Drzezga, A., Haslinger, B., Hennenlotter, A., Roettinger, M., et al. (2005). Vowel sound extraction in anterior superior temporal cortex. *Human Brain Mapping Nov.* 9; [Epub ahead of print].

Pandya, D. N., & Sanides, F. (1973). Architectonic parcellation of the temporal operculum in rhesus monkey and its projection pattern. *Anatomy and Embryology, 139,* 127–161.

Pons, T. P., Garraghty, P. E., Ommaya, A. K., Kaas, J. H., Taub, E., & Mishkin, M. (1991). Massive cortical reorganization after sensory deafferentation in adult macaques. *Science 252,* 1857–1860.

Poremba, A., Saunders, R. C., Crane, A. M., Cook, M., Sokoloff, L., & Mishkin, M. (2003). Functional mapping of the primate auditory system. *Science, 299,* 568–572.

Rajan, R., Aitkin, L. M., & Irvine. D. R. (1990a). Azimuthal sensitivity of neurons in primary auditory cortex of cats. II. Organization along frequency-band strips. *Journal of Neurophysiology, 64,* 888–902.

Rajan, R., Aitkin, L. M., Irvine, D. R., & McKay, J. (1990b). Azimuthal sensitivity of neurons in primary auditory cortex of cats. I. Types of sensitivity and the effects of variations in stimulus parameters. *Journal of Neurophysiology, 64,* 872–887.

Rajan, R., Irvine, D. R., Wise, L. Z., & Heil, P. (1993). Effect of unilateral partial cochlear lesions in adult cats on the representation of lesioned and unlesioned cochleas in primary auditory cortex. *Journal of Comparative Neurology, 338,* 17–49.

Rakic, P. (1981). Development of visual centers in the primate brain depends on binocular competition before birth. *Science, 214,* 928–931.

Rauschecker, J. P. (1991). Mechanisms of visual plasticity: Hebb synapses, NMDA receptors and beyond. *Physiology Review, 71,* 587–615.

Rauschecker J. P. (1995). Compensatory plasticity and sensory substitution in the cerebral cortex. *Trends Neuroscience, 18,* 36–43.

Rauschecker J. P. (1997). Processing of complex sounds in the auditory cortex of cat, monkey and man. *Acta Oto-Laryngologica: Supplementum, 532,* 34–38.

Rauschecker J. P. (1998). Cortical processing of complex sounds. *COIN, 8,* 516–521.

Rauschecker J. P. (2001). Cortical plasticity and music. *Annals of the New York Academy of Sciences, 930,* 330–336.

Rauschecker J. P. (2002). Sensory deprivation. In V. S. Ramachandran (ed.) *Encyclopedia of the Human Brain,* pp. 277–287. New York: Academic Press.

Rauschecker J. P. (2006a). Auditory plasticity. In S. Lomber, J. Eggermont (eds.). *Reprogramming the Cerebral Cortex: Plasticity Following Central and Peripheral Lesions,* Oxford University Press, Oxford, England (in press).

Rauschecker J. P. (2006b). Cortical processing of auditory space: pathways and plasticity. In F. Mast, L. Jäncke (eds.). *Spatial Processing in Navigation, Imagery, and Perception*, Springer-Verlag, New York (in press).

Rauschecker, J. P., & Harris, L. R. (1983). Auditory compensation of the effects of visual deprivation in the cat's superior colliculus. *Experimental Brain Research, 50*, 69–83.

Rauschecker, J. P., & Henning, P. (2001). Crossmodal expansion of cortical maps in early blindness. In J. Kaas (ed.). *The Mutable Brain*, pp. 243–259. Singapore: Harwood Academic Publishers.

Rauschecker, J. P., & Kniepert, U. (1994). Enhanced precision of auditory localization behavior in visually deprived cats. *European Journal of Neuroscience, 6*, 149–160.

Rauschecker, J. P., & Korte, M. (1993). Auditory compensation for early blindness in cat cerebral cortex. *Journal of Neuroscience, 13*, 4538–4548.

Rauschecker, J. P., & Singer, W. (1979). Changes in the circuitry of the kitten visual cortex are gated by postsynaptic activity. *Nature, 280*, 58–60.

Rauschecker J. P. (1981). The effects of early visual experience on the cat's visual cortex and their possible explanation by Hebb synapses. *Journal of Physiology, 310*, 215–239.

Rauschecker, J. P., & Tian, B. (2000). Mechanisms and streams for processing of "what" and "where" in auditory cortex. *Proceedings of the National Academy of Science of the United States of America, 97*, 11800–11806.

Rauschecker, J. P. and Tian, B. (2006). Hierarchic processing of communication sounds in primates. In G. Ehret and J., Kanwal (eds.). *Behavior and Neurodynamics in Auditory Communication*, pp. 205–222. Cambridge University Press, Cambridge, England.

Rauschecker, J. P., Tian, B., Korte, M., & Egert, U. (1992). Crossmodal changes in the somatosensory vibrissa/barrel system of visually deprived animals. *Proceedings of the National Academy of Science of the United States of America, 89*, 5063–5067.

Rauschecker, J. P., Tian, B., Pons, T., & Mishkin, M. (1997). Serial and parallel processing in rhesus monkey auditory cortex. *Journal of Comparative Neurology, 382*, 89–103.

Ravizza, R. J., & Masterton, B. (1972). Contribution of neocortex to sound localization in opossum (Didelphis virginiana). *Journal of Neurophysiology, 35*, 344–356.

Recanzone, G. H. (2000). Spatial processing in the auditory cortex of the macaque monkey. *Proceeding of the National Academy of Sciences of the United States of America, 97*, 11829–11835.

Recanzone, G. H., Allard, T. T., Jenkins, W. M., & Merzenich, M. M. (1990). Receptive-field changes induced by peripheral nerve stimulation in SI of adult cats. *Journal of Neurophysiology, 63*, 1213–1225.

Recanzone, G. H., Guard, D. C., Phan, M. L., & Su, T. K. (2000). Correlation between the activity of single auditory cortical neurons and sound-localization behavior in the macaque monkey. *Journal of Neurophysiology, 83*, 2723–2739.

Recanzone, G. H., Jenkins, W. M., Hradek, G. T., & Merzenich, M. M. (1992). Progressive improvement in discriminative abilities in adult owl monkeys performing a tactile frequency discrimination task. *Journal of Neurophysiology, 67*, 1015–1030.

Recanzone, G. H., Schreiner, C. E., & Merzenich, M. M. (1993). Plasticity in the frequency representation of primary auditory cortex following discrimination training in adult owl monkeys. *Journal of Neuroscience, 13*, 87–103.

Rice, C. E. (1970). Early blindness, early experience, and perceptual enhancement. *Research Bulletin of the American Foundation for the Blind, 22*, 1–22.

Rice, C. E., Feinstein, S. H., & Schusterman, R. J. (1965). Echo-detection ability of the blind: Size and distance factor. *Journal of Experimental Psychology, 70*, 246–251.

Rockland, K. S., & Ojima, H. (2003). Multisensory convergence in calcarine visual areas in macaque monkey. *International Journal of Psychophysiology, 50*, 19–26.

Röder, B., Teder-Salejarvi, W., Sterr, A., Rosler, F., Hillyard, S. A., & Neville, H. J. (1999). Improved auditory spatial tuning in blind humans. *Nature, 400*, 162–166.

Romanski, L. M., & Goldman-Rakic, P. S. (2002). An auditory domain in primate prefrontal cortex. *Nature Neuroscience, 5*, 15–16.

Romanski, L. M., Tian, B., Fritz, J., Mishkin, M., Goldman-Rakic, P. S., & Rauschecker, J. P. (1999). Dual streams of auditory afferents target multiple domains in the primate prefrontal cortex. *Nature Neuroscience, 2*, 1131–1136.

Sadato, N., Pascual-Leone, A., Grafman, J., Ibanez, V., Deiber, M.-P., Dold, G., & Hallett, M. (1996). Activation of the primary visual cortex by Braille reading in blind subjects. *Nature, 380*, 526–528.

Sathian, K., & Zangaladze, A. (2001). Feeling with the mind's eye: the role of visual imagery in tactile perception. *Optometry and Vision Science, 78*, 276–281.

Scott, S. K., Blank, C. C., Rosen, S., & Wise, R. J. (2000). Identification of a pathway for intelligible speech in the left temporal lobe. *Brain, 123 Pt 12*, 2400–2406.

Singer, W. (1995). Development and plasticity of cortical processing architectures. *Science, 270*, 758–764.

Stricanne, B., Andersen, R. A., & Mazzoni, P. (1996). Eye-centered, head-centered, and intermediate coding of remembered sound locations in area LIP. *Journal of Neurophysiology, 76*, 2071–2076.

Stryker, M. P., & Sherk, H. (1975). Modification of cortical orientation selectivity in the cat by restricted visual experience: a reexamination. *Science, 190*, 904–906.

Stryker, M. P., Sherk, H., Leventhal, A. G., & Hirsch, H. V. (1978). Physiological consequences for the cat's visual cortex of effectively restricting early visual experience with oriented contours. *Journal of Neurophysiology, 41*, 896–909.

Talairach, J., & Tournoux, P. (1988). *A coplanar sterotaxic atlas of the human brain.* Stuttgart, Germany: Thieme Verlag.

Tata, M. S., & Ward, L. M. (2005a). Spatial attention modulates activity in a posterior "where" auditory pathway. *Neuropsychologia, 43*, 509–516.

Tata, M. S., & Ward, L. M. (2005b). Early phase of spatial mismatch negativity is localized to a posterior "where" auditory pathway. *Experimental Brain Research, 167*, 481–486.

Tian, B., Reser, D., Durham, A., Kustov, A., & Rauschecker, J. P. (2001). Functional specialization in rhesus monkey auditory cortex. *Science, 292*, 290–293.

Tretter, F., Cynader, M., & Singer, W. (1975). Modification of direction selectivity of neurons in the visual cortex of kittens. *Brain Research, 84*, 143–149.

Wanet-Defalque, M. C., Veraart, C., De Volder, A., Metz, R., Michel, C., Dooms, G., Goffinet, A. (1988). High metabolic activity in the visual cortex of early blind human subjects. *Brain Research, 446*, 369–373.

Warren, J. D., Zielinski, B. A., Green, G. G. R., Rauschecker, J. P., & Griffiths, T. D. (2002). Analysis of sound source motion by the human brain. *Neuron, 34*, 1–20.

Weeks, R. A., Aziz-Sultan, A., Bushara, K. O., Tian, B., Wessinger, C. M., Dang, N., Rauschecker, J. P., et al. (1999). A PET study of human auditory spatial processing. *Neuroscience Letters, 262*, 155–158.

Weeks, R., Horwitz, B., Aziz-Sultan, A., Tian, B., Wessinger, C. M., Cohen, L., Hallett, M., et al. (2000). A positron emission tomographic study of auditory localisation in the congenitally blind. *Journal of Neuroscience, 20*, 2664–2672.

Weinberger, N. M., & Diamond, D. M. (1987). Physiological plasticity in auditory cortex: rapid induction by learning. *Progress in Neurobiology, 29,* 1–55.

Wiesel, T. N., & Hubel, D. H. (1963). Effects of Visual Deprivation on Morphology and Physiology of Cells in the Cats Lateral Geniculate Body. *Journal of Neurophysiology, 26,* 978–993.

Wiesel, T. N., Hubel, D. H. (1965). Comparison of the effects of unilateral and bilateral eye closure on cortical unit responses in kittens. *Journal of Neurophysiology, 28,* 1029–1040.

Yu, J. J., & Young, E. D. (2000). Linear and nonlinear pathways of spectral information transmission in the cochlear nucleus. *Proceedings of the National Academy of Science of the United States of America, 97,* 11780–11786.

Zangaladze, A., Epstein, C. M., Grafton, S. T., & Sathian, K. (1999). Involvement of visual cortex in tactile discrimination of orientation. *Nature, 401,* 587–590.

Zatorre, R. J., Bouffard, M., Ahad, P., & Belin, P. (2002). Where is 'where' in the human auditory cortex? *Nature Neuroscience, 5,* 905–909.

Zhang, L. I., Bao, S., & Merzenich, M. M. (2001). Persistent and specific influences of early acoustic environments on primary auditory cortex. *Nature Neuroscience, 4,* 1123–1130.

Zimmer, U., & Macaluso, E. (2005). High binaural coherence determines successful sound localization and increased activity in posterior auditory areas. *Neuron, 47,* 893–905.

5

Brain Plasticity and Multisensory Experience in Early Blind Individuals

Annick Vanlierde, Laurent Renier, and Anne G. De Volder

During the first years of life, the human brain undergoes repetitive modifications in its anatomical, functional, and synaptic construction to reach the complex functional organization of the adult central nervous system. This is also the case for the visual cortex that receives visual stimuli from the environment and matures during infancy and childhood. But what about this maturation when the individual is affected by early (or congenital) blindness? The "neural Darwinism" theory predicts that when one sensory modality is lacking, as in congenital blindness, the target structures will be taken over by the afferent inputs from other senses that will promote and control their functional maturation (Edelman, 1993). This view receives support from both cross-modal plasticity experiments in animal models and functional imaging studies in man. On one hand, a reorganization of sensory representations with cross-modal expansion of nonvisual modalities into normally visual brain areas has been demonstrated, using electrode recordings, in early visually deprived animals (Rauschecker, 1995). These physiological modifications might be partly related to behavioral abilities of congenitally blind cats, who are, for instance, faster in learning tactile exploration of space or sound localization than blindfolded controls (Rauschecker & Korte, 1993). On the other hand, over the last decade, functional brain imaging like positron emission tomography (PET) has provided further insight in the maturation processes in humans and has helped elucidate the pathophysiological processes involved in brain plasticity in the absence of vision. In this chapter we present some research applications of PET

67

and rehabilitation of vision to investigate sensory substitution procedures in human blindness.

VISUAL CORTEX HYPERMETABOLISM IN EARLY BLIND INDIVIDUALS

At the end of the 1980s PET studies of regional brain glucose utilization were performed in individuals with blindness of early onset. Our initial question was, Can the denervated visual cortex recover some functions? As a first attempt to investigate brain plasticity in congenital blindness, we aimed to verify whether the striate and prestriate cortices remained active in these individuals at the adult age, after a long period of blindness.

The PET studies demonstrated a high glucose utilization at rest in sensory deprived areas (Wanet-Defalque et al., 1988). In early blind adults, affected by pregeniculate lesions from birth or in the first years of life, rates of glucose metabolism measured in primary and association visual cortex reached a level comparable to that of sighted control individuals studied with their eyes open (see Figure 5-1). Since glucose is the main substrate of the brain at all ages, including during functional activation, regional brain glucose metabolism is an index of neural and synaptic activity. The high metabolic activity in visual cortex of early blind individuals presumably reflects neuronal function, as supported by deoxyglucose studies relating energy metabolism and function (Phelps et al., 1981; Sokoloff, 1981) and thus neuronal spike discharges. By contrast, PET studies in individuals who became blind after a normal visual development ("late blindness") have consistently shown low rates of glucose utilization in the visual areas, at a level comparable to that of control subjects with eyes closed (Demer et al., 1993; Kiyosawa et al., 1989; Phelps et al., 1981; Veraart et al., 1990).

The difference in visual cortex metabolism between early and late blindness might be related to the timing of visual deprivation in relation to the development of the visual cortex. It is well established from previous studies that the density of synapses in the visual cortex undergoes drastic changes with normal development. In the newborn human visual cortex, synaptic density is comparable to the adult level. Subsequently, there is a burst of synaptogenesis during the first postnatal year, when synaptic density reaches a maximum, before it declines gradually to reach the adult level around 11 years (Huttenlocher & Dabholkar, 1997; Huttenlocher & de Courten, 1987). Although the initial increasing phase of synaptogenesis appears relatively independent from environmental conditions, the subsequent decrease in density of synapses that takes place in the visual cortex has been shown to depend critically on visual experience (Bourgeois, Jastreboff, & Rakic, 1989; Bourgeois & Rakic, 1996).

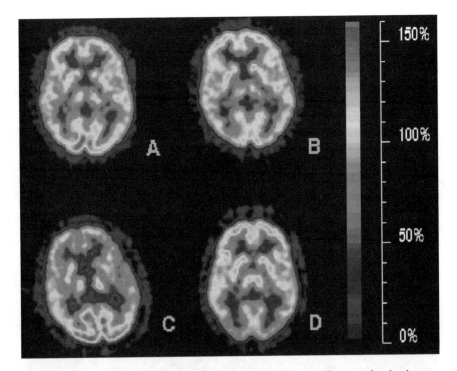

FIGURE 5–1. The top row of this picture displays PET images from a sighted volunteer studied with the eyes open (A) as compared with the eyes closed (B). Functional activation of the visual cortex is associated with elevated brain glucose metabolism (A). When an individual is affected by early blindness, an elevated metabolism is also present in the occipital cortex (C), to a level comparable to that of sighted individuals with the eyes open (A). By contrast, glucose utilization in visual areas of a late blind individual (D) is decreased, to a slightly lower level than in sighted individuals studied with the eyes closed (B). In our studies, all subjects are studied as adults. Early blind subjects became blind early in life before the age of 3 years and late blind subjects became blind after completion of visual development, at adult age. [See Color Plate]

This decreasing phase in synaptic density, called *synaptic revision*, is impaired when there is no competition between afferent inputs, as in visual deprivation. Modifications of metabolic activity can result from variations in the density of neurons and synapses as well as from changes in synaptic discharge rates (Kadekaro, Crane, & Sokoloff, 1985). It is thus reasonable to think that the metabolic increase in visual cortex of early blind individuals is due to the persistence of synaptic contacts in an unusually high density or hyperactive state, as in an activated condition (Blomqvist et al., 1994; Fox, Raichle, Mintun, & Dence, 1988).

ACTIVATION OF VISUAL AREAS USING A SENSORY
SUBSTITUTION DEVICE

Currently two main classes of vision sensory substitution devices exist, tactile (Bach-y-Rita, Kaczmarek, Tyler, & Garcia-Lara, 1998; Collins & Bach-y-Rita, 1973) and auditory, such as the vOICe (Meijer, 1992), and the prosthesis that substitutes vision with audition (PSVA) developed in our laboratory (Capelle, Trullemans, Arno, & Veraart, 1998). This device, which is shown in Figure 5–2, consists of the coupling of a rough model of the human retina with an inverse model of the cochlea, using a pixel-frequency relationship (Veraart, 1989). A head-worn TV camera allows online translation of visual patterns into sounds. When the user moves the head, visual frames are grabbed at high frequency and generate in real time the corresponding complex sounds that allow recognition. The image acquired by the camera is divided into pixels according to a two-resolution artificial retina scheme. This artificial retina con-

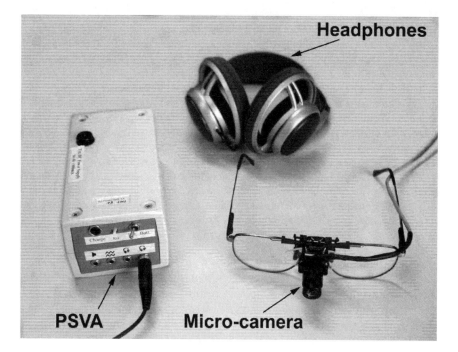

FIGURE 5–2.   The prosthesis substituting vision with audition (PSVA) consists of a miniature TV camera placed on the glasses that acquires video images of the surroundings. The camera is connected to the PSVA, which translates the images into sounds according to a transcription code (see text). The resulting signal is transmitted to the subjects by headphones.

sists of a square matrix of 8×8 pixels, with four central ones replaced by 8×8 smaller pixels (the fovea). A single sinusoidal tone is assigned to each pixel of the multiresolution image. The code of the device is based on several principles: (a) binaural balance, (b) sound frequency, (c) multi-resolution, and (d) sound intensity. Accordingly, (a) the left part of the processed image is coded by sounds transmitted mainly to the left ear of the individual, and the right part to the right ear; (b) the sound frequency increases from the bottom to the top of the processed image; (c) the multiresolution artificial retina allows separation of the processed image into two different parts, a periphery and a fovea; and (d) the intensity of each sound is modulated by the gray level of the corresponding pixel. In a previous study (Arno, Wanet-Defalque, Capelle, Catalan-Ahumada, & Veraart, 1999), we demonstrated that blindfolded sighted individuals trained to use the device acquired the ability to recognize geometric forms (visual patterns).

Use of the prosthetic device requires individuals to scan their environment by moving the head-worn TV camera. Since no head movements are allowed during PET, a graphics tablet was adapted to the setup. The patterns to be recognized were displayed within an area of 64×64 pixels at the center of the computer screen. During exploration of the graphics tablet, when a part of the artificial retina overlapped a part of the pattern, the related pixels were translated into sounds according to the same transcription code as in the original device.

The neural bases of pattern recognition were investigated with PET in blind individuals using the adapted device. For this purpose, blindfolded sighted control and early blind volunteers were enrolled in an H_2O^{15} PET study. Both groups of individuals had to perform two active auditory processing tasks: a detection task with noise stimuli and a detection task with familiar sounds. Neural activations in both conditions were compared with the activation observed during pattern recognition using auditory substitution of vision with the adapted device (Arno et al., 2001).

The results showed a differential activation pattern with the prosthetic device as a function of the visual experience. In addition to the regions involved in the recognition process in blindfolded sighted control subjects (mainly parietal areas and middle temporal gyrus), occipital areas of early blind subjects were also activated, as shown in Figure 5–3. The occipital activation, extending to parietal areas, was more important when the early blind subjects used the adapted device than during the other auditory tasks (Arno et al., 2001), suggesting that the activity of the extrastriate visual cortex of early blind individuals can be modulated by new experience (De Volder et al., 1999). The results also showed a significant difference between the two groups in the occipital cortex at rest, with the striate and the extrastriate occipital cortex displaying a higher activity level in early blind subjects compared to sighted controls, supporting the previous observations (De Volder et al., 1997; Veraart et al., 1990; Wanet-Defalque et al., 1988).

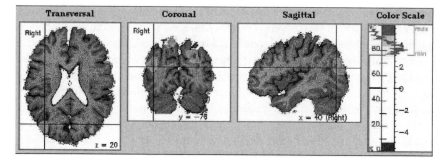

FIGURE 5–3.   Activation foci, as detected by PET, in early blind subjects during pattern recognition using the PSVA compared to an auditory detection task with noise stimuli. The statistical parametric map for this comparison is superimposed on an individual normalized MRI. Only positive difference exceeding a threshold of $p < 0.001$ (uncorrected) is shown, according to the color scale that codes the Z score. As shown on this figure, pattern recognition with auditory substitution of vision activated mainly parietal and extrastriate visual areas in early blind humans. The lines intersect on a voxel in the right middle temporal gyrus (BA 19) with a Z value of 4.52. Coordinates refer to the referential defined by the atlas of Talairach and Tournoux (1988). [See Color Plate]

Auditory substitution of vision activated Brodmann area 7, both in early blind and sighted control subjects. This common activation probably reflects the spatial processing of the task. Previous event-related potential studies (sometimes called ERP) on mental rotation have demonstrated that the same cortical areas in the parietal cortex are implicated in spatial processing in sighted and in blind individuals (Rösler, Röder, Heil, & Hennighausen, 1993). Early blind individuals are known to be able to generate spatial representation (Cornoldi, Cortesi, & Petri, 1991; Kerr, 1983; Marmor & Zaback, 1976). This is not surprising given that blind people can access spatial information from the environment through spared sensory modalities. Brodmann area 19 (in the precuneus and the middle temporal gyrus) was activated bilaterally in the early blind group during pattern recognition. In addition, the group-by-condition interaction showed that the extrastriate cortex (the left cuneus, area 18) was activated significantly more in the early blind group than in the sighted control group. These results suggest that early visual deprivation leads to a reorganization of sensory representations. Cross-modal expansion of other sensory modalities into normally visual brain areas was demonstrated also in studies with early visually deprived animals (Rauschecker, 1995) and is in agreement with electrophysiological (EEG) studies in humans (Kujala, Alho, et al., 1995; Kujala, Huotilainen, et al., 1995; Röder, Rösler, & Hennighausen, 1996). The activation of occipital cortex in early blind individuals was also reported in PET studies concerned with somatosensory processing, such as Braille reading (Büchel, Price, Frackowiak, & Friston, 1998; Sadato et al.,

1996, 1998). Our results failed to show any activation of the primary V1 area, whatever the group. The lack of V1 activation in early blind individuals was in agreement with observations made by Büchel and colleagues (1998) in the case of Braille reading but differed from the V1 activation observed by Sadato et al. (1996, 1998) in a group of blind individuals, including those who were congenitally blind. Provided there is further confirmation by additional studies on that topic, the results of the present study are in favor of a cross-modal reorganization phenomenon restricted to extrastriate areas.

FUNCTIONAL ACTIVITY OF THE DORSAL VISUAL PATHWAY IN EARLY BLIND INDIVIDUALS

As investigated in many behavioral studies since the 1970s, mental imagery seems to involve functional properties close to visual perception. It is worth noting that both processes exert an influence on each other. In spite of this close relationship between imagery and visual perception, early blind individuals are able to perform mental imagery tasks with the same efficiency as sighted ones (Vanlierde & Wanet-Defalque, 2004). Although these individuals have not had any visual experience and access their environment using nonvisual modalities, early blind individuals are able to mentally rotate tactually perceived shapes. They show an increase of reaction time that is strongly correlated with the angular disparity between two shapes in the same way as sighted individuals (Carpenter & Eisenberg, 1978; Marmor & Zaback, 1976). The metric spatial information is also preserved in their mental images. For instance, a linear relationship is observed between scanning time and distance between two objects in an imaged scene (Kerr, 1983). However, behavioral differences exist between early blind and sighted individuals in those visuospatial imagery tasks. It is difficult for early blind individuals to perform tasks requiring a large load in visuospatial working memory (Cornoldi et al., 1991; Cornoldi, Bertuccelli, Rocchi, & Sbrana, 1993) or requiring an active manipulation (Vecchi, 1998; Vecchi, Monticellai, & Cornoldi, 1995). In these specific tasks, the performance of early blind individuals is worse than that of blindfolded sighted controls.

Neuroimaging studies indicate that perception and mental imagery could share the common processing networks in the brain (O'Craven & Kanwisher, 2000; Parsons et al., 1995; Roland & Gulyas, 1995). In particular, Mellet and colleagues (Mellet, Tzourio, Denis, & Mazoyer, 1995; Mellet et al., 1996; Mellet et al., 2000) showed that the dorsal visual pathway is activated during mental imagery dealing with visuospatial information. As an attempt to investigate further the neural bases of mental imagery in early blind humans and to determine whether the dorsal pathway would be involved in visuospatial imagery in these individuals, regional cerebral blood flow was studied in early blind and blindfolded sighted control volunteers during a visuospatial imagery task (Vanlierde, De Volder, Wanet-Defalque, & Veraart, 2003). Subjects were instructed to generate a mental representation of verbally provided bi-dimensional patterns that were placed in a grid, and to assess pattern symmetry in relation to a grid axis. This condition was contrasted with a verbal memory task.

Results showed a selective activation of parieto-occipital areas during visuospatial imagery in early blind as well as in blindfolded sighted humans, as seen in Figure 5–4. Brain activation in both groups involved the precuneus, superior parietal lobule, and occipital gyrus (Brodmann 7, 7, 19, respectively). The task required the individuals to build up a pattern that was described verbally and to mentally maintain the precise location of filled-in squares inside a grid. At the end of the verbal description, a symmetry axis of the grid was provided to the subject. The subject had to then compare the location of each filled-in square in relation to this axis and evaluate the symmetry level of the pattern. Although both groups had similar task performance, they differed in their strategy. Sighted control subjects created a visual image in their minds while early blind subjects described a "coordinate X–Y" and encoded the spatial location of each square, further comparing the coordinates of the relevant squares to evaluate the symmetry level (Vanlierde & Wanet-Defalque, 2004). This different strategy was not reflected by differences in neural activation. The dorsal visual pathway was recruited in both groups during the task.

These results are in accordance with those of previous studies conducted in sighted subjects, which indicated that the same parieto-occipital areas are involved in visual perception as in mental imagery dealing with spatial components. In sighted individuals, the superior occipital and parietal areas are thought to be involved in spatial processing of visual stimuli (Haxby et al., 1991; Mishkin, Ungerleider, & Macko, 1983). Furthermore, the same brain areas are also activated in mental imagery tasks that include nonperceptual spatial information (Faillenot, Sakata, Costes, Decety, & Jeannerod, 1997; Kauff, Kassubek, Mulack, & Greenlee, 2000; Mellet et al., 1995; Mellet et al., 1996).

In early blind individuals, activation of parieto-occipital regions has been reported previously during tasks involving spatial features or spatial analyses. These areas were activated in spatial auditory localization (Weeks et al., 2000), in distance estimation using an ultrasonic device (De Volder et al., 1999), in Braille reading (Büchel et al., 1998; Sadato et al., 1996, 1998), in tactile imagery (Uhl et al., 1994), and during pattern recognition using the prosthetic device described previously and involving visuospatial working memory (Arno et al., 2001). Since visual memories are normally nonexistent in the early blind participants in the aforementioned studies, these individuals would have used spatial imagery rather than visual mental imagery during these tasks. If spatial imagery was involved, it is not surprising that parieto-occipital regions were recruited recurrently. The present study, using a complex spatial imagery task, confirmed that the dorsal visual pathway is involved in visuospatial imagery in early blind individuals in a similar way as in sighted controls. These results indicate further that this pathway can develop efficiently and remains functional in the absence of vision.

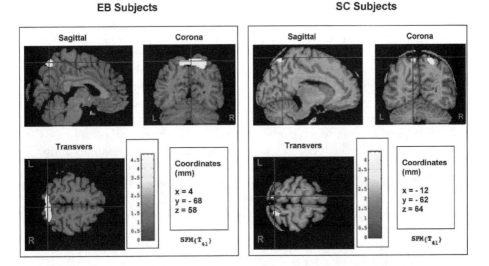

FIGURE 5–4.   Activation foci observed in visuospatial imagery as contrasted to verbal memory processing in early blind individuals (EB Subjects, left side) and in blindfolded sighted controls (SC Subjects, right side). The statistical parametric map for this comparison is superimposed on the axial, coronal, and sagittal sections of an individual normalized brain MRI. Only positive difference exceeding a threshold of $p < 0.001$ (uncorrected) is shown, according to the color scale that codes the t values. In early blind individuals, the lines intersect on a voxel in the right precuneus (BA 7) with a Z value of 4.26 ($p = 0.05$, corrected for multiple comparisons). In sighted controls, similar brain areas were activated. The lines intersect on a voxel in the left superior parietal lobule (BA 7) with a Z value of 3.81. Coordinates refer to the referential defined by the atlas of Talairach and Tournoux (1988). [See Color Plate]

FUNCTIONAL ACTIVITY OF THE VENTRAL VISUAL PATHWAY IN EARLY BLIND INDIVIDUALS

To perform visual imagery of familiar objects, knowledge referring to visual properties of these objects is required. For a sighted individual, this knowledge (*visual semantics* or sensory knowledge, e.g., the shape of a musical instrument) can be accessed by pictures and also indirectly by visual words (Caramazza, 1996). In individuals deprived of vision early in life, the knowledge of the surrounding environment must be accessed by nonvisual modalities. Several studies have indicated that mental imagery would not depend exclusively on visual experience but that mental imagery could also be obtained using other sensory modalities (Carpenter & Eisenberg, 1978; Kerr, 1983; Marmor & Zaback, 1976). However, as mentioned above, capacity limitations are observed between early blind individuals and sighted controls for mental imagery tasks (Cornoldi et al., 1991; Vecchi, 1998; Vecchi et al., 1995).

Previous neuroimaging studies have shown that common cerebral areas are involved in both perception and imagery tasks (D'Esposito et al., 1997; Kosslyn et al., 1993; Kosslyn, Thompson, & Albert, 1997; Roland & Gulyas, 1995). In particular, the ventral visual pathway, including the occipito-temporal and inferior temporal cortex, was shown to be involved in visual imagery in sighted individuals (Kosslyn, 1994; Roland & Gulyas, 1995). However, this system is deprived of any visual afferences in the blind. In order to test whether the same processes can be elicited by tactile and auditory experiences in individuals who became blind early in life, regional cerebral blood flow was assessed by PET in early blind individuals and age-matched sighted control volunteers during a mental imagery task (imagery of object shape) triggered by the sound of familiar objects. This condition was compared to passive listening to noise sounds. The aim of this study was to clarify the neural structures involved in mental representation of the shape of familiar objects and to verify whether a similar system is recruited in individuals with early-onset blindness, in whom internal representations of shape are attainable only through tactile and auditory experiences (De Volder et al., 2001).

During a training session, 33 objects were named and presented one by one to the subject. Blind subjects were required to explore each object by touching it for one minute while receiving the corresponding sound through earphones, and to build up a precise mental representation of the object, representing it as a solitary stationary object with its longer side horizontally. The same instructions were provided to sighted controls who explored the objects visually and auditorily. During the PET session, the mental imagery task required silent identification of each individual meaningful sound, provided by earphones, followed by mental retrieval of the internal representation of the related object. After the PET session, subjects were asked to retrieve the mental representation of each object and answer a series of questions on its shape attributes. A good performance was recorded in this behavioral testing in both groups, which indicated that the subjects were similarly able to generate a precise mental representation of the objects during the scans.

PET results showed a selective activation of occipito-temporal and visual association areas, particularly in the left fusiform gyrus (Brodmann 19–37), and of the cerebellar vermis during mental imagery of object shape by both groups, as shown in Figure 5–5.

The results of this experiment supported the hypothesis that mental imagery of objects recruits the ventral visual pathway extending to occipito-temporal and inferior temporal cortex in sighted individuals. Consistent with the idea that imagery and perception have common neural substrates, imagery tasks in sighted individuals have yielded activations in occipital regions, including the fusiform gyrus, especially when the tasks involved activation of visual memories (D'Esposito et al., 1997; Kosslyn et al., 1993; Roland & Gulyas, 1995). In this study, we confirmed this activation of higher-order visual asso-

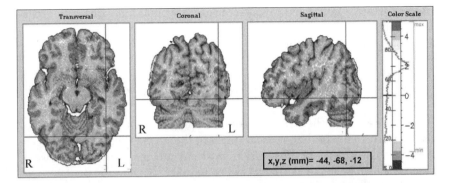

FIGURE 5-5.   Activation foci observed during mental imagery of shape as contrasted to a control auditory task (passive listening to noise stimuli) in early blind subjects. The statistical parametric map for this comparison is superimposed on the axial, coronal, and sagittal sections of an individual normalized brain MRI. Only positive difference exceeding a threshold of $p < 0.001$ (uncorrected) is shown, according to the color scale that codes the Z score. A bilateral activation of the ventral visual pathway is evident in this contrast. The intersection of the lines indicates a voxel in the left fusiform gyrus with a z value of 5.0 ($p < 0.05$ corrected for multiple comparisons). Coordinates are with reference to the Talairach and Tournoux (1988) system. [See Color Plate]

ciation cortex in a visual imagery task triggered by auditory signals. In total accordance, our findings indicated a similar involvement of the occipito-temporal cortex and a critical role of the ventral visual pathway in mental imagery in the early visually deprived individuals. According to the theory of neuronal group selection, as proposed by Edelman in 1978 (see Edelman, 1993, for a review), the functional organization of the brain is based, like in Darwin's theory of natural selection, on competition at the synaptic level. In the developing brain, selection occurs during synapse formation and elimination, which results in enormous synaptic loss during brain maturation (Changeux & Danchin, 1976). To account for this adaptive selection, transient connections, such as auditory afferences to the visual cortex (Innocenti & Clarke, 1984) or corticocortical projections between primary and secondary visual areas (Berman, 1991) have been found in the early life, which are normally withdrawn during brain development but may persist in case of sensory deprivation (Berman, 1991). These processes might form the neural basis of sensory substitution in blind humans. It is worth noting that previous results from PET studies have demonstrated that Braille reading and tactile discrimination tasks or auditory localization in early blind humans caused increased blood flow in their occipital areas (Büchel et al., 1998; Cohen et al., 1999; Sadato et al., 1996; Weeks et al., 2000). Cognitive tasks with visual components, such as visual linguistic processing (Büchel, Price, & Friston, 1998), also activated visual association areas in the ventral pathway in early blind individuals. In accordance with data obtained with evoked potentials (Uhl et al., 1994), the present results indicate that this is also the case for mental imagery.

VISUAL ILLUSIONS USING A PROSTHETIC DEVICE

To gain insight into the nature of the perception by sensory substitution of vision, we tested whether a visual illusion, the Ponzo illusion, can be perceived using our sensory substitution prosthetic device. The Ponzo illusion, which is shown in Figure 5–6, occurs when individuals overestimate the length of the horizontal bar nearest the apex (the upper one), which in reality is exactly the same length as the lower one. This perceptual phenomenon is usually considered as depending on the visual system. One of the most popular ways of explaining it is to suppose that the perceptual system interprets the figure as a flat projection of a 3-D display, or as a scene in perspective (e.g., Gregory, 1963).

Results obtained in blindfolded sighted individuals using the device to explore this illusion indicate that it is possible to perceive pure visual phenomena, e.g., a visual illusion, with a sensory substitution system (Renier et al., 2005). This illustrates the top-down influences of visual processes in full accordance with theoretical models of visual perception (Gregory, 1997). It clearly indicates the existence of a visual-like processing of sensory information gathered by the sensory substitution device. However, previous visual experience and related knowledge about visual perspective appear to be crucial factors for perceiving this illusory phenomenon since early blind individuals do not show the expected effect of the illusion when they explore the stimuli using the prosthetic device. In early blind subjects who do not have visual experi-

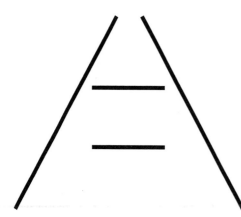

FIGURE 5–6.   Example of the stimuli used. In the Ponzo illusion, the two horizontal bars have the same length but the surrounding converging oblique lines lead to an overestimation of the horizontal bar nearest the apex.

ence but only fragmented knowledge about visual perspective, a longer period of training might be necessary to acquire the rules of visual depth perception and to become sensitive to visual illusions. Although this indicates that visual perspective requires specific visual stimulation to be developed, these observations do provide insight into the fascinating possibility that effects tied to the absence of visual experience can be compensated by means of sensory substitution.

CONCLUSION

In conclusion, early blindness seems to be associated with profound changes in the functional organization of the visual connections. Using a sensory substitution device like ours activates visual association areas in early blind humans. Perception with a sensory substitution device shares perceptual processes with normal vision, depending on visual experience and related knowledge. A functional activation of both the ventral and dorsal visual pathways is induced by specific tasks in the absence of vision.

This convergence of results suggests that the inputs from auditory and tactile modalities are capable of promoting efficient functional development of the dorsal and ventral visual pathways in the absence of vision. We hypothesize that auditory and tactile senses help create vision in the brain, at least partly, acting as a natural substitutive system for vision during brain maturation, and that this in turn enables development of the specific visual functions for which these anatomical structures are responsible. The present observations suggest that such cross-modal plasticity processes might be recruited in novel abilities with the help of sensory substitution prostheses. Additional activation studies should assess this point further, thus opening a hopeful perspective in the field of blindness rehabilitation.

ACKNOWLEDGEMENTS

The authors are grateful to the volunteers and the Oeuvre Nationale des Aveugles (ONA), Belgium for their essential collaboration. Thanks are also due to O. Collignon, B. Gerard, and Professor C. Veraart for their helpful comments and discussions. Laurent Renier and Anne G. De Volder are supported by the Belgian National Fund for Scientific Research (FNRS) as postdoctoral researcher and senior research associate, respectively. This study was supported by grants 3.4547.00 and 3.4505.04 from the Fundation for Medical and Scientific Research (Belgium) and a European Commission Quality of Life contract, No. QLG3-CT-2000-01797.

REFERENCES

Arno, P., De Volder, A. G., Vanlierde, A., Wanet-Defalque, M.-C., Streel, E., Robert, A., et al. (2001). Occipital activation by pattern recognition in the early blind using auditory substitution for vision. *NeuroImage, 13*, 632–645.

Arno, P., Wanet-Defalque, M.-C., Capelle, C., Catalan-Ahumada, M., & Veraart, C. (1999). Auditory coding of visual patterns for the blind. *Perception, 28*, 1013–1030.

Bach-y-Rita, P., Kaczmarek, K. A., Tyler, M. E., & Garcia-Lara, J. (1998). Form perception with a 49-point electrotactile stimulus array on the tongue: A technical note. *Journal of Rehabilitation Research and Development, 35*, 427–430.

Berman, N. E. J. (1991). Alterations of visual cortical connections in cats following early removal of retinal input. *Developmental Brain Research, 63*, 163–180.

Blomqvist, G., Seitz, R. J., Sjögren, I., Halldin, C., Stone-Elander, S., Widen, L., et al. (1994). Regional cerebral oxidative and total glucose consumption during rest and activation studied with positron emission tomography. *Acta Physiologica Scandinavica, 151*, 29–43.

Bourgeois, J. P., Jastreboff, P. J., & Rakic, P. (1989). Synaptogenesis in visual cortex of normal and preterm monkeys: Evidence for intrinsic regulation of synaptic overproduction. *Proceedings of the National Academy of Sciences, 86*, 4297–4301.

Bourgeois, J. P., & Rakic, P. (1996). Synaptogenesis of the occipital cortex in macaque monkey devoid of retinal input from early embryonic stages. *European Journal of Neuroscience, 8*, 942–950.

Büchel, C., Price, C., Frackowiak, R. S. J., & Friston, K. (1998). Different activation patterns in the visual cortex of late and congenitally blind subjects. *Brain, 121*, 409–419.

Büchel, C., Price, C., & Friston, K. (1998). A multimodal language region in the ventral visual pathway. *Nature, 394*, 274–277.

Capelle, C., Trullemans, C., Arno, P., & Veraart, C. (1998). A real time experimental prototype for enhancement of vision rehabilitation using auditory substitution. *IEEE Transactions on Biomedical Engineering, 45*, 1279–1293.

Caramazza, A. (1996). Pictures, words and the brain. *Nature, 383*, 216–217.

Carpenter, P. A., & Eisenberg, P. (1978). Mental rotation and the frame of reference in blind and sighted individuals. *Perception & Psychophysics, 23*, 117–124.

Changeux, J. P., & Danchin, A. (1976). Selective stabilisation of developing synapses as a mechanism for the specification of neuronal networks. *Nature, 264*, 705–712.

Cohen, L. G., Weeks, R. A., Sadato, N., Celnik, P., Ishii, K., & Hallett, M. (1999). Period of susceptibility for cross-modal plasticity in the blind. *Annals of Neurology, 45*, 451–460.

Collins, C. C., & Bach-y-Rita, P. (1973). Transmission of pictorial information through the skin. *Advances in Biological and Medical Physics, 14*, 285–315.

Cornoldi, C., Cortesi, A., & Petri, D. (1991). Individual differences in the capacity limitations of visuo-spatial short-term memory: Research on sighted and totally congenitally blind people. *Memory & Cognition, 19*, 459–468.

Cornoldi, C., Bertuccelli, B., Rocchi, P., & Sbrana, B. (1993). Processing capacity limitations in pictorial and spatial representations in the totally congenitally blind. *Cortex, 29*, 675–689.

Demer, J. L. (1993). Positron emission tomographic studies of cortical function in human amblyopia. *Neuroscience and Biobehavioral Reviews, 17*, 469–476.

D'Esposito, M., Detre, J. A., Aguirre, G. K., Stallcup, M., Alsop, D. C., Tipett, L. J., et al. (1997). A functional MRI study of mental-image generation. *Neuropsychologia, 35*, 725–730.
De Volder, A. G., Bol, A., Blin, J., Robert, A., Arno, P., Grandin, C., et al. (1997). Brain energy metabolism in early blind subjects: Neural activity in the visual cortex. *Brain Research, 750*, 235–244.
De Volder, A. G., Catalan-Ahumada, M., Robert, A., Bol, A., Labar, D., Coppens, A., et al. (1999). Changes in occipital cortex activity in early blind humans using a sensory substitution device. *Brain Research, 826*, 128–134.
De Volder, A. G., Toyama, H., Kimura, Y., Kiyosawa, M., Nakano, H., Vanlierde, A., et al. (2001). Auditory triggered mental imagery of shape involves visual association areas in early blind humans. *NeuroImage, 14*, 129–139.
Edelman, G. M. (1993). Neural Darwinism: selection and reentrant signaling in higher brain function. *Neuron, 10*, 115–125.
Faillenot, I., Sakata, H., Costes, N., Decety, J., & Jeannerod, M. (1997). Visual working memory for shape and 3D—orientation: A PET study. *NeuroReport, 8*, 859–862.
Fox, P. T., Raichle, M. E., Mintun, M. A., & Dence, C. (1988). Nonoxidative glucose consumption during focal physiologic neural activity. *Science, 241*, 462–464.
Gregory, R. L. (1963). Distorsion of visual space as inappropriate constancy scaling. *Nature, 199*, 678–691.
Gregory, R. L. (1997). *Eye and Brain: The Psychology of Seeing*, 5th edn., Princeton University Press, Princeton NJ.
Haxby, J. V., Grady, C. L., Horwitz, B., Ungerleider, L. G., Mishkin, M., Carson, R. E., et al. (1991). Dissociation of objects and spatial visual processing patway in human extrastriate cortex. *Proceedings of the National Academy of Sciences, 88*, 1621–1625.
Huttenlocher, P. R., & Dabholkar, A. S. (1997). Regional differences in synaptogenesis in human cerebral cortex. *Journal of Comparative Neurology, 387*, 167–178.
Huttenlocher, P. R., & de Courten, C. (1987). The development of synapses in striate cortex of man. *Human Neurobiology, 6*, 1–9.
Innocenti, G. M., & Clarke, S. (1984). Bilateral transitory projection to visual areas from auditory cortex in kittens. *Developmental Brain Research, 14*, 143–148.
Kadekaro, M., Crane, A. M., & Sokoloff, L. (1985). Differential effects of electrical stimulation of sciatic nerve on metabolic activity in spinal cord and dorsal root ganglion in the rat. *Proceedings of the National Academy of Sciences, 82*, 6010–6013.
Kauff, M., Kassubek, J., Mulack, T., & Greenlee, M. W. (2000). Cortical activation evoked by visual mental imagery as measured by fMRI. *NeuroReport, 11*, 3957–3962.
Kerr, N. H. (1983). The role of vision in "visual imagery" experiments: Evidence from the congenitally blind. *Journal of Experimental Psychology: General, 112*, 265–277.
Kiyosawa, M., Bosley, T. M., Kushner, M., Jamieson, D., Alavi, A., Savino, P. J., et al. (1989). Positron emission tomography to study the effect of eye closure and optic nerve damage on human cerebral glucose metabolism. *American Journal of Ophtalmology, 108*, 147–152.
Kosslyn, S. M. (1994). *Image and brain: The resolution of the imagery debate*. Cambridge, MA: MIT Press.
Kosslyn, S. M., Alpert, N. M., Thompson, W. L., Maljkovic, V., Weise, S. B., Chabris, C. F., et al. (1993). Visual-mental imagery activates topographically-organized visual cortex: PET investigations. *Journal of Cognitive Neuroscience, 5*, 263–287.

Kosslyn, S. M., Thompson, W. L., & Alpert, N. M. (1997). Neural systems shared by visual imagery and visual perception: A positron emission tomography study. *Neuroimage, 6,* 320–334.

Kujala, T., Alho, K., Kekoni, J., Hämäläinen, H., Reinikainen, K., Salonen, O., et al. (1995). Auditory and somatosensory event-related brain potentials in early blind humans. *Experimental Brain Research, 104,* 519–526.

Kujala, T., Huotilainen, M., Sinkkonen, J., Ahonen, A. I., Alho, K., Hämäläinen, M. S., et al. (1995). Visual cortex activation in blind humans during sound discrimination. *Neuroscience Letters, 183,* 143–146.

Marmor, G. S., & Zaback, L. A. (1976). Mental rotation by the blind: Does mental rotation depend on visual imagery? *Journal of Experimental Psychology: Human Perception, 2,* 515–521.

Mellet, E., Tzourio-Mazoyer, N., Bricogne, S., Mazoyer, B., Kosslyn, S. M., & Denis, M. (2000). Functional anatomy of high-resolution visual mental imagery. *Journal of Cognitive Neuroscience, 12,* 98–109.

Mellet, E., Tzourio, N., Crivello, F., Joliot, M., Denis, M., & Mazoyer, B. (1996). Functional anatomy of spatial mental imagery generated from verbal instruction. *Journal of Neuroscience, 16,* 6504–6512.

Mellet, E., Tzourio, N., Denis, M., & Mazoyer, B. (1995). A positron emission tomography study of visual and mental spatial exploration. *Journal of Cognitive Neuroscience, 7,* 433–445.

Meijer, P. B. L. (1992). An experimental system for auditory image representations, *IEEE Transactions on Biomedical Engineering, 39,* 112–121.

Mishkin, M., Ungerleider, L. G., & Macko, K. A. (1983). Object vision and spatial vision: two cortical pathways. *Trends in Neurosciences, 6,* 414–417.

O'Craven, K. M., & Kanwisher, N. (2000). Mental imagery of faces and places activates corresponding stimulus-specific brain regions. *Journal of Cognitive Neuroscience, 12,* 1013–1023.

Parsons, L. M., Fox, P. T., Downs, J. H., Glass, T., Hirsch, T. B., Martin, C. C., et al. (1995). Use of implicit motor imagery for visual shape discrimination as revealed by PET. *Nature, 375,* 54–58.

Phelps, M. E., Mazziotta, J. C., Kuhl, D. E., Nuwer, M., Packwood, J., Metter, J., et al. (1981). Tomographic mapping of human cerebral metabolism : visual stimulation and deprivation. *Neurology, 31,* 517–529.

Rauschecker, J. P. (1995). Compensatory plasticity and sensory substitution in the cerebral cortex. *Trends in Neurosciences, 18,* 36–43.

Rauschecker, J. P., & Korte, M. (1993). Auditory compensation for early blindness in cat cerebral cortex. *Journal of Neuroscience, 13,* 4538–4548.

Renier, L., Laloyaux, C., Collignon, O., Tranduy, D., Vanlierde, A., Bruyer, R., et al. (2005). The Ponzo illusion with auditory substitution of vision in sighted and early blind subjects. *Perception, 34,* 851–867.

Röder, B., Rösler, F., & Hennighausen, E. (1996). Event-related potentials during auditory and somatosensory discrimination in sighted and blind human subjects. *Cognitive Brain Research, 4,* 77–83.

Roland, P. E., & Gulyas, B. (1995). Visual memory, visual imagery and visual recognition of large field patterns by human brain: Functional anatomy by positron emission tomography. *Cerebral Cortex, 1,* 79–93.

Rösler, F., Röder, B., Heil, M., & Hennighausen, E. (1993). Topographic differences of slow event-related brain potentials in blind and sighted human subjects during haptic mental rotation. *Cognitive Brain Research, 1,* 145–159.

Sadato, N., Pascual-Leone, A., Grafman, J., Ibanez, V., Deiber, M.-P., Dold, G., et al. (1996). Activation of the primary visual cortex by Braille reading in blind subjects. *Nature, 380,* 526–528.

Sadato, N., Pascual-Leone, A., Grafman, J., Ibanez, V., Deiber, M.-P., Dold, G., et al. (1998). Neural network for Braille reading by the blind. *Brain, 121,* 1213–1229.

Sokoloff, L. (1981). Relationships among local functional activity, energy metabolism and blood flow in the central nervous system. *Federal Proceedings, 40,* 2311–2316.

Talairach, J., & Tournoux, P. (1988). *Co-planar stereotaxic atlas of the human brain.* New York: Thieme Medical Publishers.

Uhl, F., Kretschmer, T., Lindinger, G., Goldenberg, G., Lang, W., Oder, W., et al. (1994). Tactile mental imagery in sighted persons and in patients suffering from peripheral blindness early in life. *Electroencephalography and Clinical Neurophysiology, 91,* 249–255.

Vanlierde, A., De Volder, A. G., Wanet-Defalque, M.-C., & Veraart, C. (2003). Occipito-parietal cortex activation during visuo-spatial imagery in early blind humans. *NeuroImage, 19,* 698–709.

Vanlierde, A., & Wanet-Defalque, M.-C. (2004). Abilities and strategies of blind and sighted subjects in visuo-spatial imagery. *Acta Psychologica, 116,* 205–222.

Vecchi, T. (1998). Visuo-spatial imagery in congenitally totally blind people. *Memory, 6,* 91–102.

Vecchi, T., Monticellai, M. L., & Cornoldi, C. (1995). Visuo-spatial working memory: Structures and variables affecting a capacity measure. *Neuropsychologia, 11,* 1549–1564.

Veraart, C. (1989). Neurophysiological approach to the design of visual prostheses: A theoretical discussion. *Journal of Medical Engineering & Technology, 13,* 57–62.

Veraart, C., De Volder, A. G., Wanet-Defalque, M.-C., Bol, A., Michel, C., & Goffinet, A. M. (1990). Glucose utilization in human visual cortex is respectively elevated and decreased in early versus late blindness. *Brain Research, 510,* 115–121.

Wanet-Defalque, M.-C., Veraart, C., De Volder, A., Metz, R., Michel, C., Dooms, G., et al. (1988). High metabolic activity in the visual cortex of early blind human subjects. *Brain Research, 446,* 369–373.

Weeks, R., Horwitz, B., Aziz-Sultan, A., Tian, B., Wessinger, C. M., Cohen, L. G., et al. (2000). A positron emission tomography study of auditory localization in the congentally blind. *Journal of Neurocience, 20,* 2664–2672.

6

Braille, Plasticity, and the Mind

Peter Melzer and Ford Ebner

In this chapter, we examine parts of the brain that are engaged when people read Braille with their fingertips. The primary tool of our research is functional magnetic resonance imaging (fMRI), and we illustrate the methods used to extract information about local cerebral information processing from fMRI data with examples from our research.

fMRI exploits the proportionality of nerve cell activity and local cerebral blood flow (lCBF). The pioneering observations of Roy and Sherrington (1890) on cerebral blood supply and brain function, and the development of tracer methods by Kety and Schmidt (1948) to measure lCBF a half a century later were groundbreaking milestones in the investigation into the relationship between blood flow and neural activity. Yet another 50 years have passed, and the type of neural activity associated with lCBF still receives intense scrutiny to the present day (Arthurs & Boniface, 2002; Caesar, Thomsen, & Lauritzen, 2003; Logothetis, Pauls, Augath, Trinath, & Oeltermann, 2001). lCBF and neural activity are coupled under normal physiological conditions (Sokoloff, 1996). However, the precise coupling mechanisms may vary throughout the brain and are not fully understood (Gotoh et al., 2001). In spite of this incomplete understanding, blood-flow-based methods have been developed aggressively for mapping neural function in humans. Changes in lCBF can be determined non-invasively with the systemic administration of diffusible tracer compounds containing short-lived radionuclides the distribution of which can be imaged with positron emission tomography (PET; Fox, Mintun, Raichle, & Herscovitch, 1984) and single photon emission tomography (SPECT; Holman, Lee, Hill, Lovett, & Lister-James, 1984). In contrast, with fMRI of blood oxygen level-dependent (BOLD) signals (Kwong et al., 1992; Ogawa et al., 1992) and optical imaging of intrinsic signals (OIS; Malonek & Grinvald, 1997), radioactive compounds are not needed. fMRI and OIS measure changes in the proportion of oxygenated and deoxygenated hemoglobin that occur concomitant with increases in lCBF as redox state-dependent changes in red light reflected from the Fe/heme complex and shifts in the nuclear resonance of protons in surrounding water molecules, respectively. Among the four imaging techniques, OIS is the most invasive method in humans because it requires craniotomy and removal of the dura to expose the brain (Cannestra, Blood, Black, & Toga, 1996). fMRI is the least invasive method, since this method requires neither the administration of radiopharmaceuticals nor brain exposure.

PET has been widely employed to investigate the reorganization of cerebral function in people with severe visual disabilities. Imaging of the cerebral use of glucose with PET has shown that occipital regions that process visual information in sighted people remain metabolically active in people with severe visual disability (Wanet-Defalque et al., 1988). The metabolic rate appeared diminished in the adventitiously disabled and elevated in the congenitally disabled (Veraart et al., 1990). Likewise, a SPECT study showed elevated lCBF in people with early visual disability (Uhl, Franzen, Podreka, Steiner, & Deecke, 1993), and most intriguingly, PET of lCBF demonstrated that these regions were activated during Braille reading (Büchel, Price, Frackowiak, & Friston, 1998; Sadato et al., 1996). The temporal resolution of lCBF measurements with PET is constrained by the limitation that 1–2 min are needed for a freely diffusible tracer (e.g., $H_2^{15}O$) to equilibrate in the brain before scanning (Petersen, Fox, Posner, Mintun, & Raichle, 1988) under the assumption that lCBF and neural activity are in a steady state during this time. In contrast, fMRI may detect neural activation in brain structures within seconds; therefore this method is suitable for the examination of more rapid changes in cerebral activity, with greater temporal resolution than PET.

Because of the greater temporal resolution compared with PET, we used fMRI to map local cerebral activation during Braille reading. As an indicator of neural activity, local BOLD signal change was analyzed for its strength of correlation with the tasks and region-specific differences in fluctuations in signal strength. lCBF may change with neural activation within 4 sec (Malonek et al., 1997), and the temporal resolution was set to that time frame accordingly. The changes in brain activation we observed are therefore slow compared to the underlying millisecond changes in neural discharge activity. However, we were able to establish a relationship between the imaged cerebral activation and neural activity recorded with electroencephalography (EEG). Finally, we were able to demonstrate that Braille readers with different histories show differences in the magnitude of local cortical activation related to the reading of disjointed words or a text. We discuss the brain plasticity that may be involved, the possible functional roles of occipital and temporal lobe activation during Braille reading, and the implications for language processing. We conclude with an appraisal of the weaknesses and strengths of fMRI for brain studies.

MATERIALS AND METHODS

Participants

Nineteen Braille readers (11 female and 8 male; 1 Asian, 4 African Americans, and 14 Caucasians; 4 left- and 15 right-handers) and 1 Braille-naïve right-handed male were the participants in the studies described in this chapter. They were between 22 and 57 years of age (median age 37). The Braille readers were assigned to one of four groups: Early (E), Intermediate (I), Late (L), or Sighted (S).

Group E: Five participants had lost eyesight at birth and could not recall any visual experience. The visual disability was caused by retinopathy of prematurity (4 participants) or undisclosed reasons (1 participant).

Group I: Five participants had some visual function at birth and four held visual memories. However, four developed a severe visual disability within 7 years after birth and one within 13 years. The causes were microphthalmia, macular degeneration, congenital glaucoma, Steven Johnson syndrome, and accident.

Group L: Five participants had progressive retinal degeneration glaucoma, retinitis pigmentosa, or Stargart's syndrome but still maintained residual contrast and color vision or they had lost vision adventitiously as adults (retinal inflammation, accident).

Group S: Four participants were sighted Braille instructors who were able to read Braille by touch.

The participants with early and intermediate visual disability began to learn Braille between the ages of 5 and 7 whereas the participants with late visual disability and the sighted readers learned Braille in their teenage years or later.

Functional Magnetic Resonance Imaging

Stimuli. All participants wore earplugs; those with eyesight were blindfolded. The functional runs consisted of four 40-s epochs of resting alternated with reading. The participants had practiced the tasks in previous simulator training. The participants were asked to read silently one-syllable nouns (10% abstract) embossed on Dymo labelmaker tape in grade I Braille (i.e., each letter was embossed separately). During a separate run, they read from an article in the *National Geographic* magazine embossed in grade II Braille (i.e., contractions were used). Three participants were asked to alternate between epochs of noun and text reading in an additional run. Though each participant had a preferred reading hand, the index finger of which was primarily used to palpate the Braille dots, both hands were used for moving along the text line. All runs were repeated in a second scanning session with different imaging planes.

Scanning.   fMRI from six 5-mm thick contiguous slices were acquired with a General Electric Corp. Signa 1.5 T MR scanner. In the first scanning session, the imaging planes were tilted ~45° dorso-rostrally. In the second session, the slices were aligned parallel to the plane transecting the anterior and posterior commissure, extending from the dorsal boundary of the thalamus to the superior colliculus. During the first scanner runs, T_1-weighted anatomical images were obtained at 256×256 pixels in a 24×24 cm field of view. In the subsequent runs, T_2^*-weighted functional images were acquired with a gradient echo EPI pulse sequence (flip angle 90°, TE = 60 ms, TR = 4 s) at 64×64 pixels while the participants executed their tasks. The smallest brain tissue volume imaged during fMRI was therefore $3.5 \times 3.5 \times 5$ mm and the acquisition rate of the images was 0.25 per s.

Data analysis.   Cerebral activation maps were constructed by calculating the pixel-by-pixel correlation of the change in BOLD signal with the *box car* function of resting and reading at $r \geq 0.45$ (Strupp, 1996). The activated regions were superimposed on the corresponding anatomical images, and regions of interest were selected using anatomical landmarks. The average suprathreshold BOLD signal was measured in primary somatic sensory/motor cortex and in regions that receive visual input in sighted persons in the parietal, temporal, and occipital lobes. The averages were converted into z-scores: the difference between the BOLD signal at each time point and the mean BOLD signal at "rest" divided by the standard deviation of the BOLD signal at "rest." As a measure of the tightness of the link between cerebral activation and reading, correlation coefficients were calculated for the correlations between the time course of the z-scores and the *box car* curve. Furthermore, the local time courses of z-scores were subjected to a spectral analysis using Fourier transformations.

Statistics.   Statistical analyses were carried out with SAS (SAS Institute, Cary, NC). The correlation coefficients were weighted by the prevalence of the subjects with suprathreshold activation and normalized by transformation into Van der Waerden scores. They were then subjected to an analysis of variance in a nested design using general linear models with regions of interest as main effect and number of words read as associated effect. Side, subject, and onset of disability were considered nesting effects. The null hypotheses were tested for type IV sums of squares. Unequal sample sizes were adjusted using least-squares means. The effect of onset of the visual disability was tested with Bonferroni corrections and adjusted means. Lateralization of the expanse of activation was tested with a paired student's t test on the ranks of percentage side-to-side differences in the number of activated pixels between homotopic areas. The power of the peaks in the spectra of the time courses of z-scores was compared following the same procedure as used with the correlation coefficients. In addition, the association between the strengths of correlation and peak power was examined using Spearman's rank-order correlation.

Electroencephalography

EEGs were recorded, in sessions separate from fMRI, from select participants of each group and a male sighted right-hander naïve in Braille.

Stimuli. The sighted participants wore blindfolds during the entire session. Each epoch of recording lasted 2.5 min. During the epochs, the participants were asked to either rest motionless in silence or palpate one-syllable nouns or text embossed in Braille as in the fMRI sessions. Each task was repeated five times according to a randomized schedule.

Recordings. EEGs were recorded from monopolar Ag/AgCl button electrodes attached to the scalp at four homotopic sites over each cortical hemisphere (I-410 BCS, J&J Engineering, Inc., Poulsbo, WA). The recording sites were Fp1, Fp2, C3, C4, P3, P4, O1, and O2 according to the International Ten-Twenty System (Jaspers, 1958). Additional electrodes were attached to the earlobes and the neck as reference and ground, respectively. The impedance at each recording channel was routinely checked to remain at $\sim$5 kOhms. The digitized raw EEG from the eight scalp sites was sampled in 10 s bins at a sampling rate of 512 per s. In addition, spectral power was recorded online with a fast Fourier-transforming amplifier. The average EEG power was determined for increments of 2 Hz between 0 and 19 Hz as well as for the bands between 7 and 13 Hz (α), 13 and 19 Hz (β), and 36 and 43 Hz (γ). Bins contaminated with artifacts owing to eye movements were excised from the recordings post hoc, and the mean power in the spectral bands was determined for each 2.5 min epoch of recording. Eventually, the natural logarithms of the left-to-right ratios in α, β, and γ power recorded at homotopic locations were calculated for each bin and mean ratios were determined for the entire epoch.

Statistical analyses. The mean EEG power and the mean side-to-side ratios over the five episodes of resting and reading constituted the average result for a given participant. Average ratios were transformed into Van der Waerden scores for normalization, and the scores were subjected to an analysis of variance for recording site as main effect using a hierarchical nested design, general linear models, and tests of the null hypothesis using type III errors for the nesting effects (SAS; SAS Institute, Cary, NC). Subsequent pair-wise com-

parisons of the mean ratios between recording sites, tasks, and groups were carried out with a Bonferroni correction.

RESULTS

Time Course of Cortical Activation

Our functional imaging study essentially followed a block design alternating
between two mental states: resting and reading or reading nouns and reading
text. The strength of the correlation between changes in cerebral BOLD signal
and the switch in mental state were taken as indicators of cerebral activation.

In the first functional run of an fMRI session, the image slices were positioned to transect the primary visual area, as well as the primary somatic sensory and motor areas of cerebral cortex (Figure 6–1A). Primary sensory areas
are cortical regions in which the main ascending sensory pathways terminate.
Foci of activation during noun reading compared with resting are shown superimposed on the image stacks from a sighted instructor (Figure 6–1B) and a
reader with early visual disability (Figure 6–1C).

The observed cerebral activation was mapped to cortical areas that Brodmann (1909) distinguished based on cytoarchitectonic differences (Figure 6–2)
and are thus prefixed BA for Brodmann area. The task bilaterally activated
primary somatic sensory (BA 1–3), motor (BA 4) and premotor (BA 6) areas
(arrows) in the sighted instructor (Figure 6–1B) as well as in the reader with
early visual disability (Figure 6–1C). In addition, the latter had foci of activation within the area where primary visual cortex is situated in sighted people
(BA 17). Primary visual cortex contains a prominent white band at mid-depth
of the gray matter named in honor of the Italian anatomist Francisco Gennari (1750–97) as *Gennari's stria*. The band can be utilized in magnetic resonance imaging as a morphological landmark (Walters et al., 2003). We shall
call primary visual cortex (BA 17) *striate* cortex and the cortex between striate cortex and primary somatic sensory and primary auditory cortex *extrastriate* cortex. Striate and extrastriate activation remained subthreshold in the
sighted Braille instructor (Figure 6–1B). In contrast, Braille reading produced
prominent bilateral foci of activation in both cortical regions in the reader
with visual disability (Figure 6–1C), particularly in the occipital (BA 18 &19)
and temporal (BA 39 & 40) lobes. The occipito-temporal activation was more
prominent contralateral to the reading hand (Figure 6–1C; large white arrowhead). Only a few small foci were observed ipsilaterally (Figure 6–1C; large
black/white arrowheads).

Striate cortex activation occurred whether or not visually disabled readers
had experienced patterned vision during infancy. The BOLD signal increased
and decreased commensurate with reading and resting in somatic sensory and
motor cortex (Figure 6–1D) as well as in occipital cortex (Figure 6–1E). Though
each trace represents the change in BOLD signal of a reader with a different

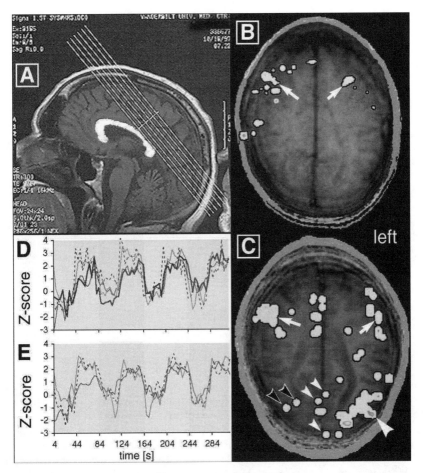

FIGURE 6–1.   Cerebral activation during Braille reading. The planes of the six contiguous functional images (lines) are shown superimposed on an anatomical scan in the sagittal plane near the midline (A). Nouns were read silently. Cerebral activation was considered above threshold when the activation correlated with reading at $r \geq 0.45$. Activated foci are shown superimposed on the stack of six slices for a sighted instructor (B) and a reader who lost eyesight at birth (C), both reading Braille with the fingertips. Both hands were used in the task and therefore primary somatic sensory and primary motor cortex were activated on both sides (arrows). In addition, cerebral activation was prominent in the occipital lobes of the reader with visual disability where visual information is processed in sighted people (arrowheads). A number of the foci were located in the otherwise primary visual area known as *striate* cortex (small white arrowheads). *Extrastriate* cortex was activated ipsilaterally in small foci (black arrowheads) and contralaterally in a large area (large white arrowhead). Time courses of activation are shown for a reader with early (dashed line), intermediate (light gray line) and late (dark gray line) visual disability and a sighted reader (solid line) in primary somatic sensory and motor cortex (D) and occipital cortex (E). The epochs of reading are shaded. *Source:* P. Melzer, D. R. Pickens, R. R. Price, V. L. Morgan, F. J. Symons, and R. S. Wall (1998). Reading Braille predominantly activates extrastriate cortex in persons with severe visual disability: a fMRI study. *Proceedings of the Sixth Scientific Meeting of the International Society for Magnetic Resonance in Medicine*, 1514. Copyright 1988 by International Society for Magnetic Resonance in Medicine. Reprinted with permission. [See Color Plate]

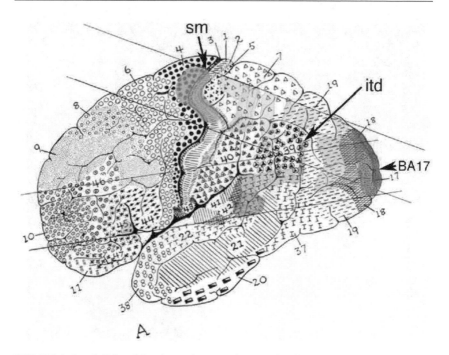

FIGURE 6–2.   fMRI and Brodmann's cortical map. The illustration was adapted from
Brodmann (1909). Brodmann divided cortex into numbered areas that he distinguished
based on cytoarchitectonic characteristics (symbols and hatchings). His scheme is in use
still today. The two sets of superimposed parallel lines constitute the borders between which
functional images were acquired in separate runs. The shading identifies regions where
foci of cerebral activation were detected. The activated regions discussed in greatest detail
in this chapter consist of Brodmann areas (BAs) 1–3 in postcentral gyrus (primary somatic
sensory cortex) and BA 4 in precentral gyrus (primary motor area) lumped together (sm),
BA 39 (dorsal inferior temporal gyrus labeled itd), as well as BA 17 (*striate* cortex).

background, the time courses overlap to a substantial degree. However, close
examination showed that the shape of the time courses varied considerably
between cortical regions, and that this variation resulted in remarkable differences in local coefficients of correlation.

Correlational Strength of Cortical Activation

The observations on the tightness of the association between Braille reading
and cortical activation have been published earlier in detail (Melzer et al.,
2001). In this chapter, we highlight essential findings of the current investigation. The readers with the greatest and most comparable reading fluency were
the participants with early (group E) and intermediate (group I) loss of eyesight
groups. They read 0.5–1.0 "one-syllable noun per s." Using their data, acti-

vated cortical regions could be divided into three classes of responders with statistically significantly different strengths of correlation.

The greatest correlation coefficients ($r > 0.65$) were found in somatic sensory (BA 3) and motor (BA 4) cortex where touch information enters cortex and palpation of the Braille is controlled. Similar strength of correlation was found in the posterior parietal cortex (BA 5, BA 7, BA 39, and BA 40) receiving input from primary somatic sensory cortex (Jeannerod, 1988). BA 7 is engaged in the tactile perception of the orientation of gratings (Sathian & Zangaladze, 2002). Moreover, BA 7, BA 39, and BA 40 have been shown to be activated during visual imagery (Lambert, Sampaio, Mauss, & Scheiber, 2004; Roland & Gulyás, 1995).

Correlations were moderate ($0.50 < r < 0.60$) in occipitotemporal (BA 19 and 37), lateral occipital (BA 19), and striate cortex (BA 17). Occipitotemporal and lateral occipital cortex are engaged in word recognition (Bookheimer, Zeffiro, Blaxton, Gaillard, & Theodore, 1995; Nobre, Allison, & McCarthy, 1994) and the processing of kinetic boundaries, shapes (Van Oostende, Sunaert, Van Hecke, Marchal, & Orban, 1997), and symmetry (Sasaki, Vanduffel, Knutsen, Tyler, & Tootell, 2005). Both regions have been shown to be activated during visual imagery (Courtney & Ungerleider, 1997; Ganis, Thompson, & Kosslyn, 2004; Lambert et al., 2004; Roland & Gulyás, 1995). Büchel and colleagues (1998) observed striate cortex activation only in people who were visually disabled during adulthood and associated it solely with visual imagery. However, evidence that striate cortex plays a more profound role in the palpation and decoding of Braille dots has been provided by the finding that transcranial magnetic stimulation of this region degrades reading performance (Cohen et al., 1997).

Low correlations (i.e., $r < 0.50$) were observed in the secondary visual area (BA 18) and dorsal (BA 39) inferior temporal gyrus. The secondary visual area might have become activated during visual imagery. The dorsal inferior temporal gyrus has been implicated in the phonological processing of words (Petersen & Fiez, 1993). In addition, low correlations of cortical activation were found in ventral inferior temporal gyrus (BA 37) and the middle superior temporal area (BA 22). The foci of activation were below the imaging plane in Figure 6–1. The ventral inferior temporal site mapped onto human MT/V5 (Tootell, Dale, Sereno, & Malach, 1996). In sighted people this area and the anteriorly adjacent middle superior temporal area are not as retinotopically organized as primary visual cortex and are considered association areas that integrate more generalized, intrinsic features of visual stimuli (Courtney & Ungerleider, 1997). The two regions are near and in Wernicke's area (Bogen & Bogen, 1976; Geschwind, 1970; Mesulam, 1990) and have been demonstrated to be involved in semantic word processing (Binder, Frost, Hammeke, Rao, & Cox, 1996; Bookheimer et al., 1995; Eden & Zeffiro, 1998; Peterson et al., 1988; Shaywitz et al., 1998). The three temporal regions may thus be engaged in the processing of symbolic language in Braille readers.

Spectral Analyses

Close inspection of the BOLD signal changes revealed that low strength of correlation did not reflect merely lower cortical activation. In addition to the waxing and waning of the BOLD signal associated with the switch of mental states, signal strength appeared to oscillate at frequencies greater than the periodicity of the two states. Consistent with the findings of Bandettini, Jesmanowicz, Wong, and Hyde (1993), spectral analyses showed that the time courses were composed of one predominant periodicity of resting and reading at 0.75 per min common to all cortical regions examined (see Figure 6–3).

The spectral power at this frequency was associated significantly with the magnitude of the correlation coefficient ($r = 0.21$; $p = 0.02$). A second smaller peak commonly present in the power spectra was located at *ca.* 2.4 per minute (underlain in green in Figure 6–3). The power of this peak was not statistically significant. Therefore, the periodicity associated with the second peak was not merely a harmonic of resting and reading. Moreover, it was an effect of neither respiration (*ca.* 10 per min) nor heartbeat (*ca.* 60 per min). Intriguingly, a trough showed at this frequency in the spectra of dorsal inferior temporal cortex contralateral to the reading hand in readers with early visual disability (Figure 6–3B) and this difference was significant ($p \leq 0.05$). A third lower peak particular to this group was distinct at *ca.* 1.5 per min in the spectra from somatic sensory and motor cortex on both cortical hemispheres (Figure 6–3A; asterisks). This observation suggests that readers without visual experience process Braille differently in the cortical region that receives tactile input than readers with early visual experience. Cortical regions, therefore, appear to exhibit characteristic signatures of BOLD signal change. Moreover, the temporal pattern of BOLD responses appears to reflect differences in the readers' personal histories. Fourier analysis revealed the presence of oscillations in the BOLD signal in addition to the periodicity of resting and reading. *Wavelet* analysis provided evidence that such oscillations are associated with Braille reading (Stefansic, Morgan, Hardin, Melzer, & Ebner, 2002).

Cortical Activation and Neural Electrical Activity

Results of EEG recordings obtained from the same participants subjected to fMRI are illustrated in Figure 6–4. Only the α power differences recorded over the occipital lobes at locations O1 and O2 (Jaspers, 1958) are shown because they constitute the most interesting complement to the fMRI findings. The visually disabled reader and the sighted Braille instructor had a noticeable interhemispheric difference in α power while resting, whereas the participant unfamiliar with Braille showed no difference (Figure 6–4A). Hence, the learned skill to read by touch may generate a persistent side-to-side difference in neural activity in the occipital lobes. Moreover, the difference in α power in the visually disabled reader was strikingly greater during "reading" than during

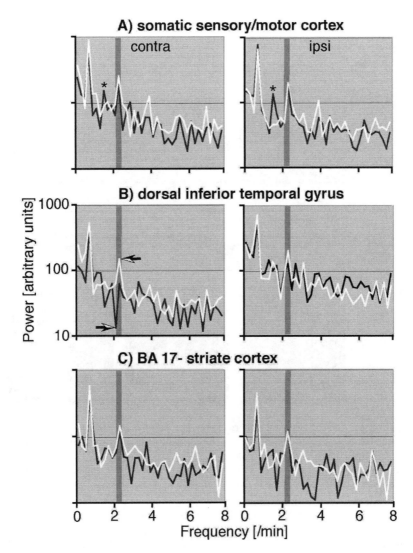

FIGURE 6–3. Oscillations of local cerebral activation. Prevalence-weighted median power spectra of local time courses of activation in the hemisphere contralateral (contra) and ipsilateral (ipsi) to the reading hand. Power in arbitrary units is plotted versus frequency for five readers with loss of eyesight at birth (black line) and five readers who were visually disabled in early childhood (white line). Spectra are shown for primary somatic sensory and primary motor cortex (A), dorsal inferior temporal gyrus (B) and *striate* cortex (C). The highest peak common to the three regions in both groups of readers is located at the periodicity of resting and reading (i.e., 0.75 per min). The second highest peak represents an about three-times faster oscillation (shaded). It is present in the three regions of both groups except contralateral dorsal inferior temporal gyrus of the readers with early loss of eyesight (B, arrows). The difference in power between the two groups is statistically significant ($p \leq$ 0.05). In addition, readers with early loss of eyesight exhibited a third, lesser peak at about twice the frequency of resting and reading in primary somatic sensory and motor cortex on both sides (A, asterisks).

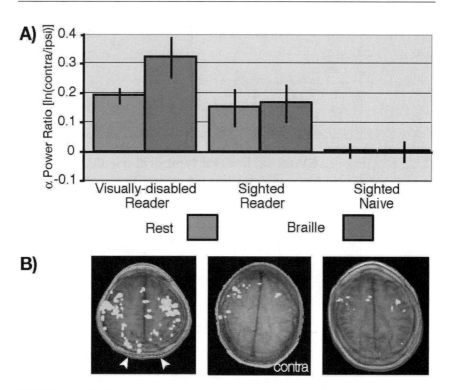

FIGURE 6–4.   EEG activity and cerebral activation. Results are shown from a reader who lost eyesight before 7 years of age (left), a sighted Braille instructor (middle), and a participant naïve in Braille (right) resting and palpating nouns embossed in Braille with the fingertips. (A) The contra-to-ipsilateral ratios in α band power ($n = 5$; mean $\pm$ standard deviation) recorded with scalp electrodes over occipital cortex (locations indicated by arrowheads in B) show stronger contralateral power at rest which increased significantly ($p \leq 0.05$) during reading. The instructor also showed increased contralateral α power at rest. However, the augmentation during reading remained negligible. The naïve participant did not exhibit any side-to-side differences under either condition. (B) Functional magnetic resonance images of cerebral activation during noun palpation from the same participants are shown superimposed on stacks of anatomical slices. Contralateral to the hand touching the Braille is on the right (contra). The participant with visual disability showed prominent occipital activation absent from the sighted participants.

"rest," whereas in the Braille instructor this increase was marginal, and it was completely absent from the naive participant. The two sighted participants did not show occipital activation during Braille reading in fMRI, whereas the visually disabled reader had prominent foci of activation (Figure 6–4B). In accord, the activated areas were significantly larger on the hemisphere contralateral to the reading hand across all readers (paired t test, $t = 5.17$, $p \leq 0.0001$). The enhancement of the side-to-side difference in EEG α power in favor of the dominant hemisphere during development has been considered to constitute a robust indicator of functional brain maturation (Fox, Bell, & Jones, 1992), and the differences observed in the present study may reflect the recruitment of the occipital lobes for Braille reading. The contralateral dominance of EEG power is consistent with the observation of others recording event-related DC potentials that occipital cortex is activated by Braille reading in people with early loss of eyesight (Uhl, Franzen, Lindinger, Lang, & Deecke, 1991). In further agreement, event-related potentials recorded over contralateral occipital cortex after tactile stimulation of an index finger were greater at 250 ms in people with early visual disability than in sighted people Kujala et al., 1995). Taken together, these results suggest that EEG and fMRI may constitute powerful complements revealing different, but mutually affirmative, features of the neural processing for tactile perception.

Task-Related Differences in Cortical Activation

In addition to temporal aspects of BOLD signal change, we examined whether the magnitude of the cortical activation differed dependent on the nature of the reading task. We investigated whether reading words in context evoked regionally different magnitudes of activation than reading disjointed nouns. Preliminary findings of this examination have been presented in abstract form (Melzer, Pickens, Price, Morgan, Wall, et al., 1998). We observed that, indeed, cortical regions were activated differentially when readers alternated between epochs of noun and text reading.

Figure 6–5 summarizes the results from a reader who had lost eyesight owing to retinopathy of prematurity and was highly fluent in Braille. The BOLD signal was recorded from two differently oriented sets of images in separate functional runs. The imaging planes of the two sets are shown superimposed on a sagittal anatomical image (Figure 6–5A and 6–5B). One set covered the inferior temporal and occipital lobes. The other transected the superior pre- (motor cortex) and postcentral (somatic sensory cortex) gyri as well as striate cortex at the occipital pole. Foci of statistically significant ($p \leq 0.05$) BOLD signal change recorded at the middle of the stacks were overlaid over the corresponding anatomical images (Figure 6–5C and 6–5D). Compared with the BOLD response to noun reading, the response to text reading was greater (red/yellow) in somatic sensory and motor cortex contralateral to the reading hand (i.e., in this reader, the left hemisphere). In addition, text reading led to greater increases in BOLD signal in striate cortex (BA 17). In contrast, the BOLD response to noun reading was commonly greater in extrastriate occipital and temporal cortex (blue/purple).

Age at Loss of Vision

To test whether the age at which vision was lost played a fundamental role in the observed differential cortical activation, data were collected in separate functional runs from the participants of the four different groups: early (group E),

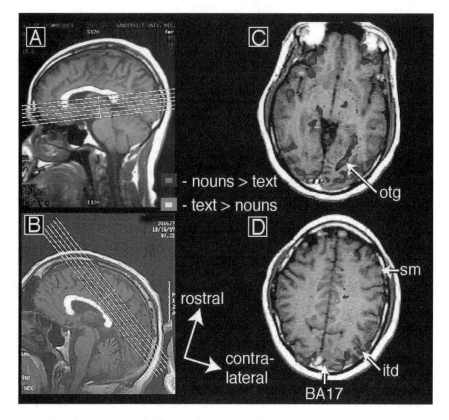

FIGURE 6–5.   Mapping of differential activation. fMRI results from a reader with early visual disability who read nouns and text alternately. Stacks of six contiguous functional images were either oriented parallel to the line transecting the anterior and posterior commissure (A) or oblique slicing through the primary somatic sensory and motor areas as well as *striate* cortex (B) in separate functional runs. The corresponding cerebral activation near the middle of the stacks is shown superimposed on anatomical scans (C, D). Activation during noun reading that was statistically significantly ($p \leq 0.01$) greater than that during text reading is shown in blue/purple. The converse is shown in red/yellow. In this reader, noun reading resulted in stronger activation in the contralateral occipito-temporal gyrus (otg), ventral *striate* cortex (BA 17) and posterior dorsal inferior temporal cortex. In contrast, text reading provided stronger activation in primary somatic sensory and motor cortex (sm), dorsal *striate* cortex (BA 17) and anterior contralateral dorsal inferior temporal cortex (itd). [See Color Plate]

intermediate (group I), late (group L) and sighted (group S). In these runs, epochs of "rest" were alternated with noun or text reading to avoid possible interactions between the BOLD responses to the two tasks. In the above analyses on correlational strength, occipital activation remained subthreshold in Braille instructors. However, small foci of activation were detected in a

number of instructors imaged for the present study, and the results were included in the analyses below. The magnitude of local BOLD signal change was
expressed as z-scores for comparison. The z-scores obtained during text reading were subtracted from those achieved during noun reading. The means of
the differences for each group and their standard errors are plotted in the
graphs of Figure 6–6.

In four instances (Figure 6–6; asterisks), differences in z scores between
text and noun reading attained statistical significance ($p \leq 0.05$) refuting the

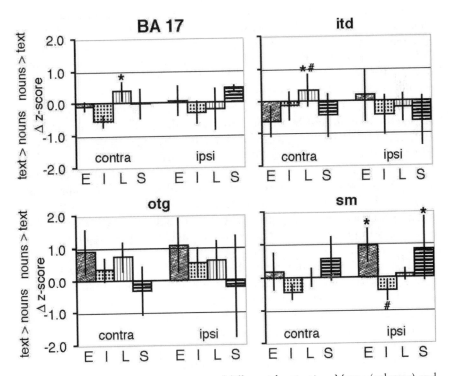

FIGURE 6–6. Quantitative comparison of differential activation. Means (columns) and
standard errors of the mean (bars) of the differences in local activation during noun and
text reading are plotted for *striate* cortex (BA 17), dorsal inferior temporal gyrus (itd),
occipito-temporal gyrus (otg), and primary somatic sensory and motor cortex (sm) contra-
(contra) and ipsilateral (ipsi) to the reading hand of the groups of five readers with early
(E), intermediate (I), and late (L) onsets of visual disability as well as for four sighted readers (S). Resting was alternated with reading text or nouns in separate functional runs. The
differences were calculated with magnitudes of activation expressed in z-scores. A positive
difference indicates that reading nouns activated cortex more than reading text. The converse is indicated by a negative difference. Asterisks label differences in activation that were
statistically significant ($p \leq 0.05$). Pound signs label differential activation that was statistically significantly ($p \leq 0.05$) different from that in readers with early loss of eyesight.

null hypothesis that the differences equaled 0. However, we observed only two instances in which the differential activation in intermediate, late, and sighted subjects differed significantly from that observed in early loss subjects (i.e., readers without visual experience—see Figure 6–6; pound signs). One instance resulted from increased activation during text reading in somatic sensory and motor cortex ipsilateral to the reading hand in readers with intermediate visual disability. The other instance was the consequence of increased activation during noun reading in dorsal inferior temporal gyrus contralateral to the reading hand in readers with late visual disability. Notably, in that case the task-related activation difference was statistically significant as well. Hence, contralateral dorsal inferior temporal cortex was the only region examined that showed a statistically significant difference in activation between text and noun reading and a statistical significant difference in this activation between the readers with early and late loss of eyesight. This finding suggests that the language processing in specific locations in the dorsal temporal lobe is influenced by early visual experience.

Striate cortex (BA 17) showed the smallest differences in activation among the four groups. However, trends were discernible. The readers with early and intermediate visual disability tended toward greater activation with text reading than the readers with late visual disability and the sighted instructors. In addition, the dorsal inferior temporal activation appeared greater with text reading on both sides across all groups. The somatic sensory and motor cortex ipsilateral to the reading hand was more activated with noun reading in the readers with early visual disability and the sighted readers, suggesting that they used the nonreading hand more vigorously when nouns were read.

The most coherent differences between noun and text reading were observed in the occipito-temporal gyrus. Common to the four groups, nouns increased the BOLD signal more than text in all readers with visual disability, and this difference was greatest on both sides in the readers with early loss of eyesight. In contrast, the mean differences were smallest and opposed in the sighted readers.

These findings are consistent with the notion discussed in the section on correlational strength that ventral temporal cortex is involved in word recognition and suggest that its recruitment for this task may be greatest when eyesight is lost early.

DISCUSSION

In this chapter we described results from three approaches to determine differences in cortical activation acquired with fMRI, which is a noninvasive method to map changes of local cerebral blood flow (lCBF) related to nerve cell activity (Sokoloff, 1996). Two of the three approaches (i.e., the analyses of stimulus/ response correlation and spectral composition of time course data) exploit temporal features of the recorded change in blood oxygen level-dependent (BOLD) signal strength. Both approaches affirmed a tight link between stimulus and BOLD response consistent with the electrical activity of the nerve cells recorded with EEG.

Our approaches to examine the time courses of the BOLD response furthermore permitted us to distinguish local differences in the temporal *signature* of the responses. These differences may be used to identify foci of brain plasticity and attribute novel functional roles to cortical regions. In the third approach, we used the differences in magnitude of the cerebral BOLD response to reading words with and without syntax to uncover brain regions engaged in the processing of language and to differentiate between Braille readers with diverse developmental histories.

Brain Plasticity

It has been long recognized that the brain is plastic and a loss of function in one cortical area can be partially compensated with recruitment of another area for the affected function (Forel, 1907). In human (Huttenlocher, de Courten, Garey, & Van der Loos, 1982) and nonhuman primate visual cortex (Bourgoise & Rakic, 1993), the number of synapses increases at an estimated rate of >5000 synapses during the first 8 months after birth and subsequently declines. During the period of synaptic elimination, the neural circuitry is particularly dependent on sensory experience, and the mature connections are thought to be stabilized by the synchrony of pre- and postsynaptic activity (Hebb, 1976). In this section, we describe mechanisms underlying cortical plasticity that may be pertinent to people with severe visual disability.

Plasticity within sensory pathways.   Functional representations in a sensory pathway develop first in the brainstem, then in thalamus, and finally in cortex (Melzer, Welker, Dörfl, & Van der Loos, 1994). Hubel, Wiesel, and LeVay (1977) were the first to demonstrate that the retinal representation in striate cortex of cats and primates is dependent on intact input from the eyes. The terminal fields of the thalamocortical afferents from both eyes originally overlap but segregate into domains of ocular dominance during development. The closing of one eye or the blockade of the electrical activity of its optic nerve just after the eyes open results in the shrinkage of the terminal fields of the deactivated sensory inputs to striate cortex. The endings of the active afferents from the used eye remain expanded (Antonini & Stryker, 1993; Chapman, Jacobson, Reiter, & Stryker, 1986). The afferents from thalamus to cortex are reactive to such activity-based modification only within a limited time window during postnatal development. However, during this epoch, reactivation of the silenced input can reverse the shift in ocular dominance toward the newly opened, previously closed eye. The window of plasticity is termed the critical period for ocular dominance plasticity.

A similar set of events occurs in the somatic sensory system. In mice, the removal of three whisker follicles in neonates results in the expansion of the cortical representation of the adjacent whiskers into the territory that normally receives the sensory input from the removed follicles (Melzer, Crane, & Smith, 1993; Melzer & Smith, 1996; Van der Loos & Woolsey, 1973). This expansion is accompanied by the enlargement of terminal fields of thalamocortical afferents. However, whisker representation already enlarges in subcortical stations of the pathway (Melzer & Smith, 1996). Similarly, the removal of a forelimb in neonatal rats leads to an expansion of hind limb inputs in the brainstem relay (Lane, Bennett-Clarke, Chiaia, Killackey, & Rhoades, 1995).

The evidence is overwhelming that maps of the peripheral sensory receptor sheet remain plastic throughout life. In adult primates, the deprivation of tactile input from one finger results in the loss of its representation in primary somatic sensory cortex and an expansion of the area responding to the adjacent fingers (Kaas, 2002). In adult mice, the terminal fields of thalamic afferents to cortex remain unaltered after whisker follicle removal (Melzer & Smith, 1995) or cutting of a nerve innervating whisker follicles (Bronchti, Corthesy, & Welker, 1999; Melzer, Yamakado, Van der Loos, Welker, & Dörf, 1988) although the whisker domains in the brain expand. Thus, different mechanisms support the plastic responses during development and in maturity. This interpretation is supported by the finding that the changes induced by novel patterns of input activity in adults are produced by changes in synaptic strength of existing connections rather than to the expansion of thalamocortical fiber domains (Bear, Cooper, & Ebner, 1987; Bear & Singer, 1986; Diamond, Armstrong-James, & Ebner, 1993; Greuel, Luhmann, & Singer, 1988) although anatomical changes have been demonstrated under some conditions.

Plasticity between sensory pathways.   The reorganization of neural connectivity is not limited to the confines of a single sensory system. Tactile thalamic inputs to deprived visual cortex may evolve as a result of the reorganization of somatic sensory trigeminotectal (Rhoades, DellaCroce, & Meadows, 1981) and tectothalamic (Mooney & Rhoades, 1983) connections, and extensive rerouting of input across sensory modalities has been demonstrated in hamsters (Frost, 1982) and ferrets (Sur, Garraghty, & Roe, 1988) after the neonatal deprivation of one sensory pathway and the simultaneous elimination of the subcortical relay stations of another pathway. In these animals, the target-deprived afferents sprouted into the input-deprived nuclei, and the modality of neurons in the corresponding cortical areas was altered accordingly (Bhide & Frost, 1992; Frost & Metin, 1985; Sur, Garraghty, & Roe, 1988). Behavioral studies have shown that the primary sensory cortical areas process subcortically rerouted sensory inputs quite effectively (Pallas, 2001; Sur, Pallas, & Roe, 1990). Consistent with these findings, somatic sensory afferents have been observed to innervate normally visual thalamic nuclei in congenitally blind mice, and the aberrant innervation was seen as strengthened by the removal of somatic sensory cortex in neonates (Asanuma & Stanfield, 1990). Somatic sensory inputs to visual thalamic nuclei have been observed also in visually impaired monkeys (Irvin, Norton, Sesma, & Casagrande, 1986). However, whether these inputs become functional has not been examined to date.

Intracortical plasticity. In addition to thalamocortical afferents, connections between cortical areas may provide novel input to the de-afferented visual cortex. The mechanisms by which such corticocortical connections are "hardwired" constitute a major area of investigation in the neurosciences. Particularly, the development of connections between the cortical hemispheres through the corpus callosum has provided insights. In primates (Dehay, Horsburgh, Berland, Killackey, & Kennedy, 1989) as well as cats (Innocenti, 1981) and rats (Ivy & Killackey, 1982; Olavarria, Malache, & Van Sluyters, 1987), it appears that early in development many more neurons project in the corpus callosum than in the mature brain. The axons of callosally projecting neurons initially accumulate in great numbers in the white matter underlying cortex. Considerably fewer axons eventually succeed in establishing lasting synapses with cortical neurons. At the same time, callosally projecting neurons send collateral axons into the ipsilateral hemisphere, which are eliminated as the callosal axons stabilize (Chalupa & Killackey, 1989; Clarke & Innocenti, 1986). It remains to be resolved whether axons in the white matter are already destined to establish connections with their cortical target neurons and, hence, proceed to grow into cortex or whether the axons are eliminated in competition with others vying for access to cortical targets (Innocenti, 1995; LaMantia & Rakic, 1990). The stabilization of callosal connections, however, appears to be associated with the maturation of thalamocortical inputs (Dehay et al., 1989; Melzer, Rothblat, & Innocenti, 1988; Olavarria et al., 1987); in their absence, the transitory connections with cortical areas of other sensory modalities may persist (Clarke & Innocenti, 1990; Dehay, Kennedy, & Bullier, 1988; Innocenti, Berbel, & Melzer, 1987). EEG evidence has shown that sensory representations can reorganize in transitional cortex between primary sensory areas. An association area in the anterior ectosylvian sulcus normally dominated by visual input contains numerous neurons responding vigorously to auditory and somatic sensory stimulation in cats deprived of vision shortly after birth (Rauschecker, 1996).

Plasticity and onset of visual disability. As discussed, the mechanisms underlying cortical plasticity during brain development may differ in many ways from those in maturity. Modifications of cortical sensory representation during development may be the consequence of a wide-ranging novel organization of neural connections within and outside cortex. By contrast, such modifications in maturity may be more likely associated with the fine-tuning of existing connections. Visual experience beyond the age of 3 seems necessary for refined visual processing in adulthood (Fine et al., 2003). The onset of the visual disability may thus determine the kind of modification in neural connectivity and local cortical function, and the identification of the type of modification may assist in the development of improved therapies for restoring cortical function at different ages. Therefore, we investigated the influence of onset of the visual disability on cortical Braille processing with fMRI in readers who had no eyesight at birth, participants with early visual experience who lost vision during early childhood, participants who lost vision as adults, and sighted Braille readers.

Our findings provided evidence that striate and extrastriate "visual" cortex indeed play a role in the tactile processing of highly discriminative touch information. Activation was detected above threshold regardless of the history of the disability, though activation occurred most variably and least frequently in sighted readers. Thus, our observations do not substantiate an entirely novel functional role of occipital cortex in Braille reading peculiar to people with visual disability. Moreover, to date we were not able to detect subcortical Braille-related activation. Hence our results did not permit us to determine whether novel ascending pathways are involved in the reorganization of human occipital neural networks processing tactile information in Braille reading.

The role of visual experience. It has been reported that people with visual disability may possess reorganized finger representations in somatic sensory cortex (Sterr et al., 1998) and, perhaps because of this, demonstrate greater tactile acuity than sighted people (Goldreich & Kanics, 2003). However, Grant, Thiagarajah, and Sathian (2000) showed that tactile acuity is enhanced with practice in any adult. Sighted people were able to achieve the same level of performance with practice as those with no visual experience. The direct impact of the absence of visual input on tactile discrimination thus remains uncertain, although substantial progress has been made in recent years (Sathian, 2005).

Our study provided three indications that information processing was profoundly reorganized in the participants who had not experienced any vision. The differences in cerebral activation were detected in the dorsal inferior temporal gyrus at the borders with the parietal and occipital lobes. Cerebral activation was temporally less correlated with reading and oscillated less in the absence of visual experience. Furthermore, text reading provoked greater activation than noun reading, whereas the converse was found in readers with visual experience. This observation suggests that the absence of visual experience influenced a higher stage of information processing than that related to reading with the fingertips.

Higher Brain Function

Our analyses of strengths of correlation between task and cerebral activation provided evidence that the cortical regions activated during Braille reading were not equally engaged in the processing of the information. A high correlation of activation with reading may be interpreted as an indication of a more immediate input from the somatic sensory pathway and an earlier stage of information processing. Low correlation, by contrast, may be indicative of a higher stage of information processing in which re-entrant multimodal and/or modulatory inputs with their own delays come to bear. The regions of low correlation may thus form a matrix (Melzack, 2001) driven largely by intrinsic brain activity making sensory input appear "modulatory" (Burton, Snyder, & Raichle, 2004). Since the observed activation in dorsal inferior temporal gyrus is located in a region implicated in phonological word processing, this area may constitute part of a neural network that interfaces between the recursive computations and the phonology of language (Hauser, Chomsky, & Fitch, 2002). The fact that this area was activated during silent reading is not inconsistent with phonological processing. The skill of silent reading has emerged as mainstream practice in occidental culture only 300 years ago (Revel et al., 1989) and thus is a very recent adaptation of the cerebral language network that possibly could not have parceled into a separate neural circuitry specific to this function in such short time (Kaas, 2004; Ebbesson, 1980).

The "visual" cortical areas that were activated in the present study, including striate cortex, also become activated during mental visual imagery. Yet, visual imagery could only account for the cerebral activation in the readers with visual experience. However, mental imagery may have occurred in the readers without visual experience because they reported having nonvisual associations with the nouns; perhaps the absence of prominent oscillations of activation at a periodicity greater than that of resting and reading in dorsal inferior temporal cortex may reflect this difference. Our findings are suggestive, therefore, of a mental imagery facilitated by the temporal lobe that is independent of the modality of sensory input, and they support the interpretation that mental imagery consists of thinking in symbols rather than in pictorial images (Eco, 1979).

CONCLUSION

Nerve cells in primary somatic sensory cortex respond to a brief touch with electrical discharge within 20 ms after stimulus onset. The heightened discharge ceases commonly within a few hundred ms. Local blood flow, however, increases only 2–3 s after stimulus onset, and neurons may have altered their electrical discharge in great numbers anytime during this period. Thus it may not be possible to predict a change in blood flow from the response of a single neuron and vice versa. Indeed, Logothetis and colleagues (2001) observed that the BOLD signal change is most tightly correlated with changes in local field potentials. These potentials mostly reflect the summed electrical activity at terminations on cortical neurons. Therefore, it may be prudent to consider the recording of single cell discharge and the recording of the BOLD signal as independent methods to examine two different aspects of cerebral activation that may not be immediately causally related (Bohr, 1950). In analogy to Heisenberg's *Unschärfe*, this uncertainty in relation might preclude that the cerebral activation uncovered with fMRI can be unequivocally associated with a neural network. The "fuzziness" may be exacerbated with as complex a mental task as reading Braille serving as an example for the complementarity of brain and mind (Stent, 2004). Even so, fMRI has proved an effective mapping tool in our investigation that permitted us to shed light on the locales of plasticity and altered function in the human brain.

ACKNOWLEDGEMENTS

This study was supported in part by a gift from Irwin and Annette Eskind, a grant from Vanderbilt University's Nicholas Hobbs Society, a core grant from the National Institute of Child Health and Human Development to the Vanderbilt Center for Research on Human Development, and a core grant from the National Eye Institute to the Vanderbilt Vision Research Center.

Collaborators in this study were Robert S. Wall (Department of Hearing and Speech, Vanderbilt University School of Medicine); Victoria L. Morgan, David R. Pickens III, and Ronald R. Price (Department of Radiology and Radiological Sciences, Vanderbilt University School of Medicine); Lynette M. Henderson and Frank J. Symons (Department of Special Education, Vanderbilt University); and Fabricio Strata and James D. Stefansic (Department of Psychology, Vanderbilt University). We are indebted to Eric Hall and Theo Larrieu (Information Technology Services, Vanderbilt University) for their technical assistance and to all of the volunteers who enthusiastically accepted inconveniences to participate in our study.

REFERENCES

Antonini, A., & Stryker, M. P. (1993). Rapid remodeling of axon arbors in the visual cortex. *Science, 260,* 1819–1821.

Arthurs, J., & Boniface, S. (2002). How well do we understand the neural origins of the fMRI BOLD signal? *Trends in Neurosciences, 25,* 27–31.

Asanuma, C., & Stanfield, B. B. (1990). Induction of somatic sensory inputs to the lateral geniculate nucleus in congenitally blind mice and in phenotypically normal mice. *Neuroscience, 39,* 533–545.

Bandettini, P. A., Jesmanowicz, A., Wong, E. C., & Hyde, J. S. (1993). Processing strategies for time-course data sets in functional MRI of the human brain. *Magnetic Resonance in Medicine, 30,* 161–173.

Bear, M. F., Cooper, L. N., & Ebner, F. F. (1987). A physiological basis for a theory of synapse modification. *Science, 237,* 42–48.

Bear, M. F., & Singer, W. (1986). Modulation of visual cortical plasticity by acetylcholine and noradrenaline. *Nature, 320,* 172–176.

Bhide, P. G., & Frost, D. O. (1992). Axon substitution in the reorganization of developing neural connections. *Proceedings of the National Academy of Sciences, 89,* 11847–11851.

Binder, J. R., Frost, J. A., Hammeke, T. A., Rao, S. M., & Cox, R. W. (1996). Function of the left planum temporale in auditory and linguistic processing. *Brain, 119,* 1239–1247.

Bogen, J. E., & Bogen, G. M. (1976). Wernicke's region—Where is it? *Annals of the New York Academy of Sciences, 280,* 834–843.

Bohr, N. (1950). On the notions of causality and complementarity. *Science, 111,* 51–54.

Bookheimer, S. Y., Zeffiro, T. A., Blaxton, T., Gaillard, W., & Theodore, W. (1995). Regional cerebral blood flow during object naming and word reading. *Human Brain Mapping, 3,* 93–106.

Bourgeois, J. P., & Rakic, P. (1993). Changes of synaptic density in the primary visual cortex of the macaque monkey from fetal to adult stage. *Journal of Neuroscience, 13,* 2801–2820.

Brodmann, K. (1909). *Vergleichende Lokalisationslehre der Grosshirnrinde in ihren Prinzipien dargestellt auf Grund des Zellenbaues* [Localisation in the cerebral cortex]. Leipzip: JA Barth.

Bronchti, G., Corthesy, M. E., & Welker, E. (1999). Partial denervation of the whiskerpad in adult mice: Altered patterns of metabolic activity in barrel cortex. *European Journal of Neuroscience, 11,* 2847–2855.

Büchel, C., Price, C., Frackowiak, R. S. J., & Friston, K. (1998). Different activation patterns in the visual cortex of late and congenitally blind subjects. *Brain, 12,* 409–419.

Burton, H., Snyder, A. Z., & Raichle, M. E. (2004). Default brain functionality in blind people. *Proceedings of the National Academy of Sciences, 101,* 15500–15505.

Caesar, K., Thomsen, K., & Lauritzen, M. (2003). Dissociation of spikes, synaptic activity, and activity-dependent increments in rat cerebellar blood flow by tonic synaptic inhibition. *Proceedings of the National Academy of Sciences, 100,* 16000–16005.

Cannestra, A. F., Blood, A. J., Black, K. L., & Toga, A. W. (1996). The evolution of optical signals in human and rodent cortex. *NeuroImage, 3,* 202–208.

Chalupa, L. M., & Killackey, H. P. (1989). Process elimination underlies ontogenetic change in the distribution of callosal projection neurons in the postcentral gyrus of the fetal rhesus monkey. *Proceedings of the National Academy of Sciences, 86,* 1076–1079.

Chapman, B., Jacobson, M. D., Reiter, H. O., & Stryker, M. P. (1986). Ocular dominance shift in kitten visual cortex caused by imbalance in retinal electrical activity. *Nature, 324,* 154–156.

Clarke, S., & Innocenti, G. M. (1986). Organization of immature intrahemispheric connections. *The Journal of Comparative Neurology, 251,* 1–22.

Clarke, S., & Innocenti, G. M. (1990). Auditory Neurons with Transitory Axons to Visual Areas Form Short Permanent Projections. *European Journal of Neuroscience, 2,* 227–242.

Cohen, L. G., Celnik, P., Pascual-Leone, A., Corwell, B., Faiz, L., Dambrosia, J., et al. (1997). Functional relevance of cross-modal plasticity in blind humans. *Nature, 389,* 180–183.

Courtney, S. M., & Ungerleider, L. G. (1997). What fMRI has taught us about human vision. *Current Opinion in Neurobiology, 7,* 554–561.

Dehay, C., Kennedy, H., & Bullier, J. (1988). Characterization of transient cortical projections from auditory, somatosensory, and motor cortices to visual areas 17, 18, and 19 in the kitten. *The Journal of Comparative Neurology, 272,* 68–89.

Dehay, C., Horsburgh, G., Berland, M., Killackey, H., & Kennedy, H. (1989). Maturation and connectivity of the visual cortex in monkey is altered by prenatal removal of retinal input. *Nature, 337,* 265–267.

Diamond, M. E., Armstrong-James, M., & Ebner, F. F. (1993). Experience-dependent plasticity in adult rat barrel cortex. *Proceedings of the National Academy of Sciences, 90,* 2082–2086.

Ebbesson, S. O. (1980). The parcellation theory and its relation to interspecific variability in brain organization, evolutionary and ontogenetic development, and neuronal plasticity. *Cell and Tissue Research, 213,* 179–212.

Eco, U. (1979). *A theory of semiotics.* Bloomington: Indiana University Press.

Eden, G. F., & Zeffiro, T. A. (1998). Neural systems affected in developmental dyslexia revealed by functional neuroimaging. *Neuron, 21,* 279–282.

Fine, I., Wade, A. R., Brewer, A. A., May, M. G., Goodman, D. F., Boynton, G. M., Wandell, B. A., et al. (2003). Long-term deprivation affects visual perception and cortex. *Nature Neuroscience, 6,* 915–916.

Forel, A. (1907). *Hygiene of nerves and mind in health and disease.* New York: GP Putnam's Sons.

Fox, N. A., Bell, M. A., & Jones, N. A. (1992). Individual differences in response to stress and cerebral asymmetry. *Developmental Neuropsychology, 8,* 161–184.

Fox, P. T., Mintun, M. A., Raichle, M. E., & Herscovitch, P. (1984). A noninvasive approach to quantitative functional brain mapping with H2(15)O and positron emission tomography. *Journal of Cerebral Blood Flow & Metabolism, 4,* 329–333.

Frost, D. O. (1982). Anomalous visual connections to somatosensory and auditory systems following brain lesions in early life. *Developmental Brain Research, 3,* 627–635.

Frost, D. O., & Metin, C. (1985). Induction of functional retinal projections to the somatosensory system. *Nature, 317,* 162–164.

Ganis, G., Thompson, W. L., & Kosslyn, S. M. (2004). Brain areas underlying visual mental imagery and visual perception: An fMRI study. *Cognitive Brain Research, 20,* 226–241.

Geschwind, N. (1970). The organization of language and the brain. *Science, 170,* 940–944.

Gotoh, J., Kuang, T.-Y., Nakao, Y., Cohen, D. M., Melzer, P., Itoh, Y., et al. (2001). Regional differences in mechanisms of cerebral circulatory response to neuronal activation. *American Journal of Physiology-Heart and Circulatory Physiology, 280,* H821–H829.

Goldreich, D., & Kanics, I. M. (2003). Tactile acuity is enhanced in blindness. *The Journal of Neuroscience, 23,* 3439–3445.

Grant, A. C., Thiagarajah, M. C., & Sathian, K. (2000). Tactile perception in blind Braille readers: A psychophysical study of acuity and hyperacuity using gratings and dot patterns. *Percept Psychophysics, 62,* 301–312.

Greuel, J. M., Luhmann, H. J., & Singer, W. (1988). Pharmacological induction of use-dependent receptive field modifications in the visual cortex. *Science, 242,* 74–77.

Hauser, M. D., Chomsky, N., & Fitch, W. T. (2002). The faculty of language: What is it, who has it, and how did it evolve? *Science, 298,* 1569–1579.

Hebb, D. O. (1976). Physiological learning theory. *Journal of Abnormal Child Psychology, 4*, 309–314.

Holman, R. L., Lee, R. G. L., Hill, T. C., Lovett, R. D., & Lister-James, J. (1984). A comparison of two cerebral perfusion tracers, N-isopropyl I-123 p-iodoamphetamine and I-123 HIPDM, in the human. *Journal of Nuclear Medicine, 25*, 25–30.

Hubel, D. H., Wiesel, T. N., & LeVay, S. (1977). Plasticity of ocular dominance columns in monkey striate cortex. *Philosophical Transactions of the Royal Society of London. Series B. Biological Sciences, 278*, 377–409.

Huttenlocher, P. R., de Courten, C., Garey, L. J., & Van der Loos, H. (1982). Synaptogenesis in human visual cortex—Evidence for synapse elimination during normal development. *Neuroscience Letters, 33*, 247–252.

Innocenti, G. M. (1981). Growth and reshaping of axons in the establishment of visual callosal connections. *Science, 212*, 824–827.

Innocenti, G. M. (1995). Exuberant development of connections, and its possible permissive role in cortical evolution. *Trends in Neurosciences, 18*, 397–402.

Innocenti, G. M., Berbel, P., & Melzer, P. (1987). The development of transitory auditory-to-visual cortex projections in the cat. *Abstracts-Society for Neuroscience, 13*, 1024.

Irvin, G. E., Norton, T. T., Sesma, M. A., & Casagrande, V. A. (1986). W-like response properties of interlaminar zone cells in the lateral geniculate nucleus of a primate (Galago crassicaudatus). *Brain Research, 362*, 254–270.

Ivy, G. O., & Killackey, H. P. (1982). Ontogenetic changes in the projections of neocortical neurons. *Journal of Neuroscience, 2*, 735–743.

Jaspers, H. H. (1958). The ten-twenty electrode system of the International Federation. *Electroencephalography and Clinical Neurophysiology, 10*, 371–375.

Jeannerod, M. (1988). The neural and behavioural organization of goal-directed movements. In D. E. Broadbent, J. L. McGaugh, N. J. Mackintosh, M. I. Posner, E. Tulving, & L. Weiskrantz (Eds.), *Oxford Psychology Series* (Vol. 15, pp. 228–44). Oxford, UK: Clarendon Press.

Kaas, J. H. (2002). Sensory loss and cortical reorganization in mature primates. *Progress in Brain Research, 138*, 167–176.

Kaas, J. H. (2004). Evolution of somatosensory and motor cortex in primates. *The Anatomical Record. Part A. Discoveries in Molecular, Cellular and Evolutionary Biology, 281*, 1148–1156.

Kety, S. S., & Schmidt, C. F. (1948). The nitrous oxide method for the quantitative determination of cerebral blood flow in man: Theory, procedure, and normal values. *The Journal of Clinical Investigation, 27*, 476–483.

Kujala, T., Alho, K., Kekoni, J., Hämäläinen, H., Reinikainen, K., Salonen, O., et al. (1995). Auditory and somatosensory event-related brain potentials in early blind humans. *Experimental Brain Research, 104*, 519–526.

Kwong, K. K., Belliveau, J. W., Chesler, D. A., Goldberg, I. E., Weisskopf, R. M., Poncelet, B. P., et al. (1992). Dynamic magnetic resonance imaging of human brain activity during primary sensory stimulation. *Proceedings of the National Academy of Sciences, 89*, 5675–5679.

LaMantia, A. S., & Rakic, P. (1990). Axon overproduction and elimination in the corpus callosum of the developing rhesus monkey. *The Journal of Neuroscience, 10*, 2156–2175.

Lambert, S., Sampaio, E., Mauss, Y., & Scheiber, C. (2004). Blindness and brain plasticity: Contribution of mental imagery? An fMRI study. *Brain Research. Cognitive Brain Research, 20*, 1–11.

Lane, R. D., Bennett-Clarke, C. A., Chiaia, N. L., Killackey, H. P., & Rhoades, R. W. (1995). Lesion-induced reorganization in the brainstem is not completely expressed in somatosensory cortex. *Proceedings of the National Academy of Sciences, 92*, 4264–4268.

Logothetis, N. K., Pauls, J., Augath, M., Trinath, T., & Oeltermann, A. (2001). Neurophysiological investigation of the basis of the fMRI signal. *Nature, 412*, 150–157.

Malonek, D., Dirnagl, U., Lindauer, U., Yamada, K., Kanno, I., & Grinvald, A. (1997). Vascular imprints of neuronal activity: Relationships between the dynamics of cortical blood flow, oxygenation, and volume changes following sensory stimulation. *Proceedings of the National Academy of Sciences, 94*, 14826–14831.

Malonek, D., & Grinvald, A. (1997). Vascular regulation at sub millimeter range. Sources of intrinsic signals for high resolution optical imaging. *Advances in Experimental Medicine & Biology, 413*, 215–220.

Melzack, R. (2001). Pain and the neuromatrix in the brain. *Journal of Dental Education, 65*, 1378–1382.

Melzer, P., Crane, A. M., & Smith, C. B. (1993). Mouse barrel cortex functionally compensates for deprivation produced by neonatal lesion of whisker follicles. *European Journal of Neuroscience, 5*, 1638–1652.

Melzer, P., Morgan, V. L., Pickens, D. R., Price, R. R., Wall, R. S., & Ebner, F. F. (2001). Cortical activation during Braille reading is influenced by early visual experience in subjects with severe visual disability: A correlational fMRI study. *Human Brain Mapping, 14*, 186–195.

Melzer, P., Pickens D. R., Price, R. R., Morgan, V. L., Symons F. J., & Wall, R. S. (1998). Reading Braille predominantly activates extrastriate cortex in persons with severe visual disability: a fMRI study. *Proceedings of the Sixth Scientific Meeting of the International Society Magnetic Resonance in Medicine*, 1514.

Melzer, P., Pickens, D. R., Price, R. R., Morgan, V. L., Wall, R. S., & Ebner F. F. (1998). Cerebral activation during reading nouns and text in Braille: A fMRI study. *Radiology, 209P*, 243.

Melzer, P., Rothblat, L. A., & Innocenti, G. M. (1988). Lesions involving the optic radiation in kittens modify the postnatal development of corticocortical connections. *Acta Anatomica, 132*, 83.

Melzer, P., & Smith, C. B. (1995). Whisker follicle removal affects somatotopy and innervation of other follicles in adult mice. *Cerebral Cortex, 5*, 301–306.

Melzer, P., & Smith, C. B. (1996). Plasticity of metabolic whisker maps in somatosensory brainstem and thalamus of mice with neonatal lesions of whisker follicles. *European Journal of Neuroscience, 8*, 1853–1864.

Melzer, P., Welker, E., Dörfl, J., & Van der Loos, H. (1994). Maturation of neuronal metabolic responses to vibrissa stimulation in the developing whisker-to-barrel pathway of the mouse. *Brain Research. Developmental Brain Research, 77*, 227–250.

Melzer, P., Yamakado, M., Van der Loos, H., Welker, E., & Dörfl, J. (1988). Plasticity in the barrel cortex of adult mouse: Effects of peripheral deprivation on the functional map; a deoxyglucose study. *Abstracts-Society for Neuroscience, 14*, 844.

Mesulam, M.-M. (1990). Large-scale neurocognitive networks and distributed processing for attention, language and memory. *Annals of Neurology, 28*, 597–613.

Mooney, R. D., & Rhoades, R. W. (1983). Neonatal enucleation alters functional organization in hamster's lateral posterior nucleus. *Brain Research, 285*, 399–404.

Nobre, A. C., Allison, T., & McCarthy, G. (1994). Word recognition in the human inferior temporal lobe. *Nature, 372*, 260–263.

Ogawa, S., Tank, D. W., Menon, R. S., Ellermann, J., Kim, S., Merkle, H., et al. (1992). Intrinsic signal changes accompanying sensory stimulation: Functional brain mapping with magnetic resonance imaging. *Proceedings of the National Academy of Sciences, 89,* 5951–5955.

Olavarria, J., Malache, R., & Van Sluyters, R. C. (1987). Development of visual callosal connections in neonatally enucleated rats. *The Journal of Comparative Neurology, 260,* 321–348.

Pallas, S. L. (2001). Intrinsic and extrinsic factors that shape neocortical specification. *Trends in Neurosciences, 24,* 417–423.

Petersen, S. E., & Fiez, J. A. (1993). The processing of single words studied with positron emission tomography. *Annual Review of Neuroscience, 16,* 509–530.

Petersen, S. E., Fox, P. T., Posner, M. I., Mintun, M. A., & Raichle, M. E. (1988). Positron emission tomographic studies of the cortical anatomy of single-word processing. *Nature, 331,* 585–589.

Rauschecker, J. P. (1996). Substitution of visual by auditory inputs in the cat's anterior ectosylvian cortex. *Progress in Brain Research, 112,* 313–323.

Revel, J., Orest, R., Flandrin, J.-L., Gélis, J., Foisil, M., & Goulemot, J. M. (1989). Forms of privatization. In P. Ariès (Ed.) G. Duby (Series Ed.) & R. Chartier (Vol. Ed.) *A history of private life. Vol III. Passions of the renaissance* (pp. 161–363). Cambridge: Harvard University Press.

Rhoades, R. W., DellaCroce, D. D., & Meadows, I. (1981). Reorganization of somatosensory input to superior colliculus in neonatally enucleated hamsters: Anatomical and electrophysiological experiments. *Journal of Neurophysiology, 46,* 855–877.

Roland, P. E., & Gulyás, B. (1995). Visual imagery and visual representation. *Trends in Neurosciences, 17,* 281–287.

Roy, C. S., & Sherrington, C. S. (1890). On the regulation of blood supply of the brain. *Journal of Physiology (London) 11,* 85–108.

Sadato, N., Pascual-Leone, A., Grafman, J., Ibanez, V., Deiber, M.-P., Dold, G., et al. (1996). Activation of the primary visual cortex by Braille reading in blind subjects. *Nature, 380,* 526–528.

Sasaki, Y., Vanduffel, W., Knutsen, T., Tyler, C., & Tootell, R. (2005). Symmetry activates extrastriate visual cortex in human and nonhuman primates. *Proceedings of the National Academy of Sciences, 102,* 3159–3163.

Sathian, K. (2005). Visual cortical activity during tactile perception in the sighted and the visually deprived. *Developmental Psychobiology, 46,* 279–286.

Sathian, K., & Zangaladze, A. (2002). Feeling with the mind's eye: Contribution of visual cortex to tactile perception. *Behavioural Brain Research, 135,* 127–132.

Shaywitz, S. E., Shaywitz, B. A., Pugh, K. R., Fulbright, R. K., Constable, R. T., Mencl, W. B., et al. (1998). Functional disruption in the organization of the brain for reading in dyslexia. *Proceedings of the National Academy of Sciences, 95,* 2636–2641.

Sokoloff, L. (1996). Cerebral metabolism and visualization of cerebral activity. In R. Greger, & U. Windhorst (Eds.), *Comprehensive human physiology: From cellular mechanisms to integration* (Vol. 1, pp. 579–602). Berlin: Springer-Verlag.

Stefansic, J. D., Morgan, V. L., Hardin, D., Melzer, P., & Ebner, F. F. (2002). Temporal frequency analysis of fMRI time courses of Braille readers with the continuous wavelet transform. *Proceedings of the Tenth Scientific Meeting of the International Society Magnetic Resonance in Medicine,* 1434.

Stent, G. S. (2004). Paradoxes of free will and the limits of human reason. *Proceedings of the American Philosophical Society, 148,* 205–212.

Sterr, A., Müller, M. M., Elbert, T., Rockstroh, B., Pantev, C., & Taub, E. (1998). Perceptual correlates of changes in cortical representation of fingers in blind multifinger Braille readers. *The Journal of Neuroscience, 18,* 4417–4423.

Strupp, J. P. (1996). Stimulate: A GUI based fMRI analysis software package. *NeuroImage, 3,* S607.

Sur, M., Garraghty, P. E., & Roe, A. W. (1988). Experimentally induced visual projections into auditory thalamus and cortex. *Science, 242,* 1437–1441.

Sur, M., Pallas, S. L., & Roe, A. W. (1990). Cross-modal plasticity in cortical development: Differentiation and specification of sensory neocortex. *Trends in Neurosciences, 13,* 227–233.

Tootell, R. B. H., Dale, A. M., Sereno, M. I., & Malach, R. (1996). New images from human visual cortex. *Trends in Neurosciences, 19,* 481–489.

Uhl, F., Franzen, P., Lindinger, G., Lang, W., & Deecke, L. (1991). On the functionality of the visually deprived occipital cortex in early blind persons. *Neuroscience Letters, 124,* 256–259.

Uhl, F., Franzen, P., Podreka, I., Steiner, M., & Deecke, L. (1993). Increased regional blood flow in inferior occipital cortex and cerebellum of early blind humans. *Neuroscience Letters, 150,* 162–164.

Van der Loos, H., & Woolsey, T. A. (1973). Somatosensory cortex: Structural alterations following early injury to sense organs. *Science, 179,* 395–398.

Van Oostende, S., Sunaert, S., Van Hecke, P., Marchal, G., & Orban, G. A. (1997). The kinetic occipital (KO) region in man: A fMRI study. *Cerebral Cortex, 7,* 690–701.

Veraart, C., De Volder, A. G., Wanet-Defalque, M.-C., Bol, A., Michel, C., & Goffinet, A. (1990). Glucose utilization in human visual cortex is abnormally elevated in blindness of early onset but decreased in blindness of late onset. *Brain Research, 510,* 115–121.

Walters, N. B., Egan, G. F., Kril, J. J., Kean, M., Waley, P., Jenkinson, M., & et al. (2003). In vivo identification of human cortical areas using high-resolution MRI: An approach to cerebral structure-function correlation. *Proceedings of the National Academy of Sciences, 100,* 2981–2986.

Wanet-Defalque, M.-C., Veraart, C., De Volder, A., Metz, R., Michel, C., Dooms, G., et al. (1988). High metabolic activity in the visual cortex of early blind human subjects. *Brain Research, 446,* 369–373.

7

Visual Cortical Involvement During Tactile Perception in Blind and Sighted Individuals

K. Sathian and Simon Lacey

In this chapter we review recent research findings which establish that visual areas of the cerebral cortex are intimately involved in tactile perception not only in visually deprived individuals but also in those who have normal sight. The question still remains as to why such cross-modal recruitment of visual cortex occurs and whether the underlying reasons differ in the sighted and the blind. We outline attempts that have been made to address these issues and offer our own perspective on the current state of affairs. We begin with an account of cross-modal recruitment of visual cortex during tactile perception in blind persons, turn next to work with persons with normal sight, and summarize the few studies that have examined the effect of short-term visual deprivation.

INVOLVEMENT OF VISUAL CORTICAL AREAS IN TACTILE PERCEPTION IN BLIND INDIVIDUALS

Rats deprived of vision neonatally show alterations in somatosensory receptive fields in the whisker barrel representation in somatosensory cortex (Toldi, Farkas, & Völgyi, 1994), as well as novel somatosensory responsiveness in visual cortex (Toldi, Rojik, & Feher, 1994). Correspondingly, blind humans demonstrate more extensive somatosensory cortical responses compared to sighted humans during Braille reading (Pascual-Leone & Torres, 1993) and vibrotactile frequency discrimination (Burton, Sinclair, & McLaren, 2004), in addition to widespread changes in occipital cortex.

An early report of cross-modal plasticity in blind humans used positron emission tomographic (PET) scanning to show that visual cortical areas in the occipital lobe were more active metabolically in early blind individuals compared to late blind and sighted individuals (Veraart et al., 1990). This was taken to mean greater synaptic activity in the early blind, possibly due to in-complete developmental pruning of synapses. Subsequently, many PET and functional magnetic resonance imaging (fMRI) studies found medial occipital cortical regions of blind subjects to be recruited during tactile reading of Braille or embossed Roman letters (Amedi, Raz, Pianka, Malach, & Zohary, 2003; Büchel, Price, Frackowiak, & Friston, 1998; Burton, McLaren, & Sinclair, 2006; Burton, Snyder, Diamond, & Raichle, 2002; Melzer et al., 2001; Sadato et al., 1996; Sadato et al., 1998; Sadato, Okada, Honda, & Yonekura, 2002). Such activations were noted to be specific to early blind subjects (Cohen et al., 1999; Sadato et al., 2002), whereas late blind and sighted subjects deacti-vated these regions (Sadato et al., 2002).

Complementing these activation studies, transcranial magnetic stimulation (TMS) over medial occipital cortex was demonstrated to impair identification of Braille or Roman characters by blind subjects, in contrast to sighted subjects whose performance on tactile identification of Roman letters was unaffected by occipital TMS (Cohen et al., 1997). As in the activation studies cited above, TMS over medial occipital cortex interfered with Braille reading in early blind but not the late blind individuals (Cohen et al., 1999), implying that visual cortical involvement in Braille reading depends on cross-modal plasticity dur-ing a critical period of visual development. Further evidence for the functional role of visual cortex in Braille reading comes from the report of an early blind person who, after an infarct of bilateral occipital cortex, became unable to read Braille (Hamilton, Keenan, Catala, & Pascual-Leone, 2000).

However, these interesting studies in the blind left open whether the ob-served visual cortical involvement reflected tactile sensory processing or higher-order cognitive processes including attention and language because the tactile reading tasks were generally contrasted with low-level conditions. In fact, numerous studies that focus on various aspects of language have shown visual cortical activity in the blind. Tasks studied included verb generation in response to tactile (Burton et al., 2006; Burton, Snyder, Conturo, et al., 2002) or auditory (Amedi et al., 2003; Burton, Snyder, Diamond, & Raichle, 2002) input, and verbal recall in the absence of any sensory input (Amedi et al., 2003). Such activity is more extensive in the early blind (Burton, Diamond, & McDermott, 2003; Burton, Snyder, Conturo, et al., 2002; Burton, Snyder, Diamond, et al., 2002) and stronger during semantic processing than phono-logical processing (Burton et al., 2003). Moreover, its strength correlates with semantic and syntactic complexity (Röder, Stock, Bien, & Rösler, 2002) and with performance on verbal recall (Amedi et al., 2003).

These studies permit the conclusion that visual cortex is active during language processing in blind individuals, but the extent of its involvement in tactile processing is still unclear although a few studies have been designed to examine this issue. When blind subjects discriminated angles or the width of grooves cut in homogeneous Braille fields, there was less activation in medial occipital cortex, compared to that during Braille reading (Sadato et al., 1996). These tasks also activated ventral occipital cortex in blind subjects but deactivated the region around secondary somatosensory cortex (S2), whereas sighted subjects activated this region but deactivated medial and ventral occipital regions (Sadato et al., 1996; Sadato et al., 1998). Vibrotactile frequency discrimination evoked extensive responses in visual cortex in congenitally blind subjects, with less extensive responses in late blind subjects (Burton et al., 2004). Category-selectivity during haptic perception of 3-D form, similar to that noted in sighted subjects (discussed below), was found in inferotemporal cortex of blind subjects, although the category-selective voxels were located more ventrally in blind compared to sighted subjects (Pietrini et al., 2004). Most of these studies, unfortunately, employed rest controls, so that the influence of sensory and linguistic processes could not be distinguished. A study of Braille reading that did attempt to control for linguistic processes, using an auditory word control, found medial occipital cortical activity in late blind but not early blind subjects, although both groups activated superior occipital and fusiform cortex during Braille reading (Büchel et al., 1998). Thus, more incisive investigation is required to address the degree to which cross-modal recruitment of visual cortex occurs during tactile processing in blind individuals.

MENTAL IMAGERY IN BLIND INDIVIDUALS

Individuals who are blind do experience mental imagery, albeit not visually based in congenitally blind persons, whereas in those with acquired blindness, the use of visual imagery declines with time (Hollins, 1989). A classic mental imagery task, originally introduced for visually presented stimuli (Shepard & Metzler, 1971), involves mental rotation. Blindness, especially if congenital, slows mental rotation of haptic stimuli (Marmor & Zaback, 1976), suggesting that visual imagery can facilitate haptic perception. Event-related potential (ERP) studies have shown that slow negativities normally recorded over parietal cortex during mental rotation of haptic stimuli extend posteriorly over occipital cortex in blind persons (Röder, Rösler, & Hennighausen, 1997; Rösler, Röder, Heil, & Hennighausen, 1993). Likewise, relatively greater occipital negativity was observed in blind than sighted subjects during mental imagery of feeling textures with the fingertips (Uhl et al., 1994). In more recent PET studies, early blind and sighted subjects activated similar areas during mental imagery: superior occipital and superior parietal areas during spatial imagery (Vanlierde, De Volder, Wanet-Defalque, & Veraart, 2003) and occipito-temporal areas during form imagery that was visually based in sighted subjects and haptically based in blind subjects (De Volder et al., 2001), although there was more extensive activation in early blind subjects in the latter task.

INVOLVEMENT OF VISUAL CORTICAL AREAS IN TACTILE PERCEPTION IN SIGHTED INDIVIDUALS

It has become clear recently that a number of visual cortical areas are active during tactile tasks even in sighted people. While the tasks used in some of these studies differed from those in work with blind people, the findings raise the possibility that visual deprivation may simply amplify the normal range of cross-modal recruitment. The first study to show that extrastriate visual cortical areas are active during tactile perception came from our laboratory (Sathian, Zangaladze, Hoffman, & Grafton, 1997), a PET study using tactile discrimination of grating orientation with stimuli being presented to the immobilized fingerpad. A contrast between this task and a control task requiring discrimination of grating groove width yielded activation at a focus in extrastriate visual cortex, close to the parieto-occipital fissure. Others had found this focus to be active during visual discrimination of grating orientation (Sergent, Ohta, & MacDonald, 1992). We were concerned that parieto-occipital cortical activation in our task might have been merely an epiphenomenon. We therefore used TMS to test whether disrupting the function of this cortical region interfered with tactile perception. We were able to demonstrate that TMS applied directly over the locus of PET activation and at sites close to it (but not at more distant sites) significantly impaired performance in the grating orientation task, with no effect on discrimination of grating groove width (Zangaladze, Epstein, Grafton, & Sathian, 1999). This allowed us to conclude that the activation found on PET scanning was functionally meaningful.

The grating orientation task can be considered a macrospatial task, and the groove width discrimination task, microspatial (groove widths ≤ 3 mm). Our observations implicating visual cortical processing in the former but not the latter task fit with the idea that vision is generally superior to touch for perceiving macrospatial features, the reverse being true for microspatial features (Heller, 1989), and with psychophysical work suggesting that macrospatial tactile tasks are preferentially associated with visual processing (Klatzky, Lederman, & Reed, 1987). Analogous findings were reported in another TMS study (Merabet et al., 2004) using repetitive TMS (rTMS) at 1 Hz, which decreases cortical excitability. The study was based on the dissociation between subjective magnitude estimates of perceived interdot distance, which increase with physical interdot distance (up to 8 mm), and those of perceived roughness, which peak at intermediate values (around 3 mm). The chief result was that rTMS over primary somatosensory cortex (S1) impaired judgments of roughness but not interdot distance, whereas rTMS over medial occipital cortex affected judgments of distance but not roughness. Further, a congenitally blind patient who suffered a stroke that damaged occipital cortex bilaterally was found to have normal roughness judgments but defective judgments of interdot spacing (Merabet et al., 2004).

In another PET study from our laboratory (Prather, Votaw, & Sathian, 2004), we investigated the mental rotation of tactile stimuli, upside-down Js, presented in one of two mirror-image configurations. Contrasting a mental rotation condition (stimuli at a 135–180° angle with respect to the long axis of the finger) with a pure mirror-image discrimination condition (stimuli at 0°) revealed activity in the left anterior intraparietal sulcus (aIPS), at a focus that is also active during mental rotation of visual stimuli (Alivisatos & Petrides, 1997). Posterior parietal cortex had been implicated in the mental rotation of tactile stimuli in earlier ERP studies (Röder et al., 1997; Rösler et al., 1993), but these could not achieve very precise localization. Other groups found that an area involved in perception of visual motion, the middle temporal complex, is also recruited during presentation of tactile motion stimuli, even in the absence of any task (Blake, Sobel, & James, 2004; Hagen et al., 2002). Additionally, the tactually perceived direction of motion can influence the visually perceived direction during bisensory (visual and tactile) evaluation of a rotating globe (Blake et al., 2004; James & Blake, 2004), which suggests that both sensory modalities engage a common representation.

Within the ventral visual pathway, which is specialized for form processing, a region termed the lateral occipital complex (LOC) is selective for visually presented objects compared to lower-level visual stimuli (Malach et al., 1995). We found in a PET study that, relative to a condition requiring discrimination of bar orientation, tactile discrimination of two-dimensional forms presented to the immobilized fingerpad activated the right LOC (Prather et al., 2004). In a related fMRI study from our laboratory (Stoesz et al., 2003), the same form-discrimination task evoked greater activity in the LOC bilaterally than a task requiring detection of a gap in a bar. The LOC is also recruited during haptic object identification using active manual exploration, as revealed by numerous fMRI studies (Amedi, Jacobson, Hendler, Malach, & Zohary, 2002; Amedi, Malach, Hendler, Peled, & Zohary, 2001; Deibert, Kraut, Kreman, & Hart, 1999; James et al., 2002; Reed, Shoham, & Halgren, 2004; Stoeckel et al., 2003; Zhang, Weisser, Stilla, Prather, & Sathian, 2004). Multisensory object-selective activity in the LOC is stronger for graspable visual objects compared to other visual stimuli, and does not appear to extend to the auditory modality (Amedi et al., 2002). In addition, the LOC appears to be necessary for both visual and haptic shape processing, as shown by studies of patients with lesions involving this region. One patient with a lesion of the left occipito-temporal cortex, that probably included the LOC, had visual agnosia (a specific inability to recognize objects), which was not surprising given the lesion location. However, this patient also turned out to have tactile agnosia although somatosensory cortex and elementary somatic sensation were intact (Feinberg, Rothi, & Heilman, 1986). Another patient developed bilateral lesions of the LOC, with associated impairments in learning unfamiliar objects using either touch or vision (James, James, Humphrey, & Goodale, 2006). Together with cross-modal priming (visuo-haptic) effects observed psychophysically (Easton, Greene, Srinivas, 1997; Easton, Srinivas, & Greene, 1997; Reales & Ballesteros, 1999) and in fMRI studies (Amedi et al., 2001; James et al., 2002), cross-modal interference effects in memory tasks (Lacey & Campbell, 2006a, b), and category-specific representations that overlap between visual and haptic modalities (Pietrini et al., 2004), these studies suggest that both visual and haptic shape perception may engage a unitary neural representation.

Face perception is a special case of form perception. Clearly, sighted humans perform face recognition using vision virtually exclusively, but they can also identify faces haptically, and cross-modal transfer can be demonstrated between the visual and haptic modalities (Kilgour & Lederman, 2002). Similar to the patients described earlier in the studies of object perception, a prosopagnosic patient (i.e., one who could not recognize faces visually) was found to be unable to recognize faces haptically (Kilgour, de Gelder, & Lederman, 2004). These behavioral studies suggest that, as for object perception, visual and haptic face perception tap into a common neural substrate. However, fMRI studies to date do not support this idea. Haptic face recognition activates the left fusiform gyrus, in contrast to the right fusiform gyrus for the visual modality (Kilgour, Kitada, Servos, James, & Lederman, 2005), and face-selective voxels in ventral and inferior temporal cortex are mostly non-overlapping between the two modalities (Pietrini et al., 2004). Further studies are needed to resolve the neural basis of bisensory face perception and its differences from bisensory object perception.

VISUAL IMAGERY AND MULTISENSORY REPRESENTATIONS

Based on the studies reviewed in the preceding section, it is evident that visual cortical processing is intimately involved in normal tactile perception in sighted persons, especially during macrospatial tasks. Moreover, such processing is highly task specific, so extrastriate visual cortical areas that are known to be specialized for particular visual tasks are involved during performance of the same tasks tactually. So "visual" cortex is not devoted solely to vision. Is this due to visual imagery? In fact, our subjects consistently report mental visualization of tactile stimuli during macrospatial tasks such as discrimination of grating orientation or tactile form, which are associated with visual cortical recruitment, but not during microspatial tasks such as discrimination of grating groove width or gap detection, which do not tend to involve visual cortical activity (Sathian et al., 1997; Stoesz et al., 2003; Zangaladze et al., 1999). One might speculate that visual imagery is occasioned by subjects' relative unfamiliarity with the tactile stimuli or tasks used; indeed, such cross-modal translation has been proposed to occur commonly, especially when complex information is being processed (Freides, 1974).

Self-reports of mental visualization of tactile stimuli are supported by an fMRI study from our group (Zhang et al., 2004) showing that interindividual variations in the magnitude of haptic shape-selective activity in the right LOC (ipsilateral to the hand used for haptic perception) were strongly predicted by a multiple regression on two scores indexing the vividness of visual imagery, one pertaining to everyday situations and employing the Vividness of Visual Imagery Questionnaire (VVIQ; Marks, 1973), and the other pertaining to visual imagery occurring during haptic shape perception. In contrast, activation strengths in the left LOC were uncorrelated with these visual imagery scores, pointing to a role for factors other than visual imagery in cross-modal visual cortical recruitment (Zhang et al., 2004). It has been argued that LOC activity during haptic perception is not due to visual imagery because visual imagery evoked much less activity in the LOC than haptic object recognition (Amedi et al., 2001). However, this reduced activation might have been due to object familiarity or the lack of a requirement to maintain images online during the entire scan. Nonetheless, other possible explanations should be considered for visual cortical recruitment during tactile perception. Vision and touch can both encode spatial properties of objects such as shape, and visual cortical activation during tactile perception might reflect a spatial representation rather than a specifically visual image. Thus, there could be direct, bottom-up somatosensory projections into the visual cortical areas that are implicated in tactile perception, as opposed to the top-down projections from prefrontal into visual cortical areas that would be required to support a process such as visual imagery. We are now exploring the analysis of fMRI data to reveal effective connectivity, using structural equation modeling based on the correlation matrix between the time courses of fMRI activity in various regions. In a study of this ilk (Peltier et al., 2006), we investigated connectivity between haptically shape-selective regions in the hemisphere contralateral to the sensing hand. Both bottom-up and top-down paths were found, in a network comprising foci in the postcentral sulcus (corresponding to Brodmann's area 2 of S1), the intraparietal sulcus (IPS), and the LOC. This suggests that potential neural substrates exist in relation to visual cortical involvement during haptic shape perception for both visual imagery and multisensory representations.

Recent behavioral studies have addressed the nature of visuo-haptic representations using interference tasks in a cross-modal memory paradigm. In one such study (Lacey & Campbell, 2006a), participants encoded familiar and unfamiliar objects visually (without touching them) or haptically (in the absence of vision) while performing a concurrent visual, verbal, or haptic interference task. The visual and verbal interference tasks disrupted encoding of unfamiliar objects and reduced subsequent cross-modal recognition significantly. The haptic interference task had no effect, and familiar objects were unaffected by any form of interference. These results suggested that encoding in both modalities resulted in a common representation linked to a strategy of covert verbal description. Interference might have been more important for the unfamiliar objects because cross-modal memory for familiar objects is probably supported by closely interconnected representations in several formats, for example, visual, verbal, and haptic (Lacey & Campbell, 2006a).

In a follow-up study, Lacey and Campbell (2006b) compared the effects of both visually and haptically presented spatial and nonspatial interference tasks on cross-modal memory for unfamiliar objects. The visual nonspatial tasks involved looking at static or dynamic visual noise. The spatial tasks were to track a dot appearing at random locations on a screen, and to follow a sequence of flashing LEDs in a 3-D array. The haptic tasks were based on the taxonomy of haptic exploratory procedures (EPs) developed by Lederman & Klatzky (1987), avoiding or utilizing those EPs that are specialized for spatial information. The haptic nonspatial tasks were to hold a distractor object, either without or with manipulation. These were static and dynamic analogs of the visual tasks. The haptic spatial tasks were to trace around 2-D or 3-D patterns concealed from view. The results were straightforward: Regardless of whether the interference occurred during encoding or retrieval, cross-modal memory was disrupted by spatial but not nonspatial interference, irrespective of the modality in which the interference task was presented. These findings argue for a spatial representation of unfamiliar objects that is accessible via both vision and touch. It remains to be seen whether this implies a single, multisensory spatial representation or separately derived spatial representations for vision and touch that can be compared effectively.

Some neurophysiological and neuroanatomic studies in monkeys have contributed to our understanding of the basis for cross-modal recruitment of visual cortex. Certain neurons in area V4 (a nonprimary area in the ventral visual pathway) were found to be selective for the orientation of a tactile grating but only when the tactile grating served as a cue for matching to a subsequently presented visual stimulus and not when it was task-irrelevant; such responses were absent in primary visual cortex (V1) (Haenny, Maunsell, & Schiller, 1988). Since selectivity for tactile grating orientation depended on the tactile stimulus being relevant, it must have been based on top-down rather than bottom-up inputs. This insightful study is consistent not only with the possibility of a multisensory representation for grating orientation, suggested by the imaging studies referred to earlier (Sathian et al., 1997; Sergent et al., 1992), but also with the idea that top-down mechanisms can engage such representations. Multisensory inputs have been found in early sensory cortical areas that are generally considered to be unisensory, including V1 (Falchier, Clavagnier, Barone, & Kennedy, 2002; Rockland & Ojima, 2003) and auditory association cortex (Schroeder et al., 2001; Schroeder et al., 2003; Schroeder &

Foxe, 2002). Analysis of the laminar profile of these projections indicates the likely presence of both top-down (Falchier et al., 2002; Rockland and Ojima, 2003; Schroeder et al., 2003; Schroeder & Foxe, 2002) and bottom-up (Schroeder et al., 2003; Schroeder & Foxe, 2002) inputs. Overall, then, the evidence favors the existence of multisensory representations that are flexibly accessible via both vision and touch, and involving interactions between bottom-up sensory inputs and top-down processes such as visual imagery.

EFFECTS OF SHORT-TERM VISUAL DEPRIVATION ON VISUAL CORTICAL RESPONSES TO TOUCH

The consequences of short-term visual deprivation of normally sighted individuals have attracted recent interest. After only 2 hours of blindfolding, subjects showed significant deactivation during tactile form discrimination and gap detection in regions that are intermediate in the hierarchy of visual shape processing (V3A and ventral IPS), as well as task-specific increases in activation in blindfolded relative to control subjects, favoring the form over the gap task, along the IPS and in regions of frontal and temporal cortex (Weisser, Stilla, Peltier, Hu, & Sathian, 2005). Over a longer period (5 days) of blindfolding, occipital cortex becomes responsive during tactile discrimination of Braille characters, and TMS over occipital cortex becomes able to disrupt Braille reading (Pascual-Leone & Hamilton, 2001). These findings suggest that cross-modal plasticity may not require new connections but could operate on pre-existing interactions between sensory modalities. Thus, visual deprivation might act to amplify the range of cross-modal recruitment that has been demonstrated under conditions of normal vision. It remains for future research to define fully the effects of short-term, long-term, and congenital visual deprivation with respect to specific perceptual and cognitive domains, and to relate these effects to the nature of cross-modal involvement of visual cortex in normally sighted individuals.

ACKNOWLEDGMENTS

Current research support from the National Eye Institute, the National Science Foundation, and the Veterans Administration is gratefully acknowledged.

REFERENCES

Alivisatos, B., & Petrides, M. (1997). Functional activation of the human brain during mental rotation. *Neuropsychologia, 36*, 111–118.

Amedi, A., Jacobson, G., Hendler, T., Malach, R., & Zohary, E. (2002). Convergence of visual
    and tactile shape processing in the human lateral occipital complex. *Cerebral Cortex,
    12*, 1202–1212.
Amedi, A., Malach, R., Hendler, T., Peled, S., & Zohary, E. (2001). Visuo-haptic object-
    related activation in the ventral visual pathway. *Nature Neuroscience, 4*, 324–330.
Amedi, A., Raz, N., Pianka, P., Malach, R., & Zohary, E. (2003). Early 'visual' cortex acti-
    vation correlates with superior verbal memory performance in the blind. *Nature Neu-
    roscience, 6*, 758–766.
Blake, R., Sobel, K. V., & James, T. W. (2004). Neural synergy between kinetic vision and
    touch. *Psychological Science, 15*, 397–402.
Büchel, C., Price, C., Frackowiak, R. S. J., & Friston, K. (1998). Different activation pat-
    terns in the visual cortex of late and congenitally blind subjects. *Brain 121*, 409–419.
Burton, H., Diamond, J. B., & McDermott, K. B. (2003). Dissociating cortical regions acti-
    vated by semantic and phonological tasks: A FMRI study in blind and sighted people.
    Journal of Neurophysiology, 90, 1965–1982.
Burton, H., McLaren, D. G., & Sinclair, R. J. (2006). Reading embossed capital letters:
    An fMRI study in blind and sighted individuals. *Human Brain Mapping, 27*, 325–339.
Burton, H., Sinclair, R. J., & McLaren, D. G. (2004). Cortical activity to vibrotactile stim-
    ulation: An fMRI study in blind and sighted individuals. *Human Brain Mapping, 23*,
    210–228.
Burton, H., Snyder, A. Z., Conturo, T. E., Akbudak, E., Ollinger, J. M., & Raichle, M. E.
    (2002). Adaptive changes in early and late blind: A fMRI study of Braille reading. *Jour-
    nal of Neurophysiology, 87*, 589–607.
Burton, H., Snyder, A. Z., Diamond, J. B., & Raichle, M. E. (2002). Adaptive changes in
    early and late blind: A fMRI study of verb generation to heard nouns. *Journal of Neuro-
    physiology, 88*, 3359–3371.
Cohen, L. G., Celnik, P., Pascual-Leone, A., Corwell, B., Faiz, L., Dambrosia, J., et al.
    (1997). Functional relevance of cross-modal plasticity in blind humans. *Nature, 389*,
    180–183.
Cohen, L. G., Weeks, R. A., Sadato, N., Celnik, P., Ishii, K., & Hallett, M. (1999). Period
    of susceptibility for cross-modal plasticity in the blind. *Annals of Neurology, 45*, 451–460.
Deibert, E., Kraut, M., Kremen, S., & Hart, J., Jr. (1999). Neural pathways in tactile object
    recognition. *Neurology, 52*, 1413–1417.
De Volder, A. G, Toyama, H., Kimura, Y., Kiyosawa, M., Nakano, H., Vanlierde, A., et al.
    (2001). Auditory triggered mental imagery of shape involves visual association areas in
    early blind humans. *NeuroImage, 14*, 129–139.
Easton, R. D., Greene, A. J., & Srinivas, K. (1997). Transfer between vision and haptics:
    Memory for 2-D patterns and 3-D objects. *Psychonomics Bulletin & Review, 4*, 403–410.
Easton, R. D., Srinivas, K., & Greene, A. J. (1997). Do vision and haptics share common
    representations? Implicit and explicit memory within and between modalities. *Journal
    of Experimental Psychology: Learning, Memory, & Cognition, 23*, 153–163.
Falchier, A., Clavagnier, S., Barone, P., & Kennedy, H. (2002). Anatomical evidence of
    multimodal integration in primate striate cortex. *Journal of Neuroscience, 22*, 5749–5759.
Feinberg, T. E., Rothi, L. J., & Heilman, K. M. (1986). Multimodal agnosia after unilateral
    left hemisphere lesion. *Neurology, 36*, 864–867.
Freides, D. (1974). Human information processing and sensory modality: Cross-modal
    functions, information complexity, memory and deficit. *Psychological Bulletin, 81*,
    284–310.

Haenny, P. E., Maunsell, J. H. R., & Schiller, P. H. (1988). State dependent activity in monkey visual cortex. II. Retinal and extraretinal factors in V4. *Experimental Brain Research*, 69, 245–259.

Hagen, M. C., Franzen, O., McGlone, F., Essick, G., Dancer, C., & Pardo, J. V. (2002). Tactile motion activates the human middle temporal/V5 (MT/V5) complex. *European Journal of Neuroscience*, 16, 957–964.

Hamilton, R., Keenan, J. P., Catala, M., & Pascual-Leone, A. (2000). Alexia for Braille following bilateral occipital stroke in an early blind woman. *NeuroReport*, 11, 237–240.

Heller, M. A. (1989). Texture perception in sighted and blind observers. *Perception & Psychophysics*, 45, 49–54.

Hollins, M. (1989). Understanding blindness. Hillsdale, NJ: Lawrence Erlbaum Associates.

James, T. W., & Blake, R. (2004). Perceiving object motion using vision and touch. *Cognitive, Affective, & Behavioral Neuroscience*, 4, 201–207.

James, T. W., Humphrey, G. K., Gati, J. S., Servos, P., Menon, R. S., & Goodale, M. A. (2002). Haptic study of three-dimensional objects activates extrastriate visual areas. *Neuropsychologia*, 40, 1706–1714.

James, T. W., James, K. H., Humphrey, G. K., & Goodale, M. A. (2006). Do visual and tactile object representations share the same neural substrate? In M. A. Heller & S. Ballesteros (Eds.), *Touch and blindness: Psychology and neuroscience* (pp. 139–55). Mahwah, NJ: Lawrence Erlbaum Associates.

Kilgour, A. R., de Gelder, B., & Lederman, S. (2004). Haptic face recognition and prosopagnosia. *Neuropsychologia*, 42, 707–712.

Kilgour, A. R., Kitada, R., Servos, P., James, T. W., & Lederman, S. J. (2005). Haptic face identification activates ventral occipital and temporal areas: An fMRI study. *Brain and Cognition*, 59, 246–257.

Kilgour, A. R., & Lederman, S. (2002). Face recognition by hand. *Perception & Psychophysics*, 64, 339–352.

Klatzky, R. L., Lederman, S. J., & Reed, C. (1987). There's more to touch than meets the eye: The salience of object attributes for haptics with and without vision. *Journal of Expimental Psychology: General*, 116, 356–369.

Lacey, S., & Campbell, C. (2006a). Mental representation in visual/haptic crossmodal memory: evidence from interference effects. *Quarterly Journal of Experimental Psychology*, 59, 361–376.

Lacey, S., & Campbell, C. (2006b). Object representation in visual/haptic crossmodal memory. Abstract, 7th International Multisensory Research forum.

Lederman, S. J., & Klatzky, R. L. (1987). Hand movements: A window into haptic object recognition. *Cognitive Psychology*, 19, 342–368.

Malach, R., Reppas, J. B., Benson, R. R., Kwong, K. K., Jiang, H., Kennedy, W. A., et al. (1995). Object-related activity revealed by functional magnetic resonance imaging in human occipital cortex. *Proceedings of the National Academy of Sciences*, 92, 8135–8139.

Marks, D. F. (1973). Visual imagery differences in the recall of pictures. *British Journal of Psychology*, 64, 17–24.

Marmor. G. S., & Zaback, L. A. (1976). Mental rotation by the blind: Does mental rotation depend on visual imagery? *Journal of Experimental Psychology: Human Perception & Performance*, 2, 515–521.

Melzer, P., Morgan, V. L., Pickens, D. R., Price, R. R., Wall, R. S., & Ebner, F. F. (2001). Cortical activation during Braille reading is influenced by early visual experience in subjects with severe visual disability: A correlational fMRI study. *Human Brain Mapping, 14,* 186–195.

Merabet, L., Thut, G., Murray, B., Andrews, J., Hsiao, S., & Pascual-Leone, A. (2004). Feeling by sight or seeing by touch? *Neuron, 42,* 173–179.

Pascual-Leone, A., & Hamilton, R. (2001). The metamodal organization of the brain. *Progress in Brain Research, 134,* 427–445.

Pascual-Leone, A., & Torres, F. (1993). Plasticity of the sensorimotor cortex representation of the reading finger in Braille readers. *Brain, 116,* 39–52.

Peltier, S., Stilla, R., Mariola, E., LaConte, S., Hu, X., & Sathian, K. (2006). Activity and effective connectivity of parietal and occipital cortical regions during haptic shape perception. *Neuropsychologia,* in press.

Pietrini, P., Furey, M. L., Ricciardi, E., Gobbini, M. I., Wu, W.-H. C., Cohen, L., et al. (2004). Beyond sensory images: Object-based representation in the human ventral pathway. *Proceedings of the National Academy of Sciences, 101,* 5658–5663.

Prather, S. C., Votaw, J. R., & Sathian, K. (2004). Task-specific recruitment of dorsal and ventral visual areas during tactile perception. *Neuropsychologia, 42,* 1079–1087.

Reales, J. M., & Ballesteros, S. (1999). Implicit and explicit memory for visual and haptic objects: Cross-modal priming depends on structural descriptions. *Journal of Experimental Psychology: Learning, Memory, & Cognition, 25,* 644–663.

Reed, C. L., Shoham, S., & Halgren, E. (2004). Neural substrates of tactile object recognition: An fMRI study. *Human Brain Mapping, 2,* 236–246.

Rockland, K. S., & Ojima, H. (2003). Multisensory convergence in calcarine visual areas in macaque monkey. *International Journal of Psychophysiology, 50,* 19–26.

Röder, B., Rösler, F., & Hennighausen, E. (1997). Different cortical activation patterns in blind and sighted humans during encoding and transformation of haptic images. *Psychophysiology, 34,* 292–307.

Röder, B., Stock, O., Bien, S. N. H., & Rösler, F. (2002). Speech processing activates visual cortex in congenitally blind humans. *European Journal of Neuroscience, 16,* 930–936.

Rösler, F., Röder, B., Heil, M., & Hennighausen, E. (1993). Topographic differences of slow event-related potentials in blind and sighted adult human subjects during haptic mental rotation. *Cognitive Brain Research, 1,* 145–159.

Sadato, N., Okada, T., Honda, M., & Yonekura, Y. (2002). Critical period for cross-modal plasticity in blind humans: A functional MRI study. *NeuroImage, 16,* 389–400.

Sadato, N., Pascual-Leone, A., Grafman, J., Deiber, M.-P., Ibanez, V., & Hallett, M. (1998). Neural networks for Braille reading by the blind. *Brain, 121,* 1213–1229.

Sadato, N., Pascual-Leone, A., Grafman, J., Ibanez, V., Deiber, M.-P., Dold, G., & Hallett, M. (1996). Activation of the primary visual cortex by Braille reading in blind subjects. *Nature, 380,* 526–528.

Sathian, K., Zangaladze, A., Hoffman, J. M., & Grafton, S. T. (1997). Feeling with the mind's eye. *NeuroReport, 8,* 3877–3881.

Schroeder, C. E., & Foxe, J. J. (2002). The timing and laminar profile of converging inputs to multisensory areas of the macaque neocortex. *Cognitive Brain Research, 14,* 187–198.

Schroeder, C. E., Lindsley, R. W., Specht, C., Marcovici, A., Smiley, J. F., & Javitt, D. C. (2001). Somatosensory input to auditory association cortex in the macaque monkey. *Journal of Neurophysiology, 85,* 1322–1327.

Schroeder, C. E., Smiley, J., Fu, K. G., McGinnis, T., O'Connell, M. N., & Hackett, T. A. (2003). Anatomical mechanisms and functional implications of multisensory convergence in early cortical processing. *International Journal of Psychophysiology, 50,* 5–17.

Sergent, J., Ohta, S., & MacDonald, B. (1992). Functional neuroanatomy of face and object processing. A positron emission tomography study. Brain, 115, 15–36.

Shepard, R. N., & Metzler, J. (1971). Mental rotation of three-dimensional objects. Science, 171, 701–703.

Stoeckel, M. C., Weder, B., Binkofski, F., Buccino, G., Shah, N. J., & Seitz, R. J. (2003). A fronto-parietal circuit for tactile object discrimination: An event-related fMRI study. NeuroImage, 19, 1103–1114.

Stoesz, M., Zhang, M., Weisser, V. D., Prather, S. C., Mao, H., & Sathian, K. (2003). Neural networks active during tactile form perception: Common and differential activity during macrospatial and microspatial tasks. International Journal of Psychophysiology, 50, 41–49.

Toldi, J., Farkas, T., & Völgyi, B. (1994). Neonatal enucleation induces cross-modal changes in the barrel cortex of rat. A behavioural and electrophysiological study. Neuroscience Letters, 167, 1–4.

Toldi, J., Rojik, I., & Feher, O. (1994). Neonatal monocular enucleation-induced cross-modal effects observed in the cortex of adult rat. Neuroscience, 62, 105–114.

Uhl, F., Kretschmer, T., Lindinger, G., Goldenburg, G., Lang, W., Oder, W., et al. (1994). Tactile mental imagery in sighted persons and in patients suffering from peripheral blindness early in life. EEG & Clinical Neurophysiology, 91, 249–255.

Vanlierde, A., De Volder, A. G., Wanet-Defalque, & M.-C., Veraart, C. (2003). Occipito-parietal cortex activation during visuo-spatial imagery in early blind humans. NeuroImage, 19, 698–709.

Veraart, C., De Volder, A. G., Wanet-Defalque, M.-C., Bol, A., Michel, C., & Goffinet, A. M. (1990). Glucose utilization in human visual cortex is abnormally elevated in blindness of early onset but decreased in blindness of late onset. Brain Research, 510, 115–121.

Weisser, V., Stilla, R., Peltier, S., Hu, X., & Sathian, K. (2005). Short-term visual deprivation alters neural processing of tactile form. Experimental Brain Research, 166, 572–582.

Zangaladze, A., Epstein, C. M., Grafton, S. T., & Sathian, K. (1999). Involvement of visual cortex in tactile discrimination of orientation. Nature, 401, 587–590.

Zhang, M., Weisser, V. D., Stilla, R., Prather, S. C., & Sathian, K. (2004). Multisensory cortical processing of object shape and its relation to mental imagery. Cognitive, Affective, & Behavioral Neuroscience, 4, 251–259.

8

The Behavioral and Neurophysiological Effects of Sensory Deprivation

Ione Fine

Normally, sensory processing is organized in a modular fashion with sensory information passing from the relevant sensory organ (whether it be retina or cochlea) to a hierarchy of specialized cortical regions which process increasingly complex attributes of the incoming sensory information. But when a sense is lost, especially early in life, significant cortical reorganization is observed. A large body of research has begun to describe the positive aspects of this reorganization, characterizing how processing of the remaining intact senses may adapt to compensate for the missing sense. However, though less studied, neural reorganization also has potential negative effects, resulting in a gradual deterioration in the ability to process the missing sense.

As will be described, plasticity as a result of sensory deprivation depends on a variety of factors. One important factor is age of deprivation, since cortex tends to be more plastic at an early age. Consequently, those that lose a sense early in life tend to show fairly dramatic changes in cortical processing. Normally, these changes that occur as a result of early sensory deprivation are of benefit to the individual, playing an important role in allowing the individual to make better use of his or her remaining senses. However, if there is an opportunity for the missing sense to be restored later in life, when cortex is no longer plastic, then these adaptations become maladaptive and can seriously limit an individual's ability to make use of the restored sense. Indeed, as will be described, those who are deprived of a sense (whether audition or vision) early in life generally find it impossible to make functional use of that sense if it is restored in adulthood.

There also seems to be a strong interaction between the cortical hierar-chy and plasticity. The critical period for primary sensory areas seems to end at a relatively early age, and the scope for plasticity after the critical period tends to be extremely limited. In comparison, the critical period for areas fur-ther along the sensory hierarchy may extend into later childhood, and may even remain plastic in adulthood. Thus, the developmental time course for plasticity varies dramatically across different sensory areas.

Although early stages of sensory pathways seem to be primarily driven by a single sensory modality, later stages of sensory processing tend naturally to be more heavily modulated by cross-modal influences. It seems plausible that higher-level sensory areas that normally show significant cross-modal modu-lation would, when their primary input is lost, be more easily biased toward the remaining senses.

Understanding reorganization as a result of sensory deprivation has sig-nificant implications for both restorative surgeries and rehabilitation training. First, deterioration as a result of sensory deprivation can seriously limit the ability to restore sight, either through standard medical interventions or through implantation of a sensory prosthesis. Second, understanding the cortical changes that occur as a result of deprivation may help guide clinicians towards devel-oping rehabilitation strategies that are suited to take advantage of the natural plasticity of the brain.

COMPENSATING FOR A MISSING SENSE: AFTER LOSING A SENSE, THERE ARE IMPROVEMENTS IN THE ABILITY TO USE THE REMAINING SENSES

Because people who are blind cannot write things down, they tend to rely heavily on short- and long-term memory to perform a variety of tasks, such as remembering appointments or phone numbers. Not surprisingly, this seems to result in better memory for tasks such as remembering verbal lists (Amedi, Raz, Pianka, Malach, & Zohary, 2003). This has led to a joke in the blind commu-nity: When a blind individual forgets a phone number or a name, they may be asked by a blind friend in a concerned tone of voice, "Are you quite sure you are really blind?"

Rehabilitation training is based on the understanding that individuals who have a reduced or missing sense can develop alternative strategies and abilities to compensate, such as developing better verbal memory to compensate for not being able to write notes. However, while there is an extensive animal literature examining both compensatory neural plasticity and the effects of sensory deprivation within visual and auditory cortex (Hunt et al., 2005; Pal-las, Razak, & Moore, 2002; Rauschecker, 1995; Sur, Pallas, & Roe, 1990), the underlying neurophysiological changes that underlie these compensatory im-provements in behavior are only now beginning to be studied in humans. This chapter focuses on studies examining plasticity as a result of sensory deprivation within humans. While the animal literature has provided great insights into the neural mechanisms underlying plasticity, it is perfectly plausible that the extent and the nature of plasticity differs enormously between humans and animals.

The growing literature examining the neural site of behavioral modifications in humans relies primarily on using functional magnetic resonance imaging (fMRI). fMRI is based on a modification of standard clinical magnetic resonance imaging techniques. However, in fMRI, the pulse sequence used to acquire images of the brain is designed to differentiate between the different magnetic properties of oxygenated and deoxygenated blood. When a region of cortex is active, the vascular system provides an oversupply of oxygenated blood. By measuring the relative amounts of oxygenated and deoxygenated blood, it is possible to determine which regions of cortex are active for a given task over a time scale of a few seconds.

Blind Individuals Are Better Than Sighted Individuals at Certain Tactile and Auditory Tasks

People who are blind often have had extensive practice with various tactile and auditory tasks such as reading Braille and navigating using a cane. There is now growing evidence that blind individuals can be better than sighted individuals in certain tasks involving both touch and hearing (Rauschecker, 1995). Blind subjects are better than the sighted at identifying changes in auditory pitch (Gougoux et al., 2004) and auditory spatial tasks (determining where in space a tone came from) in the periphery (Lessard, Pare, Lepore, & Lassonde, 1998; Roder, 1999). This is true even for tones localized in distant space beyond the reach of the subject (Voss et al., 2004). Curiously, this superior ability for blind individuals to localize sounds is particularly pronounced with monaural presentation. This has led to the suggestion that the superior auditory localization abilities of the blind are based on better use of the subtle spectral cues produced from "shadowing" by the head and ear pinna (Doucet et al., 2005).

Sighted teachers of Braille read using the shadows of the dots on the paper, not by touch, suggesting that the tactile discriminations required to read Braille by touch are difficult for the sighted (see Merabet, Pitskel, Amedi, & Pascual-Leone, chapter 3, this volume). Consistent with this observation, blind subjects tend to be better than sighted subjects at some (though not all) tactile discrimination tasks (Grant, Thiagarajah, & Sathian, 2000). For example, in a tactile grating discrimination task, blind subjects had thresholds that were on average 50% lower than those of sighted subjects (Van Boven, Hamilton, Kauffman, Keenan, & Pascual-Leone, 2000), with differences between blind and sighted subjects being largest for the dominant "reading" finger. In many, though not all, of the tactile and auditory tasks that show differences between blind and sighted individuals, there is a difference in performance between early and late blind subjects, with the performance of late blind subjects often resembling that of sighted subjects. One possibility is that there is a greater potential for cortical plasticity when deprivation occurs at an early age. However, it should be noted that early blind subjects tend both to use a cane more frequently and competently and to read Braille more fluently than late blind subjects (though there are, of course, many exceptions), so the level of practice with sensory substitution tasks presumably differs between the two groups. It may of course be the case that this difference in behavior between early and late blind subjects is due to underlying differences in cortical plasticity between the two groups. However complex factors such as societal and familial expectations and an individual's self-confidence as a blind person are likely to also play an important role.

Deaf Individuals Are Better at Certain Visual Tasks

Sign language contains large amounts of visual form and motion information. There is now extensive evidence for differences in motion processing between deaf signers, fluent hearing signers (hearing children of deaf parents), and hearing subjects that seem to correlate with the unique demands of understanding sign language. For example, in sign language the two speakers maintain eye contact, and as a result, signing occurs mostly in the lower visual field. Both deaf and fluent hearing signers are better at detecting a motion target or discriminating direction of motion in the right visual field than non-signers. The right visual field advantage is thought to be due to the right visual field projecting to the left hemisphere, which is responsible for language processing in the majority of individuals. Enhanced motion processing in the right visual field may provide a route by which high quality visual motion information is provided to language areas of the brain (Bosworth & Dobkins, 1997; Bosworth & Dobkins, 1999; Bosworth & Dobkins, 2002a; Bosworth & Dobkins, 2002b).

Subjects who are deaf also tend to be better than both hearing subjects and hearing signers at distributing attention to the periphery and at performing peripheral visual tasks (Bavelier et al., 2000; Bosworth & Dobkins, 2002a; Loke & Song, 1991; Neville & Lawson, 1987; Parasnis & Samar, 1985; Proksch & Bavelier, 2002; Rettenbach, Diller, & Sireteanu, 1999). One possibility is that an enhanced sensitivity to peripheral visual stimuli may help compensate for the loss of the auditory cues that often direct our attention to objects outside the central focus of attention.

Sign language also relies heavily on facial expression, which is used to provide both emphasis and punctuation. Facial expressions signal lexical and syntactic structures, such as questions and adverbs. These linguistic facial expressions differ from emotional expressions in their scope and timing and in the facial muscles that are used. To take an example from McCullough and colleagues (2005), the lips pressed together and protruded indicates an effortless action, whereas the tongue protruded slightly means carelessly. These expressions accompanying the same verb (e.g., "drive") convey very different meanings (to drive effortlessly vs. drive carelessly). Obviously being sensitive to these facial expressions is crucial for learning sign language. It has been found that fluent hearing and deaf signers perform significantly better than nonsigners in distinguishing among similar faces (e.g., on the Benton Faces Test, Benton & Van Allen, 1972), in identifying emotional facial expressions, and in discriminating local facial features (Arnold & Murray, 1998; Goldstein, Sexton, & Feldman, 2000; McCullough & Emmorey, 1997).

COMPENSATING FOR A MISSING SENSE: WHAT IS THE NEURAL BASIS?

So, what are the neural substrates that underlie improvements in performance after loss of a sense? Take, for example, improved auditory and tactile processing in blind subjects. Improved auditory and tactile performance might be due to changes within auditory and somatosensory cortex (*compensatory hypertrophy*). Alternatively, these improvements might be due to *cross-modal plasticity* whereby visual cortex, deprived of its usual input, begins to respond to auditory and/or tactile information.

Analogously, in the case of deaf subjects, these improvements might be due either to modifications in the way that visual cortex processes visual information (*compensatory hypertrophy*), or to changes within auditory cortex (*cross-modal plasticity*).

Blind Individuals Show Compensatory Hypertrophy Within Both Somatosensory and Auditory Cortices

There is a significant amount of evidence for compensatory hypertrophy in blind subjects. For example, stimulation of the reading finger of blind Braille readers results in expanded areas of scalp-recorded somatosensory evoked potentials (Pascual-Leone & Torres, 1993) and in changes within the representation of reading fingers within somatosensory cortex, as measured using magnetic source imaging (Sterr et al., 1998; Sterr, Muller, Elbert, Rockstroh, & Taub, 1999). Analogous topographic changes have been noted in animals trained with tactile discrimination tasks (Recanzone, Jenkins, Hradek, & Merzenich, 1992; Recanzone, Merzenich, Jenkins, Grajski, & Dinse, 1992).

Reported changes included a doubling of the size of the hand representation in those blind subjects who read with three fingers, as well as a topographic disorganization that seemed to result in perceptual "smearing" or uncertainty about which finger was stimulated. This may be due to the need in readers of Braille who use three fingers to fuse input transmitted over all three fingers, so that the incoming information can be processed as a whole (Sterr et al., 1998). This deterioration in the ability to identify which finger is being stimulated suggests that dramatic reorganization of an area has the potential to undermine the ability of the reorganized region of cortex to perform its primary functions. Presumably the improved ability to integrate information across the three fingers while reading Braille outweighs any functional disadvantages resulting from the deterioration in the ability to determine which finger was stimulated.

Analogous changes have also been found in the auditory cortex of blind subjects using magnetic source imaging to measure responses within primary and secondary auditory areas for tone bursts. Regions responding to auditory stimulation, measured using tonotopic mapping (Elbert et al., 2002), were expanded by almost a factor of 2 in blind subjects, and N1m latencies (associated with activity in central auditory areas) were shorter in blind than in sighted individuals. However this expansion may have included a posterior shift, suggesting possible occipital (visual) cortex recruitment as well as a simple expansion of auditory areas.

Compensatory Hypertrophy in Deaf Individuals

As described, early deaf subjects perform better than hearing subjects at a variety of visual tasks. Might this better performance be mediated by changes within visual cortex? Two independent studies that measured the size of early retinotopic areas using fMRI have failed to find any difference in either the overall size of these visual areas or in the relative amounts of cortex allocated to the fovea and the periphery (Dougherty & Wandell, 2001; Fine, Finney, Boynton, & Dobkins, 2005). It seems that there are no major differences in the size or responsivity of most primary visual areas (V1–V4) between early deaf and hearing subjects.

There is some evidence that attentional effects on fMRI responses to motion within MT+ (the cortical region associated with motion processing) may be slightly different in early deaf than in hearing subjects. Bavelier and colleagues (2001, 2000) found larger attentional effects in the visual cortex of early deaf than hearing subjects and also reported an asymmetry in the extent of activity in area MT+ for early deaf and hearing subjects. In these experiments, the stimulus consisted of a full field of moving dots, and subjects were asked to attend to an annulus within the center or the periphery of the dot field. Although these effects were significant, they were not large, and a recent study that examined lateralization of motion processing in MT+ using a fairly similar stimulus and task by Fine and colleagues (2005) failed to replicate their findings. One possible explanation for the difference between these two studies may be that deaf subjects differ in their ability to allocate attention to the periphery in the presence of competing stimuli, as there were no distracting dots in the Fine et al. study (see Fine et al., 2005, for a discussion). In any case, the results of both studies suggest that changes in early areas of visual cortex as a consequence of auditory deprivation may be fairly limited in scope and magnitude, even in those that lose their hearing very early in life.

One reason for this may be that the critical period for language development is around 3 years of age, and it is presumably at this age that there is the greatest demand for recruitment of cortical resources for processing sign language. However by the age of 3, plasticity within early areas of the human visual system is likely to be fairly limited because the critical period for early visual areas ends by about 1 year of age. It is surprisingly difficult to find adult perceptual learning effects that can be definitively attributed to primary visual areas. Although researchers have found neural changes within primary visual area V1 in some electrophysiology studies in monkeys, these tend to be both restricted in magnitude and task dependent (Ghose, Yang, & Maunsell, 2002; Schoups, Vogels, Qian, & Orban, 2001). In humans, V1 changes in responsivity have been found in adults as a result of training in an orientation discrimination task using fMRI, but these changes may be partially mediated by attention (Furmanski, Schluppeck, & Engel, 2004).

One type of cortical plasticity that has been studied extensively is the "filling in" of retinal lesions (a process in which cortical neurons that subserve a retinal scotoma begin to respond to nearby intact retina. Although rapid filling has been found in cats (Gilbert & Wiesel, 1992; Kaas et al., 1990), reorganization in response to scotomas seems to occur extremely slowly in both monkeys and humans. A recent study in macaques found no evidence for remapping of regions of cortex that represented a retinal scotoma over several months (Smirnakis et al., 2005). In the case of human patients, one study examining cortical mapping in patients with well-established (several years) foveal scotomas due to macular degeneration did show remapping (Baker, Peli, Knouf, & Kanwisher, 2005) also see (Cheung & Legge, 2005). Perhaps if adult retinotopic reorganization occurs as a result of restricted visual loss, it happens extremely slowly.

Another reason why early visual areas may show so little plasticity as a result of auditory deprivation is that visual cortex is already performing a demanding host of visual functions. Any dramatic reorganization of visual cortex in response to auditory deprivation could potentially undermine the ability of visual cortex to perform basic visual functions. As described above, the changes that occur in somatosensory cortex consequent on learning to read Braille with three fingers result in worse performance in discriminating which finger has been stimulated. In the case of early visual cortex, the need to perform normal visual functions may limit the scope for changes consequent on the demands of deafness.

By contrast, one might expect more substantial reorganization in higher-level visual areas that tend to be more experience dependent. Neuronal changes as a function of learning do seem to be larger in higher visual areas

(Yang & Maunsell, 2004) though no direct electrophysiological comparisons between low- and high-level plasticity have been made to date. Neurons in higher level regions of cortex show a strong preference for stimuli that have been frequently encountered, or are behaviorally important. For example, neurons in macaque inferotemporal cortex (IT) are tuned for particular shapes, including hands and faces (Desimone, Albright, Gross, & Bruce, 1984), and these representations can be shaped by training (Logothetis, Pauls, & Poggio, 1995). Monkey face selective cells in IT show different responses to different faces, with their responses carrying identity information. The tuning of these cells seems also to be dependent on factors such as familiarity or social hierarchy (Rolls & Tovee, 1995; Young & Yamane, 1992) that are clearly highly experience dependent.

In support of the notion that plasticity increases along the visual hierarchy, it seems that adult perceptual learning may be related to the task complexity, with simpler tasks demonstrating less learning. Figure 8–1 shows perceptual learning for 16 visual tasks collated as part of a meta-review (Fine & Jacobs, 2002). The learning index on the y-axis represents the ability to perform the task on each session compared to performance on the first session (d' on each session/d' on the first session, where d' is a measure of performance). No improvement in performance would be a flat line of slope, or 0. Performance on low-level tasks shows fairly limited improvement with practice; after four sessions, the slope of the learning index averaged across various tasks defined as low level was found to be 0.17. In contrast, complex tasks that required discriminations along more than one perceptual dimension showed more than twice as much learning, with a learning slope of 0.43 (note that many of these stimuli also included external noise). High-level tasks, involving identifying or discriminating real-world natural objects, showed three times as much learning as the low level tasks, with a learning slope of 0.60. The exception was that observers showed little learning for a task in which they were asked to identify briefly presented familiar objects, possibly because identification learning had already occurred for these very familiar stimuli.

Another consideration is that that higher level visual areas, as well as being more generally plastic, may also be more susceptible to cross-modal influences than lower visual areas. For example, attentional modulation of responses to visual stimuli by auditory information has been shown to increase across the visual hierarchy (Ciaramitaro & Boynton, personal communication). Perhaps areas that normally show significant cross-modal modulation can more easily be biased towards the remaining senses (Bavelier & Neville, 2002; Calvert et al., 1997). If neurons in higher level visual areas already have access to auditory information, becoming purely visual would involve biasing their selectivity rather than responding to an entirely novel input modality.

There are, therefore, two reasons to expect greater reorganization as a function of deafness in higher than in lower-level visual areas. First, neuronal responses in higher visual areas seem to be more adaptable by experience than

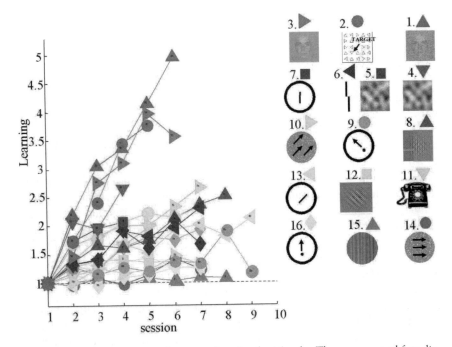

FIGURE 8–1.   Learning as a function of session for 16 tasks. These were novel face discrimination in (1) high and (3) low contrast noise; (2) simple shape search; bandpass noise
identification with (4) low and (5) high contrast noise; (6) vernier discrimination; (7) cardinal and (13) oblique orientation discrimination; spatial frequency discrimination for a
(8) complex and (12) simple plaid; direction of motion for a single dot moving in a
(9) oblique or (16) cardinal direction of motion; direction of motion discrimination for
(10) oblique and (14) cardinal directions; (11) familiar object recognition; and (15) the resolution limit for high spatial frequency gratings. *Source:* I. Fine and R. A. Jacobs (2002).
Comparing perceptual learning across tasks: A review. *Journal of Vision, 2*(5), 193. Copyright
2002 by ARVO. Adapted with permission. [See Color Plate]

in lower sensory areas, and second, neuronal responses in high-level visual
areas are influenced by auditory information, even in sighted individuals.

The effects of deafness do seem to be greater within higher-level visual
areas. For example, a recent fMRI study has demonstrated that higher level
areas of the brain involved in recognizing the emotional and linguistic content of faces (in the superior temporal sulcus and the fusiform gyrus) are reorganized in deaf signers as compared to hearing subjects (McCullough, Emmorey, & Sereno, 2005), consistent with the behavioral observation that sign
language results in an enriched processing of faces (McCullough & Emmorey,
1997). Differences between deaf and hearing individuals have also been observed within posterior parietal cortex for attentional tasks with moving dot
stimuli (Bavelier et al., 2001).

CROSS-MODAL PLASTICITY

Blind Individuals Show Cross-Modal Plasticity Within Visual Cortex

Both auditory and tactile tasks seem to activate visual cortex in blind individuals. For example, as described elsewhere in this volume (see Merabet, Pitskel, Amedi, & Pascual-Leone, chapter 3, this volume), Sadato and colleagues (Sadato, Okada, Honda, & Yonekura, 2002; Sadato et al., 1998, Sadato et al., 1996) have found that early visual areas are activated in early blind subjects for Braille reading and tactile discrimination tasks (though not passive stimulation). Disruption of occipital activation due to a stroke (Hamilton, Keenan, Catala, & Pascual-Leone, 2000) or transcranial magnetic stimulation (TMS; a coil on the surface of the head emits a short electromagnetic pulse that temporarily disrupts processing in cortical areas local to the coil) disrupts Braille reading, suggesting that these occipital responses play a functional role (Cohen et al., 1999).

It is not clear whether these cross-modal responses are dependent on loss of visual input early in development. Cross-modal responses are larger in early or congenitally blind individuals than in late blind individuals. For example, responses within occipital cortex to Braille are larger in congenital and early blind than in late blind individuals (Cohen et al., 1999; Sadato et al., 2002). Moreover, in a study examining the disruption of Braille reading TMS, only congenital and early blind subjects were affected, suggesting that the development of functionally useful cross-modal responses has a critical period (Cohen et al., 1999). On the other hand, as described elsewhere in this volume (see Merabet et al., chapter 3, this volume), learning Braille in sighted subjects was easier when the subjects were temporarily blindfolded for five days, and that this blindfolding resulted in occipital responses to Braille measured using fMRI (Pascual-Leone & Hamilton, 2001). It seems that some potential for cross-modal responses within visual cortex may exist even in sighted individuals with a normal visual history, and that these responses can be "unmasked" with a relatively short period of deprivation.

The advantages of cross-modal plasticity may go beyond simply colonizing unused regions of cortex. For example, cross-modal plasticity in Braille may be important in allowing tactile Braille to take advantage of areas such as the "word" area—a region within the midfusiform gyrus that has been shown to be selectively responsive to visual graphemes and to play an important role in reading and lexical processing (Hillis et al., 2005).

The anatomical substrates of these cross-modal influences on visual cortex are still to be determined. One possible substrate is direct monosynaptic projections from primary auditory to primary visual cortex. Direct monosynaptic projections from primary auditory cortex to both V1 and V2 have been found in adult monkeys. These auditory projections are denser in V2

than V1 and are found in portions of V1 and V2 representing the more peripheral and lower visual field (Falchier, Clavagnier, Barone, & Kennedy, 2002;
Rockland & Ojima, 2003). Alternatively, responses could be due to feedback
projections from higher-level visual or multimodal areas within parietal and
prefrontal cortex (Rockland & Ojima, 2003). These cross-modal connections
exist in adult animals with normal sensory experience, and it is plausible to
assume that these connections are likely to be more pronounced in dark-reared
animals and humans deprived from vision at an early age.

Cross-Modal Plasticity in Deaf Individuals

The majority of studies of cross-modal plasticity in deaf individuals have used
visual stimuli. This is because sign languages are visual in nature, making it
plausible that cross-modal effects will be more powerful for visual than for
tactile stimuli. However tactile cross-modal responses may exist: One magneto-
encephalography study demonstrated tactile responses within auditory cortex
of a congenitally deaf subject (Levanen, Jousmaki, & Hari, 1998) and these
cross-modal tactile responses do seem to have a behavioral correlate (Levanen,
Uutela, Salenius, & Hari, 2001).

Cross-modal plasticity for visual stimuli has been found within the primary
auditory cortex of deaf individuals (Finney, Clementz, Hickok, & Dobkins,
2003; Finney, Fine, & Dobkins, 2001) using nonlinguistic moving dot stimuli.
Hearing children of deaf adults did not show cross-modal plasticity, suggesting that lack of normal auditory input (rather than extensive experience with
a visual sign language) was necessary for cross-modal plasticity to occur (Fine
et al., 2005). Significant cross-modal responses were found only within right
auditory cortex. This region appeared to include primary, secondary, and association auditory areas—Brodmann's areas 41, 42 and 22 (Penhune, Zatorre,
MacDonald, & Evans, 1996; Rademacher et al., 2001; Westbury, Zatorre, &
Evans, 1999). The amount of activity within the region that showed cross-
modal plasticity was approximately a third of that produced in this same region
for music in hearing subjects. This recruitment of auditory cortex for visual
function may explain why, despite significant changes in white matter, deaf
subjects do not show a reduction in gray matter volume within primary auditory cortex (Emmorey, Allen, Bruss, Schenker, & Damasio, 2003). One obvious advantage of this cross-modal plasticity may be to allow visual sign language
to take advantage of connections between auditory cortex and neighboring
semantic and language processing areas.

Cross-modal plasticity seems to play a much more important role in compensating for deafness than compensatory hypertrophy. There is little evidence
for changes within visual cortex as a consequence of deafness, whereas there
are significant changes within auditory cortex (Fine et al., 2005). One possible explanation, as discussed earlier, is that visual cortex has only a limited
potential to reorganize because drastic reorganization would have the poten-

tial to undermine the ability of visual cortex to perform its primary functions. In the case of visual cortex, any disruption of the ability to perform everyday visual tasks could easily be catastrophic.

The anatomical route for cross-modal connections to auditory cortex is still a matter of speculation. As in the case of cross-modal visual responses, there are several possible anatomical routes, and it is of course possible that more than one anatomical pathway may be involved. There are exuberant projections during infancy from the visual thalamus to the primary auditory cortex (Catalano & Shatz, 1998; Ghosh & Shatz, 1992). Normally, these visual projections to the auditory cortex get pruned away over the course of development. In the case of auditory deprivation, however, the lack of functional auditory input to the auditory cortex may result in the stabilization of visual input to this area (Sur, Angelucci, & Sharma, 1999). Recently, Pallas and colleagues (2002) have demonstrated direct projections from the visual thalamus to the primary auditory cortex in early-deafened ferrets, leaving open the possibility of such projections in deaf individuals.

A second possible source of visual responses in the auditory cortex is from visual cortical areas such as V1 or V2. Projections from visual areas V1 and V2 to the auditory cortex have recently been reported in adult monkeys (Schroeder, 2004). It is plausible that these projections might be more pervasive in infancy, and it is possible that in deaf children there would be less developmental pruning of these projections.

Finally, these cross-modal responses may be the result of feedback from cortical areas responsible for processing language. At this point, a large number of studies have demonstrated responses to visual stimuli that are linguistically meaningful within auditory regions of deaf individuals (MacSweeney et al., 2002; Nishimura et al., 1999; Petitto et al., 2000). For example, Brodmann's areas 42 and 22 are activated in deaf subjects in response to visual images of sign language. Some of the areas showing visual activation in deaf subjects may normally play a role in visual language processing in hearing subjects. For example, similar regions of auditory cortex are activated by a silent lip reading task in hearing subjects as are activated by sign language in deaf subjects (Calvert et al., 1997).

The cross-modal plasticity described above presumably plays an important role in allowing the individuals to make better use of their remaining senses. However, what is the effect of cross-modal plasticity on the ability to make use of a sense if it is ever restored? One possibility is that cross-modal plasticity maintains neuronal function and connectivity within regions of cortex that might otherwise be susceptible to deterioration and cell death. According to this model, cross-modal plasticity would facilitate later recovery of vision. Alternatively, the rewiring involved in cross-modal plasticity, especially when it occurs early in development, may permanently limit the ability to regain useful sensory function.

MOLYNEAUX'S QUESTION: THE ROLE OF EXPERIENCE IN MAINTAINING SENSORY FUNCTION

Visual Processing Deteriorates in the Early Blind

> Suppose a man born blind, and now adult, and taught by his touch to distinguish between a cube and a sphere. . . . Suppose then . . . the blind man is made to see. . . . Query: whether by his sight, before he touched them, he could distinguish and tell which is the globe, which is the cube? (Locke, 1690, pp. ii, ix, 8)

Despite the philosophical and psychological interest of Molyneaux's question, cases of adult sight restoration are so rare that even now little is known about perceptual experience after long-term visual deprivation. Although the first report of recovery from blindness was in AD 1020 (von Senden, 1960) and the first clinical study of sight recovery after long-term blindness was carried out in 1728 (Cheselden, 1728), until recently only sporadic studies have been carried out (Ackroyd, Humphrey, & Warrington, 1974; Carlson & Hyvarinen, 1983; Carlson, Hyvarinen, & Raninen, 1986; Gregory & Wallace, 1963; Sacks, 1995; Valvo, 1971; Wright, Geffen, & Geffen, 1995). While these studies provide an interesting body of observations, most studies had access only to small numbers of observers (often only one) and generally only had crude measures of preoperative visual abilities. Studies were often anecdotal and qualitative, focusing on patients' ability to use their sight functionally and on their visual acuity, rather than on the neural changes consequent on visual deprivation. In addition, many patients suffered only partial deprivation. For example, Gregory and Wallace's famous patient, SB, could, in fact, count fingers preoperatively (Ackroyd et al., 1974; Gregory & Wallace, 1963), suggesting significant form vision.

In a recent study, my colleagues and I used a combination of psychophysical and neuroimaging techniques to characterize the effects of long-term visual deprivation on human cortex (Fine et al., 2003). At 3½ years old, MM lost one eye and was blinded in the other after chemical and thermal damage to his cornea. Limbal epithelial damage prevented successful replacement of MM's cornea for 40 years. As a result, he had some light perception but no experience of contrast or form. One unsuccessful corneal replacement was attempted in childhood, but he reported no visual memories or imagery.

At age 43, MM received a corneal and limbal stem-cell transplant in his right eye. His postoperative performance was tested on a wide array of tasks designed to characterize, crudely, form, motion, depth, and object and face processing. Stimuli presented to control observers were blurred using a filter designed to match MM's spatial resolution. As shown in Figure 8–2, MM had no discernable deficits in simple form tasks postoperatively. When first tested, 5 months after surgery, he perceived slight changes in the orientation of a bar and easily recognized simple shapes. He reported perceiving simple two-dimensional shapes, even immediately after surgery.

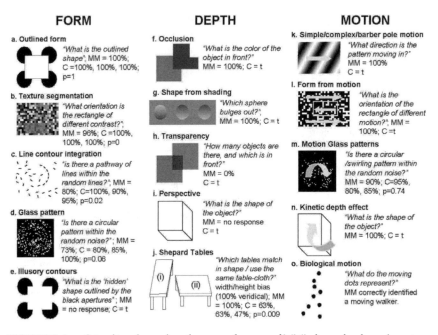

FIGURE 8–2.   Stimuli, tasks, and performance for tests of MM's form, depth, and motion processing. Stimuli presented to control observers were always blurred using a low pass filter (cutoff of 1 cycle per degree) designed to match MM's spatial resolution losses. Some tasks were trivial for control observers (t) and were not formally tested. C = control observers. *p* values, 1-tailed *t* tests. *Source:* I. Fine, A. R. Wade, A. A. Brewer, M. G. May, D. F. Goodman, G. M. Boynton, B. A. Wandell, and D. I. A. MacLeod (2003). *Nature Neuroscience,* 6(9), 915–916. Copyright 2003 by Nature Publishing Group. Adapted with permission. [See Color Plate]

Like most (Gregory & Wallace, 1963; Sacks, 1995), though not all (Ackroyd et al., 1974), sight-recovery patients, MM identified colors easily (though he occasionally had difficulty remembering the correct color name) and his equiluminance settings were normal. Differences in color processing that were observed between MM and visually normal observers were limited to color illusions based on seeing images as being three-dimensional. Ackroyd and colleagues' patient HB (1974), who, like MM, was blinded at the age of 3, had difficulty discriminating colors, though this may have been due to uncertainty about what property of the stimulus (brightness, hue, saturation) was referred to by the color name. (HB spoke English as a second language, so, unlike MM, she had no experience of English color names before the onset of blindness.)

Similarly, motion processing appears to be relatively normal in sight recovery patients. "His [SB's] only signs of appreciation were to moving objects, particularly the pigeons in Trafalgar square" (Gregory & Wallace, 1963, p. 30). Similarly, Ackroyd and colleagues (1974) reported of their patient, "She [HB] could see the pigeons as they alighted in Trafalgar Square but she said that they appeared to vanish as they came to rest." MM's color and motion processing appeared normal as well. He easily identified the direction of motion of simple and complex plaids and was susceptible to the barber pole illusion. He could segregate textured fields based on motion and could distinguish rotational Glass motion patterns (in which two successive frames differ by rotation) from random noise patterns. Surprisingly MM could use motion cues to compute three-dimensional shape, a computation thought to involve MT+ (Bradley, Chang, & Andersen, 1998; Dodd, Krug, Cumming, & Parker, 2001; Orban, Sunaert, Todd, Van Hecke, & Marchal, 1999). This sensitivity to form from motion was in striking contrast to his insensitivity to most pictorial depth cues. For example, a stationary Necker cube immediately popped-out as a cube when motion in depth was simulated. MM was also sensitive to biological motion, recognizing a point-light "Johansson" figure and even being able to determine whether the figure walked with a male or female gait. Consistent with MM's ability to perform motion tasks, when we measured fMRI responses in MM we found that responses within cortical areas responsible for motion processing were normal in area and amplitude, and showed evidence of retinotopic phase map encoding (Huk, Dougherty, & Heeger, 2002).

MM could segment texture patterns based on luminance contrast but was slightly worse than control observers at other form tasks requiring integration of texture elements, such as identifying whether a field of line contours contained a sequence of nearly collinear line segments (Field, Hayes, & Hess, 1993) and discriminating static Glass patterns (as opposed to motion Glass patterns, see previous discussion) from random noise (Glass, 1969; Lewis et al., 2002, Ross, Badcock, & Hayes, 2000). MM also had severe difficulty with "subjective contours." Though he recognized outlined two-dimensional shapes, he could not identify the same shapes in "Kanisza figures."

The literature on sight recovery seems to be in fairly good agreement that patients have difficulties projecting their two-dimensional retinal image into a three-dimensional world. Cheselden (1728) reported of his patient that he "thought no Objects so agreeable as those which were smooth and regular, though he could form no Judgment of their Shape." It was reported of Sacks' patient Virgil, "Sometimes surfaces of objects would seem to loom . . . when they were still quite a distance away; sometimes he would get confused by his own shadow . . . [Steps] posed a particular hazard. All he could see was a confusion, a flat surface of parallel and crisscrossing lines" (Sacks, 1995). Though Gregory and Wallace's patient, SB, seems to have been somewhat better at object recognition than many earlier patients (possibly due to his better preoperative acuity), he nonetheless was immune to many illusions based on perspective. One of Valvo's patients, HS, described his initial experiences after sight recovery: "I had no appreciation of depth or distance; street lights were luminous stains stuck to window panes, and the corridors of the hospital were black holes" (Valvo, 1971). It is worth noting that this patient, HS, was not deprived of sight until the age of 15. Similarly, MM had difficulty constructing a three-dimensional interpretation from his retinal image. He could exploit occlusion cues but not shading, transparency, or perspective. For example, he could not identify wire drawings of stationary Necker cubes or pyramids (regardless of their three-dimensional orientation), describing them respectively as "a square with lines" and "a triangle with lines." MM was immune to illusions based on perspective cues such as Roger Shepard's "tables" (Shepard, 1990), correctly choosing quadrilaterals of equal aspect ratios as being rotated versions of each other. Observers with normal vision tend to (mistakenly) choose very different aspect ratios of the tables even when asked to match the two-dimensional image shapes.

Possibly as a consequence of these difficulties with constructing a three-dimensional percept, sight recovery patients also consistently show difficulties recognizing even "familiar" objects and faces. Sacks (1995) observed of Virgil, "[His] cat and dog bounded in . . . and Virgil, we noted, had some difficulty telling which was which." One of the earliest recorded cases (Cheselden, 1728) describes the same confusion, "Having often forgot which was the cat and which the dog, he was ashamed to ask, but catching the cat which he knew from feeling, he was observed to look at her steadfastly and then . . . have said, So puss, I shall know you another time." Similar difficulties have been reported in a more recent case of sight recovery (Fine et al., 2003, p. 448). MM identified only 25% of common objects (Kanwisher, McDermott, & Chun, 1997), and he had difficulty judging gender or expression in faces. Like observers with prosopagnosia (Farah, Wilson, Drain, & Tanaka, 1998; Le Grand, Mondloch, Maurer, & Brent, 2001), MM seemed to rely entirely on individual features, such as the hair length or eyebrow shape. Other sight-recovery cases seem to have suffered from similar difficulties (Cheselden, 1728; Gregory & Wallace, 1963), and short-term binocular deprivation in infancy seems to result in analogous (though less striking) behavioral deficits (Le Grand et al., 2001; Le Grand, Mondloch, Maurer, & Brent, 2003). Face and object images evoked little fMRI activation within MM's lingual and fusiform gyri, whereas controls showed strong responses. These data were the first to show deficits in lingual and fusiform areas as a result of abnormal visual experience rather than as a result of neurophysiological damage.

MM showed no improvement in basic visual functions (such as acuity) over 2 years. Admittedly, no rehabilitation was carried out. However, other studies have been designed to improve vision after sight restoration, with very limited success (Carlson & Hyvarinen, 1983; Carlson et al., 1986; Fine, Smallman, Doyle, & MacLeod, 2002; Valvo, 1971). Both the motivation and intelligence of the patient seems to be critical in making cognitive use of the confusing visual world of the sight restoration patient. However, to date there is little or no evidence suggesting that the effects of early deprivation on early visual cortex are anything other than permanent after adolescence (Fine et al., 2002; Fine et al., 2003). However MM has learned to make better use of his limited visual information. As MM describes his progress in developing visual fluency, "The difference between today and over 2 years ago is that I can better guess at what I am seeing. What is the same is that I am still guessing." (http://www.sendergroup.com/mike.htm).

These results clearly have important implications for sight restoration in the early blind or congenitally blind individuals. Even if it were possible to restore "perfect optics" (i.e., to carry out a surgery that would result in perfect vision within a normal visual system), the severe neural losses that result from early deprivation, within both early and later stages of the visual hierarchy, will still severely limit the vision of any patient who had been blinded in early childhood.

Deterioration in Deaf Individuals

This same process of deterioration seems to occur after early deafness. The success of cochlear implants depends greatly upon the age of implantation. A variety of researchers have found that intervention during the first 6 months of life (whether with a hearing aid or a cochlear implant) significantly increases the level of language development, speech intelligibility, and emotional stability compared to children with later diagnosis and intervention. Even though the critical period for language development is thought to last until 7 years of age, it has generally been found that infants implanted at a very early age (younger than 18 months) have better outcomes than children implanted later in life (Geers, Nicholas, & Sedey, 2003; Svirsky, Teoh, & Neuburger, 2004; Waltzman & Cohen, 1998). Neurophysiological markers show a similar pattern: In children implanted after the age of 7 the cortical auditory evoked potential is aberrant and shows slower latencies as compared to children implanted before the age of 3 (Sharma, Dorman, & Kral, 2005).

There is some evidence that this deterioration in recovery of the ability to process auditory input may be due to cross-modal plasticity. Lee and colleagues (2001) found that the resting metabolic rate within auditory areas was inversely related to years of deafness. Children who had been deaf for a relatively short period of time showed a large drop in the resting metabolic rate within auditory cortex. In contrast, young adults who had been deaf for many years had a resting metabolic rate within auditory cortex that was close to normal levels. Performance on speech perception after cochlear implantation was inversely related to the metabolic rate pre-implantation. Speech processing outcomes were worst in those patients who showed near-normal resting metabolic activity in auditory cortex. This is consistent with the hypothesis that the maintenance of metabolic activity may be due to cross-modal plasticity, which in turn interferes with the ability to recover auditory processing abilities post-implantation.

The "critical period" for auditory development seems to depend on the task used to assess post-implantation performance. Better performance on a sound identification within a closed set of alternatives seems to depend on whether implantation occurred before the age of 4½ years. More difficult tasks involving identifying a sound from an open set of alternatives depends on whether implantation occurred before the ages of 5½ to 8½ (Harrison, Gordon, & Mount, 2005). Changing the task from a closed to open set of alternatives is likely to have resulted in the recruitment of higher stages of auditory processing in performing the task, which may explain why the effects of age of implantation last until almost 9 years of age for more complex tasks. This is consistent with work examining the effects of visual deprivation, suggesting that different regions of visual cortex vary in their developmental time courses, with higher-level visual areas continuing to retain plasticity at later ages (Fine & Jacobs, 2002; Fine et al., 2003).

In adults who have become deaf postlingually it has been found that performance in recovering speech perception is inversely related to how well the cochlear implant emulates the cortical input that had been provided by the lost cochlear mechanisms, and to the duration of deafness pre-implantation (Oh et al., 2003). This impact of deafness duration in adulthood demonstrates that deterioration in function as a result of deprivation is not limited to the effects of early deafness (Harrison et al., 2005).

IMPLICATIONS FOR REHABILITATION

As described earlier, plasticity as a result of sensory deprivation depends on a variety of factors. One important factor is age of deprivation, since cortex tends to be more plastic at an early age. Early blind and deaf subjects tend to be much more fluent at skills such as Braille, use of a cane, or sign language than later blind subjects. One reason for this may be that these skills are easier to learn at an early age, when cortex is more plastic. The greater skills of the early deprived may also be partially due to behavioral/cultural factors—early blind and deaf subjects tend to rely on Braille and sign language much more heavily than those deprived at a later age. What is most likely is that these two factors may reinforce each other: Early blind and deaf subjects learn sensory substitution skills more easily, this makes them rely on these skills more heavily, giving them practice and thereby further improving those skills. In those deprived later in life, this "circle of competency" may be much more difficult to initiate.

Understanding how plasticity may increase across the sensory hierarchy also has important implications for rehabilitation. The advantage of targeting low-level stages of processing is that any rehabilitative learning would presumably mediate a general improvement in performance. Such low-level stages of processing would presumably be modified by simple tasks such as tactile or auditory discrimination tasks. However, much of the evidence described here suggests that the effects of perceptual learning may be very limited for these simple tasks, especially in the case of visual cortex.

Alternatively, practicing higher-level tasks may result in faster and larger plasticity effects, but these learning effects would be expected to show much greater specificity for the task and the stimulus that subjects were trained on. One possibility is that training may benefit from a mixed strategy whereby time and attention are divided between key aspects of low-level processing (which would be expected to show limited improvements that would apply to a wide range of visual tasks) and higher-level tasks that are functionally important (which might show greater learning effects that are more specific in their scope). Choosing the right rehabilitation training should also consider the patient's age. A rehabilitation strategy targeting low-level processing is likely to be more successful in children than in older patients.

The possible advantages of developing coherent strategies of mixed training apply to a wide range of rehabilitation paradigms, including learning sensory substitution skills, learning strategies for dealing with low vision (such as the development of a preferred retinal location in macular degeneration, or training to reduce the effects of amblyopia), rehabilitative training after neural damage (e.g., stroke), or even learning to make the best use of a sensory prosthesis.

Normally, the cortical changes that occur as a result of sensory deprivation are of benefit to the individual, playing an important role in allowing the individual to make better use of his/her remaining senses. However, as described earlier, if there is an opportunity for the missing sense to be restored later in life then these adaptations become maladaptive and can seriously limit an individual's ability to make use of the restored sense. This is particularly troubling because restoring the missing sense can have the unintended consequence of interfering with cross-modal abilities. The decision to implant a prosthetic device or carry out a restorative surgery needs to consider not only the potential loss to any residual vision or hearing but also the potential of the device to interfere with cross-modal processing.

This leaves the field of "cutting edge" restorative surgeries and prosthetics with a dilemma. There are many sensory restoration procedures or devices currently on the market or expected soon (cortical auditory implants, visual retinal implants, epithelial stem cell replacements, retinal transplants) that offer either limited sensory restoration or have a high probability of tissue rejection or some other type of failure at some point in the individual's lifetime. As described earlier in this chapter, there are clear neurophysiological advantages to restoring a sense at as early an age as possible. However, if carried out early in life, this restorative procedure is likely to interfere with the ability to learn to navigate with a cane or read Braille. In the deaf community, this issue began to be raised and debated when cochlear implants came on the market. We may expect to see similar discussions in the blind community in the future.

Even in the case of implantation in adulthood, it is still important when evaluating outcomes to consider possible deleterious effects on cross-modal skills. Given that the ability to make use of the restored sense is often limited, any deterioration in a patients' ability to navigate with a cane, read Braille, or understand sign language can have serious consequences. Take, for example, the description of SB's ability to deal with crossing the road after a sight recovery operation (Gregory & Wallace, 1963): "He found the traffic frightening, and would not attempt to cross even a comparatively small street by himself. This was in marked contrast to his former behavior, as described to us by his wife, when he would cross any street in his own town by himself. In London, and later in his home town, he would show evident fear, even when led by a companion whom he trusted, and it was many months before he would venture alone" (p. 30). Clearly, new visual information interfered with SB's ability to use cross-modal skills that he had relied on pre-operatively.

The current assumption is that the decision to carry out a sensory restoration procedure (whether it is a prosthetic or some other type of restorative surgery) should be based on the potential to restore useful vision or audition, as compared to the risk of losing any residual sensory function and the discomfort and risks of the operation. However, as described in this chapter, cross-modal plasticity is likely to play a very significant role in compensating for sensory loss. This suggests that the possibility of a detrimental effect on skills mediated by cross-modal activity should also be borne in mind when considering sensory restoration procedures.

ACKNOWLEDGMENTS

My research described in this chapter has been supported by the National Institute of Health grant EY014645.

REFERENCES

Ackroyd, C., Humphrey, N. K., & Warrington, E. K. (1974). Lasting effects of early blindness. A case study. *The Quarterly Journal of Experimental Psychology, 26*(1), 114–124.

Amedi, A., Raz, N., Pianka, P., Malach, R., & Zohary, E. (2003). Early 'visual' cortex activation correlates with superior verbal memory performance in the blind. *Nature Neuroscience, 6*(7), 758–766.

Arnold, P., & Murray, C. (1998). Memory for faces and objects by deaf and hearing signers and hearing nonsigners. *Journal of Psycholinguistic Research, 27*, 481–497.

Baker, C. I., Peli, E., Knouf, N., & Kanwisher, N. G. (2005). Reorganization of visual processing in macular degeneration. *Journal of Neuroscience, 25*(3), 614–618.

Bavelier, D., Brozinsky, C., Tomann, A., Mitchell, T., Neville, H., & Liu, G. (2001). Impact of early deafness and early exposure to sign language on the cerebral organization for motion processing. *Journal of Neuroscience, 21*(22), 8931–8942.

Bavelier, D., & Neville, H. J. (2002). Cross-modal plasticity: Where and how? *Nature Reviews. Neuroscience, 3*(6), 443–452.

Bavelier, D., Tomann, A., Hutton, C., Mitchell, T., Corina, D., Liu, G., et al. (2000). Visual attention to the periphery is enhanced in congenitally deaf individuals. *Journal of Neuroscience, 20*(17), RC93.

Benton, A. L., & Van Allen, M. W. (1972). Prosopagnosia and facial discrimination. *Journal of Neurological Sciences, 15*(2), 167–172.

Bosworth, R. G., & Dobkins, K. R. (2002). Visual field asymmetries for motion processing in deaf and hearing signers. *Brain and Cognition, 49*(1), 170–181.

Bosworth, R. G., & Dobkins, K. R. (1999). Left-hemisphere dominance for motion processing in deaf signers. *Psychological Science, 10*(3), 256–262.

Bosworth, R. G., & Dobkins, K. R. (2002a). The effects of spatial attention on motion processing in deaf signers, hearing signers, and hearing nonsigners. *Brain and Cognition, 49*(1), 152–169.

Bosworth, R. G., & Dobkins, K. R. (2002b). Visual field asymmetries for motion processing in deaf and hearing signers. *Brain and Cognition, 49*(1), 170–181.

Bradley, D. C., Chang, G. C., & Andersen, R. A. (1998). Encoding of three-dimensional structure-from-motion by primate area MT neurons. *Nature, 392*(6677), 714–717.

Calvert, G. A., Bullmore, E. T., Brammer, M. J., Campbell, R., Williams, S. C., McGuire, P. K., et al. (1997). Activation of auditory cortex during silent lipreading. *Science, 276*(5312), 593–596.

Carlson, S., & Hyvarinen, L. (1983). Visual rehabilitation after long lasting early blindness. *Acta Ophthalmologica, 61*(4), 701–713.

Carlson, S., Hyvarinen, L., & Raninen, A. (1986). Persistent behavioural blindness after early visual deprivation and active visual rehabilitation: a case report. *The British Journal of Ophthalmology, 70*(8), 607–611.

Catalano, S. M., & Shatz, C. J. (1998). Activity-dependent cortical target selection by thalamic axons. *Science, 281*(5376), 559–562.

Cheselden, W. (1728). An account of some observations made by a young gentleman, who was born blind, or who lost his sight so early, that he had no remembrance of ever having seen, and was couch'd between 13 and 14 years of age. *Philosophical Transactions of the Royal Society of London, 402*, 447–450.

Cheung, S. H., & Legge, G. E. (2005). Functional and cortical adaptations to central vision loss. *Visual Neuroscience, 22*(2), 187–201.

Cohen, L. G., Weeks, R. A., Sadato, N., Celnik, P., Ishii, K., & Hallett, M. (1999). Period of susceptibility for cross-modal plasticity in the blind. *Annals of Neurology, 45*(4), 451–460.

Desimone, R., Albright, T. D., Gross, C. G., & Bruce, C. (1984). Stimulus-selective properties of inferior temporal neurons in the macaque. *Journal of Neuroscience, 4*(8), 2051–2062.

Dodd, J. V., Krug, K., Cumming, B. G., & Parker, A. J. (2001). Perceptually bistable three-dimensional figures evoke high choice probabilities in cortical area MT. *Journal of Neuroscience, 21*(13), 4809–4821.

Doucet, M. E., Guillemot, J. P., Lassonde, M., Gagne, J. P., Leclerc, C., & Lepore, F. (2005). Blind subjects process auditory spectral cues more efficiently than sighted individuals. *Experimental Brain Research, 160*(2), 194–202.

Dougherty, R. F., & Wandell, B. A. (2001). Personal communication, (May 7, 2001, pp. 586–98).

Elbert, T., Sterr, A., Rockstroh, B., Pantev, C., Muller, M. M., & Taub, E. (2002). Expansion of the tonotopic area in the auditory cortex of the blind. *Journal of Neuroscience, 22*(22), 9941–9944.

Emmorey, K., Allen, J. S., Bruss, J., Schenker, N., & Damasio, H. (2003). Morphometric analysis of auditory brain regions in congenitally deaf adults. *Proceedings of the National Academy of Sciences, 100*(17), 10049–10054.

Falchier, A., Clavagnier, S., Barone, P., & Kennedy, H. (2002). Anatomical evidence of multimodal integration in primate striate cortex. *Journal of Neuroscience, 22*(13), 5749–5759.

Farah, M. J., Wilson, K. D., Drain, M., & Tanaka, J. N. (1998). What is "special" about face perception? *Psychological Review, 105*(3), 482–498.

Field, D. J., Hayes, A., & Hess, R. F. (1993). Contour integration by the human visual system: Evidence for a local "association field." *Vision Research, 33*(2), 173–193.

Fine, I., Finney, E. M., Boynton, G. M., & Dobkins, K. R. (2005). Comparing the effects of auditory deprivation and sign language within the auditory and visual cortex. *Journal of Cognitive Neuroscience, 17*(10), 1621–1637.

Fine, I., & Jacobs, R. A. (2002). Comparing perceptual learning across tasks: A review. *Journal of Vision, 2*(5), 190–203.

Fine, I., Smallman, H. S., Doyle, P. G., & MacLeod, D. I. A. (2002). Visual function before and after the removal of congenital bilateral cataracts in adulthood. *Vision Research, 42*, 191–210.

Fine, I., Wade, A., Boynton, G. M. B., Brewer, A., May, M., Wandell, B., et al. (2003). The neural and functional effects of long-term visual deprivation on human cortex. *Nature Neuroscience, 6*(9), 915–916.

Finney, E. M., Clementz, B. A., Hickok, G., & Dobkins, K. R. (2003). Visual stimuli activate auditory cortex in deaf subjects: evidence from MEG. *NeuroReport, 14*(11), 1425–1427.

Finney, E. M., Fine, I., & Dobkins, K. R. (2001). Visual stimuli activate auditory cortex in the deaf. *Nature Neuroscience, 4*(12), 1171–1173.

Furmanski, C. S., Schluppeck, D., & Engel, S. A. (2004). Learning strengthens the response of primary visual cortex to simple patterns. *Current Biology, 14*(7), 573–578.

Geers, A. E., Nicholas, J. G., & Sedey, A. L. (2003). Language skills of children with early cochlear implantation. *Ear and Hearing, 24*(1 Suppl), 46S–58S.

Ghosh, A., & Shatz, C. J. (1992). Pathfinding and target selection by developing geniculocortical axons. *Journal of Neuroscience, 12*(1), 39–55.

Ghose, G. M., Yang, T., & Maunsell, J. H. (2002). Physiological correlates of perceptual learning in monkey V1 and V2. *Journal of Neurophysiology, 87*(4), 1867–1888.

Gilbert, C. D., & Wiesel, T. N. (1992). Receptive field dynamics in adult primary visual cortex. *Nature, 356*(6365), 150–152.

Glass, L. (1969). Moire effect from random dots. *Nature, 223*(206), 578–580.

Goldstein, N. S., Sexton, J., & Feldman, R. S. (2000). Encoding of facial expressions of emotion and knowledge of American Sign Language. *Journal of Applied Social Psychology, 30*, 67–76.

Gougoux, F., Lepore, F., Lassonde, M., Voss, P., Zatorre, R. J., & Belin, P. (2004). Neuropsychology: Pitch discrimination in the early blind. *Nature, 430*, 309.

Grant, A. C., Thiagarajah, M. C., & Sathian, K. (2000). Tactile perception in blind Braille readers: A psychophysical study of acuity and hyperacuity using gratings and dot patterns. *Percept Psychophysics, 62*(2), 301–312.

Gregory, R. L., & Wallace, J. G. (1963). *Recovery from early blindness: A case study.* (Experimental Psychological Society Monograph No.2) Cambridge, UK: Heffer and Sons.

Hamilton, R., Keenan, J. P., Catala, M., & Pascual-Leone, A. (2000). Alexia for Braille following bilateral occipital stroke in an early blind woman. *Neuroreport, 11*, 237–240.

Harrison, R. V., Gordon, K. A., & Mount, R. J. (2005). Is there a critical period for cochlear implantation in congenitally deaf children? Analyses of hearing and speech perception performance after implantation. *Developmental Psychobiology, 46*(3), 252–261.

Hillis, A. E., Newhart, M., Heidler, J., Barker, P., Herskovits, E., & Degaonkar, M. (2005). The roles of the "visual word form area" in reading. *NeuroImage, 24*(2), 548–559.

Huk, A. C., Dougherty, R. F., & Heeger, D. J. (2002). Retinotopy and functional subdivision of human areas MT and MST. *Journal of Neuroscience, 22*(16), 7195–7205.

Hunt, D. L., King, B., Kahn, D. M., Yamoah, E. N., Shull, G. E., & Krubitzer, L. (2005). Aberrant retinal projections in congenitally deaf mice: How are phenotypic characteristics specified in development and evolution? *The Anatomical Record. Part A, Discoveries in Molecular, Cellular, and Evolutionary Biology, 287*(1), 1051–1066.

Kaas, J. H., Krubitzer, L. A., Chino, Y. M., Langston, A. L., Polley, E. H., & Blair, N. (1990). Reorganization of retinotopic cortical maps in adult mammals after lesions of the retina. *Science, 248,* 229–231.

Kanwisher, N., McDermott, J., & Chun, M. M. (1997). The fusiform face area: a module in human extrastriate cortex specialized for face perception. *Journal of Neuroscience, 17*(11), 4302–4311.

Le Grand, R., Mondloch, C. J., Maurer, D., & Brent, H. P. (2001). Neuroperception. Early visual experience and face processing. *Nature, 410,* 890.

Le Grand, R., & Mondloch, C. J., (2003). Expert face processing requires visual input to the right hemisphere during infancy. *Nature Neuroscience, 6*(10), 1108–1112.

Lee, D. S., Sung Lee, J., Ha Oh, S., Kim, S., Kim, J., Chung, J., et al. (2001). Cross-modal plasticity and cochlear implants. *Nature, 409,* 149–150.

Lessard, N., Pare, M., Lepore, F., & Lassonde, M. (1998). Early-blind human subjects localize sound sources better than sighted subjects. *Nature, 395,* 278–280.

Levanen, S., Jousmaki, V., & Hari, R. (1998). Vibration-induced auditory-cortex activation in a congenitally deaf adult. *Current Biology, 8*(15), 869–872.

Levanen, S., Uutela, K., Salenius, S., & Hari, R. (2001). Cortical representation of sign language: Comparison of deaf signers and hearing non-signers. *Cerebral Cortex, 11*(6), 506–512.

Lewis, T. L., Ellemberg, D., Maurer, D., Wilkinson, F., Wilson, H. R., Dirks, M., et al. (2002). Sensitivity to global form in glass patterns after early visual deprivation in humans. *Vision Research, 42*(8), 939–948.

Locke, J. (1690). *Essay concerning human understanding.* New York: Dover.

Logothetis, N. K., Pauls, J., & Poggio, T. (1995). Shape representation in the inferior temporal cortex of monkeys. *Current Biology, 5*(5), 552–563.

Loke, W. H., & Song, S. (1991). Central and peripheral visual processing in hearing and nonhearing individuals. *Bulletin of the Psychonomic Society, 29,* 437–440.

MacSweeney, M., Woll, B., Campbell, R., McGuire, P. K., David, A. S., Williams, S. C., et al. (2002). Neural systems underlying British Sign Language and audio-visual English processing in native users. *Brain, 125*(Pt 7), 1583–1593.

McCullough, S., & Emmorey, K. (1997). Face processing by deaf ASL signers: evidence for expertise in distinguishing local features. *Journal of Deaf Studies and Deaf Education, 2*(4), 212–222.

McCullough, S., Emmorey, K., & Sereno, M. (2005). Neural organization for recognition of grammatical and emotional facial expressions in deaf ASL signers and hearing non-signers. *Brain Research. Cognitive Brain Research, 22*(2), 193–203.

Neville, H. J., & Lawson, D. (1987). Attention to central and peripheral visual space in a movement detection task: An event-related potential and behavioral study. II. Congenitally deaf adults. *Brain Research, 405*(2), 268–283.

Nishimura, H., Hashikawa, K., Doi, K., Iwaki, T., Watanabe, Y., Kusuoka, H., et al. (1999). Sign language 'heard' in the auditory cortex. *Nature, 397*, 116.

Oh, S. H., Kim, C. S., Kang, E. J., Lee, D. S., Lee, H. J., Chang, S. O., et al. (2003). Speech perception after cochlear implantation over a 4-year time period. *Acta-Otolaryngologica, 123*(2), 148–153.

Orban, G. A., Sunaert, S., Todd, J. T., Van Hecke, P., & Marchal, G. (1999). Human cortical regions involved in extracting depth from motion. *Neuron, 24*(4), 929–940.

Pallas, S. L., Razak, K. A., & Moore, D. R. (2002). Cross-modal projections from LGN to primary auditory cortex following perinatal cochlear ablation in ferrets. *Society for Neuroscience Abstracts, 28*, 220–228.

Parasnis, I., & Samar, V. J. (1985). Parafoveal attention in congenitally deaf and hearing young adults. *Brain and Cognition, 4*(3), 313–327.

Pascual-Leone, A., & Hamilton, R. (2001). The metamodal organization of the brain. In C. Casanova, & M. Ptito (Eds.), *Progress in Brain Research*, Vol. 134 (pp. 427–445).

Pascual-Leone, A., & Torres, F. (1993). Plasticity of the sensorimotor cortex representation of the reading finger in Braille readers. *Brain, 116*(Pt 1), 39–52.

Penhune, V. B., Zatorre, R. J., MacDonald, J. D., & Evans, A. C. (1996). Interhemispheric anatomical differences in human primary auditory cortex: Probabilistic mapping and volume measurement from magnetic resonance scans. *Cerebral Cortex, 6*(5), 661–672.

Petitto, L. A., Zatorre, R. J., Gauna, K., Nikelski, E. J., Dostie, D., & Evans, A. C. (2000). Speech-like cerebral activity in profoundly deaf people processing signed languages: Implications for the neural basis of human language. *Proceedings of the National Academy of Sciences, 97*(25), 13961–13966.

Proksch, J., & Bavelier, D. (2002). Changes in the spatial distribution of visual attention after early deafness. *Journal of Cognitive Neuroscience, 14*(5), 687–701.

Rademacher, J., Morosan, P., Schormann, T., Schleicher, A., Werner, C., Freund, H. J., et al. (2001). Probabilistic mapping and volume measurement of human primary auditory cortex. *NeuroImage, 13*(4), 669–683.

Rauschecker, J. P. (1995). Compensatory plasticity and sensory substitution in the cerebral cortex. *Trends in Neurosciences, 18*, 36–43.

Recanzone, G. H., Jenkins, W. M., Hradek, G. T., & Merzenich, M. M. (1992). Progressive improvement in discriminative abilities in adult owl monkeys performing a tactile frequency discrimination task. *Journal of Neurophysiology, 67*(5), 1015–1030.

Recanzone, G. H., Merzenich, M. M., Jenkins, W. M., Grajski, K. A., & Dinse, H. R. (1992). Topographic reorganization of the hand representation in cortical area 3b owl monkeys trained in a frequency-discrimination task. *Journal of Neurophysiology, 67*(5), 1031–1056.

Rettenbach, R., Diller, G., & Sireteanu, R. (1999). Do deaf people see better? Texture segmentation and visual search compensate in adult but not in juvenile subjects. *Journal of Cognitive Neuroscience, 11*(5), 560–583.

Rockland, K. S., & Ojima, H. (2003). Multisensory convergence in calcarine visual areas in macaque monkey. *International Journal of Psychophysiology, 50*(1–2), 19–26.

Roder, B. (1999). Improved auditory spatial tuning in blind humans. *Nature, 400*, 162–66.

Rolls, E. T., & Tovee, M. J. (1995). Sparseness of the neuronal representation of stimuli in the primate temporal visual cortex. *Journal of Neurophysiology, 73*(2), 713–726.

Ross, J., Badcock, D. R., & Hayes, A. (2000). Coherent global motion in the absence of coherent velocity signals. *Current Biology, 10*(11), 679–682.

Sacks, O. (1995). To see and not to see. In O. Sacks, *An anthropologist on mars: Seven paradoxical tales* (pp. 108–52). New York: Vintage Books, Random House.

Sadato, N., Okada, T., Honda, M., & Yonekura, Y. (2002). Critical period for cross-modal plasticity in blind humans: A functional MRI study. *NeuroImage, 16*(2), 389–400.

Sadato, N., Pascual-Leone, A., Grafman, J., Deiber, M. P., Ibanez, V., & Hallett, M. (1998). Neural networks for Braille reading by the blind. *Brain, 121*(Pt 7), 1213–1229.

Sadato, N., Pascual-Leone, A., Grafman, J., Ibanez, V., Deiber, M. P., Dold, G., et al. (1996). Activation of the primary visual cortex by Braille reading in blind subjects. *Nature, 380,* 526–528.

Schoups, A., Vogels, R., Qian, N., & Orban, G. (2001). Practising orientation identification improves orientation coding in V1 neurons. *Nature, 412,* 549–553.

Schroeder, C. E. (2004, June). *Cooperative processing of multisensory cues in auditory cortex and classic multisensory regions.* Paper presented at the International Multisensory Research Forum, Barcelona, Spain.

Sharma, A., Dorman, M. F., & Kral, A. (2005). The influence of a sensitive period on central auditory development in children with unilateral and bilateral cochlear implants. *Hearing Research, 203*(1–2), 134–143.

Shepard, R. N. (1990). *Mind sights: Original visual illusions, ambiguities, and other anomalies with a commentary on the play of mind in perception and art.* New York, NY: W. H. Freeman.

Smirnakis, S. M., Brewer, A. A., Schmid, M. C., Tolias, A. S., Schuz, A., Augath, M., et al. (2005). Lack of long-term cortical reorganization after macaque retinal lesions. *Nature, 435,* 300–307.

Sterr, A., Muller, M. M., Elbert, T., Rockstroh, B., Pantev, C., & Taub, E. (1998). Changed perceptions in Braille readers. *Nature, 391,* 134–135.

Sterr, A., Muller, M., Elbert, T., Rockstroh, B., & Taub, E. (1999). Development of cortical reorganization in the somatosensory cortex of adult Braille students. *Electroencephalograhy and Clinical Neurophysiology Supplement, 49,* 292–298.

Sur, M., Angelucci, A., & Sharma, J. (1999). Rewiring cortex: the role of patterned activity in development and plasticity of neocortical circuits. *Journal of Neurobiology, 41*(1), 33–43.

Sur, M., Pallas, S. L., & Roe, A. W. (1990). Cross-modal plasticity in cortical development: Differentiation and specification of sensory neocortex. *Trends in Neurosciences, 13*(13), 227–233.

Svirsky, M. A., Teoh, S. W., & Neuburger, H. (2004). Development of language and speech perception in congenitally, profoundly deaf children as a function of age at cochlear implantation. *Audiology & Neuro-Otology, 9*(4), 224–233.

Valvo, A. (1971). *Sight restoration after long-term blindness: The problems and behavior patterns of visual rehabilitation.* New York: American Foundation for the Blind.

Van Boven, R. W., Hamilton, R. H., Kauffman, T., Keenan, J. P., & Pascual-Leone, A. (2000). Tactile spatial resolution in blind Braille readers. *Neurology, 54,* 2230–36.

von Senden, M. (1960). *Space and sight.* Great Britain: Butler and Tanner.

Voss, P., Lassonde, M., Gougoux, F., Fortin, M., Guillemot, J. P., & Lepore, F. (2004). Early- and late-onset blind individuals show supra-normal auditory abilities in far-space. *Current Biology, 14*(19), 1734–1738.

Waltzman, S. B., & Cohen, N. L. (1998). Cochlear implantation in children younger than 2 years old. *The American Journal of Otology, 19*(2), 158–162.

Westbury, C. F., Zatorre, R. J., & Evans, A. C. (1999). Quantifying variability in the planum temporale: a probability map. *Cerebral Cortex, 9*(4), 392–405.

Wright, M. J., Geffen, G. M., & Geffen, L. B. (1995). Event related potentials during covert orientation of visual attention: Effects of cue validity and directionality. *Biological Psychology, 41*(2), 183–202.

Yang, T., & Maunsell, J. H. (2004). The effect of perceptual learning on neuronal responses in monkey visual area V4. *Journal of Neuroscience, 24*(7), 1617–1626.

Young, M. P., & Yamane, S. (1992). Sparse population coding of faces in the inferotemporal cortex. *Science, 256,* 1327–1331.

III

PERCEPTION, SENSORY SUBSTITUTION, AND COGNITIVE STRATEGIES

9

Functional Equivalence of Spatial Representations From Vision, Touch, and Hearing: Relevance for Sensory Substitution

Jack M. Loomis and Roberta L. Klatzky

One way of coping with blindness and deafness has been some form of sensory substitution—allowing one or more remaining senses to take over the functions lost as a result of the sensory loss. Because the spatial senses of vision, hearing, and touch all convey information about an individual's surroundings, they can substitute for each other to varying extents. In modern times, various inventions have facilitated sensory substitution by providing more information to the remaining senses than would be naturally available. For blind people, Braille now provides access to text, and the long cane has supplemented spatial hearing in the sensing of local features of the environment and obstacles. For deaf people, lip reading and sign language have substituted for the loss of speech perception. Finally, for people who are both deaf and blind, fingerspelling by the sender in the palm of the receiver (Jaffe, 1994) and the Tadoma method of speech reception (Reed et al., 1992) have provided means by which they can receive messages from other people. The advent of electronics in the 20th century has produced major advances in sensory substitution. For example, deaf people are now able to communicate over electronic media using text, and blind people have access to text through speech synthesis (Kurzweil, 1989) and are able to travel through unfamiliar territory with the aid of GPS-based navigation systems (e.g., Loomis, Golledge, & Klatzky, 2001).

Because the three spatial senses have all evolved in response to the demands of acting in 3-D space, it could be expected that all three share common areas of the brain. Indeed, research has shown that there are regions, like striate cortex and parietal cortex, that receive inputs from multiple sensory modalities and are involved in spatial processing (Cohen & Andersen, 2004). Thus, in spite of the huge differences in stimulation, transduction, and peripheral sensory processing, the more abstract spatial representations of the environment might well be functionally equivalent or nearly so. Prosthetic devices that help blind people perform spatial tasks often capitalize on the functional equivalence of spatial representation. In this chapter we discuss the similarities and differences in encoding by the three spatial senses, the functional equivalence (or lack thereof) of the resulting higher-level representations, and the relevance of both for thinking about sensory substitution of vision by touch or hearing in connection with spatial tasks. For other treatments of sensory substitution, see Bach-y-Rita (1972), Bach-y-Rita (2004), Kaczmarek (2000), Kaczmarek and Bach-y-Rita (1995), and Loomis (2003).

TOWARD A THEORY OF VISION SUBSTITUTION

Because the three spatial senses differ greatly in peripheral processing, the hope that touch or hearing, aided by some single device (like a tactile display driven by a video camera), can serve as wholesale replacements for vision is untenable. Thus, vision substitution needs to be directed toward enabling particular functions of everyday life. It is worthwhile reminding ourselves of some of the many diverse functions served by vision. We use vision to read text, comprehend scenes and pictures, recognize objects and people, comprehend extended events, control locomotion with respect to the immediate environment, plan and regulate travel over large distances, perform complex manual tasks, engage in skilled athletic activity (e.g., tennis), and interpret nonverbal signals during social interaction. These different functions vary tremendously in their informational requirements.

A principled approach to using touch or hearing as a substitute for vision in connection with a particular function is to (a) identify what optical, acoustic, or other information is most effective in enabling that function and (b) determine how to transform this information into sensory signals that are effectively coupled to the receiving modality. The first step, then, requires research to identify what information is necessary to perform the function. For example, consider obstacle avoidance. A person walking through a cluttered environment is able to avoid bumping into obstacles by using vision with sufficient lighting. Precisely what visual information or other form of information (e.g., ultrasonic, radar) best affords obstacle avoidance? One way to address this question is purely experimental—degrade a person's vision by limiting the field of view and spatial resolution to learn what minimum spatial bandwidth affords performance at some criterion. For example, Cha, Horch, and Normann (1992), have used pixelized displays to determine the least number of points in a square matrix of pixels—each of which varies in luminance according to the corresponding direction in the visual scene—needed for travel through an environment cluttered with obstacles (see also Pelli, 1987). An alternative approach is theoretical: Given some form of energy (e.g., microwave radiation) and sensing device (e.g, radar emitter and sensor), use ideal observer analysis to determine the least information required by a perfect perceiver to perform the task at hand. Unfortunately, we are a long way from understanding the informational requirements of most visually based activities using either of these approaches.

After one has identified what information is needed for a given function, one then needs to couple the information to the receiving modality. This coupling involves two different issues, sensory bandwidth and the specificity of higher-level representation. Sensory bandwidth refers to the information-carrying capacity of the sensory modality being used to communicate information about the external world. For example, the sensory bandwidth of a circumscribed region of retina and associated visual pathway is determined by the field of view, the spatial resolution within the field of view, and the temporal resolution. Given the informational requirements of a particular function (e.g., navigation), it must be determined whether the sensory bandwidth of the receiving modality is adequate to receive this information. For example, no one has seriously considered using the tactile sense to substitute for vision in driving a car. Regardless of how optical information is transformed for display onto the skin, it seems most improbable that the sensory bandwidth of tactile processing will ever be adequate to allow touch to substitute for this particular function. In contrast, simpler functions like using a haptic display coupled to an optical sensor to locate a visual beacon can be accomplished feasibly using tactile substitution of vision.

Even if the receiving modality has adequate sensory bandwidth to accommodate the source information, there is no guarantee that sensory substitution will be successful because the higher-level processes of vision, hearing, and touch are highly specialized for the information that typically comes through those modalities. A good illustration is the difficulty of using vision to substitute for hearing. Even though vision has greater sensory bandwidth than hearing, there is as yet no successful way of using vision to substitute for hearing in reception of the acoustic speech signal. Evidence of this is the enormous challenge in visually deciphering speech spectrograms. There is the often cited case of Victor Zue, an engineering professor who is able to translate visual speech spectrograms into his linguistic descriptions. Although his skill is impressive, what is more significant is the enormous effort required to learn this skill and the length of time needed to decode a speech spectrogram of an utterance that lasts just a couple of seconds. Thus, the difficulty of visually interpreting the acoustic speech signal indicates that presenting an isomorphic representation of the acoustic speech signal does not engage the visual system in a way that facilitates speech processing.

Although we now understand much about the sensory processing of visual, auditory, and haptic perception, we still have much to learn about the perceptual and cognitive representations of the external world created by each of these senses and the cortical mechanisms that underlie these representations. Based on what we know so far, we can identify some of the bases on which one sensory modality might substitute for another in enabling particular functions.

BASES FOR SENSORY SUBSTITUTION

Abstract Meaning

The Holy Grail of sensory substitution is to convert any sensory signal into an abstract representation (its "meaning"), which would suffice for then converting into signals for any other sensory modality. Thus, video signals conveying the content of a complex visual scene could be converted into a high-level description of the surfaces, objects, and intelligent agents within the scene, and these descriptions could be used to generate sequences of text or graphic symbols to be displayed using vision, hearing, or touch. Given the disappointments of research in artificial intelligence in producing anything remotely resembling such high level descriptions in response to unconstrained sensory input, this basis for sensory substitution will remain a dream for years to come.

Functional Equivalence

Because behavior takes place in a common 3-D physical space, coordination between the three spatial senses is to be expected. This means that the internal representations guiding action need to be commensurate to some extent. One possibility is that the modality-specific perceptual representations are isomorphic or nearly so; for example, haptic representations of 3-D shape will bear some similarity to visual representations of 3-D shape. Another possibility is that signals from the spatial senses arrive at a common region of the brain (e.g., posterior parietal cortex; see discussion to follow) and give rise to more amodal spatial representations that have lost the modality-specific features of the input sensory systems. Further treatment of functional equivalence and the lack thereof make up most of the rest of this chapter.

Synesthesia

For a few rare individuals, synesthesia is a strong correlation between perceptual dimensions or features in one sensory modality with perceptual dimensions or features in another (Harrison & Baron-Cohen, 1997; Martino &

Marks, 2001). For example, such an individual may imagine certain colors when hearing certain pitches and experience tactile sensations when hearing voices. Because of its rarity, strong synesthesia cannot be the primary basis for sensory substitution. However, much milder forms occur in the larger population, indicating reliable associations between sensory modalities that might be exploited to produce more compatible mappings between the impaired and substituting modalities. For example, Meijer (1992) has developed a device (the vOICe) that uses hearing to substitute for vision (for description of similar work, see chapter 5, this volume, by Vanlierde, Renier, and De Volder). Because of the natural correspondence between pitch and elevation in space (e.g., low-pitched tones are associated with lower elevation), the device uses the pitch of a pure tone to represent the vertical dimension of a graph or picture. The horizontal dimension of a graph or picture is represented by time or by azimuthal variation in auditory space (e.g, using stereophonic sound). For temporal representation of the horizontal dimension, a visual graph with a 45° diagonal straight line is experienced as a tone of constantly increasing pitch over time. This device is successful for conveying simple 2-D patterns and isolated shapes and is claimed to be of value for some blind people in interpreting complex images and scenes.

Rote Learning

Even when there is neither the possibility of extracting meaning using artificial intelligence algorithms nor the possibility of mapping the source information in a natural way onto the receiving modality, effective sensory substitution is not completely ruled out. Because human beings, especially at a young age, enjoy great neural plasticity and a huge capacity for learning, there is always the possibility that they can learn mappings between two sensory modalities that differ in their higher-level interpretative mechanisms (e.g., use of vision to apprehend complex auditory signals or of hearing to apprehend complex 2-D spatial images). As mentioned earlier, the vOICe developed by Meijer (1992) converts 2-D spatial images into time-varying or space-varying auditory signals. Although the device is based on the natural correspondence between pitch and height in a 2-D figure, it seems unlikely that the higher-level interpretive mechanisms of hearing are suited to handling complex 2-D spatial images usually associated with vision. Still, it is possible that if such a device were used by a blind person from early in life, the person might eventually develop the ability to interpret auditory information from unconstrained natural scenes.

Brain Plasticity

In connection with his seminal work with the Tactile Vision Substitution System, which used video information as input to an electrotactile display, Bach-y-Rita (1967, 1972) speculated that the functional substitution of vision by touch actually involved a reorganization of the brain whereby the incoming somatosensory input came to be linked to and analyzed by visual cortical areas. Though a radical idea at the time, it has recently received confirmation by a variety of studies involving brain imaging and transcranial magnetic stimulation. For example, some of the early work in this area showed that (a) the visual cortex of skilled blind readers of Braille is activated when they are reading Braille (Sadato et al., 1996) and (b) transcranial magnetic stimulation delivered to the visual cortex can interfere with the perception of Braille in blind readers (Cohen et al., 1997). Much of the new and exciting research in this area is presented elsewhere in this volume.

FUNCTIONAL EQUIVALENCE AND EQUIVALENCE LOGIC

Internal representations derived from different input modalities are functionally equivalent if they are equivalent in some of their properties such that they are treated identically by subsequent processes. For an example of functional equivalence at a very early stage of processing, consider two visual stimuli, one a circle of white light with the broad distribution of sunlight and the other a square of white light, which is the additive mixture of just two complementary wavelengths (e.g., 470 and 575 nm). Because of color metamerism established at the level of photoreceptor response, the stimuli are identical in terms of color appearance but different in terms of shape. For all cognitive tasks that depend only on the color, the perceptual representations are equivalent. This perceptual equivalence entails equivalence at many subsequent stages of processing and will be manifest behaviorally in all tasks that rely on color judgments.

Because many processes intervene between the stimuli for perception and consequent behavior, it might seem impossible to use the behavioral methods of cognitive science, like psychophysics, to focus on the perceptual and cognitive representations in the causal chain. But, of course, cognitive science has enjoyed great success in doing just this. There are basically two ways of establishing the existence of internal representations and identifying their properties: working from the stimulus and working from the response. In the former case, one uses knowledge about early processing, some of it from physiological research, to predict how the stimulus is transformed into the internal representation. This is how much of the research on perception proceeds. In working from the response side, one needs to use converging methods and look for evidence of invariance in representation, which is usually established using "equivalence logic." Typically, the converging methods are two or more tasks involving quite different behaviors. So, for example, in Figure 9–1, if two stimuli A and B are adjusted to result in equivalent performance ($P_{1A} = P_{1B}$) on behavioral Task 1 and one assumes that the processes involved in Task 1 de-

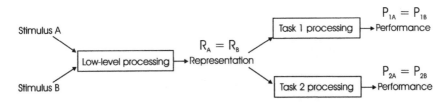

FIGURE 9–1.   Diagram illustrating the use of equivalence logic to support the idea of a common internal R_i representation as the cause of behaviors with performance levels P_{ij}.

pend only on the internal representations R_A and R_B as inputs (i.e., only internal representations that vary with the stimulus are inputs to the task-specific processes), one infers equivalent internal representations ($R_A = R_B$) or an invariance in representation. Then, if another quite different task (here Task 2) relies only on these internal representations as input, one predicts equivalence of performance on this task as well ($P_{2A} = P_{2B}$). Thus, showing that equivalent performance on one task predicts, by way of theory, equivalent performance on another is support for mediation by a common internal representation. Some examples of research using equivalence logic to establish functional equivalence of representations at different levels of visual processing are reported in the following articles: visual sensitivity (Rushton, 1965), the visual icon (Loftus, Johnson, & Shimamura, 1985), and distance perception (Philbeck & Loomis, 1997).

The importance of finding functionally equivalent representations cannot be overstated, for they are critical to decomposing the causal chain from stimulus to response into its processing stages. Once one has identified functionally equivalent representations, which necessarily are of lower dimensionality than the stimuli that give rise to them, they can be used instead of the stimuli in investigating the subsequent processing stages. Low-level perceptual equivalence, like the example of color metamerism, has been an essential tool for understanding higher processes of perception and cognition.

One form of functional equivalence derives from isomorphism of perceptual representations created by the three spatial senses (top of Figure 9–2). Under a range of conditions, it is likely that visual and haptic perception result in nearly isomorphic perceptual representations of 2-D and 3-D shape (Klatzky, Loomis, Lederman, Wake, & Fujita, 1993; Lakatos & Marks 1999; Loomis 1990). The similar perceptual representations are probably the basis both for cross-modal integration in which two senses cooperate in sensing spatial features of an object (Ernst & Banks 2002; Ernst, Banks, & Bülthoff, 2000; Heller, Calcaterra, Green, & Brown, 1999) and for the ease with which subjects can perform cross-modal matching, that is, feeling an object and then recognizing it visually (Abravanel, 1971; Behrmann & Ewell, 2003; Bushnell & Baxt, 1999; Davidson, Abbott, & Gershenfeld, 1974). Although the literature on cross-

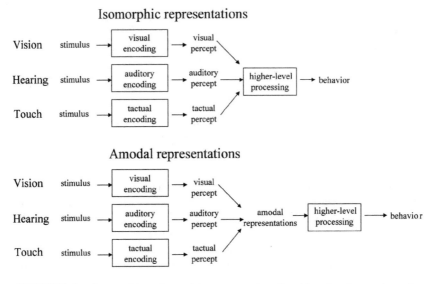

FIGURE 9–2.   Isomorphic and amodal representations for vision, hearing, and touch.

modal integration and transfer involving vision, hearing, and touch goes back decades, this is a topic that has been receiving much attention recently (e.g., Driver & Spence, 1999; Ernst & Banks, 2002; Heller et al., 1999; Martino & Marks, 2000; Massaro & Cohen, 2000; Welch & Warren, 1980).

Another form of functional equivalence would occur with the existence of amodal representations. For 3-D space perception (i.e., perceiving the direction and distance of a visible or audible target) and spatial cognition (i.e., navigating through large-scale space), it is likely that vision, hearing, and touch ultimately cause activation in common areas of the brain, like the posterior parietal cortex, with the result that the perceptual representations created by these three modalities may give rise to amodal spatial representations (bottom of Figure 9–2). For example, seeing an object, hearing sound emitted from it, and touching it with the hand or a stick, might result in the same amodal representation of its location, provided that the perceived locations have been made the same for the three senses. Once an amodal representation has been created, it then might be used to drive cognition or action in a manner that is independent of the sensory modality that gave rise to it; indeed, it might remain active even in absence of the perceptual representations that gave rise to it. Evidence for amodal representations in memory is the absence of recall of the source modality and a degree of interference by subsequent stimuli that is not specific to the source modality. Later we provide an example of this in connection with spatial updating, whereby a person maneuvers through space with respect to a target that is represented only in memory.

Our focus in the rest of chapter is on 2-D and 3-D spatial representations produced by vision, hearing, and touch. Thus, we generally are not interested in nonspatial attributes of the perceptual representations, such as color for vision, pitch for hearing, and texture for touch. Even with this focus on spatial representation, we note that because of encoding differences between the input modalities, the same nominal 2-D or 3-D stimuli (e.g., shapes for touch and vision) generally give rise to perceptual representations that are different, sometimes dramatically so. Despite these differences in encoding, functional equivalence is still possible. If one can compensate for encoding differences by adjusting the stimuli so that the perceptual representations are isomorphic or feed into amodal representations, there remains the possibility that the resulting representations will be functionally equivalent with respect to different tasks that rely on subsequent processing.

FUNCTIONAL EQUIVALENCE OF VISUAL AND TACTUAL REPRESENTATIONS

Because vision and touch both deal with the perception of shape and the perception of 3-D spatial layout, the possibility of functionally equivalent visual and tactual spatial representations has long been considered and investigated. We discuss over the next several pages some of the evidence in connection with the sensing of 2-D patterns and 3-D objects. At the outset, we recognize that the sense of touch comprises two distinct submodalities—the cutaneous sense and the kinesthetic sense (Loomis & Lederman, 1986). Among other things, the cutaneous sense provides information about mechanical forces applied to the skin surface, whereas the kinesthetic sense provides information about the relative orientations of the articulated parts of the body and changes in their orientations. The distinction between the two submodalities is primarily a functional one; at the level of mechanism, there is some blurring of the two—for example, the mechanoreceptors signaling skin stretch contribute to the sensing of hand posture (Johnson, 2002). We prefer to use the term *tactual* rather than *haptic* to refer to sensing by touch in general (Loomis & Lederman, 1986). Although haptic has come to refer to touch sensing, it also has the connotation of active control of sensing involving both the cutaneous and kinesthetic senses. Because we will be discussing cutaneous perception of 2-D patterns where active control of sensing is minimal, we prefer tactual as the encompassing term but use haptic when both submodalities are involved with active sensing.

Cutaneous Perception of 2-D Patterns

Vision and cutaneous perception of 2-D patterns both involve extended 2-D receptive surfaces that can be moved relative to the patterns being sensed. The longstanding use of cutaneous perception by the blind for reading Braille, reading printed text using electrotactile displays like the Optacon (Bliss, Katcher, Rogers, & Shepard, 1970), and recognizing raised graphics symbols indicates some degree of functional equivalence. Loomis (1981, 1982, 1990) has investigated systematically the degree of functional equivalence by comparing cutaneous recognition of raised characters felt by the index finger and visual recognition of the same characters displayed. In these experiments, the distal pad of the index finger was lowered onto the raised character without active exploration. As they are normally viewed, visual characters are more easily recognized than cutaneous patterns because of large differences in spatial resolution of the two senses. Generally, the ratio of spatial extent of the characters relative to the spatial resolution threshold is much greater for vision than for touch. To adjust for these differences, the visual characters in these experiments were either reduced greatly in angular size compared to normal (Loomis, 1990) or were subjected to optical low-pass spatial filtering (blurring) (Loomis, 1981, 1982, 1990). Either way, they were approximately matched to the cutaneous patterns in terms of the amount of sensed spatial detail. Referring back to an earlier section, this means the two modalities were effectively matched in sensory bandwidth. By assumption, this manipulation made the visual and cutaneous spatial representations of the corresponding stimuli functionally equivalent or nearly so with respect to subsequent processing stages.

Figure 9–3A shows the presumed processing stages from sensing to response selection in a model of character recognition that applies to both vision and touch. At the top is the symbolic representation of each character $(A(x,y), B(x,y) \ldots)$ as a function of the two spatial dimensions (x and y). The first two processing stages (spatial filtering and nonlinear compression of intensity) are presumed to result in the perceptual representations of the patterns (i.e., $A''(x,y), B''(x,y), \ldots$). After adjusting for differences in spatial resolution, these representations were presumed equivalent with respect to the subsequent processing stages. Subsequent stages refer to the ignoring of overall intensity in the memory representations of the patterns, computation of dissimilarities using template matching between the stimulus and each memory representation, computation of similarity from dissimilarity, and response selection using the unbiased choice model (Luce, 1963). This last step of the model is represented stochastically, with the probability of responding with each possible response being predicted for each stimulus; the matrix of such values is called a *confusion matrix*. Once the confusion matrix is predicted, overall recognition accuracy for the character set is readily computed as the mean of the diagonal cell entries (probabilities of correct recognition for the different characters). The model is quite successful in accounting for the data for both modalities (Loomis, 1990), but for present purposes, we are interested more in the similarity of recognition performance between the two modalities after matching the perceptual representations in terms of spatial detail. Figure 9–3C gives a scatterplot showing a high degree of similarity in recognition accuracy for the 23 character sets, partially represented in Figure 9–3B. Each number in the

A

Stimulus representation	$A(x,y),\ B(x,y),\ C(x,y)....Z(x,y)$
Spatial filtering	$A'(x,y) = \Sigma_i\,\Sigma_j\,A(i,j)\,\exp(-\pi((x-i)s_xc)^2+(y-j)syc)^2))$
Nonlinear compression of image	$A''(x,y) = A'(x,y)^{0.5}$
Ignore intensity	$A'''(x,y) = A''(x,y) / \Sigma_x\,\Sigma_y\,A''(x,y)$
Dissimilarity of A and B	$D(A,B) = min\Delta_x\Delta_y\,(\Sigma_x\,\Sigma_y(A'''(x,y) - B'''(x+\Delta_x,\ y+\Delta_y))^2)^{0.5}$
Similarity of A and B	$S(A,B) = \exp(-\tau D(A,B))$
Probability of B given A	$P(B|A) = S(A,B) / \Sigma_K\,(S(K,A))$

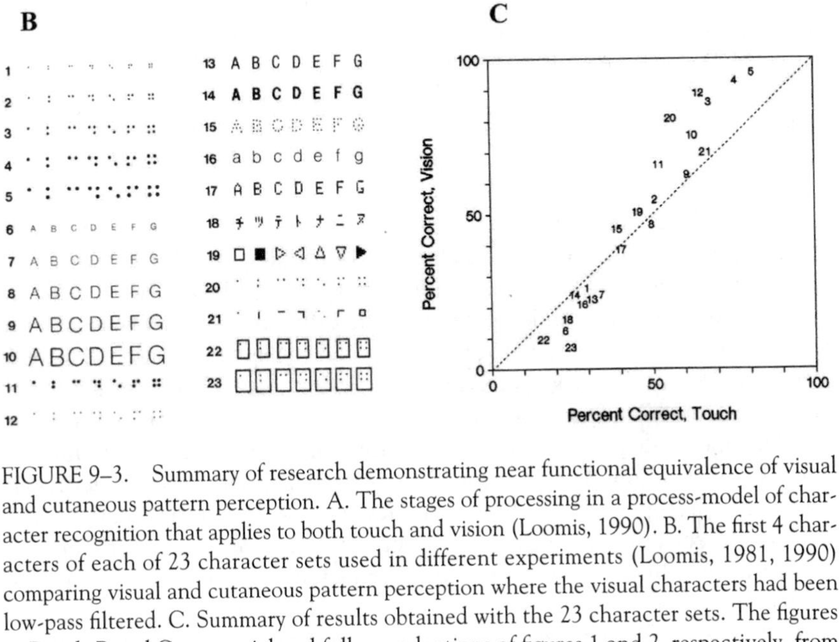

B   **C**

FIGURE 9–3. Summary of research demonstrating near functional equivalence of visual and cutaneous pattern perception. A. The stages of processing in a process-model of character recognition that applies to both touch and vision (Loomis, 1990). B. The first 4 characters of each of 23 character sets used in different experiments (Loomis, 1981, 1990) comparing visual and cutaneous pattern perception where the visual characters had been low-pass filtered. C. Summary of results obtained with the 23 character sets. The figures in Panels B and C are partial and full reproductions of figures 1 and 2, respectively, from Loomis, J. M. (1990). A model of character recognition and legibility. *Journal of Experimental Psychology: Human Perception and Performance, 16*, 106–20, published by the American Psychological Association. Reprinted with permission.

scatterplot represents one of the 23 character sets, and the abscissa and ordinate values are the percentage correct recognition accuracies, averaged over all 26 characters used in each set. Looking more at the details of the confusion matrices further indicates a high degree of functional equivalence beween the cutaneous and visual representations with respect to the subsequent processing stages in Figure 9–3A (Loomis, 1982, 1990). Still, there are some differences between the two senses. The scatterplot of Figure 9–3C indicates that even after adjusting for spatial resolution differences, vision enjoys an advantage at the upper levels of performance. Loomis (1981, 1990) has speculated that this advantage for vision accrues from the much greater amount of experience with visual character recognition. Another difference between the two senses is that the probabilities of certain confusions exhibit some small but systematic differences (Loomis, 1982).

In follow-up work Loomis (1993) has demonstrated a much clearer difference between the two senses with respect to character recognition, a difference traced to sensory processing differences. Figure 9–4A shows the stimuli and results of the experiment. The stimuli were normal and modified Braille characters presented either in isolation or in the presence of surrounds. For illustration, the four leftmost stimuli in Figure 9–4A show the Braille character T, both in isolation and in the presence of surrounds varying from sparse dots to a solid surround; the four rightmost stimuli show the modified Braille character T, this time with lines connecting the dots, in isolation and in the presence of the same three surrounds. The visual stimuli were appropriately blurred, as in the research mentioned above. The ordinate shows average recognition accuracy averaged over the 26 Braille characters as a function of the eight conditions. Visual and tactual performance was comparable for the isolated Braille characters. However, the two senses differed dramatically in how recognition performance varied as the surround changed from one with sparse dots to one with solid lines—touch improved, and vision worsened.

The likely explanation is related to basic differences between touch and vision at the earliest stages of processing. Figure 9–4B is a qualitative depiction of this difference. Whereas increasing the spatial density of points of light increases the total magnitude of neural signals, the opposite is true of touch, at least for small scale patterns presented to the finger pad. The continuum mechanics model of Phillips & Johnson (1981b) predicts that the forces acting on the mechanoreceptors in the finger pad decrease at the interior sections of a solid line. Electrophysiological (EEG) recordings from first-order afferents in monkeys show that the forces are indeed reflected in the neural responses of mechanoreceptors (Phillips & Johnson, 1981a). Figure 9–4B for touch shows qualitatively the force profiles for the dotted and solid surrounds used in the experiment by Loomis (1993). The model of character recognition (Loomis, 1990) accurately predicts the pattern of recognition accuracy for vision but not for touch. If, however, the model should be modified to account for the continuum mechanics of the skin, it ought to predict the results for touch as well. The more general point of the present discussion is that, if differences in low-level processing are compensated for by adjusting the stimuli appropriately, it should be possible to create functionally equivalent perceptual representations that are then treated equivalently by subsequent processes, like those in the model in Figure 9–3A.

Haptic Perception of 2-D Patterns

Our treatment of touch and vision so far has dealt only with recognition of simple characters. In this case, involvement of the kinesthetic submodality was

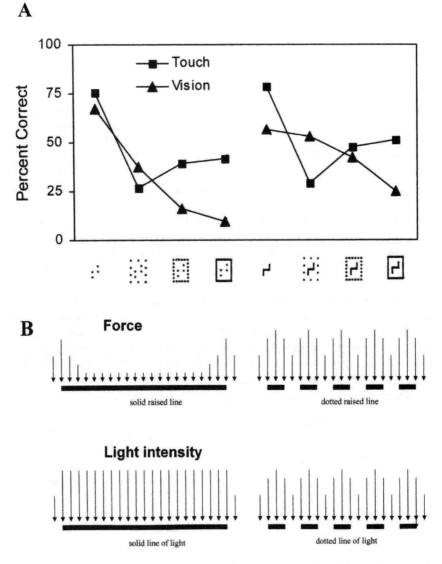

FIGURE 9–4.   A. Results of an experiment demonstrating a clear failure of functional equivalence between visual and cutaneous pattern perception (Loomis, 1993). The eight stimuli along the abscissa represent the eight conditions used in the experiment for both vision and touch. The Braille character "T" is shown in isolation at the far left. The three stimuli to the right of it represent "T" with surrounds ranging from sparse dots to solid lines. The four stimuli to the right represent the same four conditions, this time with modified Braille characters in which lines connect adjacent dots. B. Schematic depiction of how distributions of force on the skin and light intensity over the retina might differ in the response to dotted and solid lines. The figure in Panel A replots data in figure 3 from Loomis, J. M. (1993). Counterexample to the hypothesis of functional similiarity between tactile and visual pattern perception. *Perception & Psychophysics, 54,* 179–84, published by the Psychonomic Society, Inc. Data used with permission.

minimal, for the finger is essentially fixed in position. A more complex form of tactual perception is recognition of raised 2-D pictures. Because the pictures are much larger than the pad of the index finger, scanning movements of the finger along with movements of the hand are needed to sense the entire picture. Might there be functional equivalence between the visual and tactual representations under these conditions? An experiment to examine this possibility was carried out by Loomis, Klatzky, and Lederman (1991) involving the pictures of common objects. Raised pictures were used for touch and pictures were displayed on a computer monitor for vision. Because the field of view of vision is generally much larger than the effective "field of view" of sensing with the finger, the authors used computer software to reduce the instantaneous visual field of view to match the tactual "field of view." As the subject moved a pen over a touch tablet, only a portion of each picture appeared at any one moment within a small aperture fixed in the middle of the computer screen. Single and double visual apertures were used to simulate tactual exploration with one and two fingers; Figure 9–5A shows the tactual and visual "fields of view" for the two finger condition. Subjects participated in both conditions, receiving only half of the picture set in each condition. For both vision and touch, kinesthetic information from the hand and arm was used by the subject to integrate the instantaneous pattern information coming from the eye and fingerpad, respectively. The visual display was also blurred to provide the same spatial information as that conveyed by the finger(s). The recognition accuracies and response latencies in Figure 9–5B indicated nearly identical per-

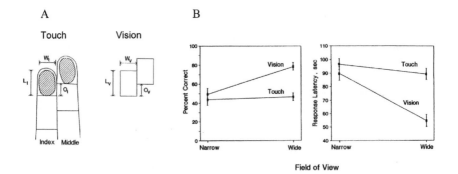

FIGURE 9–5. Summary of an experiment comparing haptic perception and visual perception of pictures in which "field of view" was matched for the two modalities (Loomis et al., 1991). A. Illustration of how computer-generated visual apertures were used to match the "fields of view" of two fingers. B. Recognition accuracies and response latencies for vision and touch in the "one-finger" and "two-finger" conditions. The figures in Panels A and B are reproductions of figures 2 and 4, respectively, from Loomis, J. M., Klatzky, R. L., & Lederman, S. J. (1991). Similarity of tactual and visual picture perception with limited field of view. *Perception, 20,* 167–77, published by Pion Ltd., London. Reprinted with permission.

formance for touch and vision with "one finger." This suggests that the spatiotemporal representations were functionally equivalent or nearly so. However, the data for "two fingers" tell a very different story. Whereas tactual performance was scarcely improved over that with one finger, visual performance improved dramatically with the increase in field of view. It would appear that the effective field of view for touch is much smaller than that for vision. Craig (1985) found a similar difficulty in integrating pattern information across adjacent fingers. It remains to be seen whether receiving much greater practice in recognizing patterns that extend over several fingers would increase the effective tactual field of view.

Haptic Perception of 3-D Shapes

In their chapter in this volume, Klatzky and Lederman discuss at length the haptic perception of 3-D shapes and haptic object recognition in relation to vision (see ch. 10 this volume). A fundamental point emerging from that discussion is that equating these two systems with respect to encoding is very challenging. In addition to differences in spatial resolution, which constrains shape processing, the two modalities differ in accessibility of material properties, cognitive emphasis on material vs. shape, and which surfaces of the object receive attention. As a result, haptic object recognition is much slower than visual object recognition, especially when efforts are made to force participants to use only shape as the basis for haptic recognition (Klatzky et al., 1993). Despite these differences, the perceptual representations are similar enough to provide a basis for cross-modal integration, where two senses cooperate in achieving a description of spatial features of an object (Ernst et al., 2000; Ernst & Banks, 2002; Heller et al., 1999). Similarity of representation is also indicated by people's ability to perform cross-modal matching tasks, as was mentioned earlier (Abravanel, 1971; Behrmann & Ewell, 2003; Davidson et al., 1974).

In lieu of fully equating the encodability of object properties by vision and haptics, some researchers have attempted to use objects that are highly differentiated in both modalities. A study that showed considerable transfer in these conditions was performed by Bushnell and Baxt (1999), who examined the ability of 5- to 6-year-olds to recognize unfamiliar objects in one modality that they had encoded with the other. Items were chosen to be distinguishable in multiple ways, including size, shape, texture, compliance, weight, and complexity. Children performed at about 75% on the haptic-to-visual task and close to 90% on the visual-to-haptic task, relative to 91% and 100% performance on the equivalent intramodal conditions (chance was 50%). Presumably, the transfer process capitalized on the capability of both modalities to encode multiple features to some extent, even if not equivalently. Given the highly differentiated stimulus set, the convergent information from coarse matches on several features would be sufficient to effect transfer.

Newell, Bülthoff, and Ernst (2003) attempted to equate shape encoding between vision and haptics more nearly by adjusting the amount of time given to the two modalities. The stimuli were shapes made from Lego bricks that were either freely touched or viewed within a transparent sphere, which allowed exposure of all surfaces through manipulation without contacting the shape directly. Subjects were given 30 seconds for vision and 60 seconds for touch to study the objects; an intra- or cross-modal recognition test followed. The mean recognition accuracies were 78% (Vision study, Vision test), 80% (Haptic study, Haptic test), 73% (Vision study, Haptic test), and 69% (Haptic study, Vision test). Although there was an advantage (approximately 10% difference) for intra-modal over cross-modal recognition, there was no effect of the learning modality. This suggests that the shape encoding was very nearly equated, with some residual modality specificity. In a comparable recognition experiment using face masks, Casey and Newell (2004) obtained similar results, but this time equating the modalities required a considerable difference in encoding duration: 1 s for vision vs. 4 min for touch!

In contrast to explicit memory tests such as cross-modal matching, Raeles and Ballesteros (1999) used an implicit memory task to study commonality of representation. The implicit task required subjects to identify fragmented pictures of real, common objects as quickly as possible, while the pictures appeared at progressively less fragmented levels. The pictures either were of previously seen or felt real objects or they represented previously unstudied objects. An advantage for previously studied objects, in terms of the level of defragmentation required for identification, would indicate implicit memory. The level of defragmentation needed for recognition was greater for previously unstudied objects than studied objects in both modalities, and more importantly, the required defragmentation levels were identical for visual and haptic pre-exposure.

Although there is an a priori expectation of functionally equivalent visual and haptic representations of shape and some supporting evidence, there is at least one clear difference between visual and haptic processing that works against it. Newell, Ernst, Tjan, and Bülthoff (2001) showed that the front surfaces are more salient in the memory representations of 3-D shapes perceived visually; in stark contrast, for shapes that could be explored manually, back surfaces were more salient in the representations. Both modalities were viewpoint-dependent, in that performance was worse if the object was rotated around its vertical axis between presentation and a recognition test in the same modality. The particularly salient finding was that when there was a modality change between presentation and test, performance improved when the object was rotated front to back along with the modality shift. Thus objects initially explored by touch were recognized better when people saw their back surface, and those initially seen from the front were recognized better when the viewed surface was rotated behind the object.

FUNCTIONAL EQUIVALENCE OF VISUAL, AUDITORY, AND LINGUISTIC REPRESENTATIONS OF LOCATION

Like physical space, the perceptual spaces for vision and hearing are three-dimensional. Perceived locations within visual and auditory space are typically specified using spherical coordinates—two for direction (azimuth and elevation) and one for distance. A perceptual dimension can exhibit error over all or part of its range. Perceptual error can be of two types: bias, which refers to deviation of the mean value from the stimulus value; or noise, which is variability about the mean. Accuracy corresponds inversely to the amount of bias, and precision corresponds inversely to the amount of noise. Both types of error have important consequences for perceptual and cognitive processes that depend upon perceived locations or any of their constituent dimensions. Our treatment here focuses on bias.

Perceived visual direction is generally veridical or very nearly so. The veridicality of perceived visual distance depends greatly on the available distance cues and state of the visual system (e.g, whether both eyes are functioning). However, there is good agreement in the literature that perceived distance is quite accurate out to 20 m or so under full-cue viewing out-of-doors (e.g., Da Silva, 1985; Foley, Ribeiro-Filho, & Da Silva, 2004; Loomis & Knapp, 2003).

Perceived auditory direction is also generally free of bias, but the precision varies with dimension—precision is considerably better for azimuth than for elevation (Gilkey, Good, Ericson, Brinkman, & Stewart, 1995; Wightman & Kistler, 1989). Perceived auditory distance generally exhibits a significant negative bias, even within 20 m. In a grassy field where reverberation cues to distance are relatively weak, perceived auditory distance was found to be roughly 50% of the source distance, which ranged from 3 to 16 m (Loomis, Klatzky, Philbeck, & Golledge, 1998). Similar methods showed more accurate perception (70–80% of source distance) in indoor environments, presumably because of the stronger reverberation cues (e.g., Klatzky, Lippa, Loomis, & Golledge, 2003; see also, Zahorik, 2002).

Perceptual representations of locations in space are generally inputs to higher-level processes serving cognition and action. An auditory example would be perceiving the pattern created by a sound source moving in the frontoparallel plane. Bias and noise associated with the successive perceived locations limit the accuracy with which such patterns can be perceived. This has implications for auditory substitution of vision. The significant noise associated with azimuth and still greater noise associated with elevation mean that attempting to convey complex 2-D visual patterns using a sound source moving in the frontoparallel plane is not likely to be useful for blind people, despite some limited successes (Hollander, 1994; Rodriguez Hernandez, Rodriguez Ramos, Chulani, Burunat, & Gonzalez-Mora, 2003).

Another example of a higher-level process is *spatial updating*, whereby a person perceives a target briefly and then mentally updates its location while moving about without further perceptual information about its location. Results of many studies have shown that after a person views a visual target and then closes both eyes, he or she can update an internal representation of its location while rotating, translating, or both (e.g., Amorim, Glasauer, Corpinot, & Berthoz, 1997; Böök & Gärling, 1981; Farrell & Robertson, 1998; Loomis, Da Silva, Fujita, & Fukusima, 1992; Loomis et al., 1998; Rieser, 1989; Rieser, Ashmead, Talor, & Youngquist, 1990; Simons & Wang, 1998; Thomson, 1983.) Other research findings have demonstrated spatial updating of auditory targets (Ashmead, DeFord, & Northington, 1995; Klatzky et al., 2003; Loomis et al., 1998; Loomis, Lippa, Klatzky, & Golledge, 2002; Speigle & Loomis, 1993) and haptic targets (Barber & Lederman, 1988; Giudice & Loomis, 2006; Hollins & Kelley, 1988; Pasqualotto, Finucane, & Newell, 2005). More recently, researchers have shown that a location specified by spatial language (i.e., an utterance such as "1 o'clock, 3 meters") can also be updated as the person moves around without perceptual access to the environment (Klatzky et al., 2003; Loomis et al., 2002).

One explanation of spatial updating posits the existence of an amodal representation of the target location, which we refer to as a "spatial image." In this explanation, there are three major processing stages: encoding, conversion to an amodal representation, and spatial updating. Figure 9–6 is a block diagram for vision, hearing, and spatial language. First, the modality-specific encoding gives rise to the visual or auditory representations (percepts) of the target locations or the linguistic meaning of the utterance. Through some additional conversion process (perhaps involving activation of posterior parietal cortex), spatial images are created. In the case of perception, these are spatially coincident with the percepts. Once created, the percepts need no longer be present for spatial updating to occur. In the case of language, imagination creates a spatial image based on prior association between perception and language. If the spatial image is indeed amodal in nature, visual percepts, auditory percepts, and linguistic meaning all referring to the same location in space and with

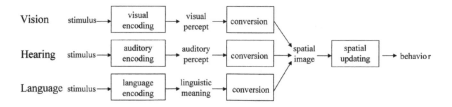

FIGURE 9–6.   Depiction of how visual and auditory perceptual representations and a linguistic representation might be converted into a common amodal representation.

the same precision will exhibit functional equivalence because as inputs to the subsequent updating process they will have equivalent effects.

Under the assumption that there are no biases associated with the conversion from percept or linguistic meaning into the spatial image, there are still distinct biases associated with the encoding and updating stages. An experimental procedure that allows for separate measurement of the encoding and updating biases makes use of spatial updating along two paths, one a direct path to the represented target location and the other an indirect path to the target (Figure 9–7). Because the spatial image is formed prior to movement along either path, the initial spatial image does not depend on the path taken, so encoding biases will be independent of the path taken as well. The centroid (spatial average) of the stopping points of the two paths is taken as an estimate of the encoded location, under the assumption that updating bias is symmetric about the encoded location (see Loomis et al., 2002, for evidence supporting this assumption). Thus, the spatial discrepancy between this location and the target location is the encoding bias. The updating bias, as stated, is the discrepancy between the stopping points of the direct and indirect paths. (We ignore encoding and updating noise here, which complicate the analysis; see Loomis et al., 2002, for the treatment of both noise and bias.)

The results of an outdoor experiment comparing vision and hearing in terms of encoding and spatial updating (Loomis et al., 1998, Experiment 3) are shown in Figure 9–8. Participants saw or heard a target that was either 3 or 10 m away, with four varying azimuths on either side of straight ahead. On some trials, participants attempted to walk directly to the location of the target while updating. On other trials (indirect path), they were led 5 m forward by the experimenter after stimulus exposure and then attempted to walk the rest of the way. The centroids of the stopping points of seven participants in each of the vision and hearing conditions are shown in the figure. The centroids for both direct and indirect paths were much closer to the targets for vision than for hearing, thus revealing larger encoding biases for hearing. These data supported the earlier generalization that visual perception of distance is more accurate than auditory perception of distance in outdoor environments. The near coincidence of the direct and indirect centroids, both for vision and hearing, indicates small updating biases for both. Because the visual targets were more accurately perceived, the updating results are not the ideal test of functional equivalence of the visual and auditory percepts. A better test would have been to have increased the distances of the auditory targets to compensate for the negative encoding biases, thus more closely equating the percepts in terms of distance. We discuss shortly a result in which better compensation for encoding biases was achieved.

The results of an experiment comparing updating performance for targets specified by spatial hearing ("3-D sound") and by spatial language (Loomis et al., 2002) are shown in Figure 9–9. In the spatial language condition, the participant heard an utterance of the form "10 o'clock, 16 feet." Ten sighted

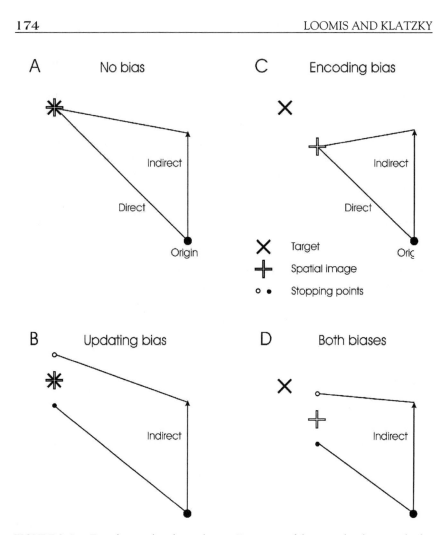

FIGURE 9–7.   Encoding and updating biases. Depiction of direct and indirect paths for various combinations of encoding bias and updating bias. When there is no encoding bias, the spatial image is coincident with the target. When there is no updating bias, the direct and indirect paths intersect at the spatial image (or target). Reproduction of figure 4 from Loomis, J. M., Lippa, Y., Klatzky, R. L., & Golledge, R. G. (2002). Spatial updating of locations specified by 3-D sound and spatial language. *Journal of Experimental Psychology: Learning, Memory, and Cognition, 28,* 335–345, published by the American Psychological Association. Reprinted with permission.

participants and six early blind participants performed updating in both conditions in an outdoor environment. The distance encoding errors for hearing were negative biases, as in the above experiment; the encoding errors for language were minimal. The analysis of updating performance indicated some small but reliable differences between hearing and spatial language, but these

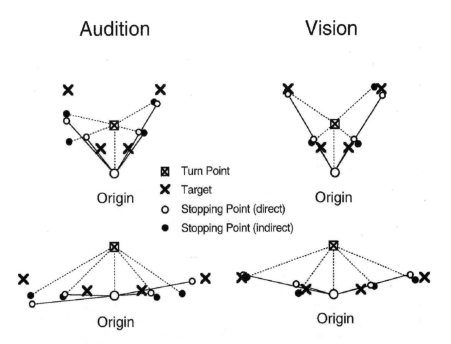

FIGURE 9–8.   Stimulus layout and results of an experiment on spatial updating of visual and auditory targets by Loomis et al., 1998. The participant stood at the origin and saw or heard a target (X) located either 3 or 10 m distant at an azimuth of –80°, –30°, 30°, or 80°. Without further perceptual information about the target, the participant attempted to walk to its location either directly or indirectly. In the latter case, the participant was guided forward 5 m to the turn point and then attempted to walk the rest of the way to the target. The open circles are the centroids of the direct path stopping points, and the closed circles are the centroids for the indirect path stopping points. Reproduction of figure 5.6 from Loomis, J. M., Klatzky, R. L., Golledge, R. G., & Philbeck, J. W. (1999). Human navigation by path integration. In R. G. Golledge (Ed.), *Wayfinding behavior: Cognitive mapping and other spatial processes* (pp. 125–151). Baltimore, MD: Johns Hopkins University Press. Reprinted with permission. [permission requested but not received]

differences were not consistent across the blind and sighted participants. Overall, the results indicate near functional equivalence of the auditory and linguistic representations with respect to updating. This result might be explained by amodal spatial images into which both percepts and linguistic representations are converted.

Updating of locations specified by vision, hearing, and spatial language were compared in a third experiment along the same lines (Klatzky et al., 2003). Whereas the preceding experiments involved updating of only a single target, probably within working memory, this experiment required the participants to spend some time first learning a layout of five target locations, one lay-

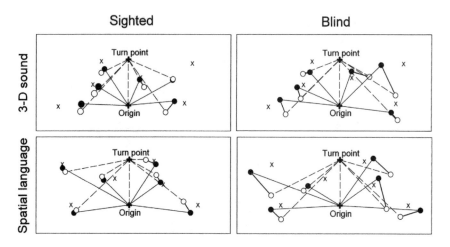

FIGURE 9–9.   Stimulus layout and results of an experiment on spatial updating of auditory targets ("3-D sound") and targets specified by spatial language (Loomis et al., 2002). The participant stood at the origin and then heard a sound at one of the locations (X) or heard an utterance specifying one of the locations (e.g., "2 o'clock, 16 feet"). Without further information about the target, the participant attempted to walk to its location either directly or indirectly. The open circles are the centroids of the indirect path stopping points, and the closed circles are the centroids of the direct path stopping points. Reproduction of figure 7 from Loomis, J. M., Lippa, Y., Klatzky, R. L., & Golledge, R. G. (2002). Spatial updating of locations specified by 3-D sound and spatial language. *Journal of Experimental Psychology: Learning, Memory, and Cognition, 28,* 335–345, published by the American Psychological Association. Reprinted with permission.

out for each input modality. Also, unlike the preceding experiments, this experiment was conducted indoors. Visual targets were identified by labels at the target locations, and auditory and language targets were identified by spoken labels. After participants had learned the targets to criterion, the updating phase of the experiment took place. On a given trial, participants were told a label, had to recall its location, and then walked to that location along a direct or indirect path. Figure 9–10 shows the data for indirect paths involving a walk forward to the turn point; data for an indirect path to the side were similar. In contrast to the two previous studies, the compression of perceived auditory distance was compensated for by using auditory targets with greater distances than the visual and language targets. As a result of this compensation, the encoded locations were similar for all three modalities, allowing for a good test of functional equivalence. The updating biases were generally larger than those for single targets (the two preceding studies). Spatial language had slightly larger updating biases than the two perceptual modalities, which did not differ. In addition, a separate analysis of updating noise showed larger noise with spatial language. Overall, the results indicated functional

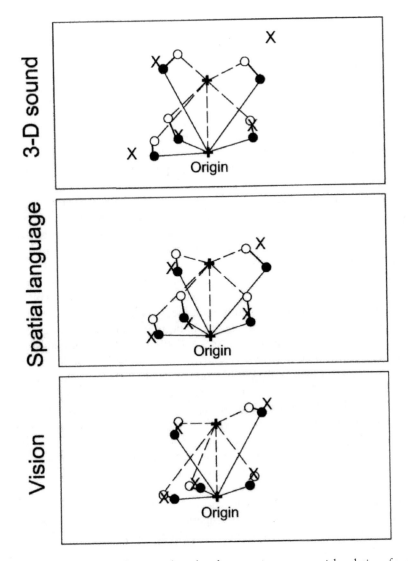

FIGURE 9–10. Stimulus layout and results of an experiment on spatial updating of auditory targets ("3-D sound"), visual targets, and targets specified by spatial language (Klatzky et al., 2003). After learning the five targets in a given modality from the origin, participants demonstrated the ability to update the target locations during the testing phase of the experiment. On each testing trial, the participant attempted to walk to one of the specified targets either directly or along an indirect path, after being led forward 2.5 m from the origin. The open circles are the centroids of the indirect stopping points, and the closed circles are the centroids of the direct stopping points. Reproduction of part of figure 4 from Klatzky, R. L., Lippa, Y., Loomis, J. M., & Golledge, R. G. (2003). Encoding, learning, and spatial updating of multiple object locations specified by 3-D sound, spatial language, and vision. *Experimental Brain Research, 149*, 48–61, published by Springer. Reprinted with permission.

equivalence between the visual and auditory representations and near functional equivalence between language and perceptual representations.

In related work, Avraamides, Loomis, Klatzky, and Golledge (2004) sought further evidence of functional equivalence between visual and language representations. Instead of performing an updating task, participants made allocentric judgments of layouts of four targets in both vision and language conditions. After learning the egocentric coordinates of the targets and their labels, participants made judgments of the distances and directions between targets for the different target pairs. Strong evidence of functional equivalence was obtained in the correlated patterns of response latencies, distance errors, and direction errors.

Because the linguistic interpretations of the utterances in the two previous studies cannot be isomorphic with the visual and auditory perceptual representations, these results support the hypothesis of a more abstract representation, here an amodal spatial image, as the basis for performing both the updating and allocentric judgment tasks.

Where might amodal representations exist in the brain? Posterior parietal cortex (PPC) has a number of characteristics indicating that it is involved in forming spatial representations from multiple modalities, particularly for purposes of action. It receives and integrates inputs from visual, somatosensory, and proprioceptive sources (Ehrsson, Spence, & Passingham, 2004; Graziano, Coke, & Taylor, 2000), and it is active in auditory spatial tasks (Arnott, Binns, Grady, & Alain, 2004; Bushara et al., 1999). Andersen and associates (reviewed in Cohen & Andersen, 2002, 2004) have used single-cell recording and computational methods to characterize spatial maps in PPC and their interrelationships. Central to their theory is the concept of a "gain field"—a modulation of the response of a cortical cell, depending on the position of the eye, head, or body, that provides a mechanism for spatial remapping. Creem and Proffitt (2001) have suggested, based on an extensive review of the literature from behavioral and brain studies, that PPC may encompass two spatial functions: perceptually directed action (how) and conscious localization (where). They have tentatively associated these functions with superior and inferior regions, respectively. In addition, PPC has been associated with visual memory (Sereno, Pitzalis, & Martinez, 2001) and imagery requiring spatial manipulation (Farah, Hammond, Levine, & Calvanio, 1988; Kosslyn & Thompson, 2003).

CONCLUDING REMARKS

Because vision, hearing, and touch operate within a common physical space, it is not surprising that the resulting spatial representations are functionally similar. Surely there is great efficiency in a cognitive architecture for which the same higher-level processes can be deployed, regardless of the sensory modality that is providing information about the surrounding space. However, because vision, hearing, and touch vary greatly in terms of the fidelity and precision with which they represent space, experiments attempting to demonstrate functional equivalence of the resulting spatial representations need to compensate for differences in encoding. In the research reviewed here comparing vision and touch, the sensory bandwidth of vision was matched to that of touch by artificially limiting the spatial resolution and/or field of view. When such adjustments for differences in encoding were made, touch and vision were found to be functionally equivalent or nearly so with respect to pattern perception. Even so, small but significant functional differences remain, but the evidence indicates that a more complete understanding of the early stages of tactual processing might trace these differences to more subtle differences in encoding, leaving the possibility of functional equivalence after further adjustments for these encoding differences.

Other studies that were reviewed were concerned with more cognitive spatial tasks, like spatial updating and judgments of allocentric direction. It is especially with such spatial cognitive tasks that one expects functional equivalence to be strongly supported after correcting for the differences in encoding of vision and hearing. Indeed, the evidence points to functional equivalence between vision and hearing with respect to spatial updating. Going further, the fact that spatial language and spatial perception result in near functional equivalence in tasks of spatial updating and allocentric judgments suggests that the spatial representations are amodal in nature.

The research reviewed is relevant to the still expanding field of sensory substitution. Although there are a number of possible bases for sensory substitution, including abstract meaning and synesthesia, the greatest hopes for successful sensory substitution would seem to lie with those electronic devices that exploit the functional equivalence of the spatial senses (vision, hearing, and touch). On the other hand, demonstrations of functional equivalence, like those reviewed here, do not justify the unbridled optimism for sensory substitution which is common on Web sites and in the popular media. These demonstrations of functional equivalence obtain only when the sensory bandwidth of one of the sensory modalities is artificially reduced to that of the other and when the two modalities are similar in terms of their higher-levels of processing. It is important to recognize that, compared to vision, touch and hearing are enormously deficient in the processing of 2-D and 3-D spatial patterns. In recognition of this, we conclude that sensory substitution using touch and hearing as the receiving modalities will be most successful when based on well-designed evaluation research and an understanding of human perceptual and cognitive processing.

ACKNOWLEDGMENTS

The authors' empirical research reported in this chapter was supported by research grants awarded from the National Eye Institute, from the National Institute of Neurological and Communicative Disorders and Stroke, and from the National Institute of Deafness and Communicative Disorders.

REFERENCES

Abravanel, E. (1971). Active detection of solid-shape information by touch and vision. *Perception & Psychophysics, 10*, 358–360.

Amorim, M.-A., Glasauer, S., Corpinot, K., & Berthoz, A. (1997). Updating an object's orientation and location during nonvisual navigation: A comparison between two processing modes. *Perception & Psychophysics, 59*(3), 404–418.

Arnott, S. R., Binns, M. A., Grady, C. L., & Alain, C. (2004). Assessing the auditory dual-pathway model in humans. *NeuroImage*, 401–408.

Ashmead, D. H., DeFord, L. D., & Northington, A. (1995). Contribution of listeners' approaching motion to auditory distance perception. *Journal of Experimental Psychology: Human Perception and Performance, 21*, 239–256.

Avraamides, M., Loomis, J. M., Klatzky, R. L., & Golledge, R. G. (2004). Functional equivalence of spatial representations derived from vision and language: Evidence from allocentric judgments. *Journal of Experimental Psychology: Learning, Memory, & Cognition, 30*, 801–14.

Bach-y-Rita, P. (1967). Sensory plasticity: Applications to a vision substitution system. *Acta Neurologica Scandanavica, 43*, 417–426.

Bach-y-Rita, P. (1972). *Brain mechanisms in sensory substitution.* New York: Academic Press.

Bach-y-Rita, P. (2004). Tactile sensory substitution studies. *Annals of the New York Academy of Sciences, 1013*, 83–91.

Barber, P. O., & Lederman, S. J. (1988). Encoding direction in manipulatory space and the role of visual experience. *Journal of Visual Impairment & Blindness, 82*, 99–106.

Behrmann, M., & Ewell, C. (2003). Expertise in tactile pattern recognition. *Psychological Science, 14*, 480–486.

Bliss, J. C., Katcher, M. H., Rogers, C. H., & Shepard, R. P. (1970). Optical-to-tactile image conversion for the blind. *IEEE Transactions on Man-Machine Systems, MMS–11*(1), 58–65.

Böök, A., & Gärling, T. (1981). Maintenance of orientation during locomotion in unfamiliar environments. *Journal of Experimental Psychology: Human Perception and Performance, 7*, 995–1006.

Bushara, K. O., Weeks, R. A., Ishii, K., Catalan, M. J., Tian, B., Rauschecker, J. P., et al. (1999). Modality-specific frontal and parietal areas for auditory and visual spatial localization in humans. *Nature Neuroscience, 2*(8), 759–766.

Bushnell, E. W., & Baxt, C. (1999). Children's haptic and cross-modal recognition with familiar and unfamiliar objects. *Journal of Experimental Psychology: Human Perception and Performance, 25*, 1867–1881.

Casey, S. J., & Newell, F. N. (2004, June). The role of familiarity in visual and haptic face recognition. Paper presented at the 2004 Eurohaptics annual meeting in Munich, Germany.

Cha, K., Horch, K. W., & Normann, R. A. (1992). Mobility performance with a pixelized vision system. *Vision Research, 32*, 1367–1372.

Cohen, L. G., Celnik, P., Pascual-Leone, A., Corwell, B., Faiz, L., Dambrosia, J., et al. (1997). Functional relevance of cross-modal plasticity in blind humans. *Nature, 389*, 180–183.

Cohen, Y. E., & Andersen, R. A. (2002). A common reference frame for movement plans in the posterio parietal cortex. *Nature Reviews: Neuroscience, 3*, 553–562.

Cohen, Y. E., & Andersen, R. A. (2004). Multisensory representations of space in the posterior parietal cortex. In G. A. Calvert, C. Spence, & B. E. Stein (Eds.), *The handbook of multisensory processes* (pp. 463–79). Cambridge, MA: MIT Press.

Craig, J. C. (1985). Attending to two fingers: Two hands are better than one. *Perception & Psychophysics, 38,* 496–511.

Creem, S. H., & Proffitt, D. R. (2001). Defining the cortical visual systems: "What", "where" and "how." *Acta Psychologica, 107,* 43–68.

Da Silva, J. A. (1985). Scales for perceived egocentric distance in a large open field: Comparison of three psychophysical methods. *American Journal of Psychology, 98,* 119–144.

Davidson, P. W., Abbott, S., & Gershenfeld, J. (1974). Influence of exploration time on haptic and visual matching of complex shape. *Perception and Psychophysics, 15,* 539–543.

Driver, J., & Spence, C. (1999). Cross-modal links in spatial attention. In G. W. Humphreys, J. Duncan, & A. Treisman (Eds.), *Attention, space, and action: Studies in cognitive neuroscience* (pp. 130–49). New York: Oxford University Press.

Ehrsson, H. H., Spence, C., & Passingham, R. E. (2004). That's my hand! Activity in premotor cortex reflects feeling of ownership of a limb. *Science, 305,* 875–877.

Ernst, M. O., & Banks, M. S. (2002). Humans integrate visual and haptic information in a statistically optimal fashion. *Nature, 415,* 429–433.

Ernst, M. O., Banks, M. S., & Bülthoff, H. H. (2000). Touch can change visual slant perception. *Nature Neuroscience, 3,* 69–73.

Farah, M. J., Hammond, K. M., Levine, D. N., & Calvanio, R. (1988). Visual and spatial mental imagery: Dissociable systems of representation. *Cognitive Psychology, 20,* 439–462.

Farrell, M. J., & Robertson, I. H. (1998). Mental rotation and the automatic updating of body-centered spatial relationships. *Journal of Experimental Psychology: Learning, Memory, and Cognition, 24,* 227–233.

Foley, J. M., Ribeiro-Filho, N. P., & Da Silva, J. A. (2004). Visual perception of extent and the geometry of visual space. *Vision Research, 43,* 2721–2733.

Gilkey, R. H., Good, M. D., Ericson, M. A., Brinkman, J., & Stewart, J. M. (1995). A pointing technique for rapidly collecting localization responses in auditory research. *Behavior Research, Instrumentation, and Computers, 27,* 1–11.

Giudice, N. A., & Loomis, J. M. (2006). Orientation specificity with vision and touch: Map learning, haptic updating, and functional equivalence. *Journal of Vision, 6,* 178a.

Graziano, M. S., Coke, D. F., & Taylor, C. S. (2000). Coding the location of the arm by sight. *Science, 290,* 1782–1786.

Harrison, J., & Baron-Cohen, S. 1997. Synaesthesia: An introduction. In S. Baron-Cohen & J. E. Harrison (Eds.), *Synaesthesia: Classic and contemporary readings.* Malden, MA: Blackwell.

Heller, M. A., Calcaterra, J. A., Green, S. L., & Brown, L. (1999). Intersensory conflict between vision and touch: The response modality dominates when precise, attention-riveting judgments are required. *Perception and Psychophysics, 61,* 1384–1398.

Hollander, A. J. (1994). *An exploration of virtual auditory shape perception.* Unpublished M. S. E. thesis, University of Washington. (Available at http://www.hitl.washington.edu/publications/hollander/)

Hollins, M., & Kelley, E. K. (1988). Spatial updating in blind and sighted people. *Perception & Psychophysics, 43,* 380–388.

Jaffe, D. L. 1994. Evolution of mechanical fingerspelling hands for people who are deaf-blind. *Journal of Rehabilitation Research and Development, 3,* 236–244.

Johnson, K. O. (2002). Neural basis of haptic perception. In H. Pashler & S. Yantis (Eds.), *Stevens handbook of experimental psychology* (3rd ed.): Vol. 1. *Sensation and perception* (pp. 537–583). New York: Wiley.

Kaczmarek, K. A. (2000). Sensory augmentation and substitution. In J. D. Bronzino (Ed.), *CRC handbook of biomedical engineering* (pp. 143.1–143.10). Boca Raton, FL: CRC Press.

Kaczmarek, K. A., & Bach-y-Rita, P. (1995). Tactile displays. In W. Barfield & T. Furness (Eds.), *Virtual environments and advanced interface design.* New York: Oxford University Press.

Klatzky, R. L., Loomis, J. M., Lederman, S. J., Wake, H., & Fujita, N. (1993). Haptic perception of objects and their depictions. *Perception and Psychophysics, 54,* 170–178.

Klatzky, R. L., Lippa, Y., Loomis, J. M., & Golledge, R. G. (2003). Encoding, learning, and spatial updating of multiple object locations specified by 3-D sound, spatial language, and vision. *Experimental Brain Research, 149,* 48–61.

Kosslyn, S. M., & Thompson, W. L. (2003). When is early visual cortex activated during visual mental imagery? *Psychological Bulletin, 129,* 723–746.

Kurzweil, R. (1989). Beyond pattern recognition. *Byte, 14,* 277.

Lakatos, S., & Marks, L. E. (1999). Haptic form perception: Relative salience of local and global features. *Perception and Psychophysics, 61,* 895–908.

Loftus, G. R., Johnson, C. A., & Shimamura, A. P. (1985). How much is an icon worth? *Journal of Experimental Psychology: Human Performance and Perception, 11,* 1–13.

Loomis, J. M. (1981). On the tangibility of letters and braille. *Perception & Psychophysics, 29,* 37–46.

Loomis, J. M. (1982). Analysis of tactile and visual confusion matrices. *Perception & Psychophysics, 31,* 41–52.

Loomis, J. M. (1990). A model of character recognition and legibility. *Journal of Experimental Psychology: Human Perception and Performance, 16,* 106–120.

Loomis, J. M. (1993). Counterexample to the hypothesis of functional similiarity between tactile and visual pattern perception. *Perception & Psychophysics, 54,* 179–184.

Loomis, J. M. (2003). Sensory replacement and sensory substitution: Overview and prospects for the future. In M. C. Roco & W. S. Bainbridge (Eds.), *Converging technologies for improving human performance: Nanotechnology, biotechnology, information technology and cognitive science* (pp. 189–98). Boston, MA: Kluwer Academic.

Loomis, J. M., Da Silva, J. A., Fujita, N., & Fukusima, S. S. (1992). Visual space perception and visually directed action. *Journal of Experimental Psychology: Human Perception and Performance, 18,* 906–921.

Loomis, J. M., Golledge, R. G., & Klatzky, R. L. (2001). GPS-based navigation systems for the visually impaired. In W. Barfield & T. Caudell (Eds.), *Fundamentals of wearable computers and augmented reality* (pp. 429–446). Mahwah, NJ: Lawrence Erlbaum Associates.

Loomis, J. M., Klatzky, R. L., Golledge, R. G., & Philbeck, J. W. (1999). Human navigation by path integration. In R. G. Golledge (Ed.), *Wayfinding: Cognitive mapping and other spatial processes* (pp. 125–151). Baltimore, MD: Johns Hopkins University Press.

Loomis, J. M., Klatzky, R. L., & Lederman, S. J. (1991). Similarity of tactual and visual picture perception with limited field of view. *Perception, 20,* 167–177.

Loomis, J. M., Klatzky, R. L., Philbeck, J. W., & Golledge, R. G. (1998) Assessing auditory distance perception using perceptually directed action. *Perception & Psychophysics, 60,* 966–980.

Loomis, J. M., & Knapp, J. M. (2003). Visual perception of egocentric distance in real and virtual environments. In L. J. Hettinger & M. W. Haas (Eds.), *Virtual and adaptive environments* (pp. 21–46). Mahwah, NJ: Lawrence Erlbaum Associates.

Loomis, J. M., & Lederman, S. J. 1986. Tactual perception. In K. Boff, L. Kaufman, & J. Thomas (Eds.), *Handbook of perception and human performance: Vol. 2. Cognitive processes and performance* (pp. 31.1–31.41). New York: Wiley.

Loomis, J. M., Lippa, Y., Klatzky, R. L., & Golledge, R. G. (2002). Spatial updating of locations specified by 3-D sound and spatial language. *Journal of Experimental Psychology: Learning, Memory, and Cognition, 28,* 335–345.

Luce, R. D. (1963). Detection and recognition. In R. D. Luce, B. R. Bush, & E. Galanter (Eds.), *Handbook of mathematical psychology: Vol. 1* (pp. 103–189). New York: Wiley.

Martino, G., & Marks, L. E. (2000). Cross-modal interaction between vision and touch: The role of synesthetic correspondence. *Perception, 29,* 745–754.

Martino, G., & Marks, L. E. (2001). Synesthesia: Strong and weak. *Current Directions in Psychological Science, 10,* 61–65.

Massaro, D.W., & Cohen, M. M. (2000). Tests of auditory-visual integration efficiency within the framework of the fuzzy logical model of perception. *Journal of the Acoustical Society of America, 108,* 784–789.

Meijer, P. B. L. (1992). An experimental system for auditory image representations. *IEEE Transactions on Biomedical Engineering, 39,* 112–121.

Newell, F. N., Bühlthoff, H. H., & Ernst, M. O. (2003, July). Cross-modal perception of actively explored objects. Paper presented at the 2003 Eurohaptics meeting in Dublin, Ireland.

Newell, F. N., Ernst, M. O., Tjan, B. S., & Bülthoff, H. H. (2001). Viewpoint dependence in visual and haptic object recognition. *Psychological Science, 12,* 37–42.

Pasqualotto, A., Finucane, C. M., & Newell, F. N. (2005). Visual and haptic representations of scenes are updated with observer movement. *Experimental Brain Research, 166,* 481–488.

Pelli, D. (1987). The visual requirements of mobility. In G. C. Woo (Ed.), *Low Vision: Principles and applications* (pp. 134–146). New York: Springer.

Philbeck, J. W., & Loomis, J. M. (1997). Comparison of two indicators of visually perceived egocentric distance under full-cue and reduced-cue conditions. *Journal of Experimental Psychology: Human Perception and Performance, 23,* 72–85.

Phillips, J. R., & Johnson, K. O. (1981a). Tactile spatial resolution: II. Neural representation of bars, edges, and gratings in monkey primary afferents. *Journal of Neurophysiology, 46,* 1192–1203.

Phillips, J. R., & Johnson, K. O. (1981b). Tactile spatial resolution: III. A continuum mechanics model of skin predicting mechanoreceptor responses to bars, edges, and gratings. *Journal of Neurophysiology, 46,* 1204–1225.

Raeles, J. M., & Ballesteros, S. (1999). Impicit and explicit memory for visual and haptic objects: Cross-modal priming depends on structural descriptions. *Journal of Experimental Psychology: Learning, Memory and Cognition, 25,* 644–663.

Reed, C. M., Rabinowitz, W. M., Durlach, N. I., Delhorne, L. A., Braida, L. D., Pemberton, J. C., et al. (1992). Analytic study of the Tadoma method: Improving performance through the use of supplementary tactual displays. *Journal of Speech and Hearing Research, 35,* 450–465.

Rieser, J. J. (1989). Access to knowledge of spatial structure at novel points of observation. *Journal of Experimental Psychology: Learning, Memory, and Cognition, 15,* 1157–1165.

Rieser, J. J., Ashmead, D. H., Talor, C. R., & Youngquist, G. A. (1990). Visual perception and the guidance of locomotion without vision to previously seen targets. *Perception, 19*, 675–689.

Rodriguez Hernandez, A. F., Rodriguez Ramos, L. F., Chulani, H. M., Burunat, E., & Gonzalez-Mora, J. L. (2003, March). Figure perception from real and virtual sounding surfaces. Paper presented at the 18th Technology and Persons with Disabilities Conference, Los Angeles, CA.

Rushton, W. A. H. (1965). The Ferrier lecture: Visual adaptation. *Proceeding of the Royal Society of London B, 162*, 20–46.

Sadato, N., Pascual-Leone, A., Grafman, J., Ibanez, V., Deiber, M-P., Dold, G., et al. (1996). Activation of the primary visual cortex by Braille reading in blind subjects. *Nature, 380*, 526–528.

Sereno, M. I., Pitzalis, S., & Martinez, A. (2001). Mapping of contralateral space in retinotopic coordinates by a parietal cortical area in humans. *Science, 294*, 1350–1354.

Simons, D. J., & Wang, R. F. (1998). Perceiving real-world viewpoint changes. *Psychological Science, 9*, 315–320.

Speigle, J. M., & Loomis, J. M. (1993) Auditory distance perception by translating observers. *Proceedings of IEEE Symposium on Research Frontiers in Virtual Reality* (pp. 92–99). Washington, DC: IEEE.

Thomson, J. A. (1983). Is continuous visual monitoring necessary in visually guided locomotion? *Journal of Experimental Psychology: Human Perception and Performance, 9*, 427–443.

Welch, R. B., & Warren, D. H. (1980). Immediate perceptual response to intersensory discrepancy. *Psychological Bulletin, 88*, 638–667.

Wightman, F. L., & Kistler, D. J. (1989). Headphone simulation of free-field listening. II: Psychophysical validation. *Journal of the Acoustical Society of America, 85*, 868–878.

Zahorik, P. (2002). Assessing auditory distance perception using virtual acoustics. *Journal of the Acoustical Society of America, 111*, 1832–1846.

10

Object Recognition by Touch

Roberta L. Klatzky and Susan J. Lederman

This chapter is organized around a series of questions. At the most general level, we pose the following question: With respect to fundamental research, what do we know about how people recognize objects by touch? Another general question is of broad concern throughout this volume: Does what we know have implications for informing and educating people who have low vision or are blind? With respect to the first question, psychological research has led to a substantial body of knowledge about haptic object recognition. With respect to the second question, we acknowledge considerable challenges in converting this work into a program for education and communication. However, the work offers the promise that if educational tools are designed to take advantage of perceptual capabilities, they will be highly useful to people who are blind or visually impaired.

When we talk informally about using touch we mean using what is technically called *the haptic system*. Haptics is the perceptual system that incorporates sensory information from the skin (cutaneous sensing) and from muscles, tendons, and joints (kinesthetic sensing). Haptic perception is typically active and under the perceiver's own control. As a result, it incorporates information about motor intentions and the outflow of movement commands. For general reviews, the reader is directed to chapters by Loomis and Lederman (1986) and by Klatzky and Lederman (2003).

Haptic object recognition involves a stream of processing that begins with exposure to a real, tangible object and ends with the formation of an internal representation of its properties. The object may or may not be familiar, and recognition may or may not include naming. As an outcome of this process, we know about haptically accessible properties of the object: what it is shaped like, how warm or cool it feels, its roughness, and so forth. Our representation may be inaccurate or incomplete, but it is the culmination of the perceptual processing stream. Here are the questions we address about haptic object recognition, as we pose them throughout the chapter.

1.   *Does visual object recognition provide a model for haptic object recognition?*

Visual and haptic object recognition share basic mechanisms, such as a progression from sensory primitives to abstract representations and use of prior knowledge and context where possible. But these general similarities notwithstanding, the two channels turn out to be quite different, and the emergent model of haptic object identification is fundamentally different from its visual counterpart.

2.   *How does haptic object recognition depend on the way people explore freely?*

Patterns of manual exploration play a critical role in what people know about objects, how they recognize them, and how they think about them once they are apprehended and named. We characterize manual exploration as involving haptic "exploratory procedures" with particular patterns, each with their own costs and benefits.
   The costs and benefits of exploration lead to further questions, including:

> *Are some properties of objects more salient, that is, stronger in our conscious experience, than others?*
>
> *Would we use touch for object recognition if vision is available, and if so, why?*
>
> *Does exploration of an object for purposes of recognition proceed in a stereotyped way, and if so, what determines the progression?*
>
> *Can we capitalize on the fact that multiple properties of objects predict their identity?*

3.   *What happens when we constrain manual exploration in space and/or time?*

We will consider how exploration and object identification change when the finger is covered with a sheath or when people explore with a rigid probe, both of which limit the spatial information available. In both cases, the direct relationship between the pressure layout on the fingertip and objects' spatial properties is eliminated, and the sensing is described as "indirect." A second type of constraint is temporal in nature. We will consider what can be learned about an object with only a very brief exposure.

4.   *Based on the fundamental research on haptic object recognition, what are the implications for education and communication in people who are blind or have low vision?*

The research we describe makes the general point that touch and vision serve complementary roles in recognizing objects. A direct implication is that although there is some utility to adapting visual displays for touch, the nature of the modality favors displaying the 3-D and material properties of objects. We will consider the challenges and opportunities of this approach. One direct implication is that 3-D displays are preferred, when possible, over raised-line drawings for conveying spatial information to the people who are blind or have low vision.

DOES VISUAL OBJECT RECOGNITION PROVIDE A MODEL FOR HAPTIC OBJECT RECOGNITION?

The first of our questions asks whether models of visual object recognition can be directly adapted to account for object recognition by touch. This is important when considering how teaching materials designed for sighted individuals should be adapted for those who are blind or have low vision. But before asking how visually based models should be adapted for haptic object recognition, we must first ask how well people can recognize objects by touch alone. Some years ago, we addressed this preliminary point in a simple study in which blindfolded sighted participants were handed a series of 100 objects—a comb, a mitten, or a tea bag—and asked to name each in turn (Klatzky, Lederman, & Metzger 1985). They could explore in any way they liked. At the time this study was performed, it was not obvious a priori what the outcome would be because touch had been thought of primarily as a poor substitute for vision. Somewhat surprisingly, then, performance was nearly 100% correct, and most responses occurred in 2 s or less. From an information-theoretic perspective, the results pointed to a virtually boundless potential for transmitting information about real, common objects over a haptic channel, given free exploration.

Figure 10–1 presents a general overview model of visual object recognition. It divides processes into three broad classes: Sensory-level processes extract primitive properties, like edges and regions of uniform color or texture. Intermediate-level processes may group these elementary features together, enlarge them, or break them apart. The familiar Gestalt psychological processes such as "grouping by similarity" are good examples. A higher-level process compares the ongoing object description to prior knowledge, ultimately producing feelings of familiarity (or not) and naming.

At first glance, one might feel that this model could be directly adapted for touch. In terms of the broad division of processes, the correspondence is fairly direct. In the details, however, the two modalities reveal themselves to be quite different. One of the principal differences is the emphasis on edge descriptions in vision. Simple line drawings can be identified readily even after brief visual exposure; these stimuli lack color, texture, or movement but still give ample information for the process to be carried to completion.

General Model of Visual Object Recognition

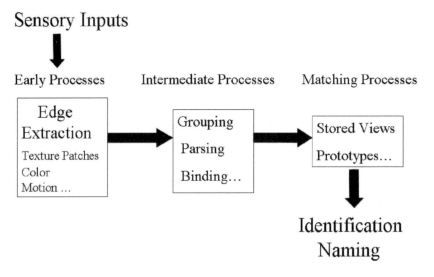

FIGURE 10–1.   A general model of visual object recognition.

Edge information, as we will see, is much harder to come by in haptic object processing and may play a subsidiary role to nonedge properties like roughness or softness when it comes to recognition. Consider the examples shown in Figure 10–2. Extracting the geometry of Braille symbols relies on a tight compromise among multiple constraints: The symbols must be big enough to overcome the blurring of shape by the fingerpad, they must be small enough to fit within the limited size of a single fingerpad, and they must be complex enough to convey the information (number of bits) required for all the alphanumeric characters (Loomis, 1990). People who are blind do read Braille, of course, but it is difficult to attain fluency. As for the second example, recognizing raised-line drawings without vision is difficult for sighted people as well as those who are blind (Lederman, Klatzky, Chataway, & Summers, 1990; Magee & Kennedy, 1980). A major problem is with intermediate-level processes (those that further process the initial pattern of light and dark elements passed forward from the retina of the eye), like parsing the lines into regions and separating the figure from the background. Another problem is that the displays must be explored over time and space, imposing the need for perceptual and/or cognitive integration. Fully 3-D forms, as in the third example, present another problem: controlling the movements that bring new surfaces into reach of the exploring fingers while controlling the exploration itself. In addition, 3-D displays demand spatiotemporal integration, much as do 2-D displays.

What's wrong with this model for touch?

- edge information is primary in vision
- edge information from touch is severely limited

Braille reading
→ limited by finger size, fingertip filtering

Recognizing raised drawings
→ limited by spatial incoherence,
   temporal integration

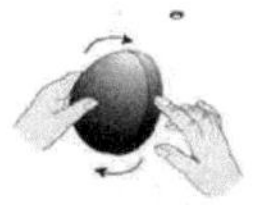

Encoding 3D contours
→ limited by motor constraints,
   kinesthetic precision, temporal
   integration

FIGURE 10–2.   Models of visual object recognition are not appropriate for haptic object recognition.

In the sections to come, we return to the issue of modeling haptic object recognition in comparison to visual recognition. Before doing so, however, we must present considerable data relating to the ways in which people explore objects they are trying to learn about and to identify.

HOW DOES HAPTIC OBJECT RECOGNITION DEPEND ON THE WAY PEOPLE EXPLORE FREELY?

When people want to learn about an object or name it using only the sense of touch, they must explore manually. That is, they manipulate it while moving their hand(s) and finger(s) actively over the object, probing and rubbing it. The regularity of their actions is striking and, as we will see, has implications for the capacities and limitations people have for perceiving objects by touch. We have developed a catalogue of touching actions (Lederman & Klatzky, 1987) that not only describes the patterns of movements that people use to explore objects but also shows how each type of movement can be linked to one or more object properties. To develop this catalogue, we used a match-to-sample task: Participants were first given a sample object and then three comparison objects. They were asked to pick the best match on a targeted object property, like surface roughness or hardness. Their exploratory hand movements were videotaped and proved to be reliably classified into what we called *exploratory procedures* (EPs). An EP is a way of feeling an object that has some invariant characteristic. For example, when people want to find out about an object's roughness, they perform an EP we call *lateral motion*. The invariant aspect of that EP is that the skin moves tangentially across the local surface of the object. In other respects, the EP can vary. People may use one finger or more, they may move quickly or slowly, or they may rub in circles or make a short sweep. The main point is that there is always tangential motion relative to the object's surface. If people are asked about some other property, say, the object's volume, they will not typically execute lateral motion. More likely is that they will enclose the object in one or more hands, which has the invariant characteristic that it maximizes the skin surface contacting the hand.

Figure 10–3 shows, in schematic form, the set of exploratory procedures that we developed. Listed with each EP is the property that elicits it. The figure shows what property is associated with what EP, but it does not explain why the association exists. That question merits a longer discussion. In another source (Klatzky & Lederman, 1999), we have addressed the causes for EP–property relationships to the extent that we have some understanding of them. For example, lateral motion is known to enhance the response of specialized sensory structures under the skin that underlie the sensation of roughness (Johnson & Lamb, 1981). It is this increase in the sensory signal from the relevant receptor population that presumably leads people to use tangential movements when they are asked to make roughness comparisons.

In a further experiment in the same series, we sought to determine what we call *costs* and *benefits* of using different EPs for learning about objects. The benefits have to do with information gathering. On this side of the equation, we ask not only how well an EP delivers information about the associated property (e.g., how well lateral motion provides information about roughness) but also how much information it delivers about other properties as well. On the other side of the equation, the costs of an EP include how long it takes to execute and whether, when it is being performed, other manual movements are locked out, precluding the performance of more than one EP at the same time.

To determine costs and benefits, we asked people to explore in a particular way while they were comparing objects on a particular property. For example, they might be asked to use lateral motion to explore when they were to compare for shape. Or they might be asked to enclose the object when they were to compare for roughness. As you might imagine, not all combinations worked. Rubbing an object on just part of its surface is not very conducive to learning about its overall shape. What that means is that any one EP usually does not provide exhaustive information about all the properties of an object.

The results of this constrained-exploration experiment are shown in Figure 10–4. The rows of the figure are EPs. The first column lists object proper-

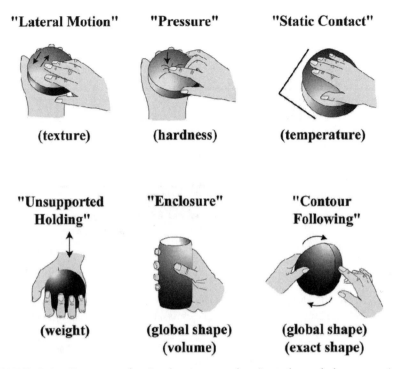

"Lateral Motion"   **"Pressure"**   **"Static Contact"**

(texture)   (hardness)   (temperature)

"Unsupported Holding"   **"Enclosure"**   **"Contour Following"**

(weight)   (global shape) (volume)   (global shape) (exact shape)

FIGURE 10–3.   Depictions of six "exploratory procedures" together with the property(ies) for which each is optimal. From S. J. Lederman and R. L. Klatzky (1987)."Hand movements: A window into haptic object recognition," *Cognitive Psychology, 22*(3), 342–68. Copyright 1987 by Elsevier. Reprinted with permission.

ties. The legend indicates how well people performed when a particular EP was required and a particular property was tested. Performance was classified as at chance (people did no better than guessing), above chance but not maximal for the given property (i.e., it was "sufficient"), maximal for the given property (i.e., the EP was "optimal"), or—in one case only—whether the EP was "necessary," meaning that it was the only EP to give above-chance information about that property.

Several things can be learned from this figure. By looking down a column, one can see how many EPs were sufficient or better for a given property. The columns are arranged so that the properties toward the left can be extracted by more EPs than the properties on the right. Looking at the column headings, it emerges that the material properties of objects (roughness, hardness, and temperature) are more accessible than the geometric properties (weight, volume, and shape), where "accessible" means that they can be extracted by multiple EPs.

By looking across a row, one can see how many properties a given EP was sufficient to extract. Some EPs extract many properties or have considerable

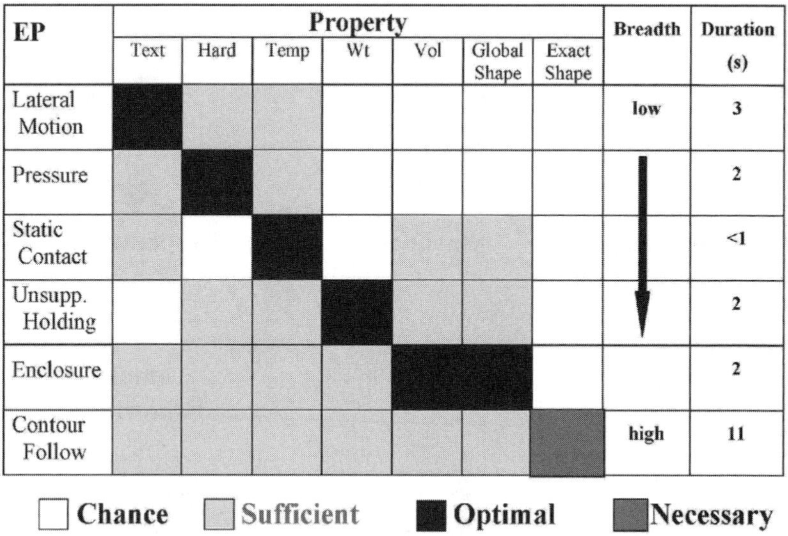

EP	Property							Breadth	Duration (s)
	Text	Hard	Temp	Wt	Vol	Global Shape	Exact Shape		
Lateral Motion	█							low	3
Pressure		█							2
Static Contact			█					↓	<1
Unsupp. Holding				█					2
Enclosure						█			2
Contour Follow							█	high	11

☐ **Chance**   ▨ **Sufficient**   ■ **Optimal**   ▧ **Necessary**

FIGURE 10–4.   Exploratory procedure (EP) costs and benefits in terms of relative EP precision (chance, sufficient, optimal, or necessary), breadth of sufficiency, and average duration.

"breadth." Others are more specialized. The rows are arranged so that broader EPs occur closer to the bottom, as shown by the descending arrow. Finally, the last column shows the average duration of the EP in the original match-to-sample task, where subjects explored freely. From this one can see that the broadest EP, contour following, was typically much slower than the others.

Contour following is the EP that is spontaneously used to extract exact shape and is necessary to achieve precise shape matching. However, the slowness of contour following is part of the message we prefaced above: There is a high cost to extracting shape information by touch. It takes a lot of time. We should also note that shape matching performance is generally much more accurate with vision than with touch (e.g., Walk & Pick, 1981).

ARE SOME PROPERTIES OF OBJECTS MORE SALIENT (STRONGER) IN OUR CONSCIOUS EXPERIENCE THAN OTHERS?

We turn next to a set of questions raised by our cost/benefit analysis of EPs. The first of these questions has to do with the salience, or impact on conscious experience, of one object property as compared to another. The cost–benefit relationships shown in Figure 10–4 indicate that material properties are more broadly available than geometric ones. That is, there are more patterns of exploration that reveal material than geometry. Moreover, precise shape, which is a geometric rather than material property, is encoded relatively inaccurately and very slowly. Does this mean that material is more salient when we feel an object freely, without vision?

To address this question, we and our colleagues Reed and Summers used a sorting task (Klatzky, Lederman, & Reed, 1987; Lederman, Summers, & Klatzky, 1996). We constructed objects that varied along several properties and asked people to sort them into bins according to their similarity. The objects were constructed by simultaneously varying geometric properties (e.g., size, shape), and material properties (e.g., roughness, hardness). There was no objectively correct response, and the dimensions were all equally discriminable. We used the pattern of sorting to determine which properties were most cognitively salient or important to the observer. For example, if size was salient, people should put all the large objects in one bin and all the small ones in another. If so, they would be mixing the objects within a bin with respect to the other properties: shape, roughness, and hardness. On this basis, the sorting pattern could be used to determine a "salience score" for each property, representing the extent to which the objects varying in that property were segregated into different bins.

There is an added manipulation in these experiments; namely, the instructions that participants were given with respect to what constituted similarity. Some subjects were told to think about similarity in terms of how the objects felt. Others were given no particular definition of similarity, but they could only feel the objects. Another group had no definition of similarity but could see the objects as well as feel them. A final group could only feel the objects, but they were told to imagine how the objects would look.

Both studies confirmed our expectations about relative dimensional salience based on costs and benefits. Considering the material properties, the salience score was higher when people felt the objects without vision or visual bias than when they saw them or imagined how they would look. When it came to the geometric properties, the salience score was higher when people saw the objects or imagined seeing them than when they merely touched them.

In short, costs and benefits affect how we think about objects. The cost of extracting geometric properties by haptic exploration means that material properties of objects become more salient when they are touched than when they are seen or visually imagined. Geometric properties become more salient when vision is present—or even imagined—than when the object is only touched.

WOULD WE USE TOUCH FOR OBJECT RECOGNITION IF VISION IS AVAILABLE, AND WHY?

Another implication of EP costs and benefits is that touching carries a cost in terms of exploration time. Why should people use touch, then, if vision is available? The answer is, of course, that it provides information that is needed but is otherwise unavailable or unreliable. Klatzky, Lederman, and Matula (1993) hypothesized that people would touch an object to encode its properties if vision did not provide reliable and accurate information, and if the information was not already available in factual memory. To test this hypothesis, we showed people pairs of real objects and asked them to say which was greater with respect to a particular property: roughness, hardness, apparent warmth, weight, size, or shape. The comparison was either easy or difficult, as in the table below.

Compared property	Difficult pair	Easy pair
Roughness	toast vs. sponge	pineapple vs. plum
Size	golf ball vs. marshmallow	penny vs. CD diskette

The results were striking. When confronted with difficult comparisons about an object's material (roughness, hardness, warmth) and also about its weight (which depends in part on material), participants touched one or both objects more than 60% of the time. When the question was about size or shape, or when it was an easy question about material properties or weight, participants rarely if ever touched the objects. As we expected, the relatively greater cost of haptic exploration than visual examination means that touch will be used only when it is particularly needed for difficult questions about properties that are not readily encoded with vision.

DOES EXPLORATION OF AN OBJECT FOR PURPOSES OF RECOGNITION PROCEED IN A STEREOTYPED WAY, AND IF SO, WHAT DETERMINES THE PROGRESSION?

Another implication of costs and benefits is that some methods of exploration quickly provide a lot of information, at a coarse level, while others more slowly provide precise information. EPs that are applicable broadly (the bottom rows in Figure 10–4) convey information about many properties, but not optimally. Among the broad EPs, contour following has a high cost in duration, leaving unsupported holding (lifting) and enclosure (grasping) as EPs that have high breadth and take relatively little time. Does this mean that those EPs will be executed early in exploration? Alternatively, if people want to find out about a particular property, such as hardness, will they execute the relevant EP (pressure) first? Coexecution is another factor in the mix: Perhaps people execute EPs early when they can be performed in tandem, which again would favor unsupported holding and enclosure (grasping and lifting).

To address this issue, Lederman and Klatzky (1990) gave participants a targeted identification task for which one property of an object was particularly diagnostic. For example, we asked them whether a noodle was a cooked noodle, for which purposes its hardness would be particularly diagnostic. (In order to determine the relative diagnosticity of properties in such questions, we performed an initial questionnaire study.)

We found that when participants were presented with a task of identifying an object for which one property was particularly relevant, they did not initially go after just that property. Rather, participants almost uniformly began the task by grasping and lifting the object—maximizing the properties that could be extracted coarsely. Only when this broadly applicable, low-cost, co-executable pair of EPs were performed did they go after other EPs that were more directly relevant to the question being asked. Thus exploration followed a two-stage sequence: first grasp and lift, then perform specialized exploration for targeted properties. When the targeted properties were associated with enclosure and unsupported holding—that is, they were revealed by grasping and lifting alone—exploration stopped at the first stage.

CAN WE CAPITALIZE ON THE FACT THAT MULTIPLE PROPERTIES OF OBJECTS PREDICT THEIR IDENTITY?

Suppose you are feeling a pear. What properties lead you to know it is a pear? It has a well-known, distinctive shape, it is smooth, and it is hand-sized. Presumably all these features act together to lead you to recognize it as a pear. Shape alone might be sufficient, and in that sense the other features are redundant, but redundant features help. It is well known from visual categorization research (e.g., Garner, 1974) that redundancy speeds object categorization, a phenomenon called redundancy gain.

With touch, redundancy gain is potentially limited by the costs of exploration. Our work has considered two kinds of costs: (a) When EPs cannot be executed together, using one EP to encode an object feature may preclude using another EP. This could block information from target features associated with the second EP. Not being able to perform the second EP means the information will not be available, and however redundant, it cannot speed categorization. (b) When EPs are executed on different regions of an object, the same locking-out can occur, not because they are motorically incompatible but because they are regionally so. In particular, exploring on a sharp edge to encode exact shape may preclude encoding texture, which requires sampling a broader region than is provided by the edge.

We demonstrated both types of blocking effects in a series of experiments. We asked subjects to categorize a set of objects by touch. In some cases, distinct categories were defined by just a single feature, such as size (all As are large, all Bs are medium, all Cs are small). In other cases, either of two features

defined a category (e.g., As are large and rough), and in other cases three features provided a redundant definition (As are large, rough, and circular).
Klatzky, Lederman and Reed (1989) conducted such a manipulation in which
the stimuli were wafer-like shapes with textured surfaces. The shape information could be found only on the edges, which provided relatively little information about texture and hardness. Accordingly, we found that redundancy
gains occurred when there were two redundant features, but when texture,
shape, and hardness were all redundant, there was no further improvement
relative to the two-feature case. We attribute this effect to both types of incompatibility described above. That is, exploring for texture and hardness pre-
cluded exploring for shape, due to movement incompatibility and concentra-
tion on different regions of the object. The failure of three-feature redundancy
to improve over two-feature redundancy is not a general rule, then, but depends
on how compatible the actions are that elicit the features in question.

To test our ideas further that incompatibilities prevent redundancy gain,
we moved to a new set of 3-D stimuli varying in curvature. Shape information was now available all over the surface. This allowed shape and roughness
to be encoded by a single motion, and redundancy gains between the two features were then seen (Lederman, Klatzky, & Reed, 1993).

We (Lederman et al., 1993; Reed, Lederman, & Klatzky, 1990) also introduced experimental manipulations that we called *redundancy withdrawal*
and *orthogonality insertion*. In the redundancy-withdrawal paradigm, we asked
subjects to categorize the same set of stimuli over a long series of trials. We
instructed them that a category was defined by only a single property, like
roughness, but in fact (without mention) there was a second property that
covaried with roughness (e.g., all rough stimuli were also round; all smooth
stimuli were oval). After subjects had performed the task for a while, we
covertly changed the stimulus set, so that the second property was no longer
a reliable cue to the category (now rough and smooth stimuli might both be
round, and only roughness defined category membership). We asked whether
categorization time would increase once previously redundant features were
held constant. If so, this would indicate that participants had been relying on
the redundant secondary dimension without having been instructed to do so.
The increase in response time would be the cost of withdrawing redundancy.
This manipulation confirmed the incompatibilities we had observed. Some
combinations of redundant features produced a cost when redundancy was
withdrawn. These were features that were extracted by compatible EPs in the
sense they could be performed together on the same region. Other feature
combinations showed little or no effect, indicating that participants had been
ignoring the redundant secondary dimension. This occurred when the features
were extracted by EPs that were motorically and/or regionally incompatible.

Orthogonality insertion is the converse of redundancy withdrawal. Now
subjects began the experiment by categorizing stimuli according to a single dimension, with other properties held constant (e.g., by categorizing by rough-

ness with constant shape). At some point in the series of trials, a previously constant attribute began to vary in a manner that was irrelevant to the targeted classification (e.g., shape began to vary while categorization continued on the basis of roughness). If participants spontaneously encoded the newly varying attribute, the time to do the classification should increase. Indeed, just such increases were found when the second attribute was extracted by the same EP that was performed to encode the first attribute.

In short, covariations among object features can speed classification when they are both diagnostic of the objects' categories. Irrelevant patterns of variation among objects from a common category can impair categorization. But whether these effects are seen when objects are categorized by touch depends on the patterns of exploration. The expected interactions among object features—positive or negative—occur only when those features are simultaneously encoded by the same EP or two compatible EPs. These constraints of commonality and compatibility are reflected in our cost–benefit analysis. Clearly, how you choose to explore manually constrains the available information and the perceptual consequences for haptic object recognition.

WHAT HAPPENS WHEN WE CONSTRAIN MANUAL EXPLORATION IN SPACE AND/OR TIME?

Up to this point, we have emphasized free exploration of objects in the service of learning about and identifying them. We turn now to what happens when exploration is constrained, either by limiting the time allowed for exploration or by limiting access to the spatial attributes of objects. Why study such constraints? We do so because the manipulations help us understand more about how object properties are encoded. Limiting the time informs us about the sequence in which object properties emerge and what can be achieved on the basis of early information. Limiting access to objects in a spatial sense tells us about the importance of shape and material information to object identification.

Cutaneous Spatial Constraints

We have approached spatial constraints in two ways, either by blocking the array of stimulation at the fingertip or by locking the joints. To understand the first of these approaches, one must be aware that some sensory receptors underneath the skin of the fingertip respond increasingly as more pressure is applied (within limits of saturation). These receptors are densely packed underneath the skin. When the responses of an entire population of the receptors beneath a skin area are considered at a single point in time, the result is an instantaneous map of the surface pressing against the skin (LaMotte & Srinivasan, 1993). For example, a Braille symbol would excite the receptors that lie below the skin contacting the raised dots more than the receptors that lie below the skin contacting the flat base. Mapping out the excitation would show higher responses in the skin areas where the dots were pressing. This spatial map of pressure is known to be important for perceiving not only geometric features of surfaces, as in Braille, but also for their nongeometric textural features as well (Hsiao, Johnson, & Twombly, 1993).

We asked what would happen to perceptual processing if the spatial pattern of forces on the fingertip were no longer available and people had access only to the summed forces as they excited receptors in skin, muscles, tendons, and joints. This is what happens, for example, when an object is explored with a tool such as a pencil. Our interest in this question stemmed in part from newly developed haptic interfaces, which similarly eliminate the pressure array on the fingertip as people explore with thimble-shaped coverings on the finger or pencil-like probes.

We eliminated the array map by covering the fingertip with a rigid sheath (Lederman & Klatzky, 1999) that capped the fingerpad from the tip of the finger to just above the most distal joint. The participants then performed in a battery of simple sensory tests and more complex haptic tests. The results showed that when the spatial deformation pattern on the fingertip is eliminated, people retain their ability to sense vibration, and they remain sensitive to gross pressure differences, but they become unable to discriminate patterns pressed against the skin. Figure 10–5 shows the decrements in performance that we found. These results, then, show that haptic perception must include the spatially distributed array of cutaneous information if fine spatial details of objects within the scale of the fingertip are to be apprehended.

Kinesthetic Spatial Constraints

In another series of studies, we considered larger-scale spatial variations that would ordinarily be encoded with contour following or the enclosure EP (Lederman & Klatzky, 2004). The subjects' task was to identify a set of common objects that were selected so that all were rigid, fairly smooth, and could not be lifted. The result of this selection was that shape information was critical to identification. We then constrained access to spatial properties by locking the subject's finger joints with splints, thus preventing execution of the enclosure EP, and by reducing the number of fingers that could be used in exploration. In the principal control condition, participants had intact kinesthetic perception from muscles, tendons, and joints, but because they wore a thick glove, they experienced sharply reduced cutaneous information relative to normal. The glove not only eliminated the precise spatial array, as in the previous study, but also damped vibration from contact. Comparisons across conditions, then, allowed us to ask how reductions in kinesthesis affected object recognition while keeping the contribution of cutaneous sensing to a minimum.

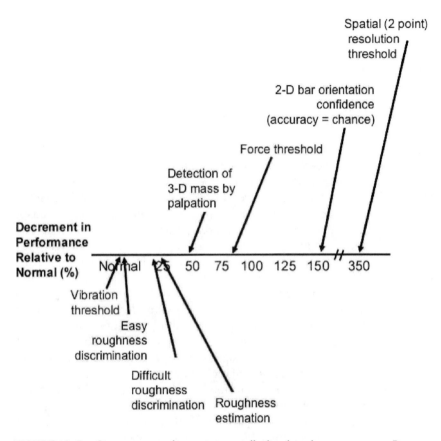

FIGURE 10–5.   Consequences of removing spatially distributed cutaenous cues. Percentage deficit in performance relative to normal baseline for multiple sensory and perceptual tasks (based on data from Lederman & Klatzky, 1999).

The results were straightforward. Losing kinesthesis impairs recognition, whether the constraint comes from reducing the number of fingers contacting the object or from splinting it so that enclosure is impossible. And the more constraints, the more the impairment. Thus, for example, exploring with a single splinted finger (maximum reduction in number of fingers as well as eliminating enclosure) led to worse performance than exploring with five splinted fingers or one unsplinted finger. However, even with such constrained kinesthetic information and substantially limited cutaneous information, subjects were still able to perform with about 80% accuracy or better.

Additional conditions in this study introduced a rigid interface between the hand and the object. They required subjects to wear a rigid sheath capping their finger or to explore the objects with a pencil-shaped probe. Performance now degenerated to about 40%. Further research is needed to understand the reasons the rigid interface reduced performance. One likely contribution is that subjects found it far more difficult to explore the objects under these conditions. In contrast to the rigid probe, a thick but compliant glove no doubt provided limited cutaneous information that helped them to maintain contact with the object while moving around it.

Temporal Constraints: Feature Availability Over Time

The costs and benefits of EPs suggest that features become available at different points in time depending on the duration of exploration and the processes that encode the explored features. In order to determine the relative availability of haptically encoded features, Lederman and Klatzky (1997) adapted a procedure called *visual search* (after Treisman & Gormican, 1988). Our adaptation is called *haptic search*. In the search paradigm, the subject must say whether a target stimulus is present in a display that contains nontarget (i.e., distractor) stimuli. A sample task is to find a horizontal line among vertical distractors. The target (horizontal) may or may not be in the display, and the number of distractors is varied.

The subject's response time for the search task is plotted as a function of the total number of items in the display including the target—if present—and the distractors. If the response time does not vary with the number of items in the display—that is, the response takes the same amount of time, whether there are few distractors or many—the target is said to "pop out." Vertical lines, for example, pop out from among horizontal ones in visual displays. A vertical line is detected at the same speed whether it is alone or among several distractors. The logic of this paradigm is that when a particular feature pops out, that feature is assumed to be extracted by specialized detectors at some point in the perceptual channel. When a feature does not pop out, it must be processed with some cost by nonspecialized processors.

The cost of processing a single item can be estimated from the response-time data as follows. The relation of response time to the number of items in the display is typically linear. That is, each additional item adds some amount of time to the total. The increment in time from a single item is estimated by the slope of the response-time function. The slope, then, indicates how much processing time must be devoted to a particular target in a particular set of distractors. It indicates the relative availability of that target among those distractors. When targets and distractors are maximally different from one another, the slope of the response-time function can be taken as a general estimate of the cost of processing the targeted feature. (The intercept of the function is also relevant but will not be discussed here; see Lederman & Klatzky, 1997.)

In order to adapt visual search to the haptic modality, we used a motorized display (Moore, Broekhoven, Lederman, & Ulug, 1991) that could transport from one to three stimuli up to simultaneously contact the fingers of each of the two hands. The fingers were positioned in finger rests with the fingerpads exposed. On any trial, from one to six fingers were contacted by a stimulus plate. The plate could have a texture, an edge, or a 3-D variation such as a ramp. It could be made of metal or wood. These variations were used to define targets and distractors for a series of trials.

The subject's task was to say whether any of the fingers were in contact with a designated target, such as a rough surface, made of raised elements, among smooth distractors. When present, the target could be the only stimulus, or it could be presented with up to five distractor stimuli (in our example, a rough target could occur with up to five smooth surfaces). On target-absent trials, from one to six fingers were contacted by distractors. This task was performed with 13 target/distractor pairings, all chosen to be highly discriminable. The target/distractor pairs fell into four sets: (a) material discriminations, such as rough surface versus smooth surface or warm (wood) versus cool (aluminum) surface; (b) discrimination of a flat surface from a surface with an abrupt spatial discontinuity, such as a raised bar; (c) discrimination between 2- and 3-D spatial layouts, such as discriminating whether a raised dot was on the left versus the right of an indentation; and (d) discrimination between two continuous 3-D contours, such as a curved surface versus a flat surface.

For each target/distractor combination, we constructed two response-time functions, one for trials in which there was a target present and one in which it was absent. The slopes of these functions indicated first whether the target popped out, and if not, the cost of processing that type of target on each additional finger. Figure 10–6 shows the two most extreme response-time functions and the associated stimuli.

The slopes of the response-time functions varied considerably, from essentially zero (i.e., pop-out) to a half second. The distribution of slope values across the various types of stimuli indicated a progression in the availability of haptic object properties, from material properties to geometric ones. The slopes of the response-time functions for material properties were small (none was greater than 36 ms and several were close to zero). Somewhat higher slope values were obtained for geometric properties that would produce a sharp discontinuity in the surface (e.g., detecting a bar in the middle of an otherwise flat surface among distractors that were entirely flat). These properties could be identified quickly by the differential intensity of pressure across the surface. Finally a third group of slopes occurred when the spatial arrangement of the surface differentiated between targets and distractors (e.g., discriminating between a dot on the right versus left of a central indentation). The slopes were highest in this third group.

These results, then, provide clear convergence with our original cost–benefit analysis. They indicate a distinction between the accessibility of material and geometric properties within the haptic system in terms of their availability over time. There is little or no cost to extracting material information from one additional finger. There is a lot of cost to determining the spatial layout of

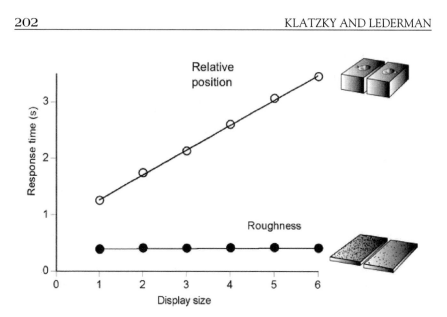

FIGURE 10–6.   Haptic search functions for material (i.e., rough-smooth) and geometric (relative position) tasks. Response time is plotted in seconds as a function of haptic display size. Linear functions are fit to the data. From S. J. Lederman and R. L. Klatzky (1997). "Relative availability of surface and object properties during early haptic processing," *Journal of Experimental Psychology: Human Perception and Performance, 23*(6), 1–28. Copyright 1997 by American Psychological Association. Reprinted with permission.

surface edges in contact with a single finger. When we feel an object, its material emerges before the spatial arrangement of its surface features, even when those features lie within the span of a fingertip.

Temporal Constraints: A Haptic Glance

Another way in which we examined the time-course of haptic feature perception was to sharply limit the amount of time that people had to contact an object and to ask them to identify the object. We call this brief exposure a *haptic glance* (Klatzky & Lederman, 1995). To implement the haptic glance, we asked subjects to move their hand downward along a rod until they contacted the object with the middle fingers. After 100 ms, a tone sounded, indicating that they should withdraw the hand. Total exposure time was approximately 200 ms. The task was then to name the object.

The objects were selected so that either shape or texture was particularly diagnostic, that is, was a strong cue to their identity. For example, a sponge could be identified by texture, or a paper clip by shape. If there was a particularly informative region, such as the lip on a measuring cup, it was placed below the hand so that it would be contacted. An additional variable in the experiment was whether the object was large or small. A large object extended beyond the outstretched fingers, although the most diagnostic area was situated for contact; a small object had an informative feature that lay entirely within the finger span.

The results are shown in Figure 10–7. The first point to note is that people could identify a substantial percentage of the objects despite such time- and space-limited exposure. The second point is that performance depended on both the size of the object's surface and its diagnostic property. Where texture was diagnostic, identification was greater when the object was larger and hence provided more surface area for the fingers to sample. Where shape was diagnostic, performance was better when the object was small, in which case the contours fell entirely within the finger span.

These results suggest that familiar objects with distinctive, diagnostic contours, along with objects for which material is highly diagnostic, can sometimes be processed sufficiently for identification even given brief exposure. A paper clip touched with the fingers, for example, provides a unique, frequently identifiable shape cue. More often, however, identification requires extended exploration, giving rise to the advantages for material properties that we have described.

EMERGENT MODEL OF OBJECT IDENTIFICATION

The research reviewed above allows us to return to the issue with which we began, namely, how people identify objects by touch in comparison to vision.

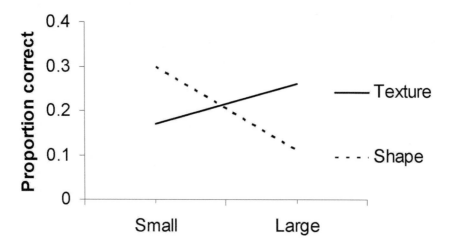

FIGURE 10–7.   Proportion correct object identification via a haptic glance (i.e., ~200 ms) as a function of size of contact area and most diagnostic attribute. From R. L. Klatzky and S. J. Lederman (1995). "Identifying objects from a haptic glance," *Perception and Psychophysics, 57*(8), 1111–23. Copyright 1995 by Psychonomic Society. Reprinted with permission.

Fundamental properties of the haptic model emerge as follows (see Klatzky & Lederman, 2000, 2003, for more extended discussion of the model):

1. Edge information is primary in visual object recognition, and a 3-D object representation can readily be obtained from a 2-D projection. In contrast, material information is, generally speaking, more accessible than geometric information in touch, and fully 3-D information is more accessible than a raised 2-D projection.

2. Touch capitalizes on redundant information about material and geometric properties in order to achieve object categorization. Common object categories are often defined by shape features, as are, for example, tables and chairs (Rosch, 1978). However, material is often diagnostic, and its greater accessibility to touch means that it can play an important role in haptic recognition.

3. Haptic object recognition unfolds over time as objects are explored. Exploration is used as needed; sometimes a simple glance may be sufficient to do the job. The exploratory sequence is governed by general cost–benefit principles and expectations about the object, which render certain features particularly diagnostic and therefore make certain EPs advantageous.

4. Object recognition requires comparison between perceptual input and memory. Models of visual recognition have suggested representations in the form of stored prototypes (Biederman, 1987) or stored views (Tarr & Bülthoff, 1995). The haptic model must, however, consider comparison to previous haptic experiences, or stored "touches."

Based on the Fundamental Research on Haptic Object Recognition, What Are the Implications for Education and Communication in People Who Are Blind or Have Low Vision?

A take-home message from our report is that touch, without vision, richly conveys a sense of real, tangible objects. Moreover, the most accessible and salient features pertain to object material and 3-D geometry. These features are conveyed by texture, heat flow, compliance, weight, and pressure differences that accompany edges or continuous 3-D contours. Communicating such information should be an important goal for purposes of education, aesthetics, or entertainment.

We envision educational programs in which simulation of tangible objects is used for courses in human anatomy, astronomy, mechanics, or molecular biology, for example. Museum artifacts might be presented over the web in arts classes. People who are blind could have access to tangibly guided tools for computer-aided design and modeling applications. Free and flexible exploration of these simulations is enabled in our ideal educational technology.

Unfortunately, this goal is far easier to express than to accomplish. There are many technical challenges. In the past decade or so, a number of devices have been developed for delivering forces to the skin that simulate contact in virtual or remote environments. The world of such force-feedback interfaces is evolving, but the predominant design at present simulates contact with an object at a single point. Textural information is limited; thermal information is nonexistent; objects are not entirely rigid. Maintaining extended contact with the object is difficult when it is felt at a single point. The interactions with these interfaces, in short, resemble those we have described in which people explore objects with a rigid probe or a sheath over the finger. Vibration and gross pressure variations can be felt, but the spatial array is absent, as are non-force-related properties.

Haptic interfaces are needed that stimulate the finger with an array of forces, that provide thermal changes, and that simulate the transition of pressure as the finger crosses a surface boundary. The simulation model must incorporate complex end-effectors and not just contact with a rigid point. To portray complex objects over remote connections, the devices will have to meet increased demands for bandwidth, storage and transmission. Libraries of objects' tangible properties must be amassed.

While these goals are enormously challenging, they are also very exciting because researchers have been developing promising new haptic technologies that may prove valuable. We look forward to educational developments that unite the needs of persons who have low vision or are blind with the marvelous perceptual capabilities of the human haptic system and the dedication of the haptic research community.

REFERENCES

Biederman, I. (1987). Recognition by components: A theory of human image understanding. *Psychological Review, 94*, 115–145.

Garner, W. P. (1974). *The processing of information and structure.* Hillsdale, NJ: Lawrence Erlbaum Associates.

Hsiao, S. S., Johnson, K. O., & Twombly, I. A. (1993). Roughness coding in the somatosensory system. *Acta Psychologica, 84*, 53–67.

Johnson, K. O., & Lamb, G. D. (1981). Neural mechanisms of spatial tactile discrimination: Neural patterns evoked by Braille-like dot patterns in the monkey. *Journal of Physiology, 310*, 117–144.

Klatzky, R. L., & Lederman, S. J. (1995). Identifying objects from a haptic glance. *Perception and Psychophysics, 57*(8), 1111–1123.

Klatzky, R. L., & Lederman, S. J. (1999). The haptic glance: A route to rapid object identification and manipulation. In D. Gopher & A. Koriat (Eds.), *Attention and performance. XVII: Cognitive regulation of performance: Interaction of theory and application* (pp. 165–196). Mahwah, NJ: Lawrence Erlbaum Associates.

Klatzky, R. L., & Lederman, S. J. (2000). L'identification haptique des objets significatifs [The haptic identification of everyday life objects]. In Y. Hatwell, A. Streri, & E. Gentaz (Eds.), *Toucher pour connacetre: Psychologie cognitive de la perception tactile manuelle* [Touching for knowing: Cognitive psychology of tactile manual perception] (pp. 109–28). Paris: Presses Universitaires de France. English translation 2003, Philadelphia: Benjamins.

Klatzky, R. L., & Lederman, S. J. (2003). Touch. In A. F. Healy & R. W. Proctor (Eds.), *Experimental psychology* (pp. 147–76). Vol. 4 in I. B. Weiner (Editor-in-Chief). *Handbook of psychology*. New York: John Wiley & Sons.

Klatzky, R. L., Lederman, S. J., & Matula, D. (1993). Haptic exploration in the presence of vision. *Journal of Experimental Psychology: Human Perception & Performance, 19*(4), 726–743.

Klatzky, R. L., Lederman, S. J., & Metzger, V. (1985). Identifying objects by touch: An "expert system." *Perception & Psychophysics, 37*(4), 299–302.

Klatzky, R., Lederman, S. J., & Reed, C. (1987). There's more to touch than meets the eye: The salience of object attributes for haptics with and without vision. *Journal of Experimental Psychology: General, 116*(4), 356–369.

Klatzky, R., Lederman, S. J., & Reed, C. (1989). Haptic integration of object properties: Texture, hardness, and planar contour. *Journal of Experimental Psychology: Human Perception & Performance, 15*(1), 45–57.

LaMotte, R. H., & Srinivasan, M. A. (1993). Responses of cutaneous mechanoreceptors to the shape of objects applied to the primate fingerpad. *Acta Psychologica, 84,* 41–51.

Lederman, S. J., & Klatzky, R. L. (1987). Hand movements: A window into haptic object recognition. *Cognitive Psychology, 19*(3), 342–368.

Lederman, S. J., & Klatzky, R. L. (1990). Haptic classification of common objects: Knowledge-driven exploration. *Cognitive Psychology, 22,* 421–459.

Lederman, S. J., & Klatzky, R. L. (1997). Relative availability of surface and object properties during early haptic processing. *Journal of Experimental Psychology: Human Perception and Performance, 23*(6), 1–28.

Lederman, S. J., & Klatzky, R. L. (1999). Sensing and displaying spatially distributed fingertip forces in haptic interfaces for teleoperator and virtual environment systems. *Presence: Teleoperators and Virtual Environments, 8*(1), 86–103.

Lederman, S. J., & Klatzky, R. L. (2004). Haptic identification of common objects: Effects of constraining the manual exploration process. *Perception & Psychophysics, 66*(4), 618–628.

Lederman, S., Klatzky, R., Chataway, C., & Summers, C. (1990). Visual mediation and the haptic recognition of twodimensional pictures of common objects. *Perception & Psychophysics, 47*(1), 54–64.

Lederman, S. J., Klatzky, R. L., & Reed, C. L. (1993). Constraints on haptic integration of spatially shared object dimensions. *Perception, 22,* 723–743.

Lederman, S., Summers, C., & Klatzky, R. (1996). Cognitive salience of haptic object properties: Role of modality-encoding bias. *Perception, 25*(8), 983–998.

Loomis, J. M. (1990). A model of character recognition and legibility. *Journal of Experimental Psychology: Human Perception & Performance, 16,* 106–120.

Loomis, J. M., & Lederman, S. J. (1986). Tactual perception. In K. Boff, L. Kaufman, & J. Thomas (Eds.), *Handbook of perception and human performance* (pp. 31-1–31-41). New York: Wiley.

Magee, L., & Kennedy, J. (1980). Exploring pictures tactually. *Nature, 283,* 287–288.

Moore, T., Broekhoven, M., Lederman, S., & Ulug, S. (1991). Q'HAND: A fully automated apparatus for studying haptic processing of spatially distributed inputs. *Behavior Research Methods, Instruments and Computers, 23*(1), 27–35.

Reed, C., Lederman, S. J., & Klatzky, R. L. (1990). Haptic integration of planar size with hardness, texture, and planar contour. *Canadian Journal of Psychology, 44,* 522–545.

Rosch, E. (1978). Principles of categorization. In E. Rosch & B. Lloyd (Eds.), Cognition and categorization (pp. 27–48). Hillsdale, NJ: Lawrence Erlbaum Associates.

Tarr, M. J., & Bülthoff, H. H. (1995). Is human object recognition better described by geon-structural-descriptions or by multiple-views? *Journal of Experimental Psychology: Human Perception and Performance, 21*(6), 1494–1505.

Treisman, A., & Gormican, S. (1988). Feature analysis in early vision: Evidence from search asymmetries. *Psychological Review, 95,* 15–48.

Walk, R. D., & Pick, H. L., Jr. (1981). *Intersensory integration and sensory integration.* New York: Plenum.

11

Training Peripheral Vision to Read

Gordon E. Legge, Sing-Hang Cheung, Susana T. L. Chung, Hye-Won Lee, Joshua Gefroh, and MiYoung Kwon

According to many surveys, difficulty with reading is the principal concern of people entering low-vision clinics. *Low vision* is sometimes defined as the inability to read the newspaper at a normal reading distance (40 cm) with best refractive correction. Age-related macular degeneration (AMD) is the leading cause of low vision in developed countries. A recent study estimated that there are 1.75 million people in the United States with AMD (Eye Diseases Prevalence Research Group, 2004). This number is projected to reach nearly three million by the year 2020. Clinical experience and laboratory research concur in showing that people with damage to the central retina from macular degeneration almost invariably have severe reading problems (Faye, 1984; Fletcher, Schuchard, & Watson, 1999; Legge, Ross, Isenberg, & LaMay, 1992; Legge, Rubin, Pelli, & Schleske, 1985; Whittaker & Lovie-Kitchin, 1993).

Macular degeneration often results in a scotoma (blind spot) in central vision, sometimes covering 10° or more of the visual field including the fovea. Figure 11–1 provides some insight about why reading with a central scotoma is difficult. The left panel shows what information is available in a single glance by a normally sighted person. Although normally sighted people have the strong impression of seeing a whole page of text at once, it has long been known that relatively few letters can be recognized with high accuracy on a single fixation. As illustrated in the left panel of Figure 11–1, the normal "visual span" for reading is about 10 letters. Characters on a line of text outside the visual span cannot be recognized reliably because of decreasing spatial resolution in peripheral vision and because of interference (crowding) between adjacent letters (cf. Bouma, 1970).

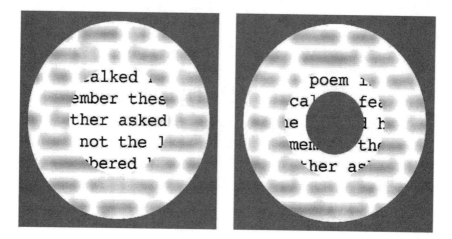

FIGURE 11–1.   Illustration of the visual span for reading. Left: The normal visual span contains about 10 recognizable letters on a line of text, "ther asked." Right: A central scotoma obscures a portion of the normal visual span, reducing the number of adjacent letters that can be recognized.

The right panel of Figure 11–1 shows a simulation of reading with a central blind spot. The two-dimensional circular region of high accuracy for letter recognition (2-D visual span) becomes ring-shaped because of the blind spot. A reader with such a blind spot will need to attend to a line of text above or below the blind spot, or to the small islands of visible text left or right of the blind spot. Regardless of the choice, we expect that the number of letters recognized on each fixation will be low; in other words, the effective visual span for reading will be reduced. As we will discuss later in this chapter, shrinkage of the visual span is likely to have an impact on reading speed. To complicate matters further, retinal disease produces blind spots having a variety of sizes and shapes, and some people have patchy retinas with more than one blind spot.

WHY READING WITH PERIPHERAL
VISION IS DIFFICULT

People with central scotomas have no choice but to use peripheral vision for reading. In this section, we briefly review three issues that are relevant to this very challenging adaptation: adoption of a preferred retinal locus, eye-movement control, and the role of magnification. In the next section, we propose that shrinkage of the visual span is a major factor limiting reading speed in peripheral vision.

Adopting a Preferred Retinal Locus Outside the Scotoma

Because the fovea is now blind, the reader must adopt a region of functioning peripheral retina for eye fixations in reading. Many people with central scotomas do learn to use a new region of retina for fixation, commonly known as the *preferred retinal locus*. There is wide interest in the factors determining the site selection for the preferred retinal locus because of the importance for rehabilitation, but this issue is not yet resolved. Explanations for PRL site selection fall into three broad categories—advantages for function (e.g., reading or mobility), optimization of visual performance (e.g., visual acuity or contrast sensitivity), and anatomical consequences of the retinotopic organization of visual cortex. For a review, see Cheung and Legge (2005). It is generally believed that a preferred retinal locus in the lower visual field below a scotoma is best for reading. Placement of the preferred retinal locus above or below the central scotoma means that letters on a fixated line of text avoid the scotoma. Despite this functional advantage for reading, results of several studies reviewed by Cheung and Legge indicate that 30–60% of AMD patients spontaneously adopt a preferred retinal locus to the left of their scotoma in the visual field. In the right panel of Figure 11–1, this is equivalent to using the portion of the visual span containing the letters "he" as the preferred retinal locus. In such a case, upcoming letters on the line of text immediately to the right of the preferred retinal locus will disappear into the scotoma.

An important issue for rehabilitation is to determine whether it is helpful to train patients with macular degeneration to use a more adaptive peripheral retinal location for reading, sometimes termed "trained retinal locus." Nilsson, Frennesson, and Nilsson (1998) have reported impressive improvements in reading speed when they trained a small group of AMD subjects to use eccentric retina below their scotomas for reading.

Eye-Movement Control

Reading involves a series of eye fixations on words, typically lasting 200–250 ms, separated by saccadic eye movements along the line of text, averaging seven to nine letters in length (cf. Rayner & Pollatsek, 1989, ch. 4). Consider the challenge of adapting oculomotor control to peripheral reading. There is evidence that it is difficult to adapt the saccadic system to use a nonfoveal retinal reference point and overcome the natural reflex to fixate text with the fovea (Peli, 1986; White & Bedell, 1990; Whittaker, Cummings, & Swieson, 1991). Such difficulties in adapting eye-movement control might explain the AMD patient's slow reading; the patient had not yet learned to control eye movements referenced to a peripheral preferred retinal locus.

Perhaps normal reading performance can be restored after oculomotor skills have been retrained. We don't think this is true. One way of assessing the

limiting role of eye movements is to test peripheral reading with a task that
minimizes or eliminates eye movements. In the method of rapid serial visual
presentation popularized by Forster (1970) for studies in cognitive psychology, words of short sentences are presented sequentially at the same place on
the computer screen. Rapid serial visual presentation eliminates the need for
between-word saccades. If problems with these saccades explain the reading
deficits of AMD subjects, we would expect rapid serial visual presentation to
result in much faster reading. Rubin and Turano (1994) did find that AMD
subjects read about 50% faster with rapid serial visual presentation compared
to conventional page text, but this improvement was not nearly enough to
restore AMD subjects to normal reading speeds. Although oculomotor recalibration is undoubtedly an important factor in learning to use peripheral
vision to read, it is certainly not the only factor limiting ultimate reading
performance.

How Much Does Magnification Help?

Another obvious issue in reading with peripheral vision is the decreased resolution of the periphery. Clinical wisdom and results of empirical studies are in
agreement that people with central scotomas benefit from magnification. In the
first study of low-vision reading in our laboratory (Legge et al., 1985), we
showed empirically that high magnification (i.e., large character size) was especially important for people with central scotomas. Unfortunately, the higher
the power of an optical magnifier, the greater the ergonomic demands. An important part of rehabilitation involves training in the effective use of magnifiers.

Figure 11–2 shows plots of reading speed versus print size, and illustrates
the effect of magnification. Print size is given in Snellen notation: 20/20 letters
subtend 5 min-arc and are at the nominal acuity limit for normal vision; 20/60
letters mark the acuity boundary for low vision. The figure shows data for one
subject with normal vision (upper curve) and one person with macular degeneration (lower curve). Both plots have a characteristic form. For the smallest character sizes, reading speed rises steeply as print size increases. Eventually, a critical print size is reached at the bend in the curve. For larger print
sizes, reading speed is constant at its maximum level.

The critical print size is larger for the person with macular degeneration,
demonstrating the need for magnification. Maximum reading speed is given
by the plateaus of the curves (dashed lines). The values here are 305 words
per min for the subject with normal vision and 132 words per min for the
subject with macular degeneration. The plateau levels show that even when
print size no longer limits reading speed, the person with macular degeneration reads more slowly than the reader with normal vision. (It should be noted
that many people with central scotomas from AMD read much more slowly
and have a more irregular curve than the AMD subject whose data are depicted in Figure 11–2.)

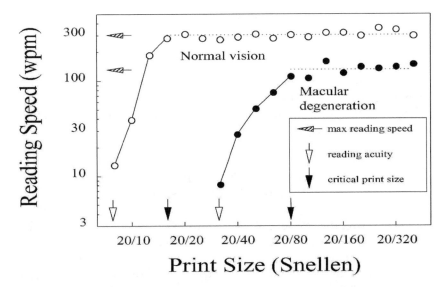

FIGURE 11–2.   Plots of reading speed (words per min) versus print size for a person with normal vision and a person with macular degeneration. Data for each person are summarized by three parameters: reading acuity (open arrow) is the smallest print size that can be read; critical print size (solid arrow) is the smallest print size that can be read at maximum speed; maximum reading speed is the reading speed on the plateau above the critical print size.

What explains the difference in maximum reading speeds between the normally sighted subject and the AMD subject? Because the AMD subject must rely on peripheral vision to read, it is possible that there are inherent differences between central and peripheral vision in the ability to read quickly. Chung, Mansfield, and Legge (1998) addressed this issue by asking the question, "Given adequate magnification and a reading task that minimizes oculomotor demand, can peripheral vision match central vision in reading speed?" Chung and colleagues measured curves of rapid serial visual presentation reading speed versus print size (similar to those in Figure 11–2) in central vision and at five retinal eccentricities ranging from 2.5–20° in the lower visual field. At each retinal eccentricity, we identified the maximum reading speed as the speed achieved on the plateau above the critical print size from curves like those in Figure 11–2. As expected, the critical print size increased in peripheral vision (from 0.16° at the fovea to 2.22° at 20° eccentricity). More importantly, the maximum reading speeds declined by about a factor of 6 from central vision to 20° eccentricity, from about 862 words per min in central vision to 143 words per min at 20° in the lower visual field. (A reading speed of 862 words per min may seem very high, even for central vision. Rapid serial visual presentation is known to yield high reading speeds because it lifts a ceiling on normal reading speed imposed by the need for eye movements. These reading speeds are typically much higher than speeds for static text. For example, Rubin and Turano (1992) reported an average reading speed of 1,171 words per min for rapid serial visual presentation text compared with 303 words per min for static text.)

Our findings imply some inherent limitation in reading with peripheral vision not associated with eye-movement control or print size. This brings us back to the visual span, the number of characters that can be recognized reliably on one fixation (Figure 11–1).

SHRINKAGE OF THE VISUAL SPAN IN PERIPHERAL VISION

Our research over the past several years points to a reduction in the size of the visual span as a key factor limiting peripheral reading speed. Figure 11–3 illustrates how we measure the visual span. We use a letter-recognition task. Our stimuli are trigrams, random strings of three letters. We use strings of letters rather than isolated letters because of their closer approximation to English text. The top row of Figure 11–3 shows that we measure performance for tri-

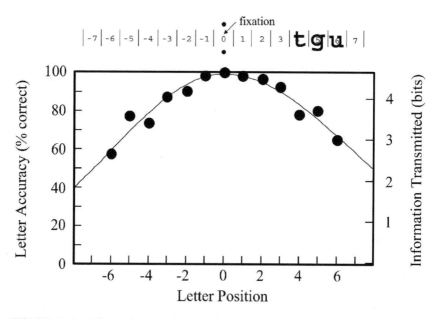

FIGURE 11–3.   The top line is a diagram showing that trigrams for measuring the visual span can be presented left or right of fixation. The graph shows a sample visual-span profile, based on a block of trigram trials. See the text for details of our method for measuring these profiles.

grams at different horizontal locations, with position indicated by the number of letter slots left or right of the midline. In Figure 11–3, "tgu" is positioned with "g" at slot +5 (negative positions refer to letters left of the midline).

In a trial, a trigram is presented very briefly, typically for 100 ms. The subject is required to report all three letters of the trigram in left-to-right order. Across a block of trials, percentage correct is accumulated for each letter slot. We refer to the resulting plot of letter accuracy versus letter position as a *visual-span profile*. The lower graph of Figure 11–3 shows a sample profile. These profiles usually peak at the midline and decline in the left and right visual fields.

We could define the size of the visual span as the breadth of the profile, measured in letter spaces, between points at some criterion accuracy level, e.g., 50% correct. Such a definition is criterion dependent and does not always capture changes in peak amplitude. Instead, we prefer a definition of visual-span size that is akin to measuring the area under the visual-span profile. In Figure 11–3, the right vertical scale of the visual-span profile shows an approximately linear transformation from percentage correct letter recognition to information transmitted in bits, ranging from 0 bits (for chance accuracy of 3.8% correct) to 4.7 bits (for 100% accuracy). (For details of this transformation, see Legge, Mansfield, & Chung, 2001, figure 10 and footnote 9.) We quantify the size of the visual span by summing across the information transmitted in each slot of the visual-span profile. The 13 slots in this sample profile transmit a total of 50.63 bits. This definition of visual-span size in bits takes into account both the breadth and height of the profile because lower or narrower visual span profiles transmit fewer bits of information.

We use a similar procedure to measure visual-span profiles in peripheral vision. The major difference is that, rather than presenting the trigrams on a horizontal line through the point of fixation, the trigrams are presented on a parallel horizontal line, displaced vertically into the upper or lower visual field. For example, for a visual-span profile at 10° in the lower visual field, slot 0 contains a letter on the vertical midline, but 10° below the point of fixation. Slots ±1, ±2, ±3 . . . ±7 are located left and right of slot zero on a horizontal line 10° below the horizontal line through fixation. We also enlarge the trigrams to exceed the critical print size for the retinal eccentricity in question.

We have measured visual span profiles out to 20° in the lower visual field (Legge et al., 2001, exp. 2).

In Figure 11–4 we show how reading speed covaries with the size of the visual span, measured in bits of information transmitted, in peripheral vision. For this graph, the visual span profiles and reading speeds were obtained from different subjects, but there is still a very strong correlation of 0.982 between the group means. The point here is that both the size of the visual span and reading speed decline together with increasing retinal eccentricity. This correlation motivates us to hypothesize that the size of the visual span is a major factor determining reading speed. The correlation between visual-span size and retinal eccentricity also suggests that sensory factors underlie the proper-

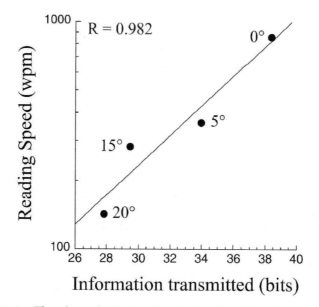

FIGURE 11–4.   The relationship between reading speed and visual-span size in peripheral vision is shown by a scatter plot of mean rapid serial visual presentation reading speeds
and mean visual-span sizes at corresponding retinal eccentricities from 0–20° in the inferior visual field. Visual-span size is given as the number of bits of information transmitted
through the visual-span profile. The reading speeds were measured by Chung et al. (1998)
and the visual spans were measured by Legge et al. (2001).

ties of the visual span. Legge (2007, ch. 3) summarizes data and theory relating
properties of the visual span to the processing characteristics of front-end visual mechanisms.

    The likely extension to low vision is that people with central-field loss who
read with peripheral vision will read slowly because of a diminished visual span.
If the visual span is a sensory bottleneck on reading, can we widen it through
training?

PERCEPTUAL LEARNING

Recent evidence for perceptual learning in the visual pathway suggests that
training may improve letter recognition or reading in peripheral vision. There
has been a flurry of recent interest in perceptual learning, that is, improved
performance on a variety of perceptual tasks following practice (cf. Fahle &
Poggio, 2002). This form of learning is presumed to be based on neural changes
in the perceptual pathways rather than on the adoption of strategic behaviors
to improve performance on a task.

In a study of perceptual learning in normal peripheral vision (Chung, Legge, & Cheung, 2004), we asked whether the visual span can be enlarged through practice, and if so, whether the improvement transfers to reading.

In our study, 18 normally sighted young adults were split into three groups of 6. Everybody received the same pre- and posttests: rapid serial visual presentation reading and visual-span measurements. Testing was conducted at 10° above fixation in the upper visual field, and 10° below fixation in the lower visual field.

The control group had no training sessions. The trained upper group was trained with repeated measurement of visual-span profiles at 10° above fixation. Training sessions occurred on four successive days, with measurement of five visual-span profiles on each day. The trained lower group received similar training at 10° below fixation. Training was done at a single character size for each subject (1.4 times larger than the critical print size), but the reading speeds were tested across a range of character sizes in the pre- and posttests. All subjects were carefully instructed about the importance of maintaining central fixation, and eye-tracking equipment was used to confirm good fixation on a subset of the subjects.

Pre- and posttest visual-span profiles for the 6 subjects in the trained-lower group are shown in Figure 11–5. The bottom row of six panels shows results in the trained field (lower field). In all cases, the posttest profiles (filled

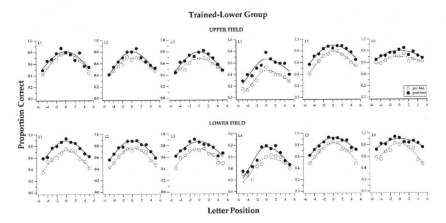

FIGURE 11–5.   Visual-span profiles are shown for 6 trained subjects (L1–L6) in a perceptual learning study (Chung, Legge, & Cheung, 2004). The 6 subjects were trained on the trigram task in peripheral vision at 10° in the lower visual field. The bottom row of panels shows visual spans before training (pretest) and after training (posttest) in the trained lower field. The upper row of panels shows pre- and posttest visual spans at 10° away from fixation in the untrained upper visual field. Reprinted from S. T. L. Chung, G. E. Legge, & S. H. Cheung, Letter recognition and reading speed in peripheral vision benefit from perceptual learning, *Vision Research, 44*, 695–709, Copyright 2004. Reprinted with permission from Elsevier.

symbols) are elevated compared with the pretest profiles (open symbols), representing better trigram letter recognition following training. The panels in the top row compare pre- and posttest results in the untrained upper visual field. In 5 of the 6 subjects, the posttest profiles are elevated, representing a substantial transfer of the training effect.

These results demonstrate an effect of perceptual learning: Training does improve letter recognition in peripheral vision. But, of greater importance to rehabilitation, does the improvement transfer to peripheral reading?

Plots of reading speed versus print size for the same 6 subjects are shown in Figure 11–6. Once again, the bottom row shows results for the trained lower visual field, and the top row for the transfer test in the upper visual field. A comparison of the pretest curves (open symbols) and posttest curves (filled symbols) shows that the effect of training is to shift the curves vertically upward. The importance of these data can be summarized in four points: (a) Following training on the letter-recognition task (trigram task), there is an increase in peripheral reading speed; (b) the training effect transfers to the untrained upper visual field; (c) the training effect generalizes across print sizes, that is, the improvement is not restricted to a single print size; and (d) training does not influence the critical print size. The results were qualitatively similar for the 6 subjects trained in the upper visual field.

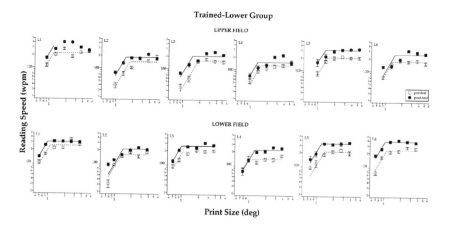

FIGURE 11–6.   Plots of reading speed versus print size are shown for the same 6 subjects (L1–L6) whose visual spans are shown in Figure 11-5. The bottom row of panels shows pre- and posttest reading speeds for the trained lower visual field, and the top row of panels shows pre-and posttest reading speeds for the untrained upper visual field. Testing was done at 10° in both the upper and lower visual fields. The data are from Chung, Legge, and Cheung (2004). Reprinted from S. T. L. Chung, G. E. Legge, & S. H. Cheung, Letter recognition and reading speed in peripheral vision benefit from perceptual learning, *Vision Research, 44*, 695–709, Copyright 2004. Reprinted with permission from Elsevier.

The six subjects in the control group had no training. Their posttest visual-span profiles showed a slight increase in size, presumably from incidental training associated with pre-and posttesting. Their pre- and posttest reading curves showed little or no difference. Overall, the pre–post differences for the control group were much smaller than the corresponding improvements demonstrated by the trained groups.

In Figure 11–7A, we summarize the effect of training on the visual-span profiles by showing the increase in the amount of letter information transmitted (increase in the area under the curve). The bars give the average increase in the number of bits transmitted—1.2 for the control group. Combining the two training groups, there is an increase of about 6 bits of information in the trained field (upper visual field for the trained upper group, and lower visual field for the trained lower group), and about 4 bits in the untrained field. Since 100% correct recognition for one letter position is equivalent to 4.7 bits, the training effect is equivalent to adding more than one perfectly recognized letter to the peripheral visual span. In principle, this extra letter could be quite advantageous for reading.

In Figure 11–7B, we summarize the pre- and posttest reading speeds by showing ratios of improvement. For the no-training group, the ratio is 1.08, which is equivalent to an 8% improvement in reading speed. Combining the

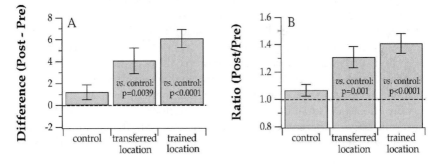

FIGURE 11–7. Summary of post–pre changes in the perceptual learning study by Chung, Legge, and Cheung (2004). The bars show mean values for the control group (no training), for performance at the trained location (combining data for those trained at 10° in the upper visual field and those trained at 10° in the lower visual field), and for performance at the transferred location (combining data across the two training groups). p values are shown for differences at the trained location or transferred location that differ significantly from the control group. A. Difference in the size of the visual span measured as the number of bits of information. B. Ratio of reading speeds with values greater than 1.0 indicating that reading speed was faster in the post test. Error bars show +1 SEM. Reprinted from S. T. L. Chung, G. E. Legge, & S. H. Cheung, Letter recognition and reading speed in peripheral vision benefit from perceptual learning, Vision Research, 44, 695–709. Copyright 2004. Reprinted with permission from Elsevier.

two training groups, the mean ratio is 1.4 (40% improvement) in the trained field, and 1.3 (30% improvement) in the transferred field.

The pre–post improvements summarized in Figure 11–7 mean that, for an average subject who went through the training in either the upper or lower visual field, the visual span got larger by the equivalent of 1+ letters, and reading speed increased by 40%. Reading speed was also improved by 30% in the untrained field. By comparison, for an average subject in the control group, reading speed improved by only 8%. We tracked retention of these improvements on 7 of our subjects over 3 months. Retention remained fairly high, with only a slight loss in performance (Chung et al., 2004).

There were three major conclusions from this study: (a) Reading in normal peripheral vision benefits from perceptual learning, with reading speed increasing by about 40%, an improvement that could be significant for rehabilitation; (b) training can be accomplished with a letter-recognition task; and (c) the training is not highly specific; Rather, it transfers from letter recognition to reading, from the upper to the lower visual field and vice versa, and across print sizes.

DEPLOYING ATTENTION TO PERIPHERAL VISION

Is our perceptual-learning effect an early sensory phenomenon, or is it due to higher level influences such as attention? The strong transfer effects—between upper and lower fields, from letter recognition to reading, and across print sizes—suggest that the perceptual learning may not have its basis in changes in the earliest cortical area V1 or other retinotopically mapped visual areas. Consistent with this supposition, recent electrophysiological studies of visual cortex in monkeys trained in perceptual-learning paradigms have shown that learning effects are small in V1 (Crist, Li, & Gilbert, 2001; Ghose, Yang, & Maunsell, 2002). There is also recent evidence that effects of learning are more evident in extrastriate cortex V4 (Rainer, Lee, & Logothetis, 2004; Yang & Maunsell, 2004).

The transfer effects we observed and the neuroscience findings just cited motivated us to consider attention as a factor mediating perceptual learning. Sperling and Reeves (1981) demonstrated that one can decouple attention from fixation and attend to targets in peripheral vision. Subsequently, there have been many studies of covert attention in which subjects fixate on a target and endeavor to deploy attention to other targets in peripheral vision. Recently it has been proposed that the choice of a site for the preferred retinal locus is determined by attentional hot spots in peripheral vision (Altpeter, Mackeben, & Trauzettel-Klosinski, 2000). The idea is that when individuals lose central vision, they may adopt a preferred retinal locus in peripheral vision that is already intrinsically better at attending. This raises the possibility that our perceptual learning effects might be explained as learning to deploy attention to peripheral vision.

We conducted a follow-up training study (Lee, Gefroh, Legge, & Kwon, 2003) with two major goals: first to replicate the perceptual learning effects observed by Chung et al. (2004), and second, to determine whether we could find correlated improvements in the ability to deploy attention to peripheral vision. If so, then attention might explain the benefit from training we observed.

The design was similar to that of the study by Chung and colleagues (2004), with a no-training group, trained upper and trained lower groups, and this time also a trained central group. (For brevity, this chapter will not deal with results from the trained central group.) As in the Chung et al. study, the pre- and posttests included measurements of reading speed and visual-span profiles. But we also included a measure of peripheral spatial attention.

Our method for assessing peripheral attention is presented in Figure 11–8. We used a lexical decision task in which subjects had to decide whether a designated three-letter string (trigram) was a word or nonword. In all the trials, tri-

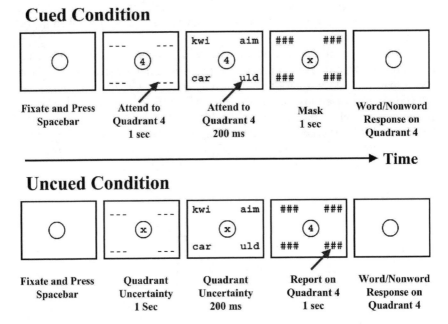

FIGURE 11–8.   Diagram illustrating our method for measuring the deployment of attention to peripheral vision. In each trial, subjects made a lexical decision, deciding whether a trigram in one of the four quadrants was a word or nonword. Attention was evaluated by comparing performance on two types of trials: cued and uncued. The top row shows the sequence of events in the attention ("cued") trials, and the bottom row shows the sequence of events in the uncued trials.

grams were presented simultaneously in the four quadrants, and the subject was required to make a lexical decision on the trigram in only one of the quadrants. Attention was evaluated by comparing performance on two types of trials: cued and uncued. The top row of Figure 11–8 shows the sequence of events in the attention ("cued") trials: fixation, then a number cue from 1 to 4 indicating which quadrant to attend to, then trigrams presented simultaneously in all four quadrants for 200 ms, and finally a postmask. The subject then decided whether the trigram in the cued quadrant was a word or nonword. If the subject was good at deploying attention to peripheral vision, the cue should have facilitated performance on the lexical decision task. The bottom row of Figure 11–8 shows the sequence of events in the uncued condition. The sequence was the same as for the cued condition except that the quadrant number did not appear until after the trigrams had been presented. For these "uncued" trials, the cue did not appear in time for selective deployment of spatial attention but only to designate the target quadrant after the stimuli had disappeared.

We measured the selective deployment of spatial attention to peripheral vision as the difference in lexical-decision performance between blocks of the cued and uncued trials. As in the Chung et al. (2004) study, training consisted purely of letter recognition in the form of visual-span measurements—4 days, five blocks per day. The attention measurement was only taken in the pre- and posttests.

We replicated all the major findings of the Chung et al. (2004) study. Panels A and B of Figure 11–9 summarize the pre–post differences in the size of the visual span (bits of information transmitted) and in reading speed.

The pre–post enlargement of the visual span for the trained subjects (trained visual field 8.79 bits, transfer field 5.15 bits) is even greater than in the Chung et al. (2004) study. The corresponding improvements in reading speed are shown by the ratios in Figure 11–9B. Expressed as percentages, training yielded an 83% increase in speed in the trained field and a 46% increase in

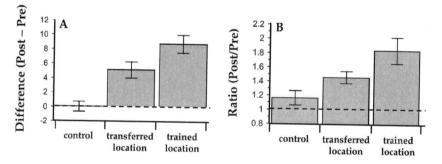

FIGURE 11–9.   Summary of post–pre changes in the study by Lee, Gefroh, Legge, and Kwon (2003), replicating the findings of Chung, Legge, and Cheung (2004). Other details are as in Figure 11-7.

the untrained field. The controls had an average increase of 16% in the posttest. This replication of the Chung et al. (2004) study confirmed that perceptual learning in peripheral vision produces an enlargement of the visual span and a corresponding increase in reading speed.

Now we can address how the training affected ability to deploy attention to peripheral vision.

Recall that attention is evaluated as the difference in performance between the cued and uncued conditions (Figure 11–8). We quantified this performance difference by a peripheral attention index (PAI), defined as: PAI = d'cued— d'uncued where d' (from signal-detection theory) is computed from proportion correct in the cued and uncued trials. A higher value of the peripheral attention index means a bigger advantage for the cued condition, i.e., a benefit attributable to deployment of spatial attention to peripheral vision.

Pre- and posttest values of the peripheral attention index for the no training, trained upper, and trained lower groups are shown in Figure 11–10. If the training effects (enlarged visual span and faster reading) were due to enhanced deployment of attention to peripheral vision, we would expect a greater pre–post difference for the peripheral-training groups. We did find an overall improvement in the peripheral attention index across groups, but no main effect of Group or Group X Pre–Post interaction. In fact, the change in the peripheral attention index was larger for the no training group (.53) than for the

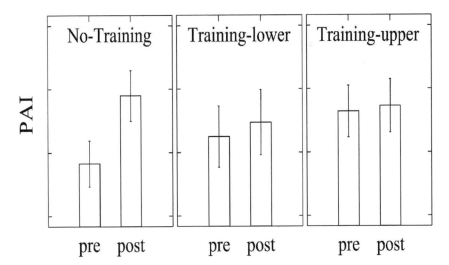

FIGURE 11–10. The peripheral attention index (PAI) is a measure of the effectiveness of deploying attention to peripheral vision: PAI = d'cued − d'uncued where d' is computed from proportion correct in the cued and uncued trials. The bars show mean values of PAI on the pre- and posttests for the control group (no training) and for groups trained at 10° in the upper and lower visual fields. Data from Lee, Gefroh, Legge, and Kwon (2003).

trained upper (.04) or trained lower (.12) groups. In other words, the pre–post changes in the peripheral attention index were uncorrelated with the training effects. Whatever changes we observed in the peripheral attention index were probably associated with the pre- and postattentional test itself, not with the letter-recognition training. We conclude from this experiment that the peripheral training effect for letter recognition and reading is robust, but that it is not accounted for by enhancing the ability to deploy attention to peripheral vision.

We are left with a puzzle to be resolved by future research. What is the locus for the perceptual learning effect? Low-level sensory factors appear to determine the shape of visual-span profiles. Training on a letter-recognition task can enlarge these profiles in peripheral vision. This perceptual learning effect appears to have its origin in higher-level visual or cognitive processing, but is not explained by changes in the ability to deploy spatial attention to peripheral vision.

SUMMARY AND CONCLUSIONS

This chapter has focused on the potential value of perceptual learning as a method for training peripheral vision to read, as summarized here:

People with central scotomas who must use peripheral vision usually read very slowly.

Reading in normal peripheral vision is slow, even when text is suitably magnified, and the need for eye movements is minimized.

Visual-span profiles provide a quantitative representation of pattern recognition relevant to reading. Information transmitted by the visual span appears to be highly correlated with reading performance.

Visual-span profiles shrink in peripheral vision. Reduction of the size of the visual span appears to be a major factor explaining slower reading in peripheral vision.

Training of peripheral vision by repetitive measurement of visual-span profiles results in larger visual spans and faster reading. The training effects transfer to different letter sizes and visual-field locations.

This training of peripheral reading and letter recognition is not explained by an enhanced ability to deploy spatial attention to peripheral vision.

We conclude with two additional questions that must be addressed in translating these findings into a useful rehabilitation strategy for patients with central-field loss. Do the beneficial effects of perceptual learning we have observed for normally sighted young adults also occur in normally sighted older adults, or in adults with macular disease? Does perceptual learning in peripheral vision play a role in the adoption of a preferred retinal locus?

ACKNOWLEDGMENTS

We thank John Rieser, Dan Ashmead, Anne Corn, Ford Ebner, and all the other organizers and participants in the workshop for providing an opportunity for an exciting and stimulating exchange of ideas. We appreciate the invitation to participate in the workshop and to contribute to this book. We also acknowledge gratefully our grant support for the research reported here from the National Eye Institute, NIH Grant EY02934.

REFERENCES

Altpeter, E., Mackeben, M., & Trauzettel-Klosinski, S. (2000). The importance of sustained attention for patients with maculopathies. *Vision Research, 40*, 1539–1547.

Bouma, H. (1970). Interaction effects in parafoveal letter recognition. *Nature, 226*, 177–178.

Cheung, S. H., & Legge, G. E. (2005). Functional and cortical adaptations to central vision loss. *Visual Neuroscience, 22*, 187–201.

Chung, S. T. L., Legge, G. E., & Cheung, S. H. (2004). Letter recognition and reading speed in peripheral vision benefit from perceptual learning. *Vision Research, 44*, 695–709.

Chung, S. T. L., Mansfield, J. S., & Legge, G. E. (1998). Psychophysics of reading. XVIII. The effect of print size on reading speed in normal peripheral vision. *Vision Research, 38*, 2949–2962.

Crist, R., Li, W., & Gilbert, C. (2001). Learning to see: Experience and attention in primary visual cortex. *Nature Neuroscience, 4*, 519–525.

The Eye Diseases Prevalence Research Group. (2004). Prevalence of age-related macular degeneration in the United States. *Archives of Ophthalmology, 122*, 564–572.

Fahle, M., & Poggio, T. (Eds.). (2002). *Perceptual learning*. Cambridge, MA: MIT Press.

Faye, E. E. (1984). *Clinical low vision* (2nd ed.). Boston, MA: Little, Brown.

Fletcher, D. C., Schuchard, R. A., & Watson, G. (1999). Relative locations of macular scotomas near the PRL: Effect on low vision reading. *Journal of Rehabilitation Research and Development, 36*, 356–364.

Forster, K. I. (1970). Visual perception of rapidly presented word sequences of varying complexity. *Perception and Psychophysics, 8*, 215–221.

Ghose, G. M., Yang, T., & Maunsell, J. H. (2002). Physiological correlates of perceptual learning in monkey V1 and V2. *Journal of Neurophysiology, 87*, 1867–1888.

Lee, H.-W., Gefroh, J., Legge, G. E., & Kwon, M. Y. (2003, November). *Training improves reading speed in peripheral vision: Is it due to attention?* Poster presented at the annual meeting of the Psychonomic Society, Vancouver, BC, Canada.

Legge G. E. (2007). *Psychophysics of Reading in Normal and Low Vision*. Mahwah, NJ: Lawrence Erlbaum Associates.

Legge, G. E., Mansfield, J. S., & Chung, S. T. L. (2001). Psychophysics of reading. XX. Linking letter recognition to reading speed in central and peripheral vision. *Vision Research, 41*, 725–734.

Legge, G. E., Ross, J. A., Isenberg, L. M., & LaMay, J. M. (1992). Psychophysics of reading. XII. Clinical predictors of low-vision reading speed. *Investigative Ophthalmology & Visual Science, 33*, 677–687.

Legge, G. E., Rubin, G. S., Pelli, D. G., & Schleske, M. M. (1985). Psychophysics of reading. II. Low vision. *Vision Research, 25,* 253–266.

Nilsson, U., Frennesson, C., & Nilsson, S. (1998). Location and stability of a newly established eccentric retinal locus suitable for reading, achieved through training of patients with a dense central scotoma. *Optometry and Vision Science, 75,* 873–878.

Peli, E. (1986). Control of eye movement with peripheral vision: Implications for training of eccentric viewing. *American Journal of Optometry & Physiological Optics, 63,* 113–118.

Rainer, G., Lee, H., & Logothetis, N. (2004). The effect of learning on the function of monkey extrastriate visual cortex. *Public Library of Science Biology, 2,* 275–283.

Rayner, K., & Pollatsek, A. (1989). *The psychology of reading.* Englewood Cliffs, NJ: Prentice-Hall.

Rubin, G. S., & Turano, K. (1992). Reading without saccadic eye movements. *Vision Research, 32,* 895–902.

Rubin, G. S., & Turano, K. (1994). Low vision reading with sequential word presentation. *Vision Research, 34,* 1723–1733.

Sperling, G., & Reeves, A. (1981). The reaction time of a shift of visual attention. In R. Nickerson (Ed.), *Attention and performance: Vol. VIII* (pp. 347–60). Hillsdale, NJ: Lawrence Erlbaum Associates.

White, J. M., & Bedell, H. E. (1990). The oculomotor reference in humans with bilateral macular disease. *Investigative Ophthalmology and Visual Science, 31,* 1149–1161.

Whittaker, S. G., Cummings, R. W., & Swieson, L. R. (1991). Saccade control without a fovea. *Vision Research, 31,* 2209–2218.

Whittaker, S. G., & Lovie-Kitchin, J. (1993). Visual requirements for reading. *Optometry and Vision Science, 70,* 54–65.

Yang, T., & Maunsell, J. H. (2004). The effect of perceptual learning on neuronal responses in monkey visual area V4. *Journal of Neuroscience, 24,* 1617–1626.

12

Strategies of Maintaining Dynamic Spatial Orientation When Walking Without Vision

Peg A. Cummins and John J. Rieser

When people explore and find their way within their home neighborhoods it is useful for them to keep track of dynamic changes in their distance and direction toward remembered landmarks. Persons born without vision often experience difficulty with skillful orientation, which can make it more difficult to figure out routes to intended destinations and revise routes in response to changes in the familiar environment.

Consider two of the ways such difficulties can be explained. First, spatial representation explanations posit that not-so-good spatial orientation occurs because people fail to call to mind two-dimensional representations of their surroundings and instead act on one-dimensional representations (representations of specific routes consisting of when to turn and when to continue walking straight ahead). What is not known is whether they are able, in principle, to generate and call to mind two-dimensional representations. Alternatively, updating explanations posit that not-so-good spatial orientation occurs whether or not people form a two-dimensional representation because they fail to keep up to date on changing self-to-object distances and directions when they move—they are deficient at knowing how to couple their locomotion with representations of things in their surroundings in order to keep up to date on their changing spatial orientation.

Much research supports these two alternatives. It is important to note that the responses of individual participants with congenital blindness are quite variable with some performing on par with sighted participants. The hypothesis motivating this study is that forming two-dimensional spatial representations is a critical problem, not updating, for some who are not so good at dynamic spatial orientation. We describe two studies to evaluate this hypothesis. Experiment 1 was aimed at comparing the dynamic spatial orientation strategies of congenitally blind versus blindfolded sighted persons. The results are consistent with the hypothesis that many congenitally blind persons do not keep a two-dimensional representation of their surroundings in mind when they walk from place to place in our test conditions. Experiment 2 was a training study. Congenitally blind persons who performed poorly in the first experiment volunteered to try to learn a "Braille cell" strategy for forming two-dimensional representations of their surroundings and using these to keep up to date on dynamic changes in spatial orientation.

The results of the first experiment indicate that the congenitally blind participants generally did not use two-dimensional representations to guide their judgments. The results of the second experiment indicate that the congenitally blind persons who performance was not so good in the first experiment improved significantly after short-term training to keep two-dimensional, not one-dimensional, representations in mind during the tests.

Previous research (Mou, McNamara, Valiquette, & Rump, 2004; Easton & Sholl, 1995) has demonstrated that when sighted individuals look at the spatial layout of objects in a room or a town, their mental representation of the arrangement of objects or figures is biased in the orientation from which it was viewed. The mental representation of the particular perspective is resistant to change until the people walk to another location. This effect is characterized by slower responses to orientation problems involving alternate perspectives.

To illustrate, participants with normal vision learned the arrangement of objects observed from one perspective (Rieser, 1989). After learning the layout of the objects, they were instructed to point to each of the objects while blindfolded. They did so under two conditions: (a) after imagining they had rotated their facing direction while standing in place and (b) after imagining that they had translated to a new position, that is moving along any straight-line path without changing their facing direction.

If the spatial representation constructed was not biased in the direction from which it was initially viewed, then the two conditions should have produced similar results. Significant differences in responses were found, however. The participants took less time and produced smaller errors when imagining that they had translated to a new position than they had when they imagined rotating to a new position. This suggests that when one initially constructs a two-dimensional mental representation of a scene, the representation is good enough to perceive the dynamic changes in self-to-object distances and directions when one walks a straight-line path. The evidence for this is that when the participants translated by stepping along any straight-line path, their responses were equivalent to those produced when they learned the layout of the objects initially.

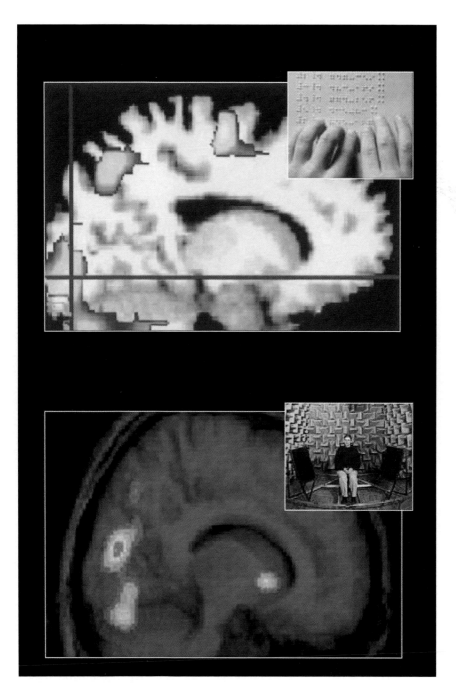

FIGURE 3–1

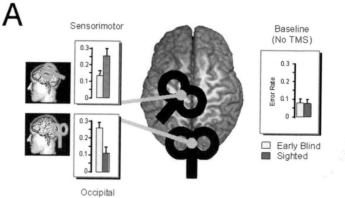

Sensorimotor

Baseline
(No TMS)

Occipital

Early Blind
Sighted

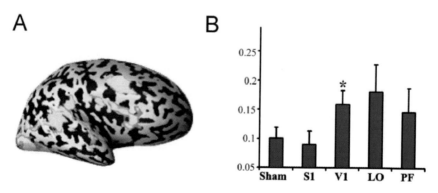

FIGURE 3–2

A

B

FIGURE 3–3

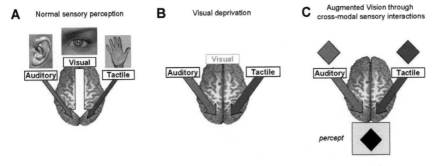

FIGURE 3–4

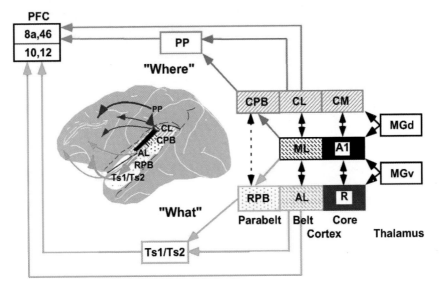

FIGURE 4–1

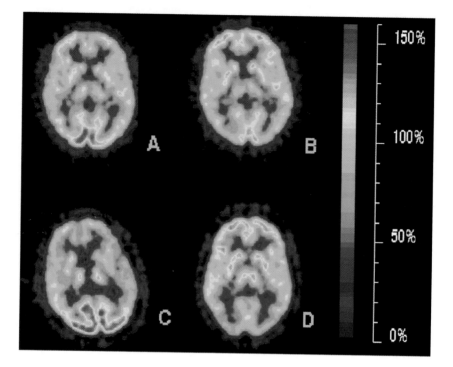

FIGURE 5–1

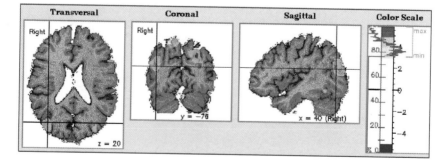

FIGURE 5–3

EB Subjects

SC Subjects

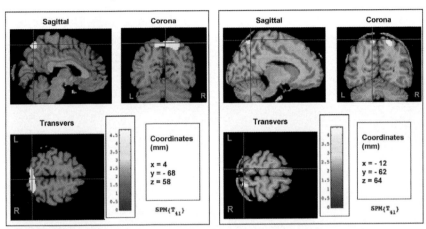

FIGURE 5–4

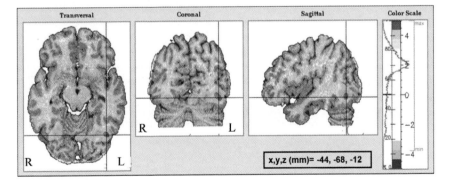

FIGURE 5–5

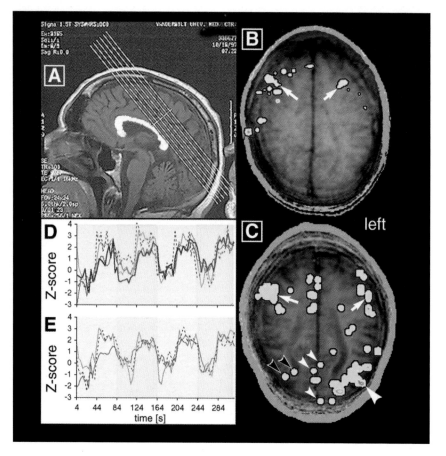

FIGURE 6–1

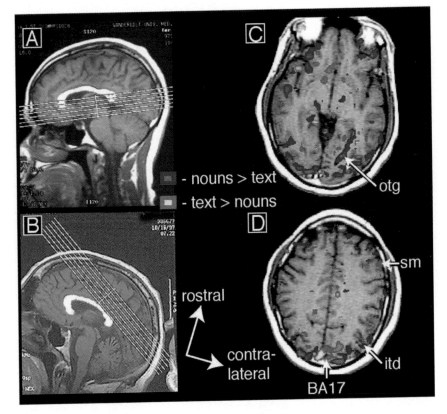

FIGURE 6–5

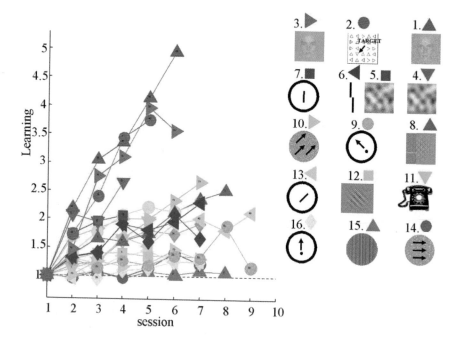

FIGURE 8–1

FORM

a. Outlined form

 "What is the outlined shape", MM = 100%; C =100%, 100%, 100%; p=1

b. Texture segmentation

"What orientation is the rectangle of different contrast?", MM = 96%; C =100%, 100%, 100%; p=0

c. Line contour integration

"is there a pathway of lines within the random lines?", MM = 80%; C=100%, 90%, 95%; p=0.02

d. Glass pattern

"Is there a circular pattern within the random noise?"; MM = 73%; C = 80%, 85%, 100%; p=0.06

e. Illusory contours

"What is the 'hidden' shape outlined by the black apertures"; MM = no response; C = t

DEPTH

f. Occlusion

"What is the color of the object in front?" MM = 100%; C = t

g. Shape from shading

"Which sphere bulges out?", MM = 100%; C = t

h. Transparency

"How many objects are there, and which is in front?" MM = 0% C = t

i. Perspective

"What is the shape of the object?" MM = no response C = t

j. Shepard Tables

 "Which tables match in shape / use the same table-cloth?" width/height bias (100% veridical); MM = 100%; C = 63%, 63%, 47%; p=0.009

MOTION

k. Simple/complex/barber pole motion

"What direction is the pattern moving in?" MM = 100% C = t

l. Form from motion

"What is the orientation of the rectangle of different motion?", MM = 100%; C =t

m. Motion Glass patterns

"Is there a circular /swirling pattern within the random noise?" MM = 90%; C=95%, 80%, 85%; p=0.74

n. Kinetic depth effect

"What is the shape of the object?" MM = 100%; C = t

o. Biological motion

"What do the moving dots represent?" MM correctly identified a moving walker.

FIGURE 8–2

CP-8

In contrast, when they imagined a position with a new facing direction, as when they were instructed to imagine rotating in place, they were slower and less accurate. This task, which required participants to employ an alternate perspective, demanded additional cognitive processing. These results suggest that the spatial representation in effect was not sufficient for the successful completion of the task. Participants may have used other means to solve the problem. For example, they may have tried to calculate the difference that would result from the new movement, or prior to completing the task the participants may have attempted to manipulate the representation that was in effect so that it reflected the viewpoint demanded of the task (Rieser, Guth, & Hill, 1982).

These results indicate that when the spatial representation fits the orientation of one's current point of view, translations (that is, walking along straight-line paths) facilitates little or not at all one's awareness of one's changing spatial orientation within the space, even when imagining those relations from a novel position. For rotations, however, walking to turn in place to face a new direction facilitates keeping up to date in the changes in perspective (Mou et al., 2004; Presson & Montello, 1994; Rieser, 1989).

We hypothesize this occurs because one's spatial representation is coupled with kinesthetic information resulting when one moves from place to place. Thus, as one turns, his or her spatial representation reflects each new perspective. Rieser and Pick (2002) suggested this spontaneous coupling of the two sources of information that supports navigation in the absence of visual, tactual, or auditory information. The results obtained by our participants demonstrated effectively the facility of locomotion in maintaining orientation. When an individual is permitted to turn when completing an orientation task, then the spatial representation in effect at that moment in time is free to vary with the orientation of the observer.

People with normal visual functioning readily construct two-dimensional mental representations of environmental spaces when they travel within familiar places and keep up to date on dynamic changes in their self-to-object distances and directions. It might be that some individuals who are congenitally totally blind cannot construct two-dimensional spatial representations of the environment, or it might be that some can construct two-dimensional representations and create them after they have moved to a new position—but they may do so in retrospect.

The purpose of Experiment 1 was to investigate the hypothesis that persons with congenital blindness tend to construct one-dimensional spatial representations. In addition we tested to find out whether it is more difficult to maintain spatial orientation after simple rotations in perspective (walking to turn in place) versus simple translations (walking without turning, along a straight-line path). The results of Experiment 1 indicated that persons with congenital blindness tended to have difficulty with keeping up to date on rotations in perspective, and that keeping up to date on translations in perspective was not as difficult. The "mental rotation" hypothesis is that the difficulties were caused by deficits in their mental representations. Experiment 2 was an intervention study. It was aimed at teaching congenitally blind persons whose dynamic spatial orientation was not so good in Experiment 1 to use an image of a Braille cell as a template for representing their immediate surroundings. The results show that short-term training was highly effective at improving the dynamic spatial orientation of the participants, all of whom were congenitally blind.

EXPERIMENT 1

In the first experiment, two groups of participants, blindfolded sighted individuals and those who were congenitally totally blind, walked eight multisegmented routes within an unidentified space. A rolling walker as is commonly used in rehabilitation centers was used to guide each participant. After walking the routes, they pointed to their starting positions using a pointer that was mounted on the walker.

The participants walked the routes under two conditions: an imagined surround and a virtual ganzfeld. In the imagined surround condition, they received instructions to imagine the position of familiar objects as they occurred in a familiar setting and navigate within the experimental site as though the objects occupied the same positions at the site. In the virtual ganzfeld condition they received no prior instructions to assist them in maintaining orientation.

In each of the two surround conditions the forms of locomotion were varied. In a "translation plus rotation" condition, the participants walked the routes as they normally would; that is, they either translated by moving forward or they rotated as the configuration of the route demanded. In the "translation only" condition, they walked the routes without changing their heading. In this condition when the route turned to the left or right they side-stepped to the left or right as demanded of the route; when the route was behind them they stepped backwards.

The possible outcomes that might result from the different conditions depend on the type of mental representation these individuals constructed when navigating within the experimental site. Those individuals who initially constructed a sequentially ordered representation of their paths of travel in the virtual ganzfeld condition might have (a) continued to construct a sequentially ordered representation of a familiar environment in the imagined surround condition, (b) constructed a spatial representation of a familiar environment in the imagined surround condition and coupled their movement with that representation, or (c) constructed a spatial representation of a familiar environment in the imagined surround condition but failed to update it by coupling their movement with the represented surrounding environment.

In the first instance, no difference in orientation performance in the two surround conditions would be evident. In the second case, navigation in the imagined surround condition would result in improved performance. In the last case, the participant would be faster and more accurate when oriented in the direction in which he or she had originally imagined the setting and slower when having to imagine a perspective that was different from the original perspective.

The dependent variables were latency and accuracy. The independent variables were surround (imagined surround or virtual ganzfeld) and movement type (translations only or translations plus rotations). To ensure that the participants were able to use the pointer effectively when pointing at the target and to provide a measure of optimal performance, a baseline condition was administered. In this condition the participant pointed at a coat rack that was positioned randomly within arm's reach around them. On average, the participants produced errors that were less than 10°.

In all of the succeeding analyses, a 2 × 2 × 2 (Visual Status × Surround × Movement Type) mixed factorial analysis of variance with repeated measures on the last two conditions was performed on error and latency data. The alpha level was set at 0.05. The variable and absolute errors and latencies obtained in the surround by movement-type trials were compared to those obtained in the baseline condition.

Results

Variable error. The data subjected to analysis were the standard deviations of the eight trials for each participant in the four surround by movement-type conditions. Only movement type had significant effects on accuracy, $F(1,13) = 24.63, p = 0.001$. The main effects of surround and of visual status were not significant, $F(1,13) = .29, p = 0.60$, and $F(1,13) = 1.76, p = 0.21$, respectively. No significant interactions were evidenced in the surround by visual status conditions, $F(1,13) = 0.38, p = 0.55$, the movement by visual status condition, $F(1,13) = 0.05, p = 0.83$, the surround by movement condition, $F(1,13) = 0.76, p = 0.40$, or the surround by movement type by visual status conditions, $F(1,13) = 1.24, p = 0.29$).

Variable error was compared with the variable error data obtained in the baseline condition. The results showed that variable error was significantly different in the baseline condition. Both groups of participants produced less variable error when pointing at the coat rack than they did when pointing at their starting positions following both surround and movement conditions.

Absolute error. The data subjected to analysis were mean errors of the eight trials for each participant in the four surround by movement-type conditions. Analysis of Variance (ANOVAs) showed that movement type had significant effects on accuracy, $F(1,13) = 21.09, p = .001$. The main effect of surround was not significant, $F(1,13) = .141, p = .713$. The main effect of visual status was not significant, $F(1,13) = 1.46, p = .248$, nor were the interactions between surround and visual status, $F(1,13) = .481, p = .50$, and movement type and visual status, $F(1,13) = .306, p = .59$. There were no significant interactions between surround and movement type, $F(1,13) = .382, p = .55$. Surround by movement type by visual status was also not significant, $F(1,13) = 1.22, p = .29$.

To examine the differences between absolute error in the four surround by movement conditions and the baseline condition, paired-sample t tests were run separately on sighted subjects wearing blindfolds and those who were blind. Significant differences were found in all conditions for both groups of participants, with all subjects being more accurate when pointing at the coat rack.

Latency. The data used were the median of the eight trials in each of the four surround by movement conditions. The main effects of movement type, $F(1,13) = 1.37, p = .26)$ and surround, $F(1,13) = 2.53, p = 0.14$ were not significant. There were no significant interactions between surround and movement type, $F(1,13) = 1.74, p = .21$, surround and group, $F(1,13) = 1.03, p = 0.33$, movement type and group, $F(1,13) = 0.16, p = 0.90$, or surround, movement type, and group, $F(1,13) = 0.88, p = 0.37$. There were significant differences between the two groups on latency, $F(1,13) = 4.51, p = .05$. The sighted subjects were significantly faster at pointing to their points of origin than were the subjects who were blind, $F(1,13) = 4.87, p = 0.05$.

We examined the difference in latency in the four surround by movement-type conditions and the baseline condition in which participants pointed at the coat rack. The latency scores of the two groups were tested separately with a paired-sample t test. No significant differences in latencies were found for the sighted subjects in any of the four test conditions and the baseline condition. Significant differences were found, though, for the participants who were blind. They were significantly faster when pointing at the coat rack than when pointing at their starting positions in the two virtual ganzfeld conditions, whether walking via translations plus rotations ($t = 5.64, p = 0.001$) or translations only ($t = 5.59, p = 0.001$), and in the imagined surround conditions while walking via translations plus rotations ($t = 5.55, p = 0.001$) and translations only ($t = 8.48, p = 0.001$). There were no significant differences in latency between the four surround by movement-type conditions.

EXPERIMENT 2

It was anticipated in Experiment 1 that the participants who were congenitally totally blind would not spontaneously construct mental representations that were spatial in structure. In Experiment 2, we assessed a strategy for the construction of a two-dimensional representation of environmental space. Individuals who were congenitally blind used a highly familiar spatial image, the Braille cell, which was to serve as a framework against which their movement could be perceived. The advantages of using a Braille cell are (a) When viewing the Braille cell the observer "sees" the whole cell under his or her fingertip. There is no need to reconstruct the parts of the object or figure viewed into its totality, as is the case when a figure or object is traced with the fingers or hands; (b) the Braille cell is (at least) two-dimensional in structure, thus providing a template from which individuals can construct their mental representation of the environment; and (c) because individuals who are congenitally blind know and use Braille, they should find its construction as a mental image effortless. Braille is a medium these individuals use daily. Its features were mastered through repetition. Because responses are automatic they require no load on working memory.

Experiments 1 and 2 were the same except that the participants were asked to construct an image of the Braille cell rather than reconstruct an image of a familiar surrounding. Again, we anticipated the participants who were congenitally blind would not construct mental representations spontaneously that were spatial in structure and couple their movement with that representation. The implementation of a strategy employing a familiar image, a Braille cell, to which movement could be coordinated might result in improvement in orientation tasks involving locomotion. It was hypothesized that when this method is employed, individuals could use the image of the Braille cell as a frame of reference against which their positions within the experimental space could be understood. This method, however, had at least one serious drawback. The representation constructed would be fixed in orientation. As a result, the layout would best be understood from one perspective—the upright position of the Braille cell. When the participants rotated to the right or to the left or turned around in the translations plus rotation condition, their perspectives no longer matched the mental representation of the Braille cell. The altered perspectives would be more difficult to construct and, therefore, would place greater demands on processing time and possibly be less accurate.

Results

Variable error.   Both surround and movement-type conditions resulted in significant main effects on accuracy. The Braille cell condition produced significantly less variability than did the virtual ganzfeld condition, $F(1,7) = 12.63, p = 0.009$, and translation alone resulted in significantly less variable error, $F(1,7) = 18.97, p = 0.003$. No significant interactions were revealed, $F(1,7) = 0.05, p = 0.82$.

The variability error scores were submitted to a paired-sample t test to determine whether there were any differences in variable error under the four surround by movement conditions when compared to the coat rack condition. Significant differences were revealed between the variable responses in the coat rack and surround by movement conditions. The subjects produced less variable errors when pointing to the position of the coat rack.

Absolute error.   ANOVAs showed that both movement type and surround had significant effects on performance, $F(1,7) = 19.39, p = .003$ and $F(1,7) = 10.12, p = 0.02$, respectively. Interactions between movement type and surround were not significant, $F(1,7) = 0.11, p = 0.75$.

The absolute error scores were submitted to a paired-sample t test to determine whether there were any differences in absolute error under the four surround by movement-type conditions when compared to the coat rack condition. Significant differences were revealed between the average responses in the coat rack and surround by movement conditions. The subjects, on average, produced less error when pointing to the position of the coat rack.

Latency.   The data used were median performances of each subject in each of the surround by movement conditions. The main effects of movement type, $F(1,7) = 0.96, p = .36$, and surround, $F(1,7) = 1.98, p = 0.20$, were not significant. There were no significant interactions between surround and movement type, $F(1,7) = 1.54, p = 0.25$. A paired-samples t test revealed significant differences between pointing responses when pointing at the coat rack in the baseline condition and pointing in the four surround by movement conditions. The participants were significantly slower at pointing at the target when translating and rotating in both the virtual ganzfeld, $t = 3.18, df = 7$, $p = .02$ (two-tailed), and Braille cell conditions, $t = 2.82, df = 7, p = 0.03$ (two-tailed), and when translating alone in the virtual ganzfeld, $t = 3.61$, $df = 7, p = .02$ (two-tailed), and Braille cell condition, $t = 4.77, df = 7, p = .01$ (two-tailed).

As in Experiment 1, the latency responses of these participants were equivalent during all walking conditions but significantly different from those attained during the baseline condition when participants pointed at the coat rack. These results indicate that the participant's strategy for solving the orientation problems when walking in the four surround by movement-type conditions were similar to each other but were different from that used for solving the orientation task when pointing at the coat rack. This conclusion is supported by their responses when walking in the translation only condition. Their reaction times should have been equivalent to those obtained when pointing at the coat rack if the spatial representation in effect at the time had been sufficient to solve the orientation problem. Instead, the reaction times in both movement conditions were equivalent. The responses of the participants suggests the orientation problem was "figured out" following movement. When they constructed spatial representations, as they would have been required to do when imagining they walked the routes using the Braille cell, they did so only after moving the required paths to their final position. From this we can conclude these individuals did not construct spatial representations while in transit and, therefore, did not couple kinesthetic information with their representations.

The spatial framework provided by the Braille cell facilitated performance of individuals who are congenitally blind on the spatial orientation task involving movement along different paths of travel. With varying degrees of success, these participants were able to use their image of the position of the dots in an imagined Braille cell to keep track of dynamic changes in spatial orientation when they walked. The representational strategy was more effective during the more difficult rotation trials than during the easier translation trials.

The responses of all participants were more accurate when they translated than when they translated and rotated. Because the participants constructed spatial representations of the Braille cell in that condition, it is not improbable to conclude that the strategy used, at least in this condition, was to construct a spatial representation after they had completed walking the route. These results suggest orientation is more easily achieved when the spatial representation in effect matches one's current perspective. Rotations introduced an element of error into the participants' responses. In a few cases, their responses were wildly off target, suggesting they may have depended primarily on sequentially arranged mental representation when walking the routes and were unable to convert that representation into spatial information or to use an alternate strategy that was effective in solving the problem.

GENERAL DISCUSSION

Why is it that so many people who have not experienced vision have difficulty keeping track of their positions relative to the objects and places that make up their environments? Centuries ago Molyneux (1690, 1978) noted that spatial learning seemed especially difficult for his wife and others who were blind. Our chapter suggests that visual experiences provide a special advantage for learning about environments and dynamic spatial orientation (it may not provide as much advantage for perceiving and learning about objects). The two experiments summarized here indicate that the dynamic spatial orientation (that is, keeping up to date on changes in self-to-object distances and directions) of persons who are congenitally blind can sometimes be improved through short-term instruction designed to encourage them to apply their expert knowledge of Braille cells as a prototype for keeping their surroundings in mind.

Our studies assessed the dynamic spatial orientation of adults, not children, but we believe it has useful implications for the teaching and learning of children born blind or with severely impaired vision. Children who are born without vision can readily obtain information about the position of objects in near space from sound and touch. Previous research suggests, however, that touch does not initially inform blind children of where an object is, and instead it informs them of the object's shape and purpose. For example, Adelson and Fraiberg (1974) asked congenitally blind children to reach for objects that made a noise. Their research suggested that the property of "where" an object is does not develop until the end of the first year or early in the second— well after sighted children begin learning about objects in their surrounding environments. Not only does reaching develop later, but children who are congenitally totally blind also crawl at a later age, a factor that delays their learning the layout of their environments including the relative position of objects and themselves within space. Why?

Initially, children who are congenitally blind need to rely on information that they can hear or touch or move to. Unlike information afforded by vision, the chance to continuously touch things while one moves is very short-lived, and the chance to hear continuous changes in perspective is limited as well. This resulting lack of reliability may interfere or prevent some children from establishing dynamic spatial orientation skills when they become mobile. Bayesian approaches to understanding the object and environment perception suggest that different sources of information are weighted differently in what people know and represent (Ernst, Banks, & Bulthoff, 2000; Cheng, Shettleworth, Huttenlocker, & Rieser, under review, 2006). Little or nothing is known about how vision and visual experience is weighted in such perceptual representations. We think that more needs to be known in order to understand how different types of information are integrated to form perceptual representations of surrounding environments explored by walking.

REFERENCES

Adelson, E., & Fraiberg, S. (1974). Gross motor development in infants blind from birth. *Child Development, 45,* 114–126.

Cheng, K., Shettleworth, S., Huttenlocher, J., & Rieser, J. (under review). Intregrating spatial information.

Easton, R. D., & Sholl, M. J. (1995). Object-array structures, frames of reference, and retrieval of spatial knowledge. *Journal of Experimental Psychology: Learning, Memory, and Cognition, 21,* 483–500.

Ernst, M. O., Banks, M. S., & Bulthoff, H. H. (2000). Touch can change slant perception. *Nature Neuroscience, 3,* 69–73.

Molyneaux, W. Cited in Locke, J. (1690/1978). *An essay concerning human understanding.* A. S. Pringle-Pattison (Ed.). Atlantic Highlands, NJ: Humanities Press.

Mou, W., McNamara, T. P., Valiquette, C. M., & Rump, B. (2004). Allocentric and egocentric updating of spatial memories. *Journal of Experimental Psychology: Learning, Memory, and Cognition, 30,* 142–157.

Presson, C. C., & Montello, D. R. (1994). Updating after rotational and translational body movements: Coordinate structure of perspective space. *Perception, 23,* 1447–1455.

Rieser, J. J. (1989). Access to knowledge of spatial structure at novel points of observation. *Journal of Experimental Psychology: Learning, Memory, and Cognition, 15,* 1157–1165.

Rieser, J. J., Guth, D. A., & Hill, E. W. (1982). Mental processes mediating independent travel: Implications for orientation and mobility. *Journal of Visual Impairment and Blindness, 76,* 213–218.

Rieser, J. J., & Pick, H. L. (2002). The perception and representation of human locomotion. In W. Prinz & B. Hommel (Eds.), *Common mechanisms in perception and action: Attention and performance XIX* (pp. 177–93). Oxford, UK: Oxford University Press.

13

Spatial Reference Frames Used in Mental Imagery Tasks

Fred W. Mast and Tino Zaehle

Spatial orientation is a fundamental ability. We move in 3-D space and must be able to orient ourselves and navigate in space. Spatial information is processed continuously and the spatial relations between objects in the environment and our own position in space are updated continuously. But how does the brain solve this problem? The problem of space has interested researchers for centuries. In the eighteenth century the philosopher Immanuel Kant proposed that space and time do not really exist in the world outside but that they are the necessary conditions of perception, imposed by our own minds. No perception is possible outside the boundaries of time and space. Kant believed that the axioms of geometry are known a priori and do not depend on experience. This view has been debated fiercely in analytical philosophy with little or no impact on disciplines other than philosophy. Almost two centuries later, however, the ethologist and later Nobel prize winner (1973) Konrad Lorenz wrote a famous article on Kant's notion of a priori (Lorenz, 1941, 1982). Lorenz argued that Kant's notion of a priori is true from an ontological perspective. However, like human organs, the a priori is also the result of biological evolution and therefore can be considered as the result of an adaptive mechanism. Lorenz reinterpreted Kant's a priori as a posteriori in terms of human phylogeny.

Lorenz initiated an evolutionary view to the study of cognitive abilities, which marked a conceptual milestone in the rise of behavioral research. In particular, survival of humans and animals seems almost uncertain without them performing well in spatial orientation and navigation. It is important to keep the adaptive value of spatial cognitive abilities in mind, but for the understanding of the mechanisms that underlie spatial abilities, the phylogenetic perspective takes a back seat. It is the experimental and clinical research that promotes a steadily increasing wealth of knowledge in distinct areas of spatial processing. In this chapter we focus on the spatial frame of reference and how it is used in cognitive tasks, in particular mental imagery tasks. Special emphasis will be given to the neuronal mechanisms associated with the frame of reference. Not only do we focus on spatial behavior but we also bridge the gap to socially relevant issues such as when we attribute intentional states to others.

SPATIAL COGNITION AND MULTIMODAL PERCEPTION

The study of spatial processes has become a unique and fascinating field for cognitive scientists. It involves cognitive operations like spatial reasoning, as well as relatively low-level sensorimotor processes. Interestingly, the mechanisms on these levels do not operate in complete isolation but rather are nested and intertwined. This implies that the brain structures involved in reflexive behavior and early perception can be influenced by cognitive factors, and likewise, cognitive processes can be modified depending on the sensory input.

The following example will illustrate this point. The vestibulo-ocular reflex (VOR) connects the vestibular end-organ to the eye muscles in such a way that moving the head in one direction induces a compensatory eye movement in the opposite direction. This reflex helps stabilize the image of the world on the retina when we move our heads. The VOR is based on a network of neurons in the brainstem and cerebellum. An organization of excitatory and inhibitory synapses ensures a rigid kind of push–pull mechanism of this reflex. The VOR starts with sensory input (acceleration detected by vestibular receptors) proceeding to a motor command, which then leads to a movement of the eye. Even though this neuronal organization suggests an automatically operating reflex, this picture is far from being complete. Barr, Schultheis, and Robinson (1976) showed that the gain of the VOR can be modified by *imagined* target distance as if the subjects were actually viewing a near or far target. This finding demonstrated that a reflex even as simple as the VOR can be modified by influences of purely cognitive origin such as when targets are imagined near or far.

The example above illustrates yet another important aspect. What appears to us as a purely visual perception is hardly ever mediated exclusively by the visual system. For example, when we keep the gaze fixed on a visual target while walking, we are normally not aware that a stable visual percept is possible only because the vestibular system compensates for the head movements, thus keeping the eyes on target. This can be easily demonstrated when we hold a newspaper at comfortable reading distance and move the head repeatedly from left to right, as if we were saying "no" in nonverbal terms (i.e., a yaw head-on-trunk rotation of about 50° amplitude with a velocity of roughly 100° per s) while the newspaper stays in place. We are still able to read nearly perfectly even though only rarely do we actually shake the head when at the same time reading the newspaper. Interestingly, however, we are much less able to read when we keep the head still but now move the newspaper from left to right with the same speed we moved the head. The visual stimulus (the newspaper in this case) appears rather blurred even though the movement of the stimulus with respect to the head is identical in both situations. We get a much better visual percept when the vestibular and the visual system are stimulated simultaneously. The visual system alone cannot compensate for the rapid changes of target position, and thus reading proficiency declines when the newspaper moves with the head held in place. The latencies for smooth pursuit eye movements are higher than those for the VOR.

The example of the VOR illustrates that the processing of spatial information is essentially *multimodal*. Unlike, for example, the perception of color, the processing of spatial information includes a variety of sensory modalities. Even though visual perception appears to us in many ways to be the dominant modality, the processes that underlie visual perception often involve nonvisual sensory information. The visual system is engaged in several mutual interactions with other sensory systems (e.g., see Brandt, Bartenstein, Janek, & Dieterich, 1998, and Brandt et al., 2002, for the mutual inhibition of visual and vestibular information). These intracortical interactions are particularly interesting in the context of this book because they may enable cross-modal compensation, which builds on already existing neural connections. These connections can account for improvements in performance in persons who are blind even though visual experience will remain absent. We use the term *cross-modal* in the context of compensation only (i.e., when a sensory input is missing) and otherwise refer to the term *multimodal* for all interactions among the senses.

The major focus of this contribution is on spatial cognition, in particular, on mental imagery abilities. The involvement of mental imagery in several motor and perception tasks has been shown in psychophysical as well as in neuroimaging studies. For the improvement of motor skills, for example, mental practice and motor imagery can be nearly as effective as physical practice (e.g., Yue & Cole, 1992; Yue, Wilson, Cole, & Darling, 1996, but see also Herbert, Dean, & Gandevia, 1998, showing no effect of imagery training on executed movements). Taken together, we think mental imagery can play a major role in better understanding how influences of purely cognitive origin can change performance in perception and motor tasks. We hope this knowledge can be explored for potential use in the domains of rehabilitation and plasticity research for blind individuals.

To what extent higher cognitive influences are conveyed via the same neuronal connections used for mutual sensory interactions is not yet clear. In a recent study (Mast, Merfeld, Kosslyn, 2006) we examined performance in visual mental imagery tasks during caloric vestibular stimulation. The logic of this experiment was the following: Vestibular stimulation deactivates (or inhibits) early visual cortex as revealed by several studies, which are based on different techniques (PET: Wenzel et al., 1996; Doppler-Sonography: Tiecks,

Planck, Haberl, & Brandt, 1996; fMRI: Bense, Stephan, Yousry, Brandt, & Dieterich, 2001). Research using neuroimaging has shown that early visual cortex is involved when subjects generate richly detailed images (images of high visual resolution; see Klein et al., 2004; Kosslyn & Thompson, 2003). Combining these two independent lines of research we expected, and in fact found, impaired performance in visual mental imagery during simultaneous caloric stimulation. The subjects made more errors during concomitant vestibular stimulation. No change in performance was found in a control task, which did not require the subjects to generate mental images. This finding strongly supports the role of early visual cortex in mental imagery and, in a more general sense, demonstrates that cognitive functions draw on brain mechanisms involved in early sensory perception.

SOCCER FOR VISUALLY IMPAIRED PERSONS

What kind of imagery processes are there when visual perception is no longer available? The following section will illustrate how visually impaired persons deal with spatial tasks. Brazilian soccer player Joao Silva scored nine goals in five matches. His shots hit the net without him seeing the playfield, the keeper, or any of the defenders running toward him. Joao Silva is blind and his goals helped the Brazilian team win the soccer gold medal at the Paralympics in Athens in 2004. Joao Silva plays *Football 5-a-Side*, a variation of soccer designed for visually impaired athletes. Rules are the same as in soccer with certain modifications: The ball makes a noise when it moves, the goalkeepers may be sighted and act as guides during the game, and some players may use eye patches to compensate for possible differences in the visual impairments. There are five players per team, they play on a smaller field, and there is no offside rule. Joao Silva and his teammates must have extraordinary spatial abilities even though they have no visual input on which to rely. The players must be able to generate a detailed map representing precisely the geometry of the soccer ground (the field is 20 m wide and 40 m long). Soccer is a fast game and the players must rush, stop, turn, and rush again, updating continuously where the other players are and where their own and the opponent's goal is. When we saw a short video sequence of the Paralympics final game, it was hard to tell any difference compared to soccer played by sighted people. Particularly when the players moved fast across the field, the slight differences became almost unnoticeable. Why is this at all possible?

SPATIAL IMAGERY AND NONVISUAL NAVIGATION

We begin with a brief presentation of recent research on early blind subjects by Vanlierde and Wanet-Defalque (2004). This study showed that early blind subjects performed a spatial imagery task just as well as sighted subjects. Moreover, neuroimaging revealed similar activation patterns during spatial imagery in occipitoparietal areas for blind and sighted subjects (Vanlierde, De Volder, Wanet-Defalque, & Veraart, 2003). Some previous research in nonvisual navigation has suggested that spatial imagery was not bound to the visual modality. On the one hand, Loomis and colleagues (1993) did not find significant differences in performance between sighted and blind subjects on their tests of spatial imagery. On the other hand, Rieser, Guth, and Hill (1986) found significant differences in performance between persons born without vision compared with those losing vision later in life and with blindfolded sighted persons. There are different ways to explain this discrepancy because it might reflect the different tasks used, differences in subject recruitment methods, or heterogeneity in the distribution of spatial skills.

Most of the time sighted people are fully aware of the objects behind them even though these objects are currently out of sight (this is often referred to as *back space*). Moreover, the ability of keeping track of where things are does not necessarily require the generation of visual images. The spatial knowledge we have about the environment automatically extends our field of view. The objects are out of sight but they remain spatially indexed. This means we keep in mind the location of objects even though we move while they are out of sight. Imagine, for example, a keeper in soccer who generally has a good sense of where the goal ends and where the posts are even though he rarely ever sees them. Most of the time, the keeper is somewhere in the penalty area standing a few meters in front of his goal. All of a sudden, he may need to sprint toward the center of the field in order to intercept a long pass meant to reach a striker. While he is playing the game his head is facing forward and at the same time he knows the precise location of the goal behind him (one is almost tempted to say that the fewer times he sees his goal the better his team plays).

We think it is also spatial imagery that helps blind individuals play soccer and even score from far distances. It is obvious that blind soccer players are able to keep track of where things are even though some of them have never seen the layout of the soccer ground or any of the other players. For them it is perhaps as if back space is all they have. The following section focuses on a neuroscientific perspective and addresses the question of how different spatial cognitive abilities are implemented in the brain.

NEURONAL IMPLEMENTATION OF SPATIAL INFORMATION

The role of parietal areas involved in the processing of spatial cognition has been shown in several studies. The parietal lobe seems to be the convergence zone in which spatial information is processed irrespective of the modality of the sensory input. Neurophysiological and anatomical studies in monkeys have provided direct evidence that parietal cortex contains several separate functional areas with representations of space (Andersen, Snyder, Bradley, & Xing, 1997; Jeannerod, Arbib, Rizzolatti, & Sakata, 1995; Rizzolatti, Fogassi, & Gallese, 1997). Furthermore, the parietal lobe integrates a variety of sensory modalities into a multimodal body-centered representation of space. This computational integration of proprioceptive, tactile, vestibular, and visual information is important for updating continuously the spatial coordinates while we move. The mechanisms of creating this central representation are largely unconscious.

The importance of the parietal lobe in spatial cognition has been shown in neuropsychological studies. Lesions of the posterior parietal cortex lead to a disturbance of visuospatial processing, such as extinction and unilateral spatial neglect (e.g., Marshall & Fink, 2001). Further demonstration of the important integrating role of the parietal lobe has recently been shown in patients with temporoparietal lesions exhibiting "out-of-body" experiences (Blanke, Landis, Spinelli, & Seeck, 2004). During an out-of-body experience, the awake patient reports having seen his body and the world from a location outside the physical body. These reports can be interpreted as a disintegration of information from different senses (e.g., vestibular and visual information). Taken together, the parietal lobe is a key structure for the mechanisms underlying spatial cognition and spatial orientation.

In the following section we focus on the frame of reference, which is absolutely necessary for the processing of any kind of spatial information. No meaningful processing of spatial information is possible without a frame of reference.

FRAMES OF REFERENCE

Human beings move in 3-D space and must be able to orient themselves continuously while they navigate. However, during locomotion the objects and the spatial relations between objects are not fixed but rather are subject to steady changes. The reasons for these changes are twofold. The visible objects can either move in space (e.g., when we stand at a sidewalk and observe cars passing by) or the observer moves past the stationary environment (e.g., when we walk along the sidewalk past the cars caught in a traffic jam). Therefore it is absolutely necessary that the perceptual system establishes a stable but at the same time flexible frame of reference (FoR) to code and update the spatial information of the environment that surrounds us.

At least two different FoRs can be distinguished. First, it is possible to encode or represent the location (e.g., distance, angle) of each object in relation to a personal agent such as one's own body. This type of representation is referred to as *egocentric* FoR, and it refers to subject-to-object relations. The position of objects can be coded in Cartesian coordinates defined by the polar and sagittal planes of the body with respect to head-fixed coordinates, to retinal coordinates, and so on. Second, another means of encoding spatial information is to use an FoR that is external and independent of the body. For example, imagine your living room at home and try to answer the question whether the TV or the couch is closer to the window. The window serves as a reference point to which you evaluate distance of the other two objects. No reference to the body is necessary. This type of FoR is called *allocentric* and it refers to object-to-object relations (Vogeley & Fink, 2003). In the context of this chapter we decided to restrict ourselves to this distinction even though other researchers often use more terms in addition to the egocentric and allocentric FoR (e.g., the environmental FoR).

Use of a FoR is evident in any task that requires spatial reasoning. An important feature of these tasks is that subjects judge the spatial relationships between different objects. In order to specify the location or direction of objects, a FoR is required that relates the location of an object to some other location or direction. An egocentric FoR is used to specify locations or directions with respect to the location and perspective of the body or an agent. For example, verbal descriptions of a path most frequently use an egocentric FoR. The spatial path is encoded verbally and contains a sequence of landmarks to which specific directions are anchored (e.g., "Turn to your left when you reach the church"). An allocentric FoR, however, uses a fixed coordinate system imposed externally such as geographic space, and is thus independent of the agent's position. Allocentric FoRs use survey knowledge such as information about regions or the structure of the environment (e.g., "The church is east of the lake"). When relying on an allocentric strategy people form an internal map of the environment. This map consists of survey knowledge, which is more abstract than specific sequences of movements defining a path in egocentric coordinates. The advantage of an allocentric strategy is its flexibility in spatial orientation (O'Keefe & Nadel, 1978). For example, we rely on an allocentric map when we try to find out a short cut or when we are forced to make a detour to get to a specific location. Another allocentric strategy is to memorize the map of a new city before actually going there. Moreover, an allocentric FoR enables us to orient on more general cues like directions (e.g., eastward or westward) or the position of the sun.

There is now compelling support for the fact that different FoRs not only coexist but also rely, at least partially, on separate neuronal mechanisms. This support comes from neuropsychological studies with patients who have had unilateral neglect following right inferior parietal and right prefrontal cortex lesions (Vallar, 2001). Clinical studies have shown the existence of two independent FoRs by selective impairments of either the egocentric FoR leading to body-centered neglect symptoms (Beschin, Cubelli, Della, & Spinazzola, 1997; Calvanio, Petrone, & Levine, 1987; Chokron & Imbert, 1995; Fujii, Fukatsu, Suzuki, & Yamadori, 1996; Heilman, Bowers, & Watson, 1983; Hillis, Rapp, Benzing, & Carmazza, 1998; Karnath & Fetter, 1995; Karnath, Schenkel, & Fischer, 1991; Ladavas, 1987) or the allocentric FoR leading to stimulus or object-related neglect symptoms (Caramazza & Hillis, 1990; Driver & Halligan, 1991; Hillis & Caramazza, 1991; Walker & Young, 1996; Young, Hellawell, & Welch, 1992). Moreover, Hillis and Rapp (1998) and Ota, Fujii, Suzuki, Fukatsu, and Yamadori (2001) have shown that these two FoRs can be dissociated in individual patients with unilateral neglect. Investigators in each of these studies report a double dissociation. Patients with a body-centered neglect had no impairment when an allocentric FoR was used, and, likewise, patients with an object-centered neglect had no impairment when an egocentric FoR was used. The dissociation between the two types of FoRs provides not only strong evidence for the existence of two distinct mechanisms in the human brain but also indicates a functional independence of these two systems. It should be noted, however, that these dissociations are relatively rare and that the spatial impairments frequently occur in combination (Arguin & Bub 1993; Walker 1995).

Furthermore, the idea of at least partly different neuronal mechanisms underlying allocentric and egocentric FoRs is buttressed by neuroimaging research. In two recent fMRI studies, tasks were used in which healthy subjects had to judge the localization of a visual stimulus with respect to either their own body (egocentric condition; Galati et al., 2000; Vallar et al., 1999) or to a seen object (allocentric condition; Galati et al., 2000). Both investigations revealed a bilateral, mostly right-hemispheric network associated with the egocentric FoR. This network involves the posterior parietal and premotor frontal cortex. Additionally, a small frontoparietal subset of this network was activated during allocentric spatial processing. An additional analysis in which the egocentric condition was subtracted from the allocentric condition revealed activation in the occipitotemporal region including the parahippocampus. The consistent finding of a predominantly right-hemispheric activation during egocentric and allocentric spatial judgment tasks strongly confirms the important role this hemisphere plays in computing spatial coordinates. Work of our own group confirmed further the involvement of a fronto-parietal network in spatial coding (Zaehle et al., in press). In this study, the subjects heard descriptions of spatial relations to induce egocentric and allocentric spatial coding strategies, and then they responded to spatial questions. The results demonstrate that the processing of egocentric spatial relations is mediated by medial superior-parietal areas, whereas allocentric spatial coding requires an additional involvement of right parietal cortex, the ventral visual stream, and the hippocampal formation. These data suggest a rather hierarchically organized processing system in which egocentric spatial coding requires a subsystem of the processing resources involved in the allocentric condition.

It has to be noted that all studies mentioned here instructed their participants to select a specific FoR to investigate the neuronal processes underlying allocentric and egocentric spatial coding. In a more natural setting, however, the appropriate FoR can be selected more flexibly, and this is exactly the focus of the next section.

SELECTION OF THE REFERENCE FRAME

The brain is able to select the appropriate FoR depending on the actual task at hand. First, the term *selection* does not necessarily imply a strategic decision to choose one or the other. For example, the nature of the task can favor the use of a particular FoR, or previous experience can determine which FoR is being assigned to a particular task. Most knowledge on FoRs is based on perception research, and yet relatively little is known about how the FoRs are involved in more cognitive operations when no sensory information needs to be processed. In particular, the coexistence of two FoRs can be used to simulate spatial relationships more efficiently.

Several studies have been carried out to get further insight into the representational processes that underlie mental simulations of spatial relationships. Typical paradigms use imagined viewer rotation and imagined array rotation tasks. These imagined transformations involve a mental manipulation and adoption of different FoRs. In a typical viewer rotation task, the subjects have to imagine a change of their actual viewpoint to another point of view in relation to the object they see.

A need for mental viewer rotations becomes evident in situations in which people are engaged in conversations about spatial layouts. When people are facing each other they often have conflicting spatial perspectives. To overcome this conflict, someone can choose his own perspective to describe the spatial relations within a scene (e.g., "The church would be on my left") and the person listening can perform a mental viewer rotation and thus adopt the speaker's perspective to follow the conversation. Alternatively, the person giving the explanation can just as well simulate the perspective of the other person and use that perspective (e.g., "The church would be on your right"). The mental viewer rotation uses and manipulates the egocentric FoR, but the relations between objects remain constant.

In an array rotation task, however, subjects have to imagine an object rotating to their current viewpoint. That means that they must imagine a transformation of the object-based FoR relative to a stable viewer. Object-based rotations are used quite frequently. For example, when you try to fit the luggage you packed for your trip in the back of your car, you often find yourself wondering whether you will be able to squeeze in the last two or three pieces. Before actually trying it out, you can think ahead and imagine whether a particular piece would still fit in. To do so, you can mentally rotate the object until it fits the empty space. If it fits in imagery, you may in fact try to put the real piece there. This mental rotation of an object will have used and manipulated an allocentric FoR while the egocentric reference frame remained fixed.

The typical paradigm to investigate these two categories of mental transformation comes from experiments originally designed to study cognitive development in children. Piaget and Inhelder (1956) showed children a model of three mountains and asked them how this scene would look if seen from a different view point. In a modified version of this task, children viewed arrays of abstract objects. The children were then asked to imagine how the objects would look after having imagined themselves moving around the array or after having imagined the array rotated in front of them. The former case requires the children to perform a mental viewer rotation whereas the latter requires a mental array rotation (Huttenlocher & Presson, 1973). Results showed that the relative difficulty of object and viewer transformation varied systematically depending on the questions the experimenter asked. The children performed the array rotation task faster and made fewer errors than in the viewer rotation task when they had to match the transformed array to one of several pictures (appearance questions). This pattern reversed when the children had to report which item was at a particular location (e.g., "What's on your right?") after they performed the mental transformation (item questions) (Huttenlocher & Presson, 1979).

Several subsequent studies with adolescents confirmed this finding of an interaction of the relative difficulty of making spatial judgments and the transformation performed in dependence of the format in which the questions are presented (Presson, 1982; Wraga, Creem, & Proffitt, 1999, 2000). The viewer advantage in tasks with item questions has been demonstrated in several studies (Wraga et al., 1999, 2000) and it has been suggested that the viewer advantage has ecological plausibility because most observers will have more experience with motion in a static environment (Wraga et al., 2000). This suggestion is supported by the fact that the viewer advantage disappeared when the rotation had to be performed in a plane other than the familiar horizontal plane (Carpenter & Proffitt, 2001). The orthogonality of the relationship between the viewer's orientation and the imagined rotation seems to be more important than gravity with respect to the viewer advantage (Creem, Wraga, & Proffitt, 2001).

Taken together, a wealth of behavioral research conducted over the last 50 years provides evidence for two distinct cognitive mechanisms underlying the mental operation of imagined array and viewer rotations. The development of neuroimaging technology now provides further methods to explore the neurofunctional correlates of mental spatial processing.

BRAIN ACTIVATION DURING IMAGINED OBJECT AND VIEWER ROTATIONS

Several researchers have used neuroimaging to investigate the neural mechanisms underlying mental rotations in imagery and have added to our understanding of how different FoRs are involved in cognitive tasks. Regarding the mental object rotation tasks, the results converge on consistent involvement of parietal areas. Using the task developed by Shepard and Metzler (1971), Cohen et al. (1996) reported that the mental rotation process is computed mainly in the superior parietal lobe. In some neuroimaging studies, bilateral activation in posterior parietal lobe has been reported (Cohen, et al., 1996; Jordan, Heinze, Lutz, Kanowski, & Jancke, 2001; Kosslyn, DiGiralamo, Thompson, & Alpert, 1998; Tagaris et al. 1997) whereas other research has revealed subdominant right hemispheric activation when people are engaged in mental rotation tasks (Carpenter, Just, Keller, Eddy, & Thulborn, 1999; Harris et al., 2000; Zacks, Vettel, & Michelon, 2003). Yet other researchers have reported left-sided activation in posterior parietal lobe (Alivisatos & Petrides, 1997; Just, Carpenter, Maguire, Diwadkar, & McMains, 2001; Vingerhoets et al. 2001). Evidently there is wide-ranging agreement on the parietal involvement in mental rotation but the question about the laterality is still debated.

How can we resolve these ambiguous results in functional lateralization? It is possible that different mental rotation tasks entail different task demands. Tagaris et al. (1996) concluded from their findings that an increase in the task demands in different processes, such as encoding the stimuli, mentally rotating them, judging, and finally deciding, can lead to an increased activation in the superior parietal lobe. Also, the complexity of the stimuli used in mental object rotation tasks has been shown to influence hemispheric lateralization (Corballis, 1997). Furthermore, the right hemispheric advantage shifts to a left hemispheric advantage with increasing amount of practice (Voyer, 1995). Finally, gender effects appear to influence hemispheric lateralization as well (Jordan, Wustenberg, Heinze, Peters, & Jancke, 2002).

In the preceding, we have presented behavioral evidence suggesting distinct mechanisms underlying imagined viewer rotations versus imagined object rotations. What about the neuronal mechanisms involved in these two types of tasks? It is of interest to see whether the differences on the behavioral level correspond to different neuronal mechanisms. The neural mechanisms associated with mental viewer rotations were investigated in two recent fMRI studies (Creem et al., 2001; Zacks et al., 2003). Both studies revealed a subdominant left-sided activation of the parietal cortex while participants performed an imagined viewer rotation task. Despite this parallelism, differences in task demands and associated activations exist. In the study by Creem et al., the subjects were instructed to imagine themselves positioned in the middle of an array and then to imagine a rotation around their main axis. Results showed hemodynamic increases in the posterior superior parietal cortex, with a peak of activation in the left hemisphere. In the Zacks et al. study, subjects performed an imagined viewer rotation task with visually presented arrays. In this task, participants imagined themselves moving around the array. The results showed increased activation in the left parieto-temporo-occipital junction for the mental viewer rotation task when compared to the condition in which the subjects mentally rotated the object. In comparison to Creem et al.'s results, this peak of activation was located relatively inferior. The reason for this difference is an open question. It is possible that there are, again, differences in task demands between the two studies. For example, the rotation axis of the mental self-rotation was different. Furthermore, there were also differences in how the data were analyzed. While in Creem et al.'s study the activation during the imaged viewer rotation task was analyzed relative to a non-rotational control condition, Zacks et al. reported activations associated with mental viewer rotation relative to an array rotation task.

Taken together, results of several neuroimaging studies concerning mental object rotation revealed converging evidence for an essential role of the parietal lobe. Only a small number of studies have been carried out using mental viewer rotation tasks. These studies have consistently shown activations of the left posterior parietal lobe associated with mental viewer rotation. Due to the lack of studies in which both spatial rotation processes were compared directly, neurofunctional differences between mental object rotation and mental viewer rotation are still hypothetical. However, based on behavioral research and limited evidence from neuroimaging studies, it can be assumed that mental spatial transformations are not performed by one single mechanism. There is evidence that object-based and viewer-based rotations engage, at least partly, separate neurofunctional mechanisms.

Research on the neuronal underpinnings of cognitive spatial abilities has recently gained attention in the context of research on basic social interactions. It is not by itself evident what the one has to do with the other. In the following section we outline how the human ability to understand others as intentional agents refers to perspective taking as a basic prerequisite for efficient social interactions.

PERSPECTIVE TAKING AND THEORY OF MIND

Perspective taking is the ability to adopt someone else's perspective in order to make (as we will see, not only) spatial judgments. The following example will illustrate what is meant by perspective taking and why we relate it to theory of mind. Recently, I (Mast) was in an elevator in company of several unfamiliar people. The button indicating first floor had been pushed already but the elevator doors remained wide open. So, I pushed the ▷|◁ button to close them. All the people I could see had entered the elevator already. However, as soon as the doors began to close, another person facing me told me that I had just shut someone out. "Can't you see? There was another person right in front of the elevator." As a matter of fact, I could not see this other person. She was not in my field of view. However, the person facing me saw her approaching rapidly, desperately trying to catch the elevator. When I was then accused of having shut out someone else, my accuser, facing me, did not take into account my own perspective. Had she done so, she would have been aware of the difference in perspective, which made it impossible for me to see this other person who wanted to get on the elevator. Her judgment was based on her own perspective and she did not perform a viewer rotation to take someone else's perspective (in this case mine). This example points out the importance spatial abilities can have in everyday life situations such as when we attribute to a person the responsibility for a given act. Had she imagined what I was able to see from my own perspective, she may not have blamed me for any rude and inappropriate behavior. The next paragraph emphasizes in more detail the issue of perspective taking in the context of the theory of mind.

A theory of mind is a specific cognitive ability to understand others as intentional agents, that is, to interpret their minds in terms of intentional states such as beliefs and desires. Two types of approaches for the underlying cognitive mechanisms have been developed. The *theory* theory assumes that this ability is based on an individual folk-psychological theory of the structure of the mind. A naive theory is suggested, with posits, axioms, and rules of inferences. Mental states such as beliefs or desires are theoretical entities (e.g, Churchland & Churchland, 1998; Gopnik & Wellman, 1995). Alternatively, a mental simulation (*simulation* theory) has been suggested to explain the abilities necessary for the theory of mind. This view is based on the idea that our capability of understanding the mental states of others depends on our ability to run cognitive simulations and that these simulations enable us to predict and explain the behavior of others. It is necessary to form a representation of imaginary circumstances, which is decoupled from reality (Gallagher & Frith, 2003). The simulation needs to ensure that no confusion emerges between the mental states of others and one's own mental states. Recent neurophysiological investigations (Ramnani & Miall, 2004; Vogeley et al., 2001) as well as philosophical notions (Adams, 2004) have strengthened the superiority of simulation theory in explaining how humans represent mental states of others.

An eminent feature of a cognitive simulation is the ability of putting oneself in someone else's place. Therefore, the egocentric FoR is translocated to the perspective of another agent. This demonstrates how spatial cognition is involved even in tasks that are not necessarily defined by their spatial nature. Perspective taking is assumed to be a central component in the context of reasoning about others (Ruby & Decety, 2001, 2003) and is strongly associated with the ability to represent mental states of others (Langdon & Coltheart, 2001; Vogeley & Fink, 2003).

Further evidence for an association between spatial transformation abilities and a theory of mind emerges from their apparent codevelopment in ontogenesis. The ability to "see" things from someone else's point of view, which we referred to as mental viewer rotation, develops in children around the age of 4 (Borke, 1975; Donaldson, 1978). Similarly, 4-year-olds can solve problems in a *false belief* experiment, the typical paradigm used to investigate the theory of mind in children (Perner, Leekman, & Wimmer, 1987; Wimmer & Perner, 1983).

There have been relatively few studies on blind children's development of perspective taking and a theory of mind. The findings suggest that children who are blind exhibit normal performance in perspective taking tasks (Peterson, Peterson, & Webb, 2000). Therefore, we can assume that this ability can develop without visual experiences. However, blind children's ability to solve the false-belief tasks develops later when compared to sighted people (Mc-Alpine & Moore, 1995; Minter, Hobson, & Bishop, 1998). Blind children between 5 and 9 years of age have a lower level of performance in theory of mind tasks until they are about 12 years old. A similar finding has been shown for deaf children who have grown up in hearing families (Siegal & Peterson, 1998). These results are interesting because they contrast what we know from the development of sighted children. It is important to note, however, that blind children are socially responsive and interactive with peers and teachers (Preisler, 1993). More research is needed before drawing more specific conclusions about the cognitive development of blind children.

MORE QUESTIONS

Why are blind people still able to play soccer? What is it that allows them to do so? How much vision do we need to play soccer? Is playing soccer less visual than we thought? There is no doubt that soccer is very visual when we watch it on TV (even though recent research on movement observation suggests an activation of motor areas in the brain). When it is played actively, however, there is evidently much more than just the visual system involved. Future research needs to focus on the mechanisms underlying the abilities blind players use. If they help the blind, they could help anybody who wants to improve his or her spatial abilities. Having said that, however, we have to be aware that there are limitations. Not everything is possible just because efforts are being made. Therefore, it is crucial to focus more on the conditions under which rehabilitation and recovery are possible. On the one side, this is a question of neuroanatomy, which provides the connections necessary to activate a given area. On the other side, it is a question of how cognitive operations can support rehabilitation. In this context, mental imagery is a well-studied cognitive function, and its impact on the brain has been demonstrated compellingly. Its use has not as yet been exploited.

ACKNOWLEDGMENTS

This article was supported by the Swiss National Science Foundation (grant no. 611-066052).

REFERENCES

Adams, F. E. (2004). Neural imaging and the theory versus simulation debate. *Mind & Language, 16,* 368–392.

Alivisatos, B., & Petrides, M. (1997). Functional activation of the human brain during mental rotation. *Neuropsychologia, 35*, 111–118.

Andersen, R. A., Snyder, L. H., Bradley, D. C., & Xing, J. (1997). Multimodal representation of space in the posterior parietal cortex and its use in planning movements. *Annual Review of Neuroscience, 20*, 303–330.

Arguin, M., & Bub, D. N. (1993). Evidence for an independent stimulus-centered spatial reference frame from a case of visual hemineglect. *Cortex, 29*, 349–357.

Barr, C. C., Schultheis, L. W., & Robinson, D. A. (1976). Voluntary, non-visual control of the human vestibulo-ocular reflex. *Acta Oto-Laryngologica, 81*, 365–375.

Bense, S., Stephan, T., Yousry, T., Brandt, T., & Dieterich, M. (2001). Multisensory cortical signal increases and decreases during vestibular galvanic stimulation (fMRI). *Journal of Neurophysiology, 85*, 886–899.

Beschin, N., Cubelli, R., Della, S. S., & Spinazzola, L. (1997). Left of what? The role of egocentric coordinates in neglect. *Journal of Neurology, Neurosurgery, and Psychiatry, 63*, 483–489.

Blanke, O., Landis, T., Spinelli, L., & Seeck, M. (2004). Out-of-body experience and autoscopy of neurological origin. *Brain, 127*, 243–258.

Borke, H. (1975). Piaget's mountains revisited: Changes in the egocentric landscape. *Developmental Psychology, 11*, 240–243.

Brandt, T., Bartenstein, P., Janek, A., & Dieterich, M. (1998). Reciprocal inhibitory visual-vestibular interaction. Visual motion stimulation deactivates the parieto-insular vestibular cortex. *Brain, 121*, 1749–1758.

Brandt, T., Glasauer, S., Stephan, T., Bense, S., Yousry, T. A., Deutschländer, A., et al. (2002). Visual-vestibular and visuovisual cortical interaction—new insights from fmri and PET. *Annals of the New York Academy of Sciences, 956*, 230–241.

Calvanio, R., Petrone, P. N., & Levine, D. N. (1987). Left visual spatial neglect is both environment-centered and body-centered. *Neurology, 37*, 1179–1183.

Caramazza, A., & Hillis, A. E. (1990). Spatial representation of words in the brain implied by studies of a unilateral neglect patient. *Nature, 346*, 267–269.

Carpenter, M., & Proffitt, D. R. (2001). Comparing viewer and array mental rotations in different planes. *Memory & Cognition, 29*, 441–448.

Carpenter, P. A., Just, M. A., Keller, T. A., Eddy, W., & Thulborn, K. (1999). Graded functional activation in the visuospatial system with the amount of task demand. *Journal of Cognitive Neuroscience, 11*, 9–24.

Chokron, S., & Imbert, M. (1995). Variations of the egocentric reference among normal subjects and a patient with unilateral neglect. *Neuropsychologia, 33*, 703–711.

Churchland P. M., & Churchland, P. S. (1998). *On the contrary: Critical essays, 1987–1997.* Cambridge, MA: MIT Press/Bradford Books.

Cohen, M. S., Kosslyn, S. M., Breiter, H. C., DiGirlamo, G. J., Thompson, W. L., Bookheimer, S. Y., et al. (1996). Changes in cortical activity during mental rotation. A mapping study using functional MRI. *Brain, 119* (Pt 1), 89–100.

Corballis, M. C. (1997). Mental rotation and the right hemisphere. *Brain and Language, 57*, 100–121.

Creem, S. H., Downs, T. H., Wraga, M., Harrington, G. S., Proffitt, D. R., & Downs, J. H., III. (2001). An fMRI study of imagined self-rotation. *Cognitive, Affective, & Behavioral Neuroscience, 1*, 239–249.

Creem, S. H., Wraga, M., & Proffitt, D. R. (2001). Imagining physically impossible self-rotations: geometry is more important than gravity. *Cognition, 81*, 41–64.

Donaldson, M. (1978). *Children's minds.* London: Fontana/Croom Helm.

Driver, J., & Halligan, P. W. (1991). Can visual neglect operate in object-centered co-ordinationes? An affirmative single-case study. *Cognitive Neuropsychology, 8,* 475–496.

Fujii, T., Fukatsu, R., Suzuki, K., & Yamadori, A. (1996). Effect of head-centered and body-centered hemispace in unilateral neglect. *Journal of Clinical and Experimental Neuropsychology, 18,* 777–783.

Galati, G., Lobel, E., Vallar, G., Berthoz, A., Pizzamiglio, L., & Le Bihan, D. (2000). The neural basis of egocentric and allocentric coding of space in humans: A functional magnetic resonance study. *Experimental Brain Research, 133,* 156–164.

Gallagher, H. L., & Frith, C. D. (2003). Functional imaging of 'theory of mind.' *Trends in Cognitive Sciences, 7,* 77–83.

Gopnik, A., & Wellman, H. (1995). Why the child's theory of mind really is a theory. In M. Davis, & T. Stone, (Eds). *Folk psychology: The theory of mind debate* (pp. 232–258). Oxford: Basil Blackwell.

Harris, I. M., Eganm, G. F., Sonkkila, C., Tochon-Danguy, H. J., Paxinos, G., & Watson, J. D. (2000). Selective right parietal lobe activation during mental rotation: A parametric PET study. *Brain, 123,* 65–73.

Heilman, K. M., Bowers, D., & Watson, R. T. (1983). Performance on hemispatial pointing task by patients with neglect syndrome. *Neurology, 33,* 661–664.

Herbert, R. D., Dean, C., & Gandevia, S. C. (1998). Effects of real and imagined training on voluntary muscle activation during maximal isometric contractions. *Acta Physiologica Scandivica, 163,* 361–68.

Hillis, A. E., & Caramazza, A. (1991). Deficit to stimulus-centered, letter shape representations in a case of "unilateral neglect." *Neuropsychologia, 29,* 1223–1240.

Hillis, A. E., & Rapp, B. (1998). Unilateral spatial neglect in dissociable frames of reference: A comment on Farah, Brunn, Wong, Wallace, and Carpenter (1990). *Neuropsychologia, 36,* 1257–1262.

Hillis, A. E., Rapp, B., Benzing, L., & Caramazza, A. (1998). Dissociable coordinate frames of unilateral spatial neglect: "Viewer-centered" neglect. *Brain and Cognition, 37,* 491–526.

Huttenlocher, J., & Presson, C. C. (1973). Mental rotation and the perspective problem. *Cognitive Psychology, 4,* 277–299.

Huttenlocher, J., & Presson, C. C. (1979). The coding and transformation of spatial information. *Cognitive Psychology, 11,* 375–394.

Jeannerod, M., Arbib, M. A., Rizzolatti, G., & Sakata, H. (1995). Grasping objects: The cortical mechanisms of visuomotor transformation. *Trends in Neurosciences, 18,* 314–320.

Jordan, K., Heinze, H. J., Lutz, K., Kanowski, M., & Jancke, L. (2001). Cortical activations during the mental rotation of different visual objects. *NeuroImage, 13,* 143–152.

Jordan, K., Wustenberg, T., Heinze, H. J., Peters, M., & Jancke, L. (2002). Women and men exhibit different cortical activation patterns during mental rotation tasks. *Neuropsychologia, 40,* 2397–2408.

Just, M. A., Carpenter, P. A., Maguire, M., Diwadkar, V., & McMains, S. (2001). Mental rotation of objects retrieved from memory: A functional MRI study of spatial processing. *Journal of Experimental Psychology. General, 130,* 493–504.

Karnath, H. O., & Fetter, M. (1995). Ocular space exploration in the dark and its relation to subjective and objective body orientation in neglect patients with parietal lesions. *Neuropsychologia, 33,* 371–77.

Karnath, H. O., Schenkel, P., & Fischer, B. (1991). Trunk orientation as the determining factor of the 'contralateral' deficit in the neglect syndrome and as the physical anchor of the internal representation of body orientation in space. *Brain, 114*, 1997–2014.

Klein, I., Dubois, J., Mangin, J.-F., Kherif, F., Flandin, G., Poline, J.-B., et al. (2004). Retinotopic organization of visual mental images as revealed by functional magnetic resonance imaging. *Cognitive Brain Research, 22*, 26–31.

Kosslyn, S. M., DiGirolamo, G. J., Thompson, W. L., & Alpert, N. M. (1998). Mental rotation of objects versus hands: neural mechanisms revealed by positron emission tomography. *Psychophysiology, 35*, 151–61.

Kosslyn, S. M., & Thompson, W. L. (2003). When is early visual cortex activated during visual mental imagery? *Psychological Bulletin, 129*, 723–46.

Ladavas, E. (1987). Is the hemispatial deficit produced by right parietal lobe damage associated with retinal or gravitational coordinates? *Brain, 110*, 167–180.

Langdon, R., & Coltheart, M. (2001). Visual perspective-taking and schizotypy: evidence for a simulation-based account of mentalizing in normal adults. *Cognition, 82*, 1–26.

Loomis, J. M., Klatzky, R. L., Golledge, R. G., Cicinelli, J. G., Pellegrino, J. W., & Fry, P. A. (1993). Nonvisual navigation by blind and sighted: assessment of path integration ability. *Journal of Experimental Psychology. General, 122*, 73–91.

Lorenz, K. (1941). Kants Lehre vom Apriorischen im Lichte der gegenwärtigen Biologie. *Blätter für Deutsche Philosophie, 15*, 94–125.

Lorenz, K. (1982). Kant's doctrine of the a priori in the light of contemporary biology. In H. C. Plotkin (Ed.), *Learning, development and culture: Essays in evolutionary epistemology* (pp. 121–143). New York: Wiley.

Marshall, J. C., & Fink, G. R. (2001). Spatial cognition: Where we were and where we are. *NeuroImage, 14*, S2–S7.

Mast, F. W., Merfeld, D. M., & Kosslyn, S. M. (2006). Visual mental imagery during caloric vestibular stimulation. *Neuropsychologia, 44*, 101–109.

McAlpine, L., & Moore, C. L. (1995). The development of social understanding in children with visual impairments. *Journal of Visual Impairment and Blindness, 89*, 349–358.

Minter, M., Hobson, R. P., & Bishop, M. (1998). Congenital visual impairment and 'theory of mind.' *British Journal of Developmental Psychology, 16*, 183–196.

O'Keefe, J., & Nadel, L. (1978). *The hippocampus as a cognitive map.* Oxford: Clarendon Press.

Ota, H., Fujii, T., Suzuki, K., Fukatsu, R., & Yamadori, A. (2001). Dissociation of body-centered and stimulus-centered representations in unilateral neglect. *Neurology, 57*, 2064–2069.

Perner, J., Leekman, S. R., & Wimmer, H. (1987). Three-years-olds' difficulty with false belief: The case for a conceptual deficit. *British Journal of Developmental Psychology, 5*, 125–137.

Peterson, C. C., Peterson, J. L., & Webb, J. (2000). Factors influencing the development of a theory of mind in blind children. *British Journal of Developmental Psychology, 18*, 437–447.

Piaget, J., & Inhelder, B. (1956). *The child's conception of space.* London: Routledge & Kegan Paul.

Preisler, G. M. (1993). A descriptive study of blind children in nurseries with sighted children. *Child: Care, Health and Development, 19*, 295–315.

Presson, C. C. (1982). Strategies in spatial reasoning. *Journal of Experimental Psychology. Learning, Memory, and Cognition, 8*, 243–251.

Ramnani, N., & Miall, R. C. (2004). A system in the human brain for predicting the actions of others. *Nature Neurosciences, 7*, 85–90.

Rieser, J. J., Guth, D. A., & Hill, A. W. (1986). Sensitivity to perspective structure while walking without vision. *Perception, 15,* 173–188.

Rizzolatti, G., Fogassi, L., & Gallese, V. (1997). Parietal cortex: From sight to action. *Current Opinion in Neurobiology, 7,* 562–567.

Ruby, P., & Decety, J. (2001). Effect of subjective perspective taking during simulation of action: A PET investigation of agency. *Nature Neurosciences, 4,* 546–550.

Ruby, P., & Decety, J. (2003). What you believe versus what you think they believe: a neuroimaging study of conceptual perspective-taking. *European Journal of Neuroscience, 17,* 2475–2480.

Shepard, R. N., & Metzler, J. (1971). Mental rotation of three-dimensional objects. *Science, 171,* 701–703.

Siegal, M., & Peterson, C. C. (1998). Preschoolers' understanding of lies and innocent and negligent mistakes. *Developmental Psychology, 34,* 332–341.

Tagaris, G. A., Kim, S. G., Strupp, J. P., Andersen, P., Ugurbil, K., & Georgopoulos, A. P. (1996). Quantitative relations between parietal activation and performance in mental rotation. *Neuroreport, 7,* 773–776.

Tagaris, G. A., Kim, S. G., Strupp, J. P., Andersen, P., Ugurbil, K., & Georgopoulos, A. P. (1997). Mental rotation studied by functional magnetic resonance imaging at high field (4 tesla): Performance and cortical activation. *Journal of Cognitive Neuroscience, 9,* 419–432.

Tiecks, F. P., Planck, J., Haberl, R. L., & Brandt, T. (1996). Reduction in posterior cerebral artery blood flow velocity during caloric vestibular stimulation. *Journal of Cerebral Blood Flow Metabolism, 16,* 1379–1382.

Vallar, G. (2001). Extrapersonal visual unilateral spatial neglect and its neuroanatomy. *NeuroImage, 14,* S52–S58.

Vallar, G., Lobel, E., Galati, G., Berthoz, A., Pizzamiglio, L., & Le Bihan, D. (1999). A fronto-parietal system for computing the egocentric spatial frame of reference in humans. *Experimental Brain Research, 124,* 281–286.

Vanlierde, A., De Volder, A. G., Wanet-Defalque, M.-C., & Veraart, C. (2003). Occipito-parietal cortex activation during visuo-spatial imagery in early blind humans. *NeuroImage, 19,* 698–709.

Vanlierde, A., & Wanet-Defalque, M.-C. (2004). Abilities and strategies of blind and sighted subjects in visuo-spatial imagery. *Acta Psychologica, 116,* 205–222.

Vingerhoets, G., Santens, P., Van, L. K., Lahorte, P., Dierckx, R. A., & De, R. J. (2001). Regional brain activity during different paradigms of mental rotation in healthy volunteers: A positron emission tomography study. *NeuroImage, 13,* 381–391.

Vogeley, K., Bussfeld, P., Newen, A., Herrmann, S., Happe, F., Falkai, P., et al. (2001). Mind reading: neural mechanisms of theory of mind and self-perspective. *NeuroImage, 14,* 170–181.

Vogeley, K., & Fink, G. R. (2003). Neural correlates of the first-person-perspective. *Trends in Cognitive Sciences, 7,* 38–42.

Voyer, D. (1995). Effect of practice on laterality in a mental rotation task. *Brain and Cognition, 29,* 326–335.

Walker, R. (1995). Spatial and object-based neglect. *Neurocase: Case Studies in Neuropsychology, Neuropsychiatry, and Behavioural Neurology, 1,* 371–383.

Walker, R., & Young, A. W. (1996). Object-based neglect: an investigation of the contributions of eye movements and perceptual completion. *Cortex, 32,* 279–295.

Wenzel, R., Bartenstein, P., Dieterich, M., Danek, A., Weindl, A., Minoshima, S., et al. (1996). Deactivation of human visual cortex during involuntary ocular oscillations. A PET activation study. *Brain, 119,* 101–110.

Wimmer, H., & Perner, J. (1983). Beliefs about beliefs: representation and constraining function of wrong beliefs in young children's understanding of deception. *Cognition, 13,* 103–128.

Wraga, M., Creem, S. H., & Proffitt, D. R. (1999). The influence of spatial reference frames on imagined object- and viewer rotations. *Acta Psychologica, 102,* 247–264.

Wraga, M., Creem, S. H., & Proffitt, D. R. (2000). Updating displays after imagined object and viewer rotations. *Journal of Experimental Psychology. Learning, Memory, and Cognition, 26,* 151–168.

Young, A. W., Hellawell, D. J., & Welch, J. (1992). Neglect and visual recognition. *Brain 115*(Pt 1), 51–71.

Yue, G. H., & Cole, K. J. (1992). Strength increases from the motor program: Comparison of training with maximal voluntary and imagined muscle contractions. *Journal of Neurophysiology, 67,* 1114–1123.

Yue, G. H., Wilson, S. L., Cole, K. J., & Darling, W. G. (1996). Imagined muscle contraction training increases voluntary neural drive to muscle. *Journal of Psychophysiology, 10,* 198–208.

Zacks, J. M., Vettel, J. M., & Michelon, P. (2003). Imagined viewer and object rotations dissociated with event-related FMRI. *Journal of Cognitive Neuroscience, 15,* 1002–1018.

Zaehle, T., Jordan, K., Wüstenberg, T., Baudewig, J., Dechent, P., & Mast, F. W. (In press.) *The neural basis of the egocentric and allocentric spatial frame of reference.*

14

Touch as a "Reality Sense"

Morton A. Heller and Ashley Clark

In everyday language, individuals are said to pinch themselves to test whether they are awake or sleeping. This reflects the widespread belief that touch is the sense that is the best measure of reality. We know that we can deceive vision through mirrors or other sorts of artifice, and we are often aware of illusory mistakes in our sense of sight. We see things in our sleep that we know are not there, much as we can have daydreams while awake. Some philosophers, G. H. Mead for example, ascribe our understanding of external objects to sensations of touch because "We see surfaces, but feel insides" (see Mead, 1932; Yolton, 1962, p. 15). Sometimes we fail to notice things that we should be able to see, even when they are right in front of us (e.g., Simons & Chabris, 1999). We are frequently aware of the failures of vision. However, touch is susceptible to errors, and this will be considered in this chapter.

Does touch give us an accurate "view" of the world? A common bias in the general population is that vision somehow gives us an accurate "photographic" image of the world whereas touch cannot do this. If this is the case, what about "optical" illusions? It is curious that people may hold diametrically opposed views about the senses. Thus, they assume that vision is susceptible to illusions, but at the same time, they believe that vision gives us a photorealistic image of our environment. Whereas people sometimes describe touch as a "reality sense," many researchers have ascribed numerous deficiencies to haptics, especially when pictures are the context or when pattern perception is involved (e.g., Revesz, 1950).

Our ability to rely on the senses for information about the world is a fundamental theoretical problem for psychology, for philosophy, and for understanding psychopathology. Many basic perceptual theories assume that illusory misperception is the norm, rather than the exception. On some versions of ecological psychology, however, illusions are thought to derive from degraded or impoverished stimulus information (e.g., Gibson, 1966). According to Soltis, illusions may be different from other more normal sorts of perceptual errors (Soltis, 1966). Philosophers such as Berkeley wondered about whether we could rely upon the senses and ultimately ascribed their reliability to the intervention of a deity. Conversely, clinicians often discriminate between normal and abnormal thoughts and percepts in terms of their relative correspondence with reality. If one were unable to tell whether one's cognitive states were "awake" or dream states, then there should be serious cause for concern. We assume that there may be differences in how well individuals have contact with some ultimate physical reality, and those with diminished knowledge of reality reside in different places than the rest of us.

There are a number of ways to study the relationships between the senses, and I will outline a few basic approaches that I have taken. One tack involves the examination of the relative dominance relations between the senses. If people rely more on one sense than another when they provide conflicting information, then that may provide clues about their relative utility for acquiring information about the world. Furthermore, these dominance relations may change when people suffer the degradation of a sense, as when they experience blurring of vision (Heller, 1983). Most people rely on vision for pattern perception, even when they should not. This reliance on sight may persist during the progressive deterioration of sight, and can interfere with rehabilitation and learning how to use touch for pattern perception and for mobility.

The senses may also assist each other in making perceptual judgments. Rather than simply adding information, they may function more efficiently when working together in a cooperative fashion (Heller, 1982, 1993). Thus, we may sometimes underestimate the capability of a sense such as touch when we study it in isolation because perception is normally multimodal (see Heller & Ballesteros, 2006).

An alternative way to study the relationship between the senses is to compare them directly. One may try to determine whether the senses are equally good at picking up particular sorts of information (Heller, 1982). We have been interested in discovering whether vision and touch are both susceptible to the same illusions, and whether the illusions vary in strength when they are experienced through touch or vision. The two senses may both experience the same illusions but for different reasons. Rather different causal mechanisms may be at work. This may be revealed in the susceptibility of the illusions to manipulations that are intended to weaken or strengthen them.

Results of a number of studies have shown that while illusions such as the horizontal–vertical illusion (Heller, Brackett, Salik, Scroggs, & Green, 2003a; Heller, Brackett, Wilson, Yoneyama, & Boyer, 2002c; Heller, Calcaterra, Burson, & Green, 1997; Heller & Joyner, 1993;) and the Mueller–Lyer illusion (Heller, et al., 2002c) occur in both vision and touch, they differ in strength in these two senses. Moreover, there is considerable evidence that the illusions may occur for different reasons, and that they respond differentially to some important experimental manipulations. Thus, there are reasons for believing that the senses may share some common features, but there are also some important differences in how they function.

COOPERATION BETWEEN VISION AND TOUCH: MULTIMODAL SYNERGY

Vision and touch may often function in a cooperative manner to improve the accuracy of perceptual judgments (Gibson, 1966). Touch can be used to orient stimuli for better viewing conditions, and peripheral vision may guide the hand to improve touch. There is recent evidence that noninformative vision can aid touch (e.g., Kennett, Eimer, Spence, & Driver, 2001). However, sight of hand movement and position can provide much useful information. Sight of the hand occurs during visual guidance of locomotion, but blurry vision of the hand can also lead to the improvement of information pickup.

There are a number of ways in which vision of the hand can aid haptics. First, the effect may be partially attentional. A blind person told Heller that it helped him judge patterns he felt when he "looked" at his hand, even though he did not have any light perception. He claimed that orienting his nonfunctional eyes towards his hands helped him attend to the patterns that he touched. Blurry vision of the hand may also provide spatial reference information that is lacking in blindfolded and blind states (see Millar, 1994, 2000), so blindfolded subjects are forced to rely on haptics for their sense of the upright and knowledge of the horizontal and vertical reference frames. This reference frame knowledge is especially important when haptic judgments involve stimuli that are defined by orientation, such as Braille, maps, pictures, or letter configurations. The lack of visual reference frame information may depress performance when blindfolded sighted subjects use haptics for pattern perception, so we may often underestimate the potential of haptics when we blindfold our participants. It is, then, sometimes a mistake to generalize from lower performance in blindfolded sighted subjects about the nature of touch perception, and to generate predictions about performance limitations in blind people from such limited data.

We have used stained glass and low lighting to degrade vision and manipulate visual information about the hand. Objects can be rendered invisible by turning the lights out and by interposing stained glass to blur vision and simulate very low vision. The addition of light-emitting diodes on the digits, hand, or other locations allows one to control sight of the hand and its orientation in space. The ability to see one's hand in space was found to aid performance in making judgments of the relative smoothness of textured surfaces (Heller, 1982). The subjects were able to see their hands as they touched surfaces, but they could not see the surfaces themselves because of the blurring effect of stained glass. The performance levels in touch plus blurry vision were comparable to those that were obtained when there was normal sight of the hand touching surfaces. This means that in normal bimodal conditions, subjects were not relying on sight of the textured surfaces but were using vision to guide exploration. Perhaps the effect was attentional, but it was certainly not the result of a simple addition of perceptual information about the surface textures from vision and touch. It was argued that in bimodal conditions, touch was used for information pickup, but vision was probably used for movement control.

More recently, Heller et al. (2002b) found rather dramatic improvements in performance under conditions of low lighting and blurred vision. The experiment was undertaken to attempt to clarify the causes of the advantage of the subjects with very low vision (VLV) in their interpretation of tangible perspective pictures drawn from different viewpoints. Stained glass and low lighting were used to simulate VLV. These individuals had little, if any, pattern perception. A few of them were able to see very close hand motion, and some could see the shape of a large picture window but only if the lighting were very bright. Their performance was exceptionally high and could have derived from a number of factors, including prior visual experience, increased haptic skill, the ability to see hand motion and the location of their hands in space, or the mere presence of light perception. While the VLV individuals had light perception, none could see the stimuli that they touched. Note that all of the blind individuals in this study performed far more rapidly than the sighted individuals. Even the congenitally blind participants were faster than the sighted participants, although they performed at a similar level in terms of accuracy.

In an attempt to clarify the possible source of the advantage of the VLV participants, two groups of sighted individuals were exposed to a picture matching task, but with low lighting and blurred vision. They felt the same solid shapes and tried to match tangible perspective drawings to those shapes. Room lights were turned off, and stained glass–covered goggles rendered the solid objects and tangible drawings invisible. One group of subjects had a small light emitting diode (LED) on top of their hands, but this aid was not given to the other group of subjects. The manipulation was designed to determine whether the mere presence of minimal light perception might be critical, or whether sight of the hand was important. The results indicated that low lighting per se had no effect on performance because the subjects performed like the blindfolded subjects of the main study (Heller et al., 2002b). This meant that lower performance by the blindfolded sighted subjects could not be explained in terms of the distracting effects of blindfolding. However, the subjects with the LEDs on their hands showed performance that was identical to that of the VLV subjects. This meant that sight of the hand, even when surfaces themselves could not be seen, aided haptic performance. Sight of the hand's location may help naïve subjects attend to touch. Also, it may provide a visual spatial framework to help organize pattern information. Thus, visual information about hand location and the layout of a room, even if blurry and degraded, may provide a spatial reference system to help people judge the shapes of stimuli that they touch. It was curious that most of the VLV subjects claimed that they could not see hand motion or the location of their hands in space. It is possible that self-report is not very reliable and that people may often be able to make use of information without explicit, conscious awareness of this process.

It is likely that very minimal residual vision can provide unexpected benefits to touch and to people who are visually impaired. For example, if a person can see the direction of light sources, this can aid locomotion indoors. The ability to see a light from a lamp or a window could help a person orient towards familiar landmarks. Certainly, the ability to see one's hand can aid vision in a number of ways, including altering attentional mechanisms. However, the mere presence of diffuse light perception and the ability to notice very minimal differences in brightness may aid visually impaired subjects. If a person can tell that the ground is not quite as bright as the sky, even if the horizon cannot be seen, then this could still assist in spatial orientation. A brighter "above" as compared with a somewhat darker "below" may help an individual maintain good posture, and this could aid pattern perception in tasks that are dependent on spatial reference information. This includes haptic pattern perception tasks that are orientation specific, such as Braille or embossed letters, maps, and perspective representations.

In the next section we take up the relationships between the senses when conflicting information is available to vision and to touch. Although the senses often provide consistent and redundant input, this is not always the case.

INTERSENSORY CONFLICT

The senses may sometimes yield discrepant information about objects so that a spoon that is immersed in water may appear crooked but feel straight. We often view objects through lenses or see them reflected in mirrors. These optical devices can alter our visual experiences, and we often consciously compensate for this intrusion upon our sensory capability. Thus, when making judgments about such important events as time to collision, we know that our side-view mirror alters the apparent distance of vehicles. However, people may not always have a proper understanding of the sources of conflicts between the senses, and this can yield perceptual errors. We have an intersensory conflict only if we believe that we are touching and seeing the same object. There are many instances in which we are touching and feeling the same object, but in different locations, in which case there is no real conflict. For example, if I look at the surface of my desk it appears relatively smooth (but cluttered). The underside of the desktop is not as smooth, but there is no discrepancy or conflict here. There is no reason to expect that the desk should not have a smooth top surface, since it is veneered. The underside is obviously a form of particle board that is not as smooth. I do not experience an intersensory conflict when I touch and view different objects, or in this case, different surfaces of one object.

If individuals were known to rely invariably upon one sense as opposed to another, then we would have very good information about dominance relations between the senses. Researchers have often assumed that vision is the dominant spatial sense, and it certainly is when precise judgments of form are required; vision can do this much faster than the other senses (see Warren & Rossano, 1991). However, dominance relations may change when touch is capable of rapid size estimates and sight is no longer able to claim "prior entry." The dominance of vision may often arise when people are able to make judgments much faster through that sense than others. Thus, if a normally sighted subject looks at a form while touching it, the observer probably gains adequate visual pattern information before touch can succeed, since vision operates much faster than touch. It is possible that subjects never get to know the form through touch under these circumstances. Note, too, that touch can dominate vision for texture, especially for smoother surfaces where touch excels (Heller, 1982). Dominance relations may depend upon both the speed of processing and the adequacy of a sense for picking up information about objects or surfaces (Freides, 1974).

Mirrors often induce left–right reversals, but they can also cause top-down inversions (Heller, 1992a). Many people are not aware of this effect of vertically placed mirrors. I took advantage of this lack of knowledge. In a study that pitted touch against vision, subjects felt tangible letters such as p, q, b, d, M, and W, but viewed themselves touching the letters in a vertical mirror. This caused subjects to see the inverted pattern as different than the one that was felt. The mirror induced a top-down inversion, but not a left–right reversal. In addition, subjects could see themselves approaching the stimulus from afar. An interposed panel in a mirror-tracing apparatus prevented the subjects from seeing their hands without the "benefit" of the vertical mirror. Most subjects relied on the sense of touch for their judgments and were able to ignore visual information. It was important that the subjects were told to name the letter, and the instructions were designed to avoid bias towards one sense or the other. It is likely that sight of the hand matters here, as it obviously does in other circumstances (e.g., Heller 2002b).

A reducing lens was used to generate a conflict between vision and touch in a series of experiments (Heller, Calcaterra, Green, & Brown, 1999). The subjects saw squares that were reduced in size because of the effects of the lens and then attempted to match squares of varying sizes to the discrepant stimulus. Sight of the hand aided subjects' compensation for the perceptual distortion of the lens. It was curious that very few subjects were aware of the presence of the lens, yet a number of them thought that they managed to hold their hands so that "they looked small and far away." When subjects generated their own size estimates, either through making a pincers posture with their index finger and thumb or by viewing a metric ruler, the response modality determined dominance relations. Thus, when subjects generated a haptic size estimate, they showed haptic dominance. Dominance relations are probably influenced by the speed with which subjects are able to make their responses because the use of the pincers response yielded haptic dominance, but haptic matching to an array did not.

Touch can be dominant in pattern perception tasks when sight of the hand is permitted but also in circumstances where vision is blurry by design or through the effects of disease (see Heller, 1983; 2006). The notion that vision is usually dominant over touch is an overgeneralization that does not fit the data.

It is scientifically questionable to raise the issue of "which sense is dominant?" The specific context for the problem must be specified, that is, in spatial perception, or in texture, or in emotional impact, and so forth. The problem is that sensory input can have a number of different implications for the observer, and many of them are very significant. Clearly, the emotional impact of a sense is very difficult to operationalize, but this bears on the question at hand. Few of us would assert that the sight of a needle entering our flesh lacks any emotional consequences, but the visible effects are very different than those that are tangible. It is not plausible or reasonable to attempt to compare them, nor would it make sense to try to apply the intersensory discrepancy paradigm to this problem.

The next section of this chapter concerns illusions in touch. Even though we generally obtain accurate information about the world through the sense of touch, all of the senses may be subject to error.

Haptic Illusions

We have been interested in studying haptic illusions as a way to gain insight into possible differences in how we process information in vision and touch. People have thought that touch may be less susceptible than vision to illusory misperception. Touch has been thought of as a "reality sense." This common belief may include a kernel of truth, or it may represent a groundless set of assumptions. The evidence supports both of these ideas.

There is no doubt that illusions exist in touch, and they have been studied for many years (e.g., Tsai, 1967). Illusions are powerful in haptics, and some may even be more potent than in vision. Although it is possible to attenuate the magnitude of many illusions in vision with practice and feedback, some are visually potent and may resist conscious efforts to ignore them. For example, the first author of this chapter, Morton Heller, has studied the horizontal–vertical illusion for many years and has never failed to be struck by the strength of the visual illusion. In the horizontal–vertical illusion, people overestimate the vertical of an inverted T configuration, even when the two segments are really the same length. A similar illusion occurs in touch.

It is very possible that viewing conditions may alter our perception of illusions in vision, and the same holds for touch. In vision, the orientation of patterns matters a great deal, as it does for touch. However, the consequences of changing the orientation of patterns can sometimes have very dramatic consequences for haptics, and they are not quite the same as in vision.

A number of variables may alter the strength of illusions in touch. Haptic illusions may be weakened or eliminated when inspection conditions are optimal. In addition, the position of the configuration in space is important, and illusory distortion may be altered in a different manner for haptics as opposed to vision. Perceptual skill may modify the expression of the illusions in haptics, but many of the haptic illusions can occur in people who are blind as well as in those who are sighted. These considerations are taken up in turn.

The horizontal–vertical illusion and the Muller-Lyer illusion, which is shown in Figure 14–1, are powerful illusions in the senses of vision and touch.

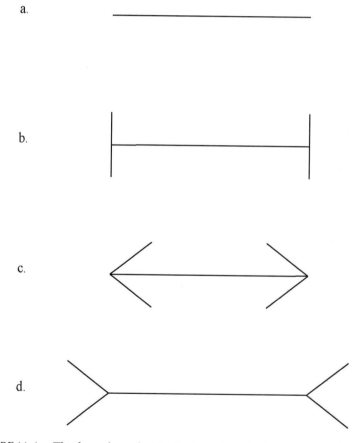

FIGURE 14–1.   This figure shows the Mueller-Lyer stimuli in the experiments described in this chapter. A. Plain line. B. Vertical ends line. C. "Wings-in" stimulus. D. "Wings-out" stimulus.

In vision, many illusions have been explained in terms of errors judging the distance of lines. A striking case is the Ponzo illusion, where the perspective induced by converging lines causes us to see a higher line near the apex as more distant and larger than a line that is lower in the picture and thereby judged as closer and smaller. Researchers have proposed that illusions may be related to mistaken impressions of depth (Fisher, 1970). This interpretation of the Mueller-Lyer illusion assumes that we see the wings-out stimuli as a corner that is further away than seen in the wings-in pattern. If both lines cover equal retinal extents, we are likely to believe that the line judged as "distant" is longer. Both of the illusions can be found in late blind persons (Heller et al., 2002c; Heller et al., 2003a) but also in persons who were born without sight. Thus, congenitally blind individuals overestimate verticals in the horizontal–vertical illusion and show overestimation of wings-out Mueller-Lyer stimuli. This means that the illusions can occur in the absence of misapplied size–constancy scaling because the presence of the illusions does not depend upon visual experience or visual imagery in persons who are blind.

Haptic illusions are also very much dependent upon size, scale, and the parts of the body that are involved in haptic exploration. Thus, the horizontal–vertical illusion was greatly diminished when subjects were limited to exploration by the fingertip and whole arm motion was prohibited (Heller et al., 1997). When subjects were not allowed to move their entire arms while exploring raised-line versions of the horizontal–vertical illusion, the normal pattern of overestimation of verticals was not found. Forcing subjects to engage in whole-arm motion (through splints) induced the illusion as subjects explored the patterns. These results were interpreted as meaning that illusory misperception is far less likely when patterns are small and can be explored with finger motion alone. The argument was that the hand is the optimal organ for picking up pattern information, and forcing larger exploratory movements (the arm space) serves to magnify illusory misperception. In some ways the hand is analogous to the fovea in the eye, except that touch may benefit from multiple foveas.

Furthermore, these results indicate the importance of scale and size for haptics. The sense of touch is not as efficient as vision in obtaining information about large scale space because this demands motion of the entire body. In large scale space, information pickup is sequential and there is a substantial load on memory. When scale is reduced, the demands of memory are diminished. Given a small space, say one that can be examined within the span of the hand (hand space), information pickup may be simultaneous, or nearly so. This reduces the demands placed upon memory and thereby aids haptics. In addition, limiting the size of objects to that of the hand allows exploration with more sensitive parts of the body, namely the fingers.

In the horizontal–vertical illusion, one normally sees overestimation of verticals, when the vertical lines are flat on a table surface. This placement induces radial scanning of verticals, where scanning motions of the index finger converge upon the body. Horizontals do not yield radial exploratory motions and are underestimated compared with verticals. However, these results are dependent upon the placement of the stimuli and restrictions in the manner in which subjects were allowed to feel the patterns.

One might expect that haptic illusions would be diminished in strength, or even eliminated, if optimal "touching positions" were adopted, or if efficient strategies for feeling the forms were permitted. On this view, haptic illusions might derive from restricting subjects to poor methods for feeling the stimuli or, perhaps, impoverished stimuli. Line drawings are not objects (Ittelson, 1996) and it is possible that the perceptual response to objects differs from perceptual response to lines or drawings (Ungerleider & Mishkin, 1982).

EXPLORATION METHOD AND THE HORIZONTAL–VERTICAL AND MUELLER-LYER ILLUSIONS

The manner in which one explores objects can influence how well the perceiver comes to know the objects. Veridical perception depends upon skilled exploration, in vision as in haptics. Artists normally use a vertical drawing table if they want to draw the human figure in correct perspective. If a drawing surface is flat or horizontal while one views a model, the artist is forced to look at the model and the drawing sequentially. This requires the individual to remember the image of the model while examining or modifying the drawing in progress. The vertical placement of the drawing allows for nearly simultaneous visual comparisons, and this reduces the demands placed on visual memory. For touch, for example, if one were to simply press one's fingers upon the surface of a cookie cutter, it would be very difficult to obtain a good idea about the outline form. Despite this, some people will spontaneously adopt poor strategies for feeling objects, just as they may walk too close to a large painting to see it properly. These comments have some bearing on haptics and illusions because the response of the observer to illusory stimuli may depend upon how they are explored haptically. Position can also matter for touch as for vision. Vertical placement may promote coding with respect to one's body, and this can aid haptics (Millar, 1994). Conceivably, vertical placement can aid haptics in much the same manner as it helps vision, but this may depend upon the task (Heller et al., in press).

Heller, Brackett, et al. (2003a) found that exploration method significantly altered illusory misperception, and the haptic horizontal–vertical illusion was greatly diminished when subjects felt solid objects rather than raised-line patterns. The critical factor was the orientation of the vertical lines because vertical with respect to gravity is not the same thing as vertical but flat on a table top. When verticals were gravitationally vertical, subjects showed overestimation of horizontals compared with verticals. This sort of negative illusion has not been reported in vision, but a weak negative illusion was previously reported for touch (Day & Avery, 1970). In both studies, the gravitationally vertical placement yielded overestimation of horizontals, despite very different experimental methods. The negative illusion occurred with tangible lines and with objects, but only when the vertical segment was gravitationally vertical.

The negative horizontal–vertical illusion was found when subjects were allowed free exploration (Heller et al., 2003a). Exploration mode was studied explicitly in a further experiment, and subjects used either free exploration, measuring with multiple fingers, grasping with the index finger and thumb, or tracing with the index finger. Many blind subjects objected to the use of tracing with the index finger in other studies of haptic illusions (e.g., Heller et al., 2002c, d; 2003a). These subjects said that making size judgments with one index finger was like asking sighted subjects to look at the world with one eye. When asked, many said that they thought that it would be easier to make accurate size estimates with the use of multiple fingers to "measure" objects or lines. The results showed that the use of only the index finger greatly reduced the magnitude of the illusion. Clearly, the quality of the information that one obtains about the world depends upon how it is explored.

This statement is reinforced by studies done on the haptic Mueller-Lyer illusion. For years the strength of this illusion has been proven in vision, and most recently in touch. Even persons born without sight have shown the illusion in their size judgments of tactile Mueller-Lyer stimuli, despite their experience with the sense of touch. Some blind subjects have argued against the restrictions placed on their mode of exploration such as using an index finger only, or one and not both hands. However, their objections do not necessarily indicate that the most comfortable exploration methods are always the most efficient.

Take, for example, one experiment on the Mueller-Lyer that controlled for exploration mode of varying sizes of stimuli (Heller et al., 2005). Four lengths of lines (2.5, 5.2, 7.6, and 10.2 cm) were used per line ending (wings-in, wings-out, plain lines, and lines with vertical endings) and presented over two trials to every subject. There were four groups of blindfolded subjects who were given specific instructions to engage in an assigned exploration mode: free exploration, tracing, grasping, and measuring. The free exploration mode allowed them to touch the lines in any manner they wished, but only with their right hands. The tracing group could only use the right index finger. The measuring method indicated that they could use any two or more fingers of the right hand to explore the stimuli; and the grasping group was to use only the index finger and thumb of the right hand to approximate the extent of the line. All size judgments were made by haptic adjustment of a tangible ruler to reflect their perception of the sizes of the lines.

As expected, the effect of line ending was significant where wings-out lines were judged as significantly larger than all others. This is probably in response to the size of the entire figure, not just the line that extends from side to side, just as one may be deceived in vision by seeing the wings-out endings. An interaction effect was found between exploration and line ending; specifically, the tracing method greatly reduced the illusion, yielding much smaller measurements overall.

Finding that tracing diminished the illusion may seem surprising because it incorporated only the index finger of one hand. Yet, it bolstered the idea that more (fingers) may not always mean better in terms of haptic exploration (but see Jansson & Monaci, 2004). While tracing was helpful with Mueller-Lyer judgments, there was also an experiment on the use of both index fingers to feel the line patterns.

To learn more about the quality of information obtained through tactile exploration, Heller et al. (2005) performed another experiment allowing subjects to feel the raised lines with both index fingers. Subjects were asked to place both index fingers at or near the middle of the stimuli and move outward in opposite directions simultaneously. They could feel the line as much as possible, so long as their fingers were not moving adjacent to one another. This method also attenuated the strength of the Mueller-Lyer effect as compared to alternative exploration modes.

The effect of line ending—whether it was wings-out, wings-in, vertical ends, or plain lines—was found to be significant, especially for the wings-out pattern. The other three varieties were judged as fairly similar in length. Whereas the tracing method resulted in the percentage illusion scores ranging from 44% to approximately 4% for the smallest to largest lines, respectively, the two-finger mode reduced the illusion scores to 21.6% for the smallest and only 1.4% for the largest line size. The difference in percentage illusion scores represents a considerable change brought on by the effectiveness of two index fingers.

It would be an overgeneralization to try to say how tactile information can be processed best or that one method leads to the most accurate perception of patterns. This is certainly an empirical matter and depends upon stimulus characteristics. Nevertheless, we should give our attention to the variety of exploration modes that provide sensory input, especially in the absence of visual cues. The strength of the haptic illusion varied considerably as a function of mode of exploration, with more efficient examination methods yielding more veridical perception and much weaker illusory misperception.

THE CONSEQUENCES OF A LACK OF SIGHT AND LACK OF VISUAL EXPERIENCE

A common view has been that persons who are congenitally blind are destined to develop deficiencies in their understanding of the world because of a lack of visual experience and imagery (see Revesz, 1950). There can be little doubt that visual experience and imagery matter a great deal for one's education. However, the specific consequences of lacks in these areas need not entail the development of generalized deficiencies in spatial tasks. The evidence, to the contrary, is that increased reliance on touch for pattern perception can lead to clear advantages for haptic spatial tasks.

It is very difficult to compare sighted and blind people on haptic tasks and control for differential past experience, pattern familiarity, and levels of skill. It is hardly surprising, for example, that comparisons involving Braille reading will favor the blind (Heller, 1992b), and those involving rotated number symbols that were drawn on the skin will favor the sighted (Heller, 1989). Blind people are practiced at reading Braille, whereas it is rare for any sighted person to ever learn to read Braille words using touch. Heller has never met a sighted person with this haptic skill, but they do exist. Nor is it surprising that blind people are unfamiliar with recognition of number patterns that are drawn on the skin because blind people are much more likely to rely on Braille than upon print number configurations. Any "fair" comparisons between sighted and blind persons must use patterns that are relatively unknown to both groups of individuals, or stimuli that are equally familiar.

Blind people may hold some advantages over the sighted in haptic tasks in which pattern familiarity is equated. In a recent study of a haptic embedded figures task, blindfolded sighted, congenitally blind, late blind, and VLV subjects were exposed to tangible targets that had to be located in a complex background (Heller, Wilson, Steffen, Yoneyama, & Brackett, 2003b). If touch tends to get a global overview of a pattern but fails to "see" the local details, one might expect difficulty locating details within a complex background. The subjects were given a raised-line drawing of a target form and four picture choices and were instructed to find the picture that contained the target. They then had to show that they could locate the target in the background by tracing it with their index fingers (see Figure 14–2). In this task the late blind and VLV subjects performed far better than the blindfolded sighted subjects. The congenitally blind subjects had similar accuracy scores as the blindfolded sighted participants, but all groups of blind subjects were approximately twice as fast as the blindfolded sighted group. The results showed the advantages of haptic skill combined with prior experience with pictures. The influence of haptic skill was shown by the much faster performance by the congenitally blind than by the blindfolded sighted subjects, given nearly identical accuracy levels. The late blind and VLV subjects performed much faster and much more accurately than the blindfolded sighted subjects. The performance levels shown by the congenitally blind participants are inconsistent with the idea that there are necessary deficiencies in haptic spatial tasks in these individuals.

Blind people may outperform sighted individuals in some areas as a result of prior experience and increased familiarity (see Sathian, 2000). Sighted people are relatively unfamiliar with the use of touch for 2-D pattern perception tasks, and are much more likely to have increased exposure to 3-D forms. Indeed, the failure to identify common, familiar 3-D forms is an indication of parietal lesions (Critchley, 1953), and we have ample evidence that touch excels in perception of common, 3-D solid objects (Klatzky & Lederman, chap-

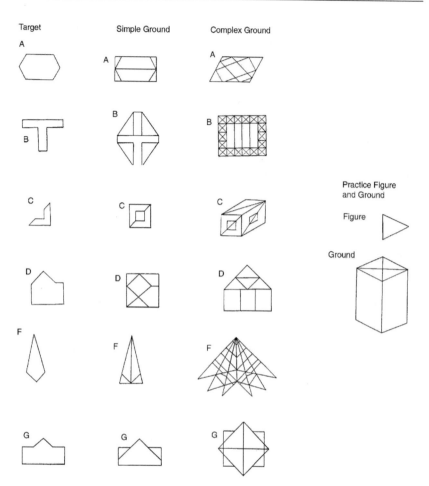

FIGURE 14–2. This figure shows the target stimuli and simple and complex backgrounds. In addition, the practice figure is present on the right. The letters correspond to the labels of the target stimuli taken from the Embedded Figures Test (Ottman, Raskin, & Witkin, 1971).

ter 10, this volume). Sighted subjects may show increased performance levels when they are given spatial reference information, either through explicit instructions, or through blurry peripheral vision that simulates very low vision.

CONCLUSIONS

Summarized in Figure 14–3 are many of the factors that influence performance in haptic tasks and whether touch is a "reality" sense; that is, whether it provides veridical information about the world. Performance levels depend upon subject

Factors Influencing Performance in Haptics

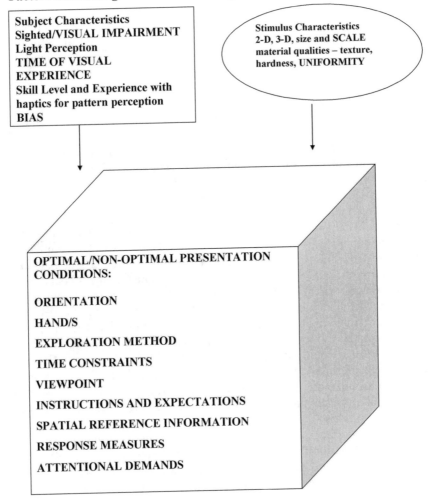

FIGURE 14–3. This figure outlines the important variables that influence performance in haptics.

variables, stimulus variables, and related information, namely whether stimulus presentation conditions are optimal or not. These are summarized in turn.

Subject experiential variables are important for haptic pattern perception. Sighted subjects may be unfamiliar with the use of touch for some forms of pattern perception tasks, and this can lower their performance during haptic scanning of 2-D arrays. Blindfolded sighted persons are not an appropriate measure of the capability of haptics because their performance can sometimes be very poor. Blind people may be more skilled and faster than blindfolded sighted people at a number of haptic pattern perception tasks, but this is very much dependent upon prior experience. For example, blind people are accurate and fast at identifying Braille configurations (Heller, 1992a); it is not surprising that sighted subjects are slower and far less accurate. Heller has found very low performance when blindfolded sighted subjects attempt to "read" two or three character grade 1 Braille words, but this is an easy task for the experienced blind reader of Braille.

Some VLV individuals, those who are functionally blind, may excel in a number of haptic pattern perception tasks. Their performance clearly excelled in picture matching, and their touch performance was actually better than that of sighted individuals in the Piagetian water level problem. This task evaluated the individuals' understanding of the horizontal and is a measure of spatial skill (Heller, Brackett, Scroggs, Allen, & Green, 2001).

The presence of light perception matters because even minimal light perception could help individuals by providing spatial reference information, that is, information about the vertical and horizontal spatial axes. This could help VLV persons as they explore stimuli that are defined by orientation, including maps, letters, or Braille patterns. It is important to note that many "blind" persons may describe themselves as completely blind when they have useful, residual vision. The ability to see the direction of strong light sources, for example, will allow an individual to locate the horizon on a bright day. This has implications for mobility. Note, too, that if individuals can see the location of their hands in space, this can aid haptics (Heller, 1993; Heller, Brackett, & Scroggs, 2002a; Heller, Brackett, Scroggs, Steffen, et al., 2002b; Heller et al., 2003b).

Stimulus characteristics are obviously important. It is not the case that one can make a cogent argument that the sense of touch invariably suffers with 2-D configurations. This is very much dependent upon pattern familiarity, complexity, and other related factors. Thus, when subjects attempted a match-to-sample task with tangible pictures, accuracy scores varied from 90–100% correct (Heller et al., 2002a). One does not see this sort of accuracy with sighted persons attempting pattern recognition with an Optacon (e.g., Heller, Rogers, & Perry, 1990). Furthermore, much lower accuracy is found for haptic face match-to-sample tasks (Kilgour & Lederman, 2002). Three-dimensional tangible faces may not be representative of many sorts of 3-D objects. Nonetheless, it is certainly very easy to engage in accurate and fast matching to sample using small tangible 2-D pictures of common and familiar objects (Heller, Brackett, & Scroggs, 2002a). Very low vision subjects had nearly perfect performance on this task (>99% correct).

Finally, the conditions of stimulus presentation matter a great deal. Just as it is possible to present stimuli under nonoptimal viewing conditions, one can present material for haptic examination in a way that is not conducive to veridical perception. Pointillist paintings can be viewed properly only at a distance, and the same holds for photorealistic paintings and photographs (see

Gibson, 1979). Similarly for touch, one may find that some viewpoints are more useful than others. The most informative viewpoint for haptic (or visual) recognition of a person would not be a top view. Also, frontal (vertical) placement aided sighted subjects as they felt rotated braille (Heller, 1992b).

Haptic mental imagery may differ from visual imagery, and this could have implications for memory tasks. It is possible that haptics and congenitally blind individuals differ from sighted persons in their memory for some forms of complex spatial layouts (see Cornoldi & Vecchi, 2000). This issue likely involves memory rather than space perception per se. We still have a great deal to learn about the nature of haptic mental imagery.

PRACTICAL PROBLEMS INVOLVING
BLINDNESS RESEARCH

Blind people are relatively rare, and those individuals who are congenitally blind are very difficult to locate for research. Studies in this area could yield very different results because of accidental differences in subject selection. This may explain some of the conflicting results in the literature, especially apparently contradictory findings that show relatively higher or lower levels of performance by blind subjects.

Age of onset of blindness and the duration of blindness are significant variables, in part because they suggest very different educational experiences. Persons blinded much later in life, as in old age, may never learn a number of haptic and mobility skills that are often acquired by blind individuals in early childhood. Moreover, older blind individuals who were blinded in childhood may have had very different educational backgrounds because they may have been educated in institutional environments, namely schools for the blind. Currently, blind children are generally mainstreamed in their education in the United States (Livingston-White, Utter, & Woodward, 1985).

Unfortunately, negative social expectations and bias play a role in the educational background and functioning of some blind people (Heller, 2000a, 2000b), especially prior to mainstreaming in schools. This problem is frequently ignored but can alter the outcome of research. For example, we have heard older blind people indicate that they thought that tasks involving tangible drawings would be too difficult, perhaps because blind people were not "meant" to "think sighted." At the start of a recent experiment on mental rotation, one congenitally blind person asked, "Can other blind people do this?" The question reflected her concern that she might not be able to succeed at a novel task. Once we indicated that other blind people completed the task, she said, "Then I can do it." Negative expectations may cause some blind individuals to perform poorly because they may expect to fail. These negative expectations may derive from experience with teachers who communicated negative impressions or from bias present within society. Whatever their source, some blind persons are convinced that they have poor spatial skills, even when the reality may be very different. Blind people are no different than sighted persons in this regard; they are influenced by the expectations of others. Researchers need to be careful to avoid communicating expectations or predictions to their subjects, be they sighted or blind.

Touch as the Harbinger of Reality

Is touch or vision the ultimate index of what is real and what is not? There are a number of ways to try to answer this question. The answer to the main question of interest depends upon how one approaches it. One can argue that the issue of which sense is "better for understanding reality" is not really scientific because it is too vague. Studies of intersensory discrepancies suggest that conflict resolution depends upon the specific attribute that one examines and the experimental methods applied. Texture either yields a compromise judgment between the senses (Lederman & Abbott, 1981), or touch dominance (Heller, 1982). Dominance relations are subject to change for dynamic stimuli (see Spence, McDonald, & Driver, 2004). Touch may dominate vision when vision is blurry or otherwise degraded due to disease or manipulations of sight (Heller, 1982, 1983). The frequently cited visual advantage in form perception is also questionable (Heller et al., 1999; Hershberger & Misceo, 1996).

When we examine the consequences of loss of a sense, the answers we get are far less equivocal. People can learn to adjust to a loss of sight, although few of us would wish to undertake this adventure. Permanent visual loss cannot be duplicated in the laboratory by blindfolding or through the use of methods to blur or otherwise degrade visual input. In many ways, touch can provide suitable substitute information for visual loss. However, it is very clear that the loss of touch information can be devastating. Very few individuals have completely lost touch input, and the loss of pain perception is likely to shorten one's life considerably. The complete loss of touch sensation is so rare that there is no common name for it in any language that we know of, but there have been a few cases reported in the medical literature of complete sensory neuropathy (see Carello & Turvey, 2000; Cole, 1995). The scant literature in this area suggests the primacy of touch information.

The picture is still murky when we examine the data on illusions and multisensory interactions. Vision and touch are susceptible to illusions, and many "optical" illusions are not merely optical. However, there are illusions that appear in vision and not in touch. Some of these illusions do not occur in touch because they may depend upon mistaken impressions of depth information (e.g., the Ponzo illusion; see Heller, Hasselbring, Wilson, Shanley, & Yoneyama, 2004), and others may occur in vision because of a greater likelihood of global processing. Vision may be more likely to process large patterns globally, that is, apprehend a larger configuration at a glance. The Mueller-Lyer illusion seems stronger in touch, but it can be attenuated (Heller et al., 2005). The horizontal–vertical illusion may not appear in the same manner in touch as in vision becasue it is so dependent upon spatial placement. Note that perceptual error is very likely in both vision and touch in states involving psychopathology. Just as people may suffer visual and auditory hallucinations, they may also experience these phenomena in touch.

A body of evidence is emerging that suggests that multimodal input may be most likely to yield the highest quality information about reality (see Heller, 1982, 2000b). This is the view expressed earlier by Gibson (1966) and much earlier by a number of philosophers. Most recently, considerable attention has been directed towards the study of intersensory interactions and multimodal facilitation (Driver & Spence, 2004; Spence et al., 2004). This multisensory research approach is likely to yield rich answers to important questions about the functioning of the senses.

ACKNOWLEDGMENTS

This research and preparation of the chapter was supported in part by NSF grant BCS-0317293 from the program in Perception, Action and Cognition.

REFERENCES

Carello, C., & Turvey, M. T. (2000). Rotational invariants and dynamic touch. In M. A. Heller (Ed.), *Touch, representation and blindness* (pp. 27–66). Debates in Psychology Series. Oxford, UK: Oxford University Press.

Cole, J. (1995). *Pride and a daily marathon.* Cambridge, MA: MIT Press.

Cornoldi, C., & Vecchi, T. (2000). Mental imagery in blind people: The role of passive and active visuospatial processes. In M. A. Heller (Ed.), *Touch, representation and blindness* (pp. 143–181). Debates in Psychology Series. Oxford, UK: Oxford University Press.

Critchley, M. (1953). *The parietal lobes.* New York: Hafner.

Day, R. H., & Avery, G. C. (1970). Absence of the horizontal-vertical illusion in haptic space. *Journal of Experimental Psychology, 83,* 172–173.

Driver, J., & Spence, C. (2004). Crossmodal spatial attention: Evidence from human performance. In C. Spence & J. Driver (Eds.), *Crossmodal space and crossmodal attention* (pp. 179–220). Oxford, UK: Oxford University Press.

Fisher, G. H. (1970). An experimental and theoretical appraisal of the perceptive and size-constancy theories of illusions. *Quarterly Journal of Experimental Psychology, 22,* 631–652.

Freides, D. (1974). Human information processing and sensory modality: Cross-modal functions, information complexity, memory and deficit. *Psychological Bulletin, 81,* 284–310.

Gibson, J. J. (1966). *The senses considered as perceptual systems.* Boston: Houghton Mifflin.

Gibson, J. J. (1979). *The ecological approach to visual perception.* Boston: Houghton Mifflin.

Heller, M. A. (1982). Visual and tactual texture perception: Intersensory cooperation. *Perception & Psychophysics, 31,* 339–344.

Heller, M. A. (1983). Haptic dominance in form perception with blurred vision. *Perception, 12,* 607–613.

Heller, M. A. (1989). Tactile memory in sighted and blind observers: The influence of orientation and rate of presentation. *Perception, 18,* 121–133.

Heller, M. A. (1992a). "Haptic dominance" in form perception: Vision versus proprioception. *Perception, 21,* 655–660.

Heller, M. A. (1992b). The effect of orientation on tactual braille recognition: Optimal "touching positions." *Perception & Psychophysics, 51,* 549–556.

Heller, M. A. (1993). Influence of visual guidance on braille recognition: Low lighting also helps touch. *Perception & Psychophysics, 54,* 675–681.

Heller, M. A. (2000a). Guest editorial: Society, science and values. *Perception, 29,* 757–760.

Heller, M. A. (Ed.). (2000b). *Touch, representation and blindness.* Debates in Psychology Series. Oxford, UK: Oxford University Press.

Heller, M. A. (2006). Picture perception and spatial cognition in visually impaired people. In M. A. Heller & S. Ballesteros, (Eds.), *Touch and blindness: Psychology and neuroscience.* Mahwah, NJ: Lawrence Erlbaum Associates.

Heller, M. A., & Ballesteros, S. (Eds.). (2006). *Touch and blindness: Psychology and neuroscience.* Mahwah, NJ: Lawrence Erlbaum Associates.

Heller, M. A., Brackett, D. D., Salik, S. S., Scroggs, E., & Green, S. (2003a). Objects, raised-lines and the haptic horizontal-vertical Illusion. *Quarterly Journal of Experimental Psychology: A, 56,* 891–907.

Heller, M. A., Brackett, D. D., & Scroggs, E. (2002a). Tangible picture matching in people who are visually impaired. *Journal of Visual Impairment and Blindness, 96,* 349–353.

Heller, M. A., Brackett, D. D., Scroggs, E., Allen, A., C., & Green, S. (2001). Haptic perception of the horizontal by blind and low vision individuals. *Perception, 30,* 601–610.

Heller, M. A., Brackett, D. D., Scroggs, E., Steffen, H., Heatherly, K., & Salik, S. (2002b). Tangible pictures: Viewpoint effects and linear perspective in visually impaired people. *Perception, 31,* 747–769.

Heller, M. A., Brackett, D. D., Wilson, K., Yoneyama, K., & Boyer, A. (2002c). Visual experience and the haptic horizontal-vertical illusion. *British Journal of Visual Impairment, 20,* 105–109.

Heller, M. A., Brackett, D. D., Wilson, K., Yoneyama, K., Boyer, A., & Steffen, H. (2002d). The haptic Muller-Lyer illusion in sighted and blind people. *Perception, 31,* 1263–1274.

Heller, M. A., Calcaterra, J. A., Burson, L. L., & Green, S., L. (1997). The tactual horizontal-vertical illusion depends on radial motion of the entire arm. *Perception & Psychophysics, 59,* 1297–1331.

Heller, M. A., Calcaterra, J. A., Green, S. L., & Brown, L. (1999). Intersensory conflict between vision and touch: The response modality dominates when precise, attention-riveting judgments are required. *Perception & Psychophysics, 61,* 1384–1398.

Heller, M. A., Hasselbring, K., Wilson, K., Shanley, M., & Yoneyama, K. (2004). Haptic illusions in the sighted and blind. In S. Ballesteros and M. A. Heller (Eds.). *Touch, blindness and neuroscience.* Madrid: UNED Press.

Heller, M. A., & Joyner, T. D. (1993). Mechanisms in the tactile horizontal/vertical illusion: Evidence from sighted and blind subjects. *Perception & Psychophysics, 53,* 422–428.

Heller, M. A., Kennedy, J. M., Clark, A., McCarthy, M., Borgert, A., Fulkerson, E., & Wemple, L. A., Kaffel, N., Duncan, A., & Riddle, T. (in press). Viewpoint and orientation influence picture recognition in the blind. *Perception.*

Heller, M. A., McCarthy, M., Schultz, J., Greene, J., Shanley, M., Clark, A., Skoczylas, S., & Prociuk, J. (2005). The influence of exploration mode, orientation and configuration on the haptic Mueller-Lyer illusion. *Perception, 34*, 1475–1500.

Heller, M. A., Rogers, G. J., & Perry, C. L. (1990). Tactile pattern recognition with the Optacon: Superior performance with active touch and the left hand. *Neuropsychologia, 28*, 1003–1006.

Heller, M. A., Wilson, K., Steffen, H., Yoneyama, K., & Brackett, D. D. (2003b). Superior haptic perceptual selectivity in late-blind and very-low-vision subjects. *Perception, 32*, 499–511.

Hershberger, W., & Misceo, G. F. (1996). Touch dominates haptic estimates of discordant visual-haptic size. *Perception & Psychophysics, 58*, 1124–1132.

Ittelson, W. H. (1996). Visual perception of markings. *Psychonomic Bulletin and Review, 3*, 171–187.

Jansson, G., & Monaci, L. (2004). Haptic identification of objects with different numbers of fingers. In S. Ballesteros & M. Heller (Eds.), *Touch, blindness and neuroscience* (pp. 209–219. Madrid: UNED Press.

Kennett, S., Eimer, M., Spence, C., & Driver, J. (2001). Tactile-visual links in exogenous spatial attention under different postures: Convergent evidence from psychophysics and ERPs. *Journal of Cognitive Neuroscience, 13*, 462–478.

Kilgour, A. R., & Lederman, S. J. (2002). Face recognition by hand. *Perception and Psychophysics, 64*, 339–352.

Lederman, S. J., & Abbott, S. G. (1981). Texture perception: Studies of intersensory organization using a discrepancy paradigm and visual vs. tactual psychophysics. *Journal of Experimental Psychology: Human Perception & Performance, 7*, 902–915.

Livingston-White, D., Utter, C., & Woodard, Q. E. (1985). Follow-up study of visually impaired students of the Michigan school for the blind. *Journal of Visual Impairment and Blindness, 79*, 150–153.

Mead, G. H. (1932). Philosophy of the present. La Salle, IL: Open Court.

Millar, S. (1994). *Understanding and representing space: Theory and evidence from studies with blind and sighted children.* Oxford, UK: Oxford University Press.

Millar, S. (2000). Modality and mind: Convergent active processing in interrelated networks. A model of development and perception by touch. In M. A. Heller (Ed), *Touch, representation and blindness* (pp. 99–141). Oxford, UK: Oxford University Press.

Ottman, P. K., Raskin, E., & Witkin, H. A. (1971). *Group Embedded Figures Test.* Palo Alto, CA: Consulting Psychologists Press.

Rock, I., & Victor, J. (1964). Vision and touch: An experimentally created conflict between the two senses. *Science, 143*, 594–596.

Revesz, G. (1950). *The psychology and art of the blind.* London: Longmans Green.

Sathian, K. (2000). Practice makes perfect: Sharper tactile perception in the blind. *Neurology, 54*, 2203–2204.

Simons, D. J., & Chabris, C. F. (1999). Gorillas in our midst: Sustained inattentional blindness for dynamic events. *Perception, 28*, 1059–1074.

Soltis, J. F. (1966). *Seeing, knowing and believing.* Reading, MA: Addison Wesley.

Spence, C., McDonald, J., & Driver, J. (2004). Exogenous spatial-cuing studies of human crossmodal attention and multisensory integration. In C. Spence & J. Driver (Eds.), *Crossmodal space and crossmodal attention* (pp. 277–320). Oxford, UK: Oxford University Press.

Tsai, L. S. (1967). Muller-Lyer illusion by the blind. *Perceptual and Motor Skills, 25*, 641–644.

Ungerleider, L. G., & Mishkin, M. (1982). Two cortical visual systems. In D. J. Ingle, M. A. Goodale, & R. J. W. Mansfield (Eds.), *Analysis of visual behavior* (pp. 169–188). Cambridge, MA: MIT Press.

Warren, D. H., & Rossano, M. J. (1991). Intermodality relations: Vision and touch. In M. A. Heller & W. Schiff (Eds.), *The psychology of touch*. Hillsdale, NJ: Lawrence Erlbaum Associates.

Yolton, J. W. (1962). *Thinking and perceiving*. La Salle, IL: Open Court.

IV
FROM
USE-ORIENTED
RESEARCH TO
APPLICATION

15

Nonvisual Sports and Art: Fertile Substrates for the Growth of Knowledge About Brain Plasticity in People Who Are Blind or Have Low Vision

Paul E. Ponchillia

Before attending the Vanderbilt University conference on brain plasticity and blindness, I was aware of the research related to human brain plasticity in people who are blind but had not thought of my own work as having a direct relationship to the science. It took only a cursory look at the brain plasticity literature in preparation for my presentation at the conference, however, to understand that much of my work is highly relevant. Part of the misunderstanding came from a lack of knowledge of what brain plasticity really is. In order to prevent confusion, the reader should know that I will use *brain plasticity* in its broadest sense (i.e., any change in brain structure or function). Examples include change in structure resulting from development, learning and experience, recovery from injury, cross-modal reorganization, network prioritization, and interrelationships.

The diversity of scientific professionals, research interests, and methodologies and the outstanding enthusiasm of the Vanderbilt conferees left me with a strong desire to contribute to the body of knowledge surrounding brain plasticity and people who are blind. The purposes of this document, which stem from that desire, include

- to describe the physical and art education skills of people who are blind, particularly as they relate to human development, the game of goalball, and stone sculpting
- to describe a personal perspective and the literature on aspects of blindness important to the interpretation and conduct of brain plasticity research in order to raise awareness about key issues, such as visual imagery, the factors affecting performance of blind participants, and enhancement of skill building among people who are blind
- to suggest possible courses of research to increase knowledge in the area of brain plasticity, as it relates to sports and art skills among children and adults who are blind
- to encourage further interaction between brain plasticity and blindness professionals

The chapter is arranged in two major sections: Physical Skills and Art Skills. Each begins with discussions of barriers to access, followed by descriptions of sports or art education camps, skills required in sports or art, their relationships to brain plasticity research, and suggestions for future research in each of the two areas.

BACKGROUND

In order to understand the perspective I bring to this subject, it is necessary to give the reader a brief overview of my background. In addition to the usual work of a university-based teacher/researcher in the field of blindness and low vision, I have also had a somewhat unique history in sports and art. I acquired total blindness some 30 years ago after being highly involved in sports as a sighted person during the first 30 years of my life. Also, I have participated as a blind athlete in the sport of goalball, and to some extent in track, for 25 years and have sculpted stone tactually for nearly that long.

In addition to these personal experiences, I have directed sports and art education camps for children with visual impairments for 19 years. At those camps I taught sports and art skills to literally hundreds of children, observed the effects of the early onset of a severe visual impairment on the development of physical and tactile skills and spatial concepts, and conducted a good deal of outcome research on camp participants.

PHYSICAL SKILLS

Barriers to Physical Skills

The term "physical skills" is broad, here focusing on those actions required to play sports activities, such as running, jumping, and throwing, but also including those required in everyday life, such as reaching, creeping, and walking. Of particular interest is the effect of early or prebirth visual impairment on the development of such skills. The physical performance of children with early onset blindness is affected to such a degree that it is rare that they have outstanding skills such as robust goalball throws or lengthy long jumps. Deficits in development are further confounded by less than adequate physical education services for children with visual impairments in public schools, and it should be noted that art education also lags. Together, these two factors combine to limit the ultimate sports and art skills of those who become blind adults. The Sports and Art Education Camps, which are described in detail later, were specifically designed to help overcome the deficits resulting from these two significant factors.

Developmental Barriers

The quality and quantity of information coming to a child with a visual impairment during early development is decreased by the fact that it is entirely or mostly gathered through the sensory modalities of audition, touch, and kinesthetics, which limit and distort that information when compared to vision (Lowenfeld, 1973). The developments of the affective, cognitive, and psychomotor domains are all affected by limited vision (Lowenfeld, 1973; Scholl, 1986). Although the focus of this section is primarily on physical skills, it is necessary to discuss the affective and cognitive domains because one's self-image and conceptual framework would be expected to affect physical performance. The development of the affective domain requires the establishment of love bonds between a parent or caregiver and the awareness of one's degree of control over his or her environment (Piaget, 1981). There is nothing about blindness itself that interferes with either of these, but a blind child's probability of being hospitalized may interfere with love bond formation, and the parent's reaction to the child's disability may cause overprotection, which can interfere with the establishment of locus of control (Lowenfeld, 1973). Poor self-image, particularly if it is from strong overprotection, could lead to a child's having little need to move or being afraid to move and could result in a stronger desire for security than for discovery. Lack of movement ultimately leads to loss of muscle mass and hypotonia (Norris, Spaulding, & Brodie, 1957). Buell (1982) believed early hypotonia to be a cause of passivity of movement later in life.

As it relates to the topic of movement and physical skill, the concept of objects and physical space is an important aspect of the development of the cognitive domain. Toddlers with severe visual impairments must come to understand their own body concepts, their relationship to objects, the relationship of objects to other objects, and ultimately, the more complex notion of the total layout of the environment in order to move through space effectively (Guth & Rieser, 1997). Bigelow (1992) felt that the common delay in mobility-related motor skills has its source in the development of object permanence, inasmuch as children who are blind must realize that objects exist (are permanent) although they are outside the limits of their remaining senses. The requirement that objects have auditory outputs in order to establish object permanence makes this aspect of development problematic because most objects are silent. It follows that if there is no awareness of objects, there is little motivation to move to retrieve them (Bigelow, 1992). Bigelow's contention regarding lack of movement surely plays a role, but movement also involves the development of psychomotor skills, such as the mechanical ability required to crawl from one point to another, to reach out to pick up a toy, or ultimately to throw, run, and jump. It is widely known that children who have early onset visual impairments have lesser physical abilities than their classmates with vision (Cratty, 1971; Fraiberg, 1968, 1977). Infants who are blind reach many postural milestones at similar times to those of sighted children, but creeping is a notable exception (Adelson & Fraiberg, 1974), and the differences between the two groups become more noticeable after age 10 to 12 years (Portfors-Yeomans & Riach, 1995).

The necessity of learning complex movements such as throwing or jumping without the benefit of visual observation appears to be especially problematic because of the role that incidental learning through observation surely plays in skill development. Whereas most would-be young athletes watch their heroes and try to emulate the details of their throwing, running, or swimming styles, children who are blind cannot get even a rough idea of the throwing, running, or swimming motion, let alone the particulars of the style, through listening or touching.

Physical Education and Barriers to Learning

It is clear that regular involvement in physical activity, sports, and recreation have a positive effect on physical and emotional well-being (Auxter, Pyfer, & Huetting, 1997; Gronmo & Augestad, 2000). Unfortunately, children who have visual impairments do not have the same degree of access to physical education and physical activities as do their sighted peers (Lieberman & Houston-Wilson, 1999). The barriers to access appear to be numerous and diverse, some relating to the prejudicial nature of human beings, some to children's reticence to try new things, and others to the weaknesses of university physical education teacher training programs or to the public school systems themselves.

Perhaps the largest source is a result of commonly held prejudicial attitudes that individuals with disabilities are helpless (Smart, 2001). Because such attitudes are expected from virtually anyone in the United States, some percentage of school administrators, fitness facility owners, physical educators, or other power holders would be expected to limit access through unintended but effectual discrimination. Also, university physical education preservice teacher training programs seldom include any specific training regarding blindness or low vision, leaving physical educators unprepared to teach children who are blind (Lieberman & Houston-Wilson, 1999). Additionally, a child's lack of skill, which affects confidence and willingness to attempt an unfamiliar athletic activity, can in turn create a vicious cycle of never participating, never learning, never participating, and so on (Ponchillia, 1995). The large size of public school classes and the resulting loss of attention to an individual student, with or without special needs, might also limit access, especially to those who could not keep up with the pace of the main body of the class (Goldfine, 1993; Trippe, 1996).

Another school-related barrier is the difficulty of finding time for physical education classes in the usually overcrowded schedules of students in the special education curriculum, which often results in the child being pulled from physical education in lieu of orientation and mobility or some other specialized service (Lieberman & Houston-Wilson, 1999).

Consequences of Limited Access and Limited Development

Poor access to quality physical education confounds the common limitations resulting from developmental lags described earlier. In addition, limited access deprives such children of the concepts and skills available through a sound physical education program. The object permanence and spatial limitations resulting from lack of vision that were described earlier have the potential of limiting movement in the environment. Furthermore, there are concepts taught within the physical education curriculum that deal with space in a sports context that are missed if instruction is withheld.

Graham, Holt, and Hale (2001), whose expertise lie in physical skills instruction, have recognized five categories that delineate various aspects of space: location, directions, levels, pathways, and extension. Location is made up of self-space and general space, where the latter comprises all the space away from self that is reachable by locomotion (e.g., the remainder of a room or playground). Directions in space are the dimensional possibilities into which children or their limbs move (e.g., up and down, forward and backward, right and left, clockwise and counterclockwise). When a child is in a standing position, levels in space are described as *low* (the space below the knees), *medium* (the space between the knees and the shoulders), and *high* (the space above the shoulders). Pathways indicate the patterns or trajectory of a child's movement or that of a thrown or struck object, such as the arched flight of a basketball shot or the curved path of a pitcher's curveball. The category extensions include the size of movements of the body or its parts in space (i.e., small or large arm circles, tucked or open forward rotating dives). Skills in self-space are taught first, and learning proceeds through complex combinations of moving through generalized space with varying directions, levels, pathways, and extensions. If Bigelow's (1992) contention that the lack of the relatively simple concept of object permanence inhibits the movement of children with early onset visual impairments, one can only imagine what the lack of these concepts inhibit. At present, there is no literature to tell us.

The sports concept of "effort" is also affected if children are deprived of physical education (Graham et al., 2001). These authors hold that there are three aspects of the concept of effort: Time is the rate at which a movement is accomplished (fast or slow); force is the degree of strength with which it is done; and flow is the degree of control one exhibits over a movement (running wildly down a hill is free flow and running down the same hill with a beanbag on top of the head is bound flow).

Fitness and Health

According to the literature, the consequences of limited access are lesser physical skills and poor fitness (Kobberling, Jankowski, & Leger, 1991; Lieberman & McHugh, 2001; Short & Winnick, 1986). Jankowski and Evans (1981) found that the physical education of children with visual impairments is insufficient to maintain normal levels of body composition, strength, and aerobic capacity. In addition to this, Sherrill (1993) stated that children with visual impairment have lower fitness in comparison to sighted peers due to lack of adequate instruction, decreased participation, and overprotection by parents and teachers. Skaggs and Hopper (1996) estimated that 36% of the visually impaired students in the United States are overweight due to a lack of physical activity.

There appears to be no literature regarding the concepts of sports "space" and "effort" among children with visual impairments. However, my experience at various sports education camps has demonstrated that direction and extension among the "space" concepts and time and force among the "effort" concepts are especially problematic. Children with visual impairments who come to the camps with limited involvement in sports and physical education often do not show the usual reaction to dive towards a goalball to block it and prevent a goal. Instead of extending knees, hips, shoulders, elbows, wrists, and fingers in a burst of speed to block a bell-filled goalball as it approaches and passes on the playing floor, many children simply stay affixed in their positions on hands and knees and make a reaching gesture towards the ball, but the effort is misdirected and significantly limited in force, timing, and speed. Such children generally throw the ball with little velocity, have difficulty lining up on parallel raised lines on a court, and seldom extend all joints in correct goalball blocking form. (See comparison of throwing form in Figure 15–1 and blocking form in Figure 15–2.)

Good

Poor

FIGURE 15–1. Comparison of poor (bottom) and good (top) throwing form.

Good

Poor

FIGURE 15–2. Comparison of poor (bottom) and good (top) blocking skills.

Physical Skills Development

The most obvious deficiency resulting from being left out of physical education class in public school is surely that of physical skills development. The lack of skills teaching in elementary and middle school grades can confound the skills deficit already apparent as a result of altered psychomotor development in early childhood. Quite simply, if children are not taught to run, jump, throw, and kick in physical education class at school, the entire burden of instruction is left to parents and others outside the educational system.

The physical skills and body mechanics that children bring to sports camps also reflect the developmental lags and lack of instruction in many of their pasts that result in limited "skills repertoire." For example, among a group of ten12-year-old children at a junior camp who are asked, "Do any of you know how to throw a softball overhand?" nine will typically answer "Yes." However, when asked to demonstrate the overhand throw, a conservative estimate is that fewer than half can actually do so. In addition, only the two or three whose parents have either taught them or arranged for special lessons will know such basic skills as standing in a "ready position," a hop or skip, a standing long jump, the "down" wrestling position, or a hook shot. A second noticeable limitation is in the mechanics of the movements required to accomplish a skill, which is most prevalent among those with early and severe visual impairments. Whereas the movements of baseball pitchers are generally smooth and quick, these children's throws have a noticeably mechanical look, one in which each part of the throw comes in jerky motions and the individual parts of the action can be recognized.

Overcoming Skills Deficits

Many of the limitations described above can be overcome through specific training regimens. Research on aerobic exercise programs for women who are blind has demonstrated that such individuals perform the movements adequately with training (Ponchillia, Powell, Felski, & Nicklawski, 1992) and that they can eliminate the fitness deficit described earlier (Blessing, McCrimmon, Stovall, & Williford, 1993). There is evidence from one of our studies (Ponchillia, Strause, & Ponchillia, 2002) that receiving physical education is an important predictor of later involvement in sports. We found that members of the United States Association of Blind Athletes who received physical education or participated in sports during junior high or high school were significantly more likely to be participating in higher level sports activities than those who did not receive those services.

Knowing that many of the access barriers to physical education are a function of serving children with visual impairments in their local schools, and knowing that it is extremely difficult to modify the system in a way that would provide an ideal physical education to them, other approaches to solving the access problem have been suggested (Ponchillia, 1995; Ponchillia, Armbruster, & Wiebold, 2005). The first approach aims to provide a useful way for anyone to adapt a simple activity, such as an elementary game, or a more complex sport, such as basketball, for use by students with visual impairments. I have proposed an AccessSports Model (ASM) (Ponchillia, 1995) for this purpose. The ASM allows professionals who have a basic knowledge of visual impairment and who know something about sports to analyze any sports activity by investigating three of the game's components: the targets or goals utilized in the sport, its boundaries, and its rules. The process requires the user to think through each of these aspects of the sport and to design adaptations needed for each. Targets or goals include balls, archery or dartboard bull's eyes, goal nets, and the like. Boundaries include the edges of playing surfaces, such as the out-of-bound lines on a football field or the edge of a shuffleboard court. Rule modifications usually simplify games by reducing the number of players, increasing the ease of scoring points, or decreasing the possibility of player injury.

A second approach to increasing access provides the adaptive skills to children in short-term specialized programs of a few days duration, and then depends on the self-determination of the children to take these ideas back to school (Ponchillia et al., 2005). Our research has demonstrated that physical skills may also be increased among students with visual impairments through short-term specialized clinics provided outside of or in conjunction with the education system.

Short-Term Training—The Sports Education Camps

In 1988, faculty members of the Department of Blindness and Low Vision Studies and the athletes of the Michigan Blind Athletic Association combined to offer the first Sports Education Camp. The camp was designed to address the well-known physical education and sports access barriers described earlier (Lieberman & Houston-Wilson, 1999; Ponchillia, 1995) and the resulting poor fitness and motor development that can be expected (Kobberling et al., 1991; Short & Winnick, 1986). The camp's purposes included (a) to empower children to self-advocate by teaching them basic sports skills, sports adaptations, and methods of assisting their physical education teacher; (b) to educate parents, teachers, and the community regarding the adaptations required for participation and regarding children's limitless potential in sports; and (c) to increase access to physical education, sports, and recreation by building a network of advocates. The original Sports Education Camp project included a weeklong residential series of sports clinics for children, a graduate-level course for teachers, parents, and "potential advocates," and the formation of a statewide management team to oversee the project and to build the statewide advocacy network. In clinics of 15 or so students, the 10- to12-year-old participants were introduced to the basic skills of running, jumping, and throwing, along with the sports of wrestling, track and field, bowling, goalball, and gymnastics. The 13- to 18-year-old athletes were also taught physical skills, but they concentrated more on the overall aspects of the sporting events as well. Each athlete generally received approximately 30 hours in clinics and/or competitions during the camp.

Phase II Initial Expansion

A Phase II expansion effort begun in 2001 resulted in a Western Michigan University (WMU) partnership with the United States Association of Blind Athletes (USABA) and an 11-state program by 2003. The WMU/USABA partnership enabled the use of the national network of the USABA, which increased abilities to fund the project, coordinate a national program, disseminate educational materials, and acquire role models and their technical expertise in sports adaptation. The Phase II sites were based on the initial model, but the sports activities differed somewhat according to the wishes of the local organizers.

The procedures used in the Phase II project proved to be extremely effective and included

- housing the administrative office and functions of the project at Western Michigan
- selecting expansion sites through competitive bidding
- providing training and an operations manual to the site personnel
- providing funding for 2 years of programming
- holding local focus groups prior to each new expansion site to organize and plan
- providing managerial support at the local camp, fostering development of statewide advocacy networks
- collecting research-based evaluation data from each site

Also, the dissemination of educational products, including the development of an online university course on teaching sports and physical skills to students with visual impairments, numerous professional presentations, a website, and journal articles were forthcoming. Network building was also successful, as measured by the fact that, although the federal support ended in 2003, 9 of the 11 expansion sites initiated during Phase II continued (Ponchillia et al., 2005).

Outcome data showed significant growth from pre- to postcamp in the young participants in physical skills, in sports knowledge, and in their opinions of themselves as athletes. (Ponchillia et al., 2005). The education received at the sports camps resulted in increased sports knowledge on a 10-item true/false test, increased distance in underhand and overhand softball throw, and increased long jump distance. In addition, camp participants were more likely to consider themselves "good athletes" following the experience than they did when they initially reported to camp.

A precamp comparison of the athletes returning to camp for a second or third time to those who were coming for the first time demonstrated that the returning group scored higher on the sports knowledge quiz, said they knew how to change a sport so they could play, reported that they played sports with other visually impaired athletes in their local area, and felt they were better in sports than other kids their age.

Most relevant to the topic of brain plasticity were the data relating to the degree of useful vision. Vision was measured by the students' response to "Which one of the following better described your vision?" "Can run safely without a guide" or "Cannot run safely without a guide." As might be expected, the children in the "can run safely" group performed at higher levels in several areas than did the children with more limited vision. This was true in the pre- and postcamp skill areas of throwing and jumping and in the gain score in these activities from pre- to postcamp. The "run safely" group was also more likely to take gym class with sighted students, play the same games in gym class as the other kids, and tell others how to change games so they could play. Although there was less significant growth in the "cannot run safely" group, these results likely were a result of the physical and conceptual delays in the group and indicated the need for longer-term training.

Brain Plasticity, Touch, and Psychomotor Skills

Brain Plasticity and Visual Impairment

The major focus of this writing is on the development and training of the psychomotor skills of people who were blind or severely visually impaired at or near birth. As described above, this group faces developmental and learning barriers, including parental overprotection, limitations of learning with little or no visual input, difficulty understanding certain spatial concepts that are complex without vision, difficulty accessing basic skills instruction in an educational system not designed for them, and problems in locating accessible venues for participating in sports activities. Conversely, our research and experience at Sports Education Camps demonstrate that such individuals are capable of learning the concepts and skills required to participate in high level sports if given specialized instruction (Ponchillia et al., 2005).

It has also been demonstrated that individuals with early onset visual impairments have a propensity for learning certain spatial and tactual skills through the processing of the multimodal potential of the occipital cortex. Hamilton and Pascual-Leone (1998) reported that peripherally blind subjects have large areas of their occipital cortex available to be recruited for the processing of tactile and auditory information. Braille reading by subjects who are blind is one such use, and it has been shown to activate the dorsal and ventral portion of the occipital cortex (Sadato et al., 1998; Sadato et al., 1996). The contention that Braille reading is a function of the occipital cortex has also been supported by a study in which interference with the function of the occipital cortex using repetitive transcranial magnetic stimulation (rTMS) results in disruption of the processing of tactile Braille reading among otherwise skilled readers (Cohen et al., 1997). Because removal of the magnetic stimulation restores the readers' original abilities, it is apparent that processing of Braille reading takes place in the occipital cortex.

The relationship between Braille reading and psychomotor sports skills may appear to be somewhat vague at first glance, but not if "touch" is defined in its broadest sense. Miller (2000), known for operationalizing the definitions of behaviors concerning the study of touch perception, believes that touch is often misunderstood. She holds that because touch is called one of the five senses, it is thought of as skin sensation, such as hot, light, pressure, temperature, pain, but touch also involves the joints and can be influenced by outside frameworks. She proposes that touch includes (a) tactual acuity; (b) characteristics of the pattern—e.g., size, features in the pattern, and saliency; (c) propensity and kinesthetic inputs from scanning movements; and (d) redundancy or coincidence of body reference. Carello and Turvey (2000) have also pointed out that touch is both perceptual and motor, and they study touch as a rotational function around the joints. They have shown how the perception of the length of long rods can be predicted based on the rotation around the wrist and elbow caused by the inertia tensor (rotation) of the rod. They discuss further how touch through an implement is not filtered through the body but functions more like a whisker or claw, sending somatosensory information directly to the brain. Accepting the premises of Miller (2000), the learning of physical skills has a somatosensory or tactual component (i.e., it is done through the complexities of touch). Also, little change in the tactual neuroprocessing occurs when an implement such as a ball is introduced. These issues are explored also in chapter 9 by Loomis and Klatzky in this volume.

Goalball, which is described in the following paragraphs, is played under blindfold, involves constant movement on foot, and yet requires keeping track of one's position on a static court marked by raised boundaries. The somatosensory task of tracking an approaching ball, coming from anywhere down court and arriving in less than 1 s, is confounded by the nonvisual spatial task of maintaining a constantly changing visual image of the location of the court and one's playing position (left side, middle, or right side). Surprisingly, this degree of nonvisual perceptual skill appears to be commonplace, since goalball is an experiment that has been designed and carried out successfully for more than 50 years by hundreds of players worldwide. As such, it provides an extremely rich medium for studying complex somatosensory/spatial interactions totally void of visual input.

Goalball is a game that was developed in Western Europe by veterans who were blinded in World War II (see United States Association of Blind Athletes at www.usaba.org). It is played exclusively by persons who are blind or those who have low vision, but all players are blindfolded during play.

The playing court and playing positions appear in Figure 15–3. Note that the sport uses a volleyball-sized playing area with two teams of three players each facing one another. The boundary and other lines shown in the figure are made tactile by placing small diameter cord under vinyl tape. Note the lines that extend into the team areas from the middle left to right and middle front to back are orientation lines to help keep players in position. The goalball itself is approximately basketball size, has thick rubber walls with several holes, and has sleigh bells placed in the unpressurized chamber. Goalball is a goal-oriented sport, scoring being much like that of soccer or hockey. If a player throws the ball underhand, rolling the ball across the floor, through the defenders at the other end, and into the net, a goal is scored (see ball approach in Figure 15–4).

Defenders make themselves into "human dams" from fingertips to outstretched toes (i.e., lying on one side with all joints extended and facing the throwing team). Goalball's popularity is surely due to the fact that players require no direct assistance from sighted people during a game. Referees are, of course sighted, but players can devote every ounce of energy they have to the game because it can be played at high levels of competence using touch (Miller's definition), hearing, and kinesthetics.

In order to play the game adequately, players must be able to throw the ball consistently from one end to the other, keeping it inside the left to right court boundaries; throw with moderate velocity; predict where the ball will go when it leaves an opposing player's hand; move quickly left to right 4 or 5 ft to block a ball; have good extended blocking form, to pass the ball to

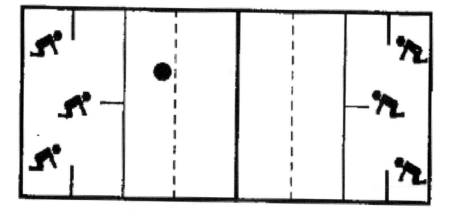

FIGURE 15–3. Goalball court diagram.

FIGURE 15–4. Example of a score about to be made.

another player; and know which opposing team member is preparing to throw the ball next.

Outstanding players know where the ball is on both ends of the court at all times; throw with pinpoint accuracy to a given location on the defenders' end; move from their position on one side to the other, throw the ball, and get back into position in seconds; throw a curving ball; throw using a complete 360 degree spin without losing track of orientation; predict in less than 1 s where the ball will be the instant it leaves the thrower's hand at the other end of the court; and make long dives to stop a ball 10 ft or more from the original defensive position.

Conversely, players who have not developed good physical skills or spatial concepts have difficulty lying parallel to the back line when blocking, throwing the ball with velocity, extending into "good" defensive blocking form, staying oriented on the court, and knowing how much force is required to stop a ball some distance from their starting defensive position. There is virtually no research that has investigated the sources of the outstanding spatial and sensory abilities of good players and the sources of the spatial difficulties of others. Perhaps the most intriguing question relates to the relationship between the sensory modalities of hearing and somatosensory input. It appears that there may be a basic conflict between the two that causes some individuals with early onset blindness to have difficulty lying parallel to the back line to block a ball. Perhaps hearing is so dominant spatially that individuals have great difficulty overcoming the tendency to go face first towards the bell sounds coming from the ball, rather than to lie perpendicular to its trajectory.

The lack of velocity in the throw of nearly all goalball players who lose vision early in life appears to be mechanical. As mentioned, their throw is not a fluid motion but is often two-handed, or if one-handed, appears awkward and out of synchronization. In fact, there are virtually no early blinded individuals who presently play goalball on the national level who can achieve the throwing speeds of equal sized teammates with acquired losses.

As mentioned earlier, inability to maintain rigid form may also relate to the possible dominance of hearing over somatosensory functions because one of the most common form irregularities has the player on both knees facing the ball as it comes, then trapping it between the legs (See Figure 15–5).

Limited ability to move around the team area freely, which is exemplified by being more or less lost on the court when attempting to get back into defensive position after throwing, is likely a problem of lack of spatial awareness (i.e., of the team area). Whereas many players who have functional vision or who lost sight as older children often move around the team area based primarily on auditory feedback, spatially limited players appear to be more dependent upon the raised surface lines.

FIGURE 15–5.   Common face-forward form irregularity of players with congenital impairments.

The concept of the use of the necessary degree of force among goalball players with early onset blindness appears to be a major problem. It is likely a function of not learning this concept in physical education class, as discussed above, or it simply may relate to not having experience in competitive sports. In any case, these problems faced by children with early blindness require serious research attention, both from basic scientists and from blindness practitioners.

Goalball as a Medium for Brain Research

Goalball would appear to be an ideal medium for plasticity research. It contains aspects of brain plasticity research reported by several well-known basic scientists (Carello & Turvey, 2000; Kennedy, 2000; Miller, 2000). In particular, Carello and Turvey's work on tools may well apply to the goalball player's ability to use inertia tensor to predict the travel path of the goalball he or she has thrown. Also, Kennedy's work is on outline drawings and the degree to which players can visualize the "diagram" of the rectangular playing area, make use of it to stay oriented within the area, and throw a goalball accurately to the opponent's end—all the while in a state of dynamic movement. Also, Miller's (2000) ideas about the effects of consistency in body reference, patterns, and redundancy on skill building appear to apply to a goalball player's ability to throw the ball with pinpoint accuracy. Although the number of goalball players is not great, it has been easy to obtain volunteers for any research we have conducted, partly because there is a strong national goalball network that holds regional tournaments and national camps annually.

The following questions appear to be appropriate using goalball:

1. How accurately can persons who are blind use the raised boundaries and their imagery to locate a target at 18 meters?
2. Does the goalball court imagery of veteran players affect brain structure, and if so, where is the change?
3. What is the multimodal relationship between the somatosensory task of defensive body alignment along the raised orientation lines and the auditory tracking of the ball?
4. Is there an auditory brain function that is dominant over the somatosensory input that drives players with early onset and severe vision loss to dive headfirst for the ball, rather than lie parallel to the goal line?

ART SKILLS

Just as it was a surprise to sports fans to discover that one of golf's best, Casey Martin, has a serious disability, few people expect someone who is blind to be an outstanding artist, and in fact, many would even wonder why someone who couldn't see would have any interest in the visual arts at all (Nelson, 2003).

However, if Day, Gaitskell, and Hurwitz's (1982) description of the role of art in the human experience holds true, that art is a means of engaging all human senses for learning and expression and creating a heightened sensitivity to the physical world that fosters a more perceptive appreciation of the environment, there is no reason to think art is unique to those with vision. In fact, many of the world's masters, including Monet, Van Gogh, and Degas, had visual impairments (Ravin & Becker, 2003). Nelson described the importance of art to people who have visual impairments and organized the work of many such artists into a national touring exhibition termed "Art of the Eye."

The integration of physical education skills and art skills into a single chapter in these pages may seem somewhat counterintuitive, since physical skills are generally viewed on one end of a continuum and art appreciation on quite another; football and sculpting do not generally appear together in the same pages, let alone in the same paragraph. However, they are combined here because they have relatedness in their relative absence from the school curricula of children with visual impairments and their absence in the daily lives of persons who are blind. In the context of this writing, they are related through their common use of touch and spatial imagery. As discussed earlier, touch, when defined in its broadest context, is a common thread that links the tactile exploration of a sculpture with orienting oneself to the raised boundaries of a goalball court. In addition, the ability of an individual who is blind to use imagery to predict the playing space of a sports activity or the space ultimately occupied by a finished piece of art also demonstrates the relatedness of art and sports. Lastly, physical and artistic skills are both areas of a great deal of experience and of intense interest to me.

Barriers to Skill and Concept Development

The barriers faced by children with visual impairments to the learning of basic art skills are much the same as those described earlier as barriers to physical and sports education—those related to early childhood development in the affective, cognitive, and psychomotor domains, and those stemming from the educational system itself. Early childhood development of drawing skills and of the somatosensory aspects of touch perception, however, appear to be sufficiently unique to require further coverage in this section. The barriers related to school programming are, essentially, identical to those described for the learning of physical skills but may not be as severe. Evaluations of our art education camps indicated that the students attending the camps were included more fully in their local art classes than are sports camp participants in physical education classes. Whereas approximately 50% of sports camp participants were fully included in physical education classes (Ponchillia, 1995), 77% of those attending our art camp in 2002 reported that they took art class with their sighted classmates (Phillips, 2002).

The Art Education Camp

The Art Education Camp is structured in the same fashion as the Sports Education Camp. The camp is a weeklong series of residential clinics that employs content experts as instructors and is primarily experiential. The annual camp serves approximately 30 students with visual impairments, who range in age from 9 to 18 years. Students attend art skills clinics that have covered stone sculpting, clay sculpting and pottery, life mask making, drawing, print making, photography, story-telling, theater, and poetry. Participants also learn ways to help their local art instructor modify art activities, how to build a portfolio, and how to exhibit and market their artwork. They also show their work in an annual exhibition through the Greater Kalamazoo Council for the Arts.

Art Concepts and Skills

Art has two orientations. The first involves creating, making, and presenting art works and engagement in the processes used to produce them. The second concerns the study of art works from a perspective of aesthetics. When people produce works of art, they learn how to express ideas and feelings and how to communicate with others, and the "viewers" grow in their abilities to understand their world when they engage with art. People who are blind or have severe low vision must accomplish this engagement with the visual arts either tactually or through limited vision, both of which cause the viewer to investigate it from a specific to general context. They must look at the aspects that are available to multiple touches of a hand, then put these pieces together to form a whole, which is the reverse of how a visual viewer perceives artwork (Hull, 2003). However, if the artwork to be viewed is small enough to grasp in both hands, visual and tactile viewing are relatively equivalent (Katz, 1989), with sight becoming more advantageous as the size of the viewed object increases beyond the range of touch.

Viewing Art Through Touch

The details of the specific characteristics, somatosensory basis, relationship to neurological networking, and cortical origins of touch will not be discussed in detail here because they will be presented by others in this book. However, it is necessary to establish certain facts about touch as it applies to viewing 2-D and 3-D objects that are crucial to understanding their application to art. Perhaps most important of all, Katz (1989) pointed out the incredible capabilities of touch, which is commonly equivalent to and sometimes better than sight for determining the characteristics of objects. Art Education Camp participants have often demonstrated this ability by pointing out flaws on the surfaces of stone sculptures that go unnoticed by sighted observers. Carello and Turvey

(2000), as well as many camp participants, have noted that active touch is generally more accurate than passive touch; that is, the continuous movement of the investigating hand increases tactile "acuity," whereas a still hand can discern little about the object. Miller (2000) has pointed out also that touch includes tactile acuity, characteristics of the pattern (e.g., size, features in the pattern, and saliency), perceptive and kinesthetic inputs from scanning movement, and redundancy or coincidence of body reference. As such, the use of consistent scanning patterns, placement of object to be viewed, viewing experience, and instruction in proper scanning and viewing techniques have benefits to those who wish to appreciate art tactually.

My experience at "touch exhibitions" demonstrates that most people, even those with visual impairments, have little idea of how to investigate an artwork efficiently by touch. When told to "go ahead and touch it," they will simply use the tip(s) of one or two fingers and "stab" lightly at random parts of the artwork. Therefore, they are getting the same random multiple mini-samplings of the artwork that Hull (2003) has described as being forced to use. However, there are methods that can improve this viewing technique. For example, Braille readers have used scanning techniques that employ the finger surfaces of both hands to give them an idea of the format of the page before they actually begin to read (Ponchillia & Ponchillia, 1996, p. 126). Putting this technique into an art context, using the palms and fingers of both hands to investigate the form of a life sized duck sculpture will immediately tell the viewer what it is, whereas it would take a great deal of time and frustration to discern that it is a duck using one fingertip multiple times. The viewing "hints" listed below come from years of sculpting experience, rather than from my research. They include

- using all possible surface area of one's palms and fingers of both hands to perceive form and the relationship among the parts of a piece
- using light touch pressure in smooth flowing movements over the surface to view textural differences
- using strong thumb pressure to discern detail within texture or inscribed markings
- using the light hairs on the backs of fingers or even one's cheek to better enjoy the beauty of a velvety soft, polished stone or wood surface
- adding oils or polishes to enhance the "softness" of a smooth stone surface
- being sure to inspect different textures for their appearance of being at varying temperatures from one another, with the smoother surfaces generally feeling cooler than those with more texture

The fact that nerve cells are concentrated in fingertips (Cholewiak & Collins, 1991) would seem to contradict the contention that the backs of fingers or even one's cheek might be superior for some uses. I have no research to support my conclusion but feel that the downy hairs on finger backs and cheek increase sensitivity and that friction is reduced due to the hair and the lighter touch pressures used there.

An academic work covering the viewing of tactile art would not be complete without the inclusion of information about the use of raised line pictures and drawings by persons who are blind. Drawing has been included as an art camp activity, primarily based on the work of Kennedy (2000) and Heller (2000), who have written extensively on their research. Although their research is basic in nature, the techniques and materials they described have guided the methods used in our drawing clinics. As Kennedy reported earlier (1993), children who are blind easily grasp the concept of using raised lines to represent the outside borders of pictures. Raised line drawings or copies of pictures are produced by drawing freehand on special devices designed for the purpose or by copying the image on heat-sensitive paper that "rises" only under the heat-absorbing black lines of the copied image and is unchanged where the copy remains white (Ponchillia & Ponchillia, 1996). In either case, children who are blind are sufficiently skilled to outperform untrained sighted children at interpreting such tactile pictures (D'Angiulli, Kennedy, & Heller, 1998).

Producing Art

Descriptions of many art projects for children and adults are available in print. Rodriguez (1984) has described numerous art activities for children in her excellent work, and projects for children and adults with visual impairments are described in a comprehensive work covering the subject of art and visual impairments recently published by Art Education for the Blind (Axel & Levent, 2003). I focus next on drawing and sculpting because of their relevance to spatial imagery and touch.

Drawing

Kennedy (1993) found that untrained people with congenital blindness could draw accurate representations of common objects. He argued that spatial perception is possible through touch as well as through sight and that the learning sequence experienced by both groups is similar. Many students at the Art Education Camp have also produced recognizable drawings that are noticeably the work of novices but virtually all demonstrate good representation of shape and size, and many employ tools of perspective, such as foreshortening, size/distance relationships, and convergence, with no instruction whatever. All the young artists who did not use such skills upon coming to the camp were able to do so after instruction. It was equally clear that the camp participants who drew were able to reproduce recognizable drawings of objects they had never seen but had only touched. The limiting factor in interpreting the child's imagery as represented by his or her drawing is in the lack of detail possible in the sketches of novice artists. It seems feasible that the production of a 3-D representation in clay or some other malleable substrate from a visual image might improve the ability to compare imagery and resulting artwork.

Sculpting

Because sculpting is three dimensional, it would appear to fit most people's perception of an art form that is within a blind person's abilities. Illustrations of the sculptures of blind people appear in the work of Revesz more than 50 years ago (Revesz, 1950), and sculpting has surely been a pastime of persons who are blind as long as humans have existed. However, there appears to be virtually nothing written by people who sculpt exclusively by touch that would help us understand the adaptive methodologies required to maintain realistic sculptures from a spatial perspective. For this reason, I focus next on the techniques I have developed over the past several years and on the visualization that must accompany them. The steps required to produce a stone sculpture are selecting and cleaning a stone, cutting out the figure, forming the figure, detailing the figure, and finishing the surface.

Selecting and cleaning.   There are two ways to begin a sculpting project, either having a figure in mind before beginning the entire project or selecting the figure to be represented by the final product by taking advantage of the natural shape of the rough stone. In either case, stones that come to the studio do so directly through the supplier from the mine, which means that it normally has an outer crumbly crust of impurities that needs to be chiseled or ground off, so that the true shape of the stone is apparent. Cleaning is important because it often changes the overall shape significantly.

If I have a preconceived idea about what figure or abstract shape I want to make, I usually call the supplier and ask someone to find a rough stone that would make a good "bear with its head up" or "whale with a high humped back." If I have no preconceived ideas about what to make, I order a stone and simply look at it from all angles and make a decision about what its natural shape will permit me to make from it. My imagery, along with touch, appears to be extremely efficient in this first step of establishing what sculpture resides within the rough form of the natural stone. In fact, I often "see" sculpting possibilities that sighted sculptors do not. However, as the form of the "piece to be" becomes more specific and begins to have body parts, eyes, body curvature, and so on, my visual imagery requires supplementation. In that case, I usually make a small clay maquette (scale model) or find an inexpensive model that is close to what I want the piece to look like. I then use this maquette throughout the remainder of the project to, in the case of the bear, furnish proportional information concerning relative neck versus total body length, leg length versus total body height, snout length versus total head length, and so forth. Visual imagery simply cannot give me that kind of detail, unless the figure is one that I have carved multiple times. However, the same weakness appears to be true among sculptors with vision because they nearly always have photographs or other visual aids to provide them the proportional details. Audiences with whom I have posed the problem "Please close your eyes and visualize the face of your mother or someone else you love very much and attempt to hold that image as long as you can" appear to reinforce my belief that it is rare to find someone who can retain a visual image long enough to furnish detailed information regarding specific characteristics, such as eye position, nose width, and mouth shape. Because I am aware of this weakness in imagery, I collect inexpensive plastic or wooden models of animals to keep in reserve for times when one of that variety might be needed.

Cutting out.   If I were making a bear standing on all four feet, I would start with a cleaned stone of blocky shape. On the part of the stone I considered to be the top of the bear's back, I would use a pointed file to scratch the general outline of the shape of the bear looking down at it from the top. I would deepen and widen the etched line with a rasp so I could place the edge of an air-powered 3-in. rotating diamond blade in the resulting groove and cut all the stone away from the outside of the line I scratched. I also commonly use an air chisel instead of the rotating blade to do this removal. The next step is to draw the legs, body, neck, and head from the side view with my point, then cut everything that isn't body, neck, or legs away with a saw or chisel. When this "cutting out" phase is done, I have a bear, but she has square legs, neck, and body.

Forming.   This phase is the slowest and requires the most work of the entire sculpting process. Either heavy wood rasps or power grinders are used to round off the square legs, body, and neck—and constant comparisons with the maquette are required to maintain the proper bear form.

Detailing.   Adding the jaw, the ears, the toes, and so forth is the most difficult spatial task of the process. The task is done with curved files called *rifflers* or with small pencil-like air-powered grinders. When this degree of detail is required, it is necessary to make a tentative etching where I believe the detail to go, and then check the placement by touch from varying perspectives. Interestingly, what appears to be the perfect placement from one tactile vantage point often turns out to be incorrect, so I take several "sightings" from different perspectives before committing to cutting deeply into the stone for the final detail.

Finishing.   The final step is to sand the surface of the piece by first using course 50 grit sandpaper to get rid of the filing and grinding marks and ending with 2000 grit paper to make the stone shine like glass. I usually go from 50 to 125, to 200, to 400, to 600, then to 2000 grit. Finishing poses a serious tactile challenge because it is easy to "hide" scratches from my fingertips by moving too quickly to the next level of sandpaper. For example, if a small scratch went unnoticed while using 100 grit paper, the 200 or 400 grit paper will polish the scratch to a point that its edges are smooth and not tactually discernible, but the scratch holds white powder that is easily visible to people with sight. Unfortunately, regardless of how much care I take, I must have visual feedback to ensure that the final piece is free of scratches. The extremely fine sandpapers (i.e., 1500 and 2000 grit) are used with water. This is done because the sandpaper "clogs" with stone dust too quickly to permit the use of a piece for more than a minute or two under dry conditions. Dipping the paper in water removes the dust from the sand, allowing for extended use of fine papers. A complication of using these fine papers is that, after sanding for a short time, it is not possible with fingertips to determine which side is the grit side and which is the nongrit side. Although the description is not pleasant, one's lightly clinched front teeth are capable of this fine tactile discrimination task. The last step in finishing a piece is polishing, which adds gloss and deepening of the stone's color. The polishing compound is one used for stone countertops, and it can be applied efficiently and evenly by touch. See finished sculptures by the author in Figures 15.6 and 15.7.

Art as a Medium for Brain Plasticity Research

Most of the research that might be interpreted as having to do with art and plasticity has been done with 2-D raised drawings (Heller, 2000; Kennedy, 2000). The major focus of the research has been the interpretation of the visual imagery of blind people by having them draw objects that they have touched but never seen. The conclusion of these important studies has been that touch provides people who are blind an image that is equivalent to that which would have resulted from vision (Kennedy, 2000). There has been some speculation that drawing and resulting 2-D pictures may not be the best way to determine the nature of the visual images of people who are congenitally blind. Lederman, Klatzky, Chataway, and Summers (1990) felt, and it seems logical, that the precision of a 3-D product would be a better measure of imagery. Also, because people who have been blind since birth are not familiar with drawing or using drawing instruments, another method may also be more effective.

The work of Hamilton and Pascual-Leone (1998) demonstrated that Braille, which is read tactually, is actually processed in the visual cortex of the occipital lobe of the brain. This cross-modal ability has allowed their subjects to use a part of the brain that, because they are blind, would otherwise not be expected to function. This leads one to speculate about what other tactile tasks might be assumed by the visual cortex.

FIGURE 15–6.   "Floe Edge," a soapstone polar bear on an ice floe by the author.

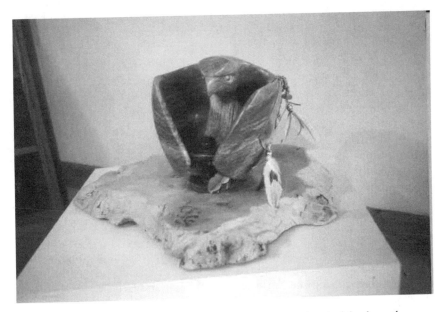

FIGURE 15–7.   "Praying," an alabaster eagle on western hemlock by the author.

These two major findings and their ramifications lead me to pose the following questions in the area of art and plasticity research:

1. Would the imagery of people who are blind be better measured through the production of three-dimensional clay or other sculpting materials than drawing?
2. Would the tactile viewing of art involve the visual cortex as Braille reading does among people who are blind?
3. Are there differences in brain structure and psychosocial attributes of blind people who have been exposed to tactile art as opposed to those who have not?
4. Are there the same differences among blind people who have been involved in producing art as opposed to those who have not?

SUMMARY

Four major points are made in this article: (a) There are barriers to the development of sports and arts skills, some inherent to nonvisual performance but others tied more to parenting and educational practices such as negative parental attitudes and lack of effective instruction; (b) Sports and arts camps for children with blindness that focus on physical skills instruction confirm that, with appropriate guidance and expectations, children can become skilled in these domains; (c) The examples of goalball and sculpting show extremely rich content domains in which high levels of nonvisual expertise can be acquired for the performance of difficult tasks; and (d) Issues surrounding skill acquisition are surely relevant to brain plasticity, since the activities are so strongly guided by vision in persons who are able to see. Furthermore, I would be remiss if I did not express my gratitude for the opportunity this chapter afforded to put brain plasticity into the context of my own life. In hindsight, I see just how phenomenally the cortical transition was made from visual to nonvisual performance in sports activities that I performed both before and after my vision loss. For example, apart from fears and early self-doubts, accomplishing a long jump appeared to be unchanged nonvisually, presumably because the imagery of the long jump pit and runway remained vivid and the thousands of jumps made with vision had set the movement deep in muscle and joint memory. Conversely, I had virtually no experience with the visual arts prior to blindness, other than taking an art history course in college. I had little interest and exhibited little aptitude until an awakening experience occurred some 2 years following blindness. My interest came thundering down on me at a tactile art exhibition I attended. I vividly recall the pure joy that overcame me when I touched a gloriously smooth and soft marble sculpture of two African faces peering at me questioningly from atop two flowing, curving, elongated, and intertwining necks! The image is still absolutely vivid these 30 years later. Again reflecting, I knew after 2 years of haptic experience that the sense was giving me highly accurate information, but I had never thought of it as pleasurable or so richly revealing as I did at the touch of that beautiful, enlightening piece. And now I fully understand that I truly was seeing the piece.

I hope the thoughts presented in this chapter have painted an adequate picture of the wealth of research opportunities available in the areas of physical and art skills and concepts among individuals who are blind or have low vision. I hope also that this and the other chapters stimulate continued cooperation between researchers in the areas of brain plasticity and blindness and low vision studies. Indeed, the opportunities for growth of knowledge through research are limitless.

REFERENCES

Adelson, E., & Fraiberg, S. (1974). Gross motor development in infants blind from birth. *Child Development, 45*, 1–126.

Auxter, D., Pyfer, J., & Huetting, C. (1997). *Principles and methods of adapted physical education and recreation* (8th ed.). St. Louis, MO: Mosby Year Book.

Axel, E. S., & Levent, N. S. (2003). Art beyond sight: A resource guide to art, creativity and visual impairment. New York, NY: American Foundation for the Blind.

Bigelow, A. E. (1992). Locomotion and search behavior in blind infants. *Infant Behavior and Development, 15*, 179–189.

Blessing, D. L., McCrimmon, D., Stovall, J., & Williford, H. N. (1993). The effects of regular exercise programs for visually impaired and sighted schoolchildren. *Journal of Visual Impairment and Blindness, 87*, 50–51.

Buell, C. E. (1982). *Physical education and recreation for the visually handicapped* (2nd ed.). Reston, VA: American Alliance for Health, Physical Education, Recreation and Dance.

Carello, C., & Turvey, M. T. (2000). Rotational invariance in dynamic touch. In M. A. Heller (Ed.), *Touch representation and blindness* (pp. 27–66). Oxford and New York, NY: Oxford Press.

Cholewiak, R. W., & Collins, A. A. (1991). Sensory and physiological bases of touch. In M. A. Heller (Ed.), *The psychology of touch*. Hillsdale, NJ: Lawrence Erlbaum Associates.

Cohen, L. G., Celnik, P., Pascual-Leone, A., Corwell, B., Falz, L., Dambrosia, J., & Honda, M., (1997). Functional relevance of cross-modal plasticity in blind humans. *Nature, 389*, 180–183.

Cratty, B. J. (1971). *Movement and spatial awareness in blind children and youth*. Springfield, IL: Charles C Thomas.

Day, M., Gaitskell, C. D., & Hurwitz, A. (1982). *Children and their art* (4th ed). New York, NY: Harcourt Brace Jovanovich.

D'Angiulli, A. D., Kennedy, J. M., & Heller, M. A. (1998). Tactile picture recognition by blind and sighted children. *Scandinavian Journal of Psychology, 39*, 187–190.

Fraiberg, S. (1968). Parallel and divergent patterns in blind and sighted infants. *Psychoanalytic Study of the Child, 23*, 264–300.

Fraiberg, S. (1977). *Insights from the blind: Comparative studies of blind and sighted infants*. New York, NY: Basic Books,

Goldfine, B. D. (1993). Incorporation of health-fitness concepts in secondary physical education curricula. *Journal of School Health, 63*, 142–147.

Graham, G., Holt, S. A., & Hale, M. P. (2001). *Children moving: A reflective approach to teaching physical education.* Mountain View, CA: Mayfield Publication.

Gronmo, S. J., & Augestad, L. B. (2000). Physical activity, self-concept, and global self-worth of blind youths in Norway and France. *Journal of Visual Impairment and Blindness, 94*, 522–526.

Guth, D. A., & Rieser, J. J. (1997). Perceptions and the control of locomotion by blind and visually impaired persons. In B. Blasch, W. Weiner, & R. Welsh (Eds.), *Foundations of orientation and mobility* (2nd ed.). New York, NY: American Foundation for the Blind.

Hamilton, R. H., & Pascual-Leone, A. (1998). Cortical plasticity associated with Braille learning. *Trends in Cognitive Science, 2*(5), 168–174.

Heller, M. A. (Ed.). (2000). *Touch, representation and blindness* (Debates in Psychology Series). Oxford, England: Oxford University Press.

Hull, J. M. (2003). The world of sight and the world of touch. In E. Axel & N. Levent (Eds.), *Art beyond sight: A resource guide to art, creativity and visual impairment* (pp. 204–208). New York, NY: American Foundation for the Blind.

Jankowski, L. W., & Evans, J. K. (1981). The exercise capability of blind children. *Journal of Visual Impairment and Blindness, 75*, 248–251.

Katz, D. (1989). *The world of touch.* (L. E. Krueger, Trans.). Hillsdale, NJ: Lawrence Erlbaum Associates.

Kennedy, J. M. (1993). *Drawing and the blind.* New Haven, CT: Yale University Press.

Kennedy, J. M. (2000). Recognizing outline pictures via touch: Alignment theory. In M. A. Heller (Ed.), *Touch, representation and blindness* (pp. 67–98). Oxford, Great Britain: Oxford University Press.

Kobberling, G., Jankowski, L., & Leger, L. (1991). The relationship between aerobic capacity and physical activity in blind and sighted adolescents. *Journal of Visual Impairment and Blindness, 85*, 382–384.

Lederman, S. J., Klatzky, R. L., Chataway, C., & Summers, C. D. (1990). Visual mediation and the haptic recognition of two dimensional pictures of common objects. *Perception & Psychophysics, 47*, 54–64.

Lieberman, L. J., & Houston-Wilson, C. (1999). Overcoming the barriers to including students with visual impairments and deaf-blindness in physical education. *Review, 31*, 129–138.

Lieberman, L. J., & McHugh, E. (2001). Health-related fitness of children who are visually impaired. *Journal of Visual Impairment and Blindness, 95*, 272–285.

Lowenfeld, B. (1973). *The visually impaired child in school.* New York, NY: John Day.

Miller, S. (2000). Modality and mind: Convergent active processing in inter-related networks as a model of development and perception by touch. In M. A. Heller (Ed.), *Touch representation and blindness* (pp. 99–142). Oxford and New York, NY: Oxford University Press.

Nelson, S. (2003). A professional artist and curator who is blind. In E. Axel & N. Levent (Eds.), *Art beyond sight: A resource guide to art, creativity and visual impairment* (pp. 26–30). New York: American Foundation for the Blind.

Norris, M., Spaulding, P. J., & Brodie, F. H. (1957). *Blindness in children.* Chicago: University of Chicago Press.

Phillips, H. (2002). *An evaluation of the art education camp for students with visual impairments.* Unpublished manuscript, Western Michigan University, Kalamazoo.

Piaget, J. (1981). *Intelligence and affectivity: Their relationship during child development.* Palo Alto, CA: Annual Reviews.

Ponchillia, P. (1995). AccessSports: A model for adapting mainstream sports activities for individuals with visual impairments. *Re:View, 27,* 5–14.

Ponchillia, P. E., Armbruster, J., & Wiebold, J. (2005). The national sports education camps project: A short-term model for introducing sports skills to students with visual impairment [Abstract]. *Journal of Visual Impairment and Blindness, 99*(11), 685.

Ponchillia, P., & Ponchillia, S. (1996). *Foundations of rehabilitation teaching with persons who are blind or visually impaired.* New York: American Foundation for the Blind.

Ponchillia, S. V., Powell, L. L., Felski, K. A., & Nicklawski, M. T. (1992). The effectiveness of aerobics exercise instruction for totally blind women. *Journal of Visual Impairment and Blindness, 86,* 174–177.

Ponchillia, P. E., Strause, B., & Ponchillia, S. V. (2002). Athletes with visual impairment: Attributes and sports participation. *Journal of Visual Impairment and Blindness, 96,* 267–272.

Portfors-Yeomans, C., & Riach, C. L. (1995). Frequency characteristics of postural control of children with and without visual impairment. *Developmental Medicine and Child Neurology, 37,* 456–463.

Ravin, J. G., & Becker, J. (2003). Historical perspective: Visual impairments of well-known artists. In E. Axel & N. Levent (Eds.), *Art beyond sight: A resource guide to art, creativity and visual impairment* (pp. 31–32). New York: American Foundation for the Blind.

Revesz, G. (1950). *Psychology and art of the blind.* London: Longmans, Green.

Rodriguez, S. (1984). *The special artist's handbook: Art activities and adaptive aids for handicapped students.* Palo Alto, CA: Dale Seymour Publications.

Sadato, M., Pascual-Leone, A., Grafman, J., Ibanez, V., Deiber, M.-P., Dold, G., & Hallett, M. (1996). Activation of the primary visual cortex by Braille reading in blind subjects. *Nature, 380,* 526–528.

Sadato, N., Pascual-Leone, A., Gradman, J., Deiber, M.-P., Ibanez, V., & Hallet, M. (1998). Neural networks for Braille reading by the blind. *Brain, 121,* 1213–1229.

Scholl, G. T. (1986). Growth and development. In G. T. Scholl (Ed.), *Foundation of education for blind and visually handicapped children and youth* (pp. 23–33). New York: American Foundation for the Blind.

Sherrill, C. (1993). *Adapted physical activity recreation and sport* (4th ed.). Dubuque, IA: Wm. C. Brown.

Short, F., & Winnick, J. (1986). The influence of visual impairment on physical fitness test performance. *Journal of Visual Impairment and Blindness, 80,* 729–731.

Skaggs, S., & Hopper, C. (1996). Individuals with visual impairments: A review of psychomotor behavior. *Adapted Physical Activity Quarterly, 13,* 16–26.

Smart, J. (2001). *Disability, society, and the individual.* Gaithersburg, MD: Aspen.

Tripp, H. (1996). Children and sports: Encouraging a healthy attitude to exercise should start in primary school. *British Medical Journal, 312,* 199–200.

16

Making the Environment Accessible to Pedestrians Who Are Visually Impaired: Policy Research

Billie Louise Bentzen

INTRODUCTION TO POLICY RESEARCH
AND ACCESSIBLE DESIGN

The Architectural Barriers Act (ABA) of 1968 was the first legislation in the United States that was concerned with making the built environment accessible to people with disabilities. Activists who were largely people with mobility impairments, including many veterans whose mobility depended on use of a wheelchair, were key advocates for this legislation. The emphasis of the ABA was on making the environment accessible to people with mobility impairments, and its applicability was limited to federal and federally-funded facilities.

Since that time several other laws have been passed that have broadened requirements for accessibility to all public accommodations, including public transportation and public rights-of-way. The legislation was also broadened to specifically include people with sensory disabilities as well as mobility impairments. Foremost among these laws is the Americans with Disabilities Act of 1990 (ADA), the first comprehensive disability rights law in the world. The ADA is a civil rights law, prohibiting discrimination on the basis of disability in employment, state and local government programs and facilities, public accommodations and services including transportation provided by public and private entities, and telecommunications.

Standards and Guidelines Are Required to Implement Disability Legislation

Implementation of disability laws requires standards and guidelines. The Architectural and Transportation Barriers Compliance Board, now commonly called the Access Board, was created by Section 502 of the Rehabilitation Act of 1973 to develop standards by which the ABA would be enforced. The Access Board is now responsible for development of guidelines for implementing the accessibility requirements of the ADA as well. These are referred to as the ADA Accessibility Guidelines, or ADAAG, originally adopted in 1991, and revised in 2004—now referred to as New ADAAG. The guidelines are the basis for enforceable standards adopted by the U.S. Departments of Justice (DOJ) and Transportation (DOT). New ADAAG was adopted by the DOT on October 30, 2006, but it has not been adopted by DOJ and DOT as of this writing.

The federal rule-making process for accessibility standards requires that the Access Board adopt accessibility guidelines, typically basing the guidelines on the input of special purpose advisory committees. The Access Board is comprised of 14 public members, a number of presidential appointees who represent a wide range of interest and knowledge regarding disabilities, and 12 members representing federal agencies such as the DOJ and DOT.

The Access Board typically appoints an advisory committee to aid in development of specific standards; committees include representatives of stakeholder groups as appropriate for a given standard. For example, the advisory committee providing input to the development of guidelines for access to public rights-of-way included members of consumer and professional groups representing people with disabilities, state departments of transportation, departments of public works, engineers, and architects. The special purpose committees and the Access Board always consider research as the basis for guidelines and technical specifications.

Before final adoption of guidelines, a public comment period is required, during which members of the public, including all stakeholder groups, are invited to submit comments and recommend changes either at public hearings or in writing. All comments and recommended changes must be considered before a standard is adopted and published in the Federal Register as a final rule.

When ADAAG was first being developed, stakeholder groups working to establish standards and guidelines for accessibility could readily understand that persons with mobility impairments, particularly people who are mobile using a wheelchair, could not travel routes including stairs or curbs, that they had limited reach ranges, and that they required more space and extra support to enable turning and transferring in toilet rooms. Standards and guidelines for modifying the physical environment to address these needs could be based largely on anthropometrics.

Environments that are accessible to people with visual impairments are ones in which there is sufficient information perceptible using low vision or other sensory modalities for them to travel about and to use facilities safely, efficiently, and gracefully, with minimal need for assistance from other people. Accessibility for people having visual impairments is usually a matter of having the right information at the right time. Having information means having choices; it means the ability to make the correct choice the first time; it means not having to engage in tiresome deductive reasoning from imprecise clues; it means not having to ask frequently for information or assistance. Having information also means being able to travel more safely. For example, an accessible pedestrian signal (APS) indicates the onset of the pedestrian phase at an intersection whose signal phases are difficult to determine by listening to traffic; a detectable warning at the bottom of a curb ramp or at a blended curb enables positive identification of the boundary between the pedestrian and vehicular ways.

Prior to the late 1970s there was little or no research on making the environment accessible to people who are blind or who have low vision. However, at that time there was an increasing awareness that the requirement for curb ramps to make public rights-of-way accessible to people with mobility impairments removed the definitive cue to blind pedestrians that they had come to the end of a sidewalk and were about to step into a street. Research was conducted to identify a surface texture or material that was sufficiently detectable to people with visual impairments to be used as a warning indicating the boundary between the pedestrian and the vehicular way (Aiello & Steinfeld, 1980).

It was recognized that protruding objects could endanger pedestrians who are blind, that signs needed to have relatively larger characters and high contrast to be legible to people who have low vision, and that elevators needed to be marked in such a way that floor numbers were legible to users who were blind or who had low vision. The first standard providing technical specifications addressing these needs was the industry standard, ANSI A117.1 1980, the *American National Standard Specifications for Making Buildings and Facilities Accessible to and Usable by Physically Handicapped People*. The ANSI A117.1, revised approximately every 5 years, is also the product of consensus among stakeholders. This standard becomes enforceable as its provisions are adopted (scoped) by building codes, and it ultimately becomes enforceable by building inspectors. Provisions of ANSI A117 1980 and its revisions formed the basis for subsequent federal standards and guidelines.

The following issues regarding accessibility for persons who are visually impaired have been addressed by research that was the basis for technical specifications in ADAAG or ANSI:

- Specifications for signs, including character height, stroke width, and spacing
- Specifications for tactile characters
- Specifications for texture of a detectable warning surface

- Specifications for depth of detectable warnings in the direction of travel
- Specifications for location of detectable warnings on curb ramps and transit platform edges
- Specifications for contrast of detectable warnings
- Specifications for the locator tone repetition rate for APS
- Caution against the use of a two-tone system for APS
- Specifications for push-button location (in the regulatory process)
- Guidelines for the content and structure of APS speech messages (in the regulatory process)
- Specifications for an extended button press to actuate special accessible features of an APS (in the regulatory process)

ACCESSIBILITY FOR PEOPLE WITH VISUAL IMPAIRMENTS OFTEN IMPROVES ACCESS FOR OTHER GROUPS

Many designs intended to make some aspect of the environment accessible to and usable by people with visual impairments have resulted in benefits for users who are not visually impaired. Truncated dome detectable warnings (see Figure 16–1), whose surface texture was identified through a long series of experiments funded by the Department of Housing and Urban Development, the Federal Highway Administration, the Urban Mass Transit Administration, the Federal Transit Administration, and Project ACTION (administered by Easter Seals) have been required at drop-offs along transit platform edges since 1991 (ADAAG, 1991).

These detectable warnings are intended to provide advance information about the precise location of these hazardous drop-offs that is perceptible both under foot and by use of a long cane. This requirement was in response to the disproportionate number of visually impaired transit riders who were experiencing falls from transit platforms (Bentzen, Jackson, & Peck, 1981; McCulley & Bentzen, 1987; McGean, 1991).

Research on the influence of detectable warnings on curb ramps, and on safety and negotiability for people with mobility impairments indicated that decreases in safety and negotiability were minimal (Bentzen, Nolin, Easton, Desmarais, & Mitchell, 1994b, 1994c; Hughes, 1995). However, there was minimal adverse influence for a very small proportion of people with mobility impairments. Therefore, it was recommended that the depth of detectable warnings (in direction of travel) on curb ramps should be as little as possible (i.e., 24 in.). A minimum depth of 24 in. had been found to be detectable on 90% of approaches by blind subjects (Peck & Bentzen, 1987). Additionally, in the first 10 years of use in the United States, 24 in. deep detectable warnings at transit platforms in San Francisco and Miami were found not only to de-

FIGURE 16–1.   Detectable warning along a platform edge in MARTA (Atlanta).

crease the number of platform edge falls by riders with visual impairments but also to decrease the overall number of platform edge falls (Bentzen, Barlow, & Tabor, 2000; McGean, 1991).

Researchers found also that truncated dome detectable warnings required near the bottom of curb ramps were judged by participants with visual impairments not only to aid in street crossing but also a majority of participants with mobility impairments felt that they were safer, had better traction, and were more stable on ramps having detectable warnings than on brushed concrete ramps (Hauger, Rigby, Safewright, & McAuley, 1996). These researchers found that 44% of participants reported they required less effort to negotiate up and down curb ramps having detectable warnings, whereas only 23% said the opposite. Thus detectable warnings benefit not only people with visual impairments but also many people with mobility impairments.

Accessible pedestrian signals that provide acoustic output during the WALK interval of the pedestrian phase have been found to decrease starting delay for all pedestrians. Examples of these signals are shown in Figure 16–2. They have been found also to decrease the average number of pedestrians who are still in the crosswalk when the green phase begins for perpendicular traffic (Hulscher, 1976; Wilson, 1980). Thus APSs not only increase the safety and

FIGURE 16–2. Top: APS installed on the pedestrian signal head, typical of older installations in the United States. Bottom: APS integrated into the pedestrian pushbutton, typical of newer installations in the United States and specified in the Access Board's Draft Guidelines for Accessible Public Rights-of-Way.

318

independence of pedestrians who are visually impaired but also benefit all pedestrians. They benefit drivers as well because there is less delay to vehicular traffic when pedestrians clear the intersection faster.

Large-print, high-contrast signs with minimal glare generally increase the speed and accuracy of reading by all people, including those having low vision, as well as increasing the distance at which signs can be read (Bentzen, 1996; Bentzen & Easton, 1996; Georgia Institute of Technology, 1985; Peter Muller-Munk Associates, 1986).

Other design modifications which have been implemented in various locations initially in order to make the environment more usable to people with visual impairments but which have been found to be appreciated by other user groups as well include high contrast handrails, high contrast stair nosings, and landscaping to indicate crosswalk location.

SPECIAL CONSIDERATION FOR POLICY RESEARCH

Unlike pure science, policy research is driven by the need for empirical research to inform decision making. Therefore, topics and timing of research as well as funding are heavily influenced by contemporary legislative and regulatory issues. Identification of a problem may begin with consumer concern and the experience of blindness professionals who persuade Congress or a regulatory body that the problem is important. Research may be undertaken to identify a solution or solutions; timing is often driven by a cycle of revision for a regulation. A solution, or technical specification, may be written based on results of research, and this solution may get approval from the stakeholders participating in the regulatory body.

During public comment other consumers or other stakeholder groups may doubt the existence of the problem or raise additional concerns about the proposed solution. This may necessitate an urgent need for additional research on the proposed standard to measure and quantify the problem or to evaluate the effect of the suggested solution on other groups. Sometimes stakeholders having other disabilities, who have not been alert to the development of a standard that addresses needs of people with visual impairments, have become concerned that implementation of a standard could have a negative impact on the group they represent. They may then advocate for additional research to determine the effect of the standard on their group, and this additional research is often undertaken.

Such nonlinear research is common in the policy arena. When research results document that the problem is of sufficient severity and the proposed solution is demonstrated to address the problem appropriately, the standards body has the substantiation needed to retain the requirement or technical specification. It is not uncommon for this see-sawing effect to continue through more than one revision cycle of a standard.

AN EXAMPLE OF DEVELOPMENT OF STANDARDS
FOR DETECTABLE WARNINGS ON CURB RAMPS
AND TRANSIT PLATFORMS

The following case study details, in chronological order, the development of standards for detectable warnings on curb ramps and transit platforms. The interplay of research, public comment, and standards development is represented in this example. I was involved extensively in research and standards setting throughout this time, so the case study represents my own perspective on events. (Keep in mind that publication dates do not necessarily indicate exactly when research was actually conducted.)

As was noted earlier, in the 1970s it was recognized that removal of the curb to promote wheelchair use created a safety problem for pedestrians who are blind. The curb is the definitive cue that informs pedestrians who are blind that they have come to the end of the sidewalk and are about to enter the street. About the same time, it was recognized that a highly disproportionate number of blind transit riders were falling from platform edges, to the track bed, sometimes resulting in death (Bentzen et al., 1981). Subsequent research confirmed the frequency of this problem (McCulley & Bentzen, 1987; McGean, 1991). It was thought that a special tactile surface on curb ramps could enable blind pedestrians to recognize when they had come to a street, and research was undertaken to identify such a surface (Aiello & Steinfield, 1980).

The earliest research to identify a warning surface for use on curb ramps emphasized only detection, by blind persons who were using a long cane, of a warning surface adjoining brushed concrete. A ribbed rubber mat was found highly detectable because it varied from concrete in texture, resiliency, and sound when tapped with a long cane (Aiello & Steinfeld, 1980). A resilient tennis court surface was found to be highly detectable to blind long-cane users (Templer & Wineman, 1980). Various steel surfaces were found to be highly detectable on the basis of differences in sound between steel and concrete when contacted by a long cane (Templer, Wineman, & Zimring, 1982).

In the ANSI Standard, A117.1-1980, what were then referred to as tactile warnings were specified for the entire walking surface of curb ramps. A strip 36 in. wide was specified along the full edge of blended curbs. A tactile warning surface was also specified for tops of stair runs except those in dwelling units, in enclosed stair towers, or to the side of the path of travel. Further, tactile warnings were specified for edges of reflecting pools that did not have railings, walls, or curbs. Tactile warnings were to consist of exposed aggregate concrete, rubber, or plastic cushioned surfaces; raised strips; or grooves. Textures had to contrast with the surrounding surface. Grooves were permitted indoors only.

Despite the standardization and the fact that grooves were not permitted outdoors, early implementations of the ANSI A117.1-1980 and subsequent ANSI A117.1-1986 standard for tactile warnings included a number of surface treatments such as grooved concrete, which had not been found to be highly detectable to pedestrians who are blind. Figure 16–3 shows design features of grooved surfaces which have been considered, whereas Figure 16–4 shows a curb ramp treatment that is not considered a detectable warning because it has not been found to be highly detectable, is not standardized, and is easily mistaken for other common features in the pedestrian environment (Bentzen

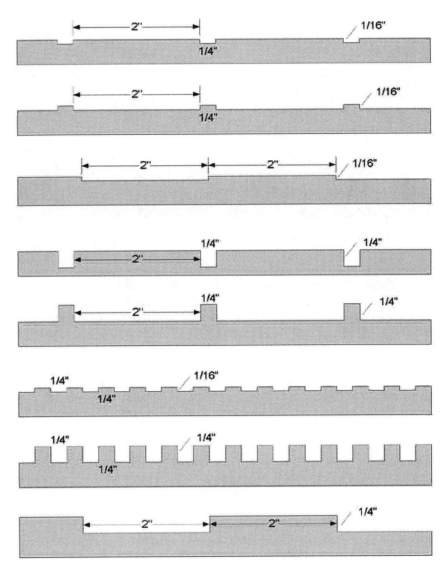

FIGURE 16–3. Cross-sections of surfaces found to be low in detectability. Drawing shows profiles of eight grooved surfaces. Grooves varied in width between 1/4 and 2 in., and in depth between 1/16 and 1/4 in.

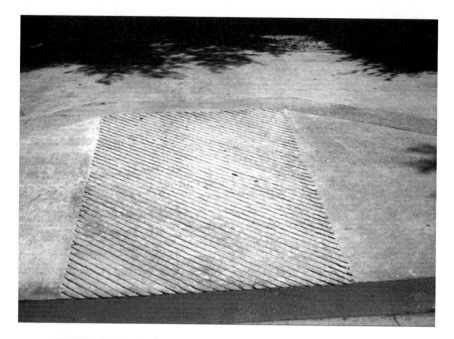

FIGURE 16–4.   Curb ramp with a minimally detectable grooved surface.

et al., 2000). Many surfaces that would have seemed likely to be highly detectable were only somewhat detectable, especially under foot.

The Urban Mass Transportation Administration (UMTA), precursor to
the Federal Transit Administration (FTA), sponsored research to identify a
warning surface that was highly detectable when it adjoined the variety of
surfaces in common use for transit platforms (Peck & Bentzen, 1987). The
researchers recognized that it was essential that warnings be highly detectable
under foot as well as by use of the long cane. A minority of people who are
legally blind regularly use a long cane for obtaining surface information as
they travel. Other people who are visually impaired use dog guides or their low
vision. To detect changes in walking surfaces, they rely on under-foot information and/or visual contrast. Low vision is quite variable; a person who often
can see streets, platform edges and stairs may sometimes be unable to see them
because of glare, poor illumination, poor visual contrast, or fatigue.

Peck and Bentzen (1987) identified two surfaces suitable for transit platform use, which were both highly detectable when used in association with
brushed concrete, exposed aggregate concrete, a frequently used resilient tile
with raised circles commonly referred to as Pirelli tile, and heavy wooden decking, representing both typical and extreme surfaces then in use on transit platforms. One experimental surface was a prototype "corduroy" surface having
raised ribs that were dome-shaped in cross section, 3/16 in. high, 3/4 in. wide,

and 2 in. apart on center. The other was a resilient rubber tile having a truncated dome pattern similar to the pattern of warning surfaces that had been in use in Japan since the 1960s.

Both of these surfaces were highly detectable to blind persons both under foot and with the use of a long cane and were more highly detectable in a noisy environment like a transit station than a rough textured steel surface or a resilient tennis court surface. The truncated dome surface was recommended for a standard warning surface because similar surfaces were being used for warnings in Japan and England, while linear surfaces were being used in Japan to attempt to provide directional guidance.

In 1991, the Access Board published ADAAG, which included scoping and technical specifications for truncated dome detectable warnings at curb-ramps, hazardous vehicular ways, reflecting pools, and edges of transit platforms having drop-offs. The ADAAG specifications were based on the research by Peck and Bentzen (1987).

ADAAG (1991) specified that:

> Detectable warnings shall consist of raised truncated domes with a diameter of nominal 0.9 in (23 mm), a height of nominal 0.2 in (5 mm) and a center-to-center spacing of nominal 2.35 in (60 mm) and shall contrast visually with adjoining surfaces, either light-on-dark or dark-on-light.
>
> The material used to provide contrast shall be an integral part of the walking surface. Detectable warnings used on interior surfaces shall differ from adjoining walking surfaces in resiliency or sound on cane-contact. (ADAAG 4.29.2)

The requirement for detectable warnings at curb ramps were as follows: "A curb ramp shall have a detectable warning complying with [ADAAG] 4.29.2. The detectable warning shall extend the full width and depth of the curb ramp." (ADAAG 4.7.7)

The requirement for detectable warnings at transit platform edges was as follows: "Platform edges bordering a drop-off and not protected by platform screens or guard rails shall have a detectable warning. Such detectable warnings shall comply with 4.29.2 and shall be 24 inches wide running the full length of the platform drop-off." (ADAAG 10.3.1 (8))

Both specifications and scoping for detectable warnings quickly became one of the most controversial issues in ADAAG. Truncated dome detectable warnings were strongly advocated by some individuals and organizations of blind travelers and by the orientation and mobility (O&M) profession. They were strongly opposed by other individuals and organizations of blind travelers and by some individuals and organizations representing people concerned with safety of persons with mobility impairments. Blind persons opposing detectable warnings at curb ramps and hazardous vehicular ways claimed that other cues were available and that detectable warnings were an unnecessary and costly feature. Additionally, concerns were expressed regarding the use of truncated dome detectable warnings on sloped curb ramps, and the possibility of trips and falls for sighted pedestrians, particularly women wearing high heels, as well as difficulty for wheelchair users in traversing ramps with additional "bumps."

These concerns led to suspension of the requirements for detectable warnings on curb ramps and hazardous vehicular ways. By 1992 some members of the ANSI A117.1 committee were no longer certain that detectable warnings were needed in any location, and all specifications for the texture and for its use in various locations were dropped from the 1992 ANSI A117. In addition, in April 1994 ADAAG requirements for truncated dome detectable warnings at curb ramps, hazardous vehicular ways, and reflecting pools were temporarily suspended while the Access Board sought additional research on the following questions.

- Are detectable warnings needed on curb ramps?
- Do detectable warnings on curb ramps help people with visual impairments?
- Do detectable warnings on curb ramps have adverse impacts on people with mobility impairments?
- Do detectable warnings at hazardous vehicular ways create hazards for women in high heels, or persons using strollers, shopping carts, and the like?

The requirement for truncated dome detectable warnings at transit platform edges remained in effect.

Research was then undertaken to answer these questions. Two research projects (Barlow & Bentzen, 1994; Bentzen & Barlow, 1995; Hauger et al., 1996) then confirmed that removal of the single reliable cue to the presence of an intersecting street, that is, the down curb, as shown in Figure 16–5, did result in the inability of even skilled, frequent blind travelers to detect some streets.

Barlow and Bentzen (1994) found that on 35% of approaches to unfamiliar streets, blind travelers using a long cane failed to detect the presence of an intersecting street before stepping into it. On 59% of trials on which the street was not detected before stepping into it, there was traffic on that street. Hauger et al. (1996) found failure to detect streets on a somewhat smaller percentage of trials.

Hauger et al. (1996) obtained subjective data from 70 research participants who were blind or who had low vision that indicated that detectable warnings were judged to be helpful. In the same project, raters viewing videotapes of the 70 participants as they crossed intersections with and without detectable warnings on curb ramps found that a higher proportion of unsuccessful crossings occurred where there were no detectable warnings than where there were detectable warnings. They also found that the visual contrast of detectable warn-

FIGURE 16–5. Where there is no difference in slope or elevation between the sidewalk and street, it is particularly difficult for pedestrians who are blind to determine when they have reached an intersecting street. Photo shows a blended curb in Portland, Oregon.

ings helped participants with low vision establish and maintain a heading toward the opposite corner. Participants using dog guides may also have been aided by the visual contrast that the dog guides appeared to head for.

Hughes (1995) conducted research in which 15 participants who were totally blind or who had low vision traveled up and down laboratory ramps having eight different tactile surfaces, of which five were truncated domes. Of the 10 participants who then responded to structured interviews including questions about their perception of the tactile surfaces, 9 said use of tactile surfaces on curb ramps would increase their safety, and 6 said that use of the tactile surfaces would make them more likely to travel by foot.

During the 7 years following the installation of detectable warnings on all platform edges in the Bay Area Rapid Transit (BART) system, platform edge accidents decreased for all riders, but especially for riders having visual impairments (McGean, 1991). In San Francisco, riders in stations having different platforms serving both BART and the San Francisco Municipal Railway (MUNI) were observed to stand at different distances from the platform edge. On BART platforms, which had 24 in deep detectable warnings along the edges, passengers tended to wait behind the warning, that is, at least 2 ft from the edge. On MUNI platforms, which did not have detectable warnings, passengers waited closer to the edge (McGean, 1991).

Objective and subjective research confirmed that truncated dome detectable warnings at transit platform edges do not adversely affect people having a variety of mobility impairments. None of the 24 participants in research by Peck and Bentzen (1987) in BART had any difficulty maneuvering across or along truncated domes or turning on truncated domes. Participants in this research reported that truncated domes would have minimal effects on their travel in BART. A few people who used canes or crutches said they felt their aids would be less likely to slip as they exited trains onto the truncated dome surface than onto smoother surfaces.

However, public comments on ADAAG and concerns expressed by people with mobility impairments prompted additional objective and subjective research to determine the effects of detectable warnings installed on slopes such as curb ramps for people with mobility impairments. Bentzen, Nolin, Easton, Desmaris and Mitchell (1994b, 1994c) videotaped 40 participants having mobility impairments that made them most likely to have difficulty on bumpy, sloping surfaces, traveling up and down, stopping, starting, and turning on nine ramps with truncated domes (4′ × 6′ and slope 1:12) and one ramp surfaced with brushed concrete. Video raters observed minimal evidence of increased effort, slipping, loss of stability, or wheel or tip entrapment on this challenging task. Participants in this research reported minimal effects of truncated domes relative to the brushed concrete surface. Figure 16–6 shows an example of a curb ramp with truncated domes along the full length of the ramp.

Hauger et al. (1996), as previously mentioned, also found minimal adverse effect of truncated domes on people with mobility impairments. In addition, they observed pedestrians at three commercial sites where shopping carts were used and where detectable warnings were installed to separate the pedestrian and vehicular ways. In 12 hours of observation, more than 1,500 pedestrians crossed the detectable warnings. No significant incidents or problems were observed for the general public, which included persons with mobility impairments, shopping carts, shopping carts with children, large gurneys, and baby carriages.

Other related questions that had been raised in public comment were investigated. Although ADAAG requires that detectable warning surfaces used indoors differ in sound on cane contact, there had been no documentation of this empirically. Bentzen and Myers (1997) tested four truncated dome products installed on an outdoor light-rail platform in Sacramento for differences in sound on cane contact. Surfaces differed significantly from one another in both objective and subjective measures of differences in sound on cane contact between the adjoining platform of pavers and the detectable warnings. Difference in sound between the warning surface and the adjoining platform surface appeared to be related to both the detectable warning material and the way in which it was installed. The detectable warning material installed with

FIGURE 16–6.   Brick detectable warning on full surface of curb ramp in Cleveland. Curb ramps having a detectable warning surface on the full length and width of a curb ramp were tested by Hauger, Rigby, Safewright, and McAuley (1996) and found to have minimal impact on people using wheelchairs and other mobility aids.

a slight gap between the warning and the substrate was most detectable on both objective and subjective measures.

Other questions were asked about contrast specifications or standardized color. ADAAG (1991) required that detectable warnings contrast visually with adjoining surfaces, either dark on light, or light on dark. A 70% contrast in light reflectance between a detectable warning and an adjoining surface was recommended in the appendix. This requirement was based on research on reading signs. Research was needed on the effects of color and contrast on detection of detectable warnings. Research undertaken by Bentzen, Nolin, and Easton (1994a) showed that the color safety yellow (ISO 2864) is so salient— even to persons having very low vision—that it is highly visible even when used in association with surfaces having light reflectance values differing by as little as 40% (new, gray-white concrete). A safety yellow detectable warning surface having a 40% reflectance difference from new concrete was subjectively judged more detectable than a darker warning surface that contrasted with new concrete by 86%. Hughes (1995) found specifically that yellow or yellow-orange warning surfaces were preferred over black warning surfaces. Nonetheless ADAAG and ANSI A117 continue to require detectable warnings to contrast only in light on dark or dark on light, except in California, where safety yellow is required.

Following publication of ADAAG in 1991, numerous manufacturers entered the market. The products differed slightly in the truncated dome dimensions and spacing as well as materials. Truncated dome products soon included resilient sheet material, dimensional pavers, tiles, polymer composites, bricks, precast concrete, stamped concrete, and applied surfaces. There were questions about detectability of the many different surfaces. The FTA sponsored laboratory research (Bentzen et al., 1994a) to evaluate the detectability of truncated dome surfaces that differed in material, dome dimensions, and dome spacing. Thirteen surfaces representing the extremes as well as the midpoints of dome dimensions and dome spacing were tested by 24 blind participants for underfoot detectability in association with four transit platform surfaces varying in roughness and resiliency. Each detectable warning surface was paired with brushed concrete, coarse exposed aggregate concrete, Pirelli tile, and wooden decking. Detection rate was greater than 95% for all but one warning surface (a prototype described as 1/4 in. cylinders that was not offered for sale).

CURRENT REGULATORY STATUS REGARDING DETECTABLE WARNINGS

The ADAAG requirement for detectable warnings on curb ramps was suspended in 1994; the suspension expired on July 26, 2001. Following the expiration of the suspension, the Federal Highway Administration advised State Departments of Transportation that detectable warnings were now required in new construction and alterations (Horne, 2002). The recommended depth of detectable warnings was 24 in. Placement of detectable warnings of that depth is shown in Figure 16–7.

The *Draft Guidelines for Accessible Public Rights-of-Way*, released in 2002 by the Access Board and revised November 23, 2005, as preliminary steps in rule-making to implement the ADA on public rights-of-way, reflected most results of research on detectable warnings up to that date. Research by Bentzen et al. (1994b) had demonstrated that truncated dome surfaces comprised of slightly larger domes, spaced a little wider apart, were nonetheless highly detectable to blind travelers. Therefore, a range of truncated dome dimensions and spacings was permitted to fulfill the standard for detectability, and a depth of only 24 in. was required to provide greater accessibility for persons having mobility impairments. The *Revised Draft Guidelines for Accessible Public Rights-of-Way*, shown in Table 16–1, contain the specifications for truncated dome detectable warnings and requirements for their installation.

By 2003, the ANSI A117 Committee had reviewed the research conducted to answer the questions proposed by the Access Board and determined that the research justified the inclusion in ANSI A117, 2003 of the dimen-

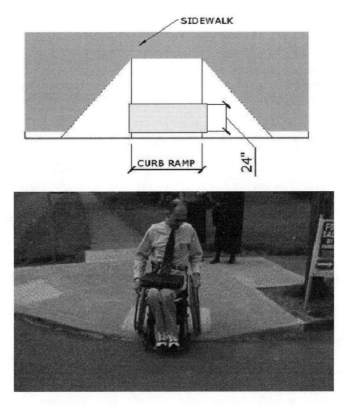

FIGURE 16–7.   Top: Diagram of placement of detectable warning at prototypical curb ramp. Bottom: Twenty-four inch deep detectable warnings 24 in. deep at a corner in Portland, Oregon.

sional specifications for detectable warnings required by the *Draft Guidelines for Accessible Public Rights-of-Way* (and the *Revised Draft Guidelines for Accessible Public Rights-of-Way*), and by New ADAAG. On January 23, 2006, the FHWA issued the following memorandum making the provisions for detectable warnings as provided in the *Revised Draft Guidelines for Accessible Public Rights-of-Way* recommended practice.

> The draft guidelines are not standards until adopted by the U.S. DOJ and the U.S. DOT. The present standards to be followed are the ADA Accessibility Guidelines (ADAAG) standards. However, the draft guidelines are the currently recommended best practices and can be considered the state of the practice that could be followed for areas not fully addressed by the present ADAAG standards. Furthermore, the draft guidelines are consistent with the ADA's requirement that all new facilities (and altered facilities to the maximum extent feasible) be designed and constructed to be accessible to and useable by people with disabilities.

R304 Detectable Warning Surfaces

R304.1 General. Detectable warnings shall consist of a surface of truncated domes aligned in a square or radial grid pattern and shall comply with R304.

R304.1.1 Dome Size. Truncated domes in a detectable warning surface shall have a base diameter of 23 mm (0.9 in) minimum to 36 mm (1.4 in) maximum, a top diameter of 50 percent of the base diameter minimum to 65 percent of the base diameter maximum, and a height of 5 mm (0.2 in).

> *Advisory R304.1.1 Dome Size. Where domes are arrayed radially, they may differ in diameter within the ranges specified.*

R304.1.2 Dome Spacing. Truncated domes in a detectable warning surface shall have a center-to-center spacing of 41 mm (1.6 in) minimum and 61 mm (2.4 in) maximum, and a base-to-base spacing of 17 mm (0.65 in) minimum, measured between the most adjacent domes.

> *Advisory R304.1.2 Dome Spacing. Where domes are arrayed radially, they may differ in center-to-center spacing within the range specified.*

R304.2 Location and Alignment

R304.2.1 Perpendicular Curb Ramps. Where both ends of the bottom grade break complying with R303.3.4 are 1.5 m (5.0 ft) or less from the back of curb, the detectable warning shall be located on the ramp surface at the bottom grade break. Where either end of the bottom grade break is more than 1.5 m (5.0 ft) from the back of curb, the detectable warning shall be located on the lower landing.

> *Advisory R304.2.1 Perpendicular Curb Ramps. Detectable warnings are intended to provide a tactile equivalent underfoot of the visible curbline; those placed too far from the street edge because of a large curb radius may compromise effective crossing analysis.*

R304.2.2 Landings and Blended Transitions. The detectable warning shall be located on the landing or blended transition at the back of curb.

R304.2.3 Alignment. The rows of truncated domes in a detectable warning surface shall be aligned to be perpendicular or radial to the grade break between the ramp, landing, or blended transition and the street.

> *Advisory R304.2.3 Alignment. Where a ramp, landing, or blended transition provides access to the street continuously around a corner, the vertical rows of truncated domes in a detectable warning surface should be aligned to be perpendicular or radial to the grade break between the ramp and the street for a 1.2 meter-wide (4.0 ft) width for each crosswalk served.*

R304.2.3 Rail Crossings. The detectable warning surface shall be located so that the edge nearest the rail crossing is 1.8 m (6 ft) minimum and 4.6 m (15 ft) maximum from the centerline of the nearest rail. The rows of truncated domes in a detectable warning surface shall be aligned to be parallel with the direction of wheelchair travel.

When New ADAAG was adopted by the DOT on October 30, 2006, the DOT reiterated their requirement for detectable warnings on curb ramps, even though this is not explicit in the New ADAAG (Transportation for Individuals with Disabilities: Adoption of New Accessibility Standards, 2006).

CONCLUSION

In access policy research both the nature of the research questions and the funding of research are driven by standards processes such as those to implement the ADA. It is not uncommon for research to be undertaken to solve a problem or to support writing of technical specifications followed by research that demonstrates that the problem exits.

Lawmakers are subject to pressure by advocates who convince them that there is a problem. Standards-setting bodies attempt to represent all stakeholders. They are therefore more likely than legislators to require objective demonstration of a problem and of the effectiveness of design solutions before making a requirement or writing technical specifications.

Policy research, like basic science, occurs over time and usually involves multiple researchers working on the same problem, as can be seen in the case study on detectable warnings presented here. Unlike basic science, however, research topics are motivated primarily by the need to make decisions regarding standards and requirements.

REFERENCES

Aiello, J., & Steinfeld, E. (1980). *Accessible buildings for people with severe visual impairment.* Washington, DC: U.S. Department of Housing Urban Development, Office of Policy Research, Report No. HUD-PDR-404.

American National Standard specifications for making buildings and facilities accessible to and usable by physically handicapped people, ANSI A117.1-1980. New York, NY: American National Standards Institute.

Americans with Disabilities Act accessibility guidelines [ADAAG] (July 26, 1991). Washington, DC: U.S. Architectural and Transportation Barriers Compliance Board. 36 CFR Part 1191.

Americans with Disabilities Act and Architectural Barriers Act Accessibility Guidelines [New ADAAG] (July 23, 2004). Washington, DC: U.S. Architectural and Transportation Barriers Compliance Board.

Barlow, J., & Bentzen, B. L. (1994). *Cues blind travelers use to detect streets.* Final report. Cambridge, MA: U.S. Department of Transportation, Federal Transit Administration, Volpe National Transportation Systems Center.

Bentzen, B. L. (1996). Transit vehicle signage for persons who are blind or visually impaired. *Journal of Visual Impairment Blindness, 90,* 352–56.

Bentzen, B. L., & Barlow, J. M. (1995). Impact of curb ramps on safety of persons who are blind. *Journal of Visual Impairment and Blindness, 89,* 319–28.

Bentzen, B. L., Barlow, J. M., & Tabor, L. (2000). *Detectable warnings: Synthesis of U.S. and international practice*, Washington, DC: U.S. Access Board.

Bentzen, B. L., & Easton, R. D. (1996). *Specifications for transit vehicle next stop messages. Final Report to Sunrise Systems*. Pembroke, MA: Sunrise Systems.

Bentzen, B. L., Jackson, R. M., & Peck, A. F. (1981). *Techniques for improving communication with visually impaired users of rail rapid transit systems*. Washington, DC: U.S. Department of Transportation, Urban Mass Transportation Administration. Report No. UMTA-MA-0036-81-3.

Bentzen, B. L., & Myers, L. A. (1997). Human factors research, appendix C in *Detectable warnings evaluation services*. Menlo Park, CA: Crain & Associates.

Bentzen, B. L., Nolin, T. L., & Easton, R. D. (1994a). *Detectable warning surfaces: Color, contrast and reflectance*. Cambridge, MA: U.S. Department of Transportation, Federal Transit Administration, Volpe National Transportation Systems Center. Report No. VNTSC-DTRS-57-93-P-80546.

Bentzen, B. L., Nolin, T. L., Easton, R. D., Desmarais, L., & Mitchell, P. A. (1994b). *Detectable warning surfaces: Detectability by individuals with visual impairments, and safety and negotiability for individuals with physical impairments*. Final report VNTSC-DTRS57-92-P-81354 and VNTSC-DTRS57-91-C-0006. Cambridge, MA: U.S. Department of Transportation, Federal Transit Administration, Volpe National Transportation Systems Center, and Project ACTION, National Easter Seal Society.

Bentzen, B. L., Nolin, T. L., Easton, R. D., Desmarais, L., & Mitchell, P. A. (1994c). *Detectable warnings: Safety & negotiability on slopes for persons who are physically impaired*. Washington, DC: Federal Transit Administration and Project ACTION of the National Easter Seal Society.

Georgia Institute of Technology. (1985). *Signage for low vision blind persons: A multidisciplinary assessment of the state of the art*. Final report. Architectural Transportation Barriers Compliance Board, Contract No. 300-83-0280.

Hauger, J., Rigby, J., Safewright, M., & McAuley, W. (1996). Detectable warning surfaces at curb ramps. *Journal of Visual Impairments and Blindness, 90*, 512–25.

Horne, D. A. (2002). Memorandum from Dwight A. Horne, Office of Program Administration, Federal Highway Administration, May 6.

Hughes, R. G. (1995). *A Florida DOT field evaluation of tactile warnings in curb ramps: Mobility considerations for the blind and visually impaired*. Chapel Hill, NC: The University of North Carolina at Chapel Hill, Highway Safety Research Center.

Hulscher, F. (1976). Traffic signal facilities for blind pedestrians. *Australian Road Research Board Proceedings, 8*, 13–26.

McCulley, R., & Bentzen, B. L. (1987). *Train platform accidents reported by visually impaired travelers: Results of a survey by the Massachusetts Commission for the Blind*. Unpublished report, Massachusetts Commission for the Blind, Boston.

McGean, T. K. (1991). *Innovative solutions for disabled transit accessibility*. Washington, DC: U.S. Department of Transportation, Urban Mass Transportation Administration. Report No. UMTA-OH-06-0056-91-8.

Peck, A. F., & Bentzen, B. L. (1987). *Tactile warnings to promote safety in the vicinity of transit platform edges*. US Department of Transportation, Urban Mass Transportation Administration, Report No. UMTA-MA-06-0120-87-1.

Peter Muller-Munk Associates. (1986). *Information systems for low vision persons*. Washington, DC: U.S. Architectural Transportation Barriers Compliance Board. ED Contract No. 300-85-0186.

Templer, J. A., & Wineman, J. D. (1980). *The feasibility of accommodating elderly and handicapped on over- and undercrossing structures.* Washington, DC: U.S. Department of Transportation, Federal Highway Administration, U.S. Government Printing Office. FHWA-RD-79-146.

Templer, J. A., Wineman, J. D., & Zimring, C. M. (1982). *Design Guidelines to make crossing structure accessible to the physically handicapped.* Washington, DC: U.S. Department of Transportation, Federal Highway Administration. Final Report #DTF-H61-80-C-00131.

Transportation for Individuals with Disabilities: Adoption of New Accessibility Standards, Final Rule, 71 Fed. Reg. October 30, 2006, 63263–63267.

Wilson, D. G. (1980). *The effect of installing an audible signal for pedestrians at a light controlled junction.* Transport Road Research Laboratory, Crowthorne, Berkshire, United Kingdom.

17

Crossing Streets Without Vision: Access to Information, Strategies for Traveling, and the Impact of Technology, Training, and Environmental Design

Richard Long

Walking without vision, or with impaired vision, while sometimes challenging, can be accomplished efficiently and safely by most people most of the time. This chapter is about the perceptual information and the associated strategies that people who are blind and visually impaired use to move about safely and efficiently in outdoor environments. It focuses on changes in recent years in the "information stream" that is available in urban street environments and the relevance of those changes for the task of crossing streets without vision or with impaired vision. The strategies that may be useful in reducing the impact of these changes when they result in limitations to travel efficiency and safety are also discussed.

As a means of introducing the concepts of access to nonvisual information and the use of strategies to support safe and efficient travel, I open the chapter with a discussion of the tasks of locating a landmark and relocating the travel path when veering from it. I then focus on the information and strategies used when completing key components of street crossings. In this discussion, round-abouts and conventional signalized intersections are compared as a means of illustrating how differences in the design and operation of intersections lead to differences in the information and strategies used by blind individuals. I close with some thoughts about training, research, technology development, and public policy as they relate to the safety and efficiency of travel by individuals with blindness and low vision, particularly in urban street settings.

Data collected from the National Health Interview Survey on Disability (1994–95) indicated that approximately 1.3 million persons reported legal blindness and an estimated 20% of legally blind individuals reported having light perception or less, representing an estimated 260,000 individuals (American Foundation for the Blind, 2006). One hundred thirty thousand individuals reported using a white cane as a mobility aid on the 1994 National Health Interview Survey on Disability (Russell, Hendershot, LeClere, Howie, & Adler, 1997). The estimated number of dog guide users among the blind population in the United States is 8,000 (Whitstock, Franck, & Haneline, 1997).

Many individuals who are blind or have low vision travel safely and independently in their communities. They learn travel-related skills, both from experience and from systematic instruction in orientation and mobility (O&M). Children with blindness and low vision often receive O&M instruction throughout their school years, and adults receive services from O&M specialists employed by state, federal, or private rehabilitation facilities. During O&M instruction, blind and low vision travelers learn to make use of auditory, vibrotactile, and (to a lesser degree) olfactory information when making travel-related decisions. Instruction also focuses on teaching individuals to perceive and evaluate various types of perceptual information relevant for travel. Travelers learn a set of strategies for accomplishing travel-related tasks, and they learn how to use the perceptual information at hand to guide decisions about the selection of strategies. The effective use of strategies, in turn, presumably is associated with safer and more efficient travel. The focus of this chapter is on the information and strategies used by travelers who are blind and visually impaired who use the long cane as their primary mobility device. The information and strategies used by dog guide users is not discussed here, primarily because the information stream and the O&M strategies of long cane users and dog guide users differ significantly.

The long cane is a probe that extends by several feet the user's preview of the environment just ahead. Effective use of the long cane (typically moved side to side while walking) usually allows individuals to determine whether the path ahead is clear of obstacles and to determine the approximate size, shape, and characteristics (e.g., roughness) of many of the obstacles and other features (e.g., changes in walking surface) they encounter while walking. The long cane also aids users in detecting changes in elevation just ahead, such as slopes, stairs, or curbs. When used properly, the long cane affords detection of objects in the area immediately in front of the user's body, with only modest reduction of detection afforded by vision during travel. However, one important exception is that the long cane does not permit users the ability to detect most objects that protrude into or overhang the travel path. LaGrow and Weessies (1994) and Jacobson (1993) describe the diverse strategies that blind and low vision travelers use to travel safely and efficiently, including the various strategies for using the long cane to gather information for safe and efficient orientation and mobility.

Consider one problem an individual walking without vision might need to solve and the information and strategies used to solve it. A traveler walking a familiar route needs to locate an object just to the side of the sidewalk in a residential area because this object serves as a landmark that allows her to locate the sidewalk leading to her house. She likely would use the strategies of widening the movement of the cane on the side of her body where the landmark is located (to ensure that the cane contacts the object) and shortening her stride when she perceives (via kinesthetic cues about the distance she has walked) that she has traveled far enough along the block and is approaching the landmark. She implements these strategies to ensure that she contacts the object with the long cane rather than walking past it. The changes in vibratory and acoustic information that occur when the cane strikes the object (as contrasted with striking the sidewalk or objects) are associated with the particular landmark she is looking for. She typically does not need to explore the object with her hands to identify it. If she is walking in an unfamiliar place, she may mentally note the characteristics of various objects and changes in surface texture, particularly their location relative to the location of choice points (e.g., turns) along the route. She may elect to identify objects by exploring them with her hands after contacting and exploring them with the long cane, as a way of learning more about the particular features in an unfamiliar place. In short, she gathers, interprets, and remembers the perceptual and spatial information that will presumably allow her to find her way more efficiently when she travels in the area again, and she pays limited attention to the information that is not relevant for wayfinding and mobility.

One strategy she may use in both familiar and unfamiliar areas is to "follow along" the grassline at the sidewalk edge with the long cane, a strategy called *shorelining*. Using this strategy helps her locate intersecting sidewalks to her side, and thus this strategy is often used when anticipating a turn onto an adjacent sidewalk just ahead (Jansson, 1990). Auditory information also may be useful for locating objects at the side of the path (provided they are large enough and close enough) and for the task of following along. For example, travelers may hear the sound that is reflected from an object to the side of the travel path. They can often detect and follow a building line using auditory cues, just as in indoor environments they can use their hearing to locate open doorways and intersecting hallways.

Suppose travelers inadvertently veer from the travel path into a driveway in an unfamiliar residential area. Here, as with the task of locating a landmark, information relevant to recovering the travel path and line of travel must be obtained, interpreted, and acted on via the application of problem solving strategies that have proven to be effective in the past. As in the landmark location task above, travelers use auditory or tactile information, combined with their knowledge of the typical spatial arrangement of features (e.g., street, sidewalk, grassline, driveway) in environments like the one being negotiated to determine that they have veered and to determine the direction of veer. They then implement a set of strategies that usually permit them to relocate the path. Travelers who veer into a driveway will often detect (hear and feel) that a veer has occurred when their cane contacts the grassline in front of them instead of the hard surface of the sidewalk. The fact that the sounds of vehicles are farther away than before is a clue that they have veered away from the street they were walking along rather than toward it. They then probe with the long cane to the left and right to locate the sidewalk (instead of grass or other landscape features). If they encounter grass on both sides, they know that this usually means that they have veered away from the street they were walking along, rather than toward it, and thus they conclude they must move toward the street to relocate the sidewalk.

Vision is not essential for accomplishing tasks like locating a landmark beside a path and recovering from veer, and these tasks often can be accomplished readily using nonvisual information to guide decision making. Tactual, auditory, and kinesthetic information often is as effective, or nearly so, as visual information in accomplishing many travel-related tasks. This is particularly true when the information needed for task performance is within reach of the long cane. When information must be obtained from environmental features that are beyond the reach of the cane, it is primarily the sounds these features produce, or the sounds they reflect, that provide information for travelers who are blind. When distal features do not make or reflect sounds, when travelers cannot hear the direct or reflected sounds they make, or when they cannot extract information for decision making from what they hear, they may not be able to travel as safely or as efficiently as an individual with typical vision. The sounds of traffic movement and the reflected sound from a building line are two examples of distal sound cues that may or may not be available to a traveler who is blind. Also, actions based on the perception of distal sound sources may not be as precise as actions based on visual cues because vision has much greater resolution than other perceptual systems. However, individuals using hearing alone often can determine the position of distal objects or features well enough to locate them with the long cane and explore them with their hands. This permits them to gather more information, if desired, about their size and shape and their spatial relationship to other environmental features they can hear.

In most situations and most of the time, the proximal and distal perceptual information that is available to travelers with blindness and low vision, coupled with effective use of strategies, results in safe and efficient travel. As travelers gain experience in using strategies in various environments and in familiar and unfamiliar environments, they become accustomed to perceiving, making decisions based on those perceptions, evaluating the effectiveness of the decisions, and initiating the perception-action-perception cycle again. When information is not available or not adequate for moving efficiently and safely along a route, travelers must find ways to get enough information to move about safely and efficiently. Sometimes they solicit assistance from others to obtain the information necessary for travel, such as when they ask (usually by pointing and asking a sighted person to "correct" their pointing direction) for the direction they must walk in order to locate a doorway to a business while on the sidewalk. If the strategies used to solve a particular travel-related problem are not effective as determined by the information stream they produce, then new strategies must be tried and evaluated.

The urban street environment is an ideal, if challenging, laboratory for studying the information needs and mobility-related strategies used by pedestrians who are blind. Intersections in this environment have undergone significant changes in recent years, driven primarily by the increasing number of vehicles on U.S. roadways and the need to move them as efficiently as possible. For example, traffic engineers now routinely use vehicle-actuated traffic signal timing to move vehicles more efficiently through intersections. Actuated intersections often are equipped with pedestrian pushbuttons, and pedestrians must push the button to receive a walk signal and have adequate time to cross the street. (Prior to the advent of actuated signalization, most pedestrian and vehicle signals were fixed-timed, regulated by a clock, and had vehicle signal phases in each direction of travel that were long enough to permit pedestrians to cross without the need to push a pedestrian pushbutton). Because pushing the pedestrian pushbutton is often important for making low-risk crossings, and because its presence and its location relative to the desired crossing point is important, blind individuals, like sighted individuals, should have access to pedestrian pushbuttons themselves and to the information they provide. As awareness of this need for equal access to information grows, accessible pedestrian signals will become more common at traditional intersections in the United States. Barlow, Bentzen, and Bond (2005) have demonstrated that without access to pedestrian signal status, blind individuals are at increased risk when crossing streets at actuated intersections.

Other changes to the streetscape also have an effect on individuals traveling nonvisually. Many intersections have become wider and their signal phases have become more complex, presumably making them more difficult for blind pedestrians to "decipher" auditorially. Also, engineers are are increasingly using blended curbs, in which the entire curbline at an intersection is level with the roadway, as well as splitter and median islands. These features can pose challenges for street detection for the pedestrian who relies on nonvisual cues.

Another example of the changing urban streetscape that creates challenges for travelers who are blind is the advent of roundabout intersections. Figure 17–1 illustrates some of the features of modern roundabouts. Roundabouts are relatively new in the United States, but they are ubiquitous in Europe and in Australia. They are circular intersections with unique design and traffic control features, including yield control for entering traffic and approaches that are designed to limit vehicle speed on the approaches and in the circulatory roadway. Roundabouts facilitate the efficient, safe movement of vehicle traffic without the need for traffic signals and the queuing that signals create, thus there is great enthusiasm on the part of engineers and designers for installing these intersections. However, roundabouts pose some unique challenges for the traveler who is blind.

Consider the information demands and the strategies used when crossing streets, particularly the differences in crossing at traditional signalized intersections and at roundabout intersections. The four components of the street-crossing task are to (a) determine the characteristics of the intersection, (b) locate the optimal place to begin the crossing, (c) face directly toward the desired end point of the crossing, (c) cross at a relatively low-risk time, and (d) maintain one's bearing toward the desired point when crossing—in other words, reduce or avoid veering.

Consider the task of determining, nonvisually, the characteristics of the intersection one is approaching. At a prototypical signalized intersection, the traffic lanes are usually perpendicular or parallel to the sidewalks, and thus the sounds of vehicles moving perpendicular to one's line of travel is an im-

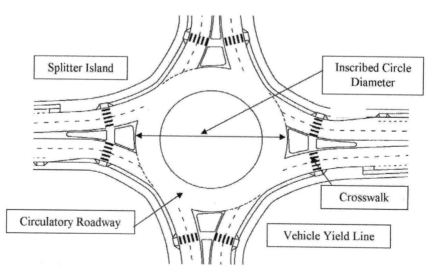

FIGURE 17–1.   Schematic of a typical modern roundabout.

portant auditory cue that an intersection is just ahead. Individuals who are blind listen to traffic sounds in various directions, usually through several signal cycles if the intersection is unfamiliar, to determine the characteristics of "traditional" intersections. In contrast, traffic moving through a roundabout produces a different pattern of sound. Because vehicles approaching a roundabout on the street parallel to a pedestrian's approach are deflected away from the center of the intersection by the central island, and because they do not stop at the circulatory roadway unless there is a vehicle in the roadway, it may appear to a traveler who is blind that there is a rightward curve in the road rather than an intersection. As a result, a traveler who is blind may walk past a roundabout intersection and turn 90° to his or her initial line of travel without being aware that he or she is now walking on another street. Because roundabouts are relatively new and unfamiliar to many blind individuals, and because they are becoming more common, it is important that strategies are developed to increase the likelihood that pedestrians who are blind can recognize that they are arriving at a roundabout. One possibility is to provide travelers with a means of previewing routes in advance, perhaps by "virtual travel" via a GPS-based navigation device or on the Web, or by using acoustic virtual reality technology. There also may be benefits to developing technologies that can communicate important features of intersections in "real time" via cell phones as they arrive at an intersection. One challenge in regard to conveying information about intersection geometry and operational characteristics to travelers is the need to develop effective strategies for conveying both spatial and nonspatial information quickly, effectively, and in ways that allow users to tailor the information flow to their own preferences for both content and delivery format. I am part of a research team, funded by the National Institute on Disability and Rehabilitation Research, that is working on development of verbal descriptions of intersections and on strategies for effectively delivering spatial and nonspatial information to pedestrians who are blind.

Another possibility is to develop training protocols that can be implemented in actual travel environments, and that permit travelers who are blind to learn the unique acoustic "signatures" of roundabout intersections and differentiate them from traditional rectilinear intersections. With experience and training, it is likely that many individuals will be able to distinguish roundabouts from other types of intersections, just as they currently differentiate other types of intersections (e.g., stop controlled and signalized intersections). Research is needed to determine the type and degree of experience and/or training that pedestrians who are blind need in order to distinguish the perceptual (acoustic) characteristics of various types of intersections, including roundabouts. For example, can blind pedestrians differentiate the sometimes subtle differences in auditory motion paths of vehicles at roundabouts and traditional intersections given competing sound sources, and can they accurately associate these differences with the various types of intersections they encounter? The experience of travelers and their O&M instructors at distinguishing various features of traditional intersections leads to the conclusion that many travelers will, with training and experience, be able to make these discriminations reliably.

In regard to information for locating the desired place to stand while waiting to cross the street, blind (or sighted) pedestrians' typical path of travel along a sidewalk in a residential or business environment will usually lead to the appropriate place to stand while waiting to cross the street at a typical signalized intersection. Also, blind pedestrians often use the sounds of traffic crossing in front of them to determine that they are nearing an intersection. The end of a building line offers yet another auditory "clue" that a cross street may be just ahead (although this is an ambiguous cue in the absence of prior knowledge that the end of the building line marks the end of the block and not a driveway or alleyway). The downward slope of a curb ramp may indicate that a cross street is just ahead, and, once the ramp is detected, the place to stand while waiting to cross can usually be located by probing with the long cane for the joint between the curb ramp, the gutter, and the street.

In the absence of information from traffic or curb ramps or building lines, blind individuals sometimes have difficulty detecting the presence of a cross street, and they inadvertently walk into the street. Bentzen and Barlow (1995) documented this in a study that showed that blind pedestrians stepped into the street on 39% of approaches, with the likelihood of doing so increasing as ramp slope decreased. At ramps that met the ADA standards of 1:12 slope or less (some ramps on the routes were steeper than allowed by ADAAG), individuals continued into the street on 48% of approaches.

The Americans with Disabilities Act Accessibility Guidelines (ADAAG), first published in 1991, mandate the installation of detectable warnings at new or renovated intersections. Detectable warnings, as specified in ADAAG, are a pattern of small truncated domes, which can be manufactured in various materials including resin-based material, bricks, plastics, thermoplastic, and cast iron. The truncated dome detectable warnings are installed on curb ramps at the edge of the street, covering the entire width of the ramp (or blended curb) with a depth of 24 inches. The material adds tactual information to the intersection environment that presumably reduces the likelihood that individuals who are blind walk into the cross street at an intersection without knowing they have done so. The development of standards for the design and installation of the truncated dome detectable warning material was developed by research that documented the characteristics of underfoot surfaces that were likely to be detectable with the long cane and the foot.

Now consider the information that specifies the "wait here to cross" point at a roundabout intersection. As at a rectilinear intersection, the end of a building line suggests that an intersecting street may be just ahead (although breaks in building lines can occur for other reasons, and thus other sources of information are needed to confirm this). Traffic moving across a traveler's direction of movement and in front of him also can be a cue, although, as noted earlier, vehicles are moving on curved paths rather than straight ones and thus the auditory information may be harder to interpret. In regard to the "line of travel" cue, unlike a signalized intersection where the location for crossing the street ahead is more or less in front of a pedestrian as he or she approaches the intersection, at a roundabout the crosswalk for the street perpendicular to the traveler's approach is to the traveler's side, rather than in front. This is because the crosswalks are usually set back from the intersection further at a roundabout than they are at a signalized intersection. As a result, travelers who are blind, if intending to continue straight along a road and through an intersection, must follow the sidewalk away from the roundabout for a few feet and then probe on the street side with the long cane to locate the crosswalk. This task presumably is easier if landscaping or some other environmental feature is available as an information source (e.g., a following along or trailing surface).

Another "where to cross" issue is based on the fact that roundabouts have splitter islands in the middle of the roadway. These splitter islands divide inbound and outbound traffic lanes. Splitters are often cut through and are at roadway level to facilitate travelers who use wheelchairs. One challenge for individuals who are blind is to detect the boundaries of the splitter island (i.e., the leading and trailing edge and the junction between the island and the roadway). Detectable warnings are required on splitter islands so that individuals who are blind have information they need to know the location of the splitter island.

At traditional signalized intersections, the sounds of vehicles on the parallel and perpendicular streets not only aid in locating the streets but they are also an important source of information for establishing alignment toward the opposite curb (Guth, Hill, & Rieser, 1989) and for crossing more or less directly toward the desired point on the opposite curb (Guth & Rieser, 1997). For example, individuals often use the strategy of listening to vehicles as they recede into the distance ahead of them and then turning slightly away from the point at which they last hear the vehicle. Guth et al. (1989) documented that the accuracy of alignment is approximately the same regardless of whether the traveler is listening and aligning to traffic on a parallel or perpendicular street. Precision of alignment to traffic sounds under optimal listening conditions ranged from 5 to 15°. No research has been conducted regarding alignment or crossing direction at roundabout intersections.

Presumably, alignment and crossing via a relatively straight path at a roundabout may be more difficult than these tasks at traditional intersections because, as mentioned earlier, vehicles at roundabouts are traveling on curvilinear rather than on more or less straight paths. What cues might provide alignment information at roundabout intersections? Given that the downward slope of curb ramps at roundabouts is almost always in line with the adjacent crosswalk, it could be that individuals who are blind can simply rely on the strategy of aligning with the slope of the ramp. This assumes, however, that it is possible to align to such a slope. To our knowledge, this topic has not been studied, although results of a pilot study that I conducted indicated that slope of ground may not be a useful alignment cue. Even assuming the usefulness of slope for alignment, it would not be useful at a rectilinear intersection where a single curb ramp at a corner (a common installation) is located at the apex of the curb, with one curb ramp serving both crosswalks. Following the ramp slope would result in a traveler walking into the center of the intersection. Consequently, pedestrians who are blind do not rely on direction of slope unless they know from experience that it is reliable at a particular ramp or in a particular neighborhood. Return curbs, which are vertical sided curb ramps bordered by landscaping also can potentially provide alignment information because their vertical sides are often parallel to the desired line of travel to the crosswalk and these sides can be probed with the long cane or the foot. The perceptual question here is whether an individual can take an accurate bearing with exploration of a return curb. Finally, some countries have made use of underfoot "bar tile" surfaces that are detectable underfoot and with the long cane. These surfaces are installed on curb ramps, on sidewalks adjacent to curb ramps, or in the crosswalk. They are designed to aid in establishing initial alignment and to aid in maintaining a desired line of travel while walking in the street. Because of the potential challenges in alignment and walking direction that roundabouts (particularly multilane ones) likely will pose for travelers who are blind, features like these may be important considerations. The U.S. Access Board is currently supporting research about underfoot surfaces that are useful for alignment information for travelers who are blind.

Perhaps the most important aspect of the street crossing task is to begin to cross at an appropriate (i.e., low-risk) time. At a signalized intersection, individuals who are blind usually listen for the surge of traffic on the street beside them (the parallel street) and begin walking when they hear traffic moving straight through the intersection (and not turning because vehicles can turn right on red). The accessible pedestrian signals described earlier provide additional (and sometimes the only) audible information regarding when to consider initiating a crossing. Blind travelers must "check" auditorially for turning vehicles as they initiate the crossing, just as individuals with typical vision often check visually for vehicles turning from the parallel to the perpendicular street on green. Barlow, Bentzen, and Bond (2005) have shown that when intersections are unfamiliar and relatively complex, individuals who are blind often make errors in completing the various subtasks of the crossing tasks, including the key subtask of crossing at an appropriate time.

At a roundabout, individuals (regardless of visual status) can safely begin crossing when no approaching vehicle can reach the crosswalk before the crossing is completed, or when they have determined that vehicles are slowing or have stopped to allow them to step into the crosswalk. (There typically are no traffic controls at roundabout crosswalks). The auditory information used by blind individuals to make crossing decisions at roundabouts is very different from that at signalized intersections. Instead of walking with the sound of initial vehicle movement through the intersection on the parallel street, blind individuals must detect the absence of vehicles (a challenging task as vehicles become increasingly quiet) or they must detect the sound of a slowing or stopped (i.e., yielding) vehicle amidst the sounds of other vehicles (this presumes that at least some drivers actually yield; see Geruschat & Hassan, 2005). In short, individuals must attend to a very different "array" of perceptual information at a roundabout than at a traditional intersection, and they must use a different set of strategies to initiate a crossing at a relatively low-risk time.

For the past 5 years, I have been a part of a research team funded by the National Eye Institute to conduct research about blind pedestrians' access to complex intersections. One of the team's goals in our early work was to assess the ability of individuals who were blind to make appropriate crossing judgments at roundabout intersections. In later work, we began to identify solutions to access issues that were revealed in the early studies. These studies are pertinent here because they illustrate the way that access to information and actions based on limited information can affect safety and efficiency in street crossings.

In each of the roundabout studies conducted (in Baltimore, Maryland; Tampa, Florida; Nashville, Tennessee; and Raleigh, North Carolina) travelers who were blind received a brief orientation to each roundabout under study. In general, participants in these studies were inexperienced at crossing streets at roundabout intersections other than what could be gained in a brief familiarization period. They then were asked to stand at a crosswalk, listen to vehicle movement, and indicate when they could cross from the curb to the splitter island before the next approaching vehicle reached the crosswalk. The participants did not actually cross the street. Instead, they pushed a button that was linked to a computer to indicate they believed they could cross safely. The arrival of vehicles at the crosswalk after a participant pushed the button was also recorded. By subtracting the time needed to cross from the time of arrival of the closest vehicle after the participant pushed the crossing button, we determined whether the participant would actually have been able to complete the crossing before a vehicle reached the crosswalk.

Our first study was conducted at three roundabouts in the Baltimore area with six adults who were blind and six comparison participants who were sighted (Guth, Ashmead, Long, Wall, & Ponchillia, 2005). The participants made crossing judgments at both the entry and exit lanes. The auditory information used for making crossing decisions is different in these two travel directions. Making judgments about whether vehicles are exiting requires listening "toward" the roundabout, and thus in the direction of other vehicles in or near the circulatory roadway. On the other hand, making judgments about the location and speed of entering traffic may be easier because the focus of attention is away from the potentially confusing sounds of the circulatory roadway. Our principal finding was that the safety margins were significantly shorter for the blind participants than for the sighted participants at the two higher-volume multilane roundabouts we studied but not at the low-volume, single lane roundabout. Overall, the blind participants were about 2.5 times more likely than were the sighted participants to report that they would initiate a crossing when there was not adequate time to cross. The blind participants at all three roundabouts tended to detect the onset of a crossable gap about 3 s after the sighted participants did, a significant lag given the fact that gaps were often only marginally longer than the time needed to cross. This was due to the fact that blind participants tended to wait until the sound of receding traffic faded sufficiently to permit them to hear approaching vehicles before indicating they would cross. As we expected given the nature of the auditory information, exit-lane judgments were more difficult than were entry-lane judgments, probably due both to masking and to the difficulty of determining whether vehicles were exiting or continuing in the circulatory roadway.

The Baltimore study established clearly that two of the roundabouts posed challenges to access for the sample of blind participants, whereas one did not appear to do so, at least under our low traffic-volume experimental conditions. Our findings led us to conclude that some moderate- and high-volume roundabouts may pose an unacceptable level of risk for blind pedestrians, whereas some lower-volume roundabouts may not. We then conducted a second study with procedures similar to those used in Baltimore at a one lane roundabout in Tampa. Data were collected at both low and high traffic volumes (peak and non-peak travel times). As in the Baltimore study, the blind participants made more high-risk judgments than the sighted participants, and, as expected, they made high-risk judgments more often during periods of peak traffic volume (rush hours) than during periods of low-traffic volume.

The work in Baltimore and Tampa involved making judgments about crossing without actually crossing the street. This left open the possibility that participants were using different criteria than they would have had used if they actually crossed the street. To address this issue, the team conducted a third study at a relatively high-volume, two-lane roundabout in Nashville (Ashmead, Guth, Wall, Long, & Ponchillia, 2005). As at the two higher-volume roundabouts in Baltimore and the Tampa roundabout at periods with higher volume, the blind pedestrians had greater difficulty than did the sighted pedestrians when distinguishing gaps in approaching traffic that were long enough to cross from those that were not. A performance measure used for the first time in the Nashville study was the frequency of interventions by an orientation and mobility (O&M) instructor, who closely followed the participants as they crossed the street during the trials. An intervention was recorded any time the O&M instructor physically stopped the pedestrian from continuing to cross because of safety concerns. Although interventions occurred on only 6% of the trials, this rate projects to a 99% likelihood of at least one pedestrian-vehicle conflict at this intersection if a person who was blind crossed it daily for three months. (A conflict is a situation in which a crash is likely unless the driver or pedestrian takes immediate evasive action.) No interventions were recorded for the sighted comparison subjects.

This is a key finding of our work, in that it is perhaps the most compelling evidence of the challenges that roundabout intersections pose for individuals who are blind or have low vision. Many participants who were blind told us that they would not cross at the study site if they had any other option. As in our studies at other locations, drivers on the entry lanes but not on the exit lanes frequently yielded to pedestrians. The sighted comparison participants always took advantage of this yielding, but the blind participants rarely did so, particularly because of the difficulty in hearing idling vehicles over the sounds of moving vehicles, and in correctly detecting that drivers had yielded both lanes rather than the curb lane alone.

Our fourth study involved evaluating an intervention to improve access to a relatively high-volume, single-lane roundabout in Raleigh, North Carolina. This study was a follow-up to our formal (Geruschat & Hassan, 2005; Guth et al., 2005) and informal observations that at many roundabouts, few drivers yielded to pedestrians who were waiting to cross, even those who used mobility devices. In those previous studies, we also found that when a vehicle yielded, blind pedestrians often failed to detect it, which sometimes appeared to be due to ambient noise levels that made it impossible to hear the idling vehicle, sometimes because vehicles yielded so far back from the crosswalk that they could not be heard, sometimes because the vehicles themselves were quiet as they yielded, and sometimes because of a combination of these factors. In October 2004, our team built and evaluated a prototype system that used a series of in-roadway sensors to detect the presence of vehicles approaching a crosswalk and a set of decision rules to determine when a vehicle had yielded. When the system detected a vehicle that had yielded, this information was conveyed via speech messages that were presented by speakers at the crosswalk. The participants crossed with and without the system, and all trials were filmed. Although the prototype system requires more development and testing, it is clear that the information presented by the system is a useful adjunct to the "naturally" available acoustic information.

What are the implications of these findings about street crossing performance at roundabouts and traditional intersections? First, it is apparent that the auditory information that is available to travelers differs in significant ways. Travelers must be able to perceive these differences, understand their relevance for street crossing safety, and select strategies that are likely to result in relatively low-risk crossings. In regard to traditional intersections and roundabouts, it should be noted that at roundabouts, auditory information is sometimes unavailable, either because there are no vehicles at all or because the sound of approaching vehicles is masked, often by other vehicles. The participants in our roundabout studies often missed gaps in upstream traffic because they could not be certain that there were no vehicles approaching. This problem of "missed gaps" does not tend to occur at traditional intersections because of the onset of through traffic movement on the parallel street does not tend to be masked by other sounds. Finally, it should be noted that decision-making using auditory information requires more time than decision-making based on visual information. Sometimes gaps are missed because of the need to confirm that gaps long enough to cross have occurred. Our participants who were blind typically began crossing about 3 or 4 s after the beginning of a "crossable gap," whereas individuals using visual cues left the curb almost at the leading edge of the gap. The need to take time to listen and ensure that no vehicles are approaching, or that a vehicle has yielded, means that individuals who are blind miss gaps and presumably are somewhat delayed in traversing a route compared to individuals traveling with visual information.

Auditory information can be misinterpreted at both types of intersections. Individuals at traditional intersections can mistake vehicles turning with an advance green turn arrow for the through movement on the parallel street. Similarly, at a roundabout, individuals may fail to hear approaching vehicles, may misinterpret the direction of travel of vehicles they hear, or may determine that a vehicle is yielding when it is not. Also, it should be noted that the problem of missed gaps and misinterpretation of auditory information is likely to increase with the increase in electric and hybrid vehicles that make little sound other than tire noise at low speeds.

More research is needed regarding the limits of human auditory perception and typical perceptual abilities in street environments and in laboratory simulations of them. It also would be useful to investigate how varying types and levels of information are used by travelers with varying degrees of familiarity with intersection types, and how individuals differ in their knowledge of strategies for interpreting information. One example is the need for research about individuals with low vision, who rely on their vision for completing some aspects of the street crossing task and rely on other perceptual systems for other aspects. Vision is a relatively precise sense, and tactile and auditory sensory abilities have lower resolution than vision. Tactile information is typically always available (although it could be snow covered), but it may be missed by the traveler who walks to the side of it. Auditory information is intermittent and omnidirectional, but it can be missed due to masking.

How do these and other characteristics of information influence the decisions that are made about training, intersection design, and the use of technology to supplement naturally occurring information? What are the cost–benefits of adding information to the street crossing environment? How does the degree of uncertainty regarding the interpretation of information affect travelers? Can guided exposure or training regarding the usefulness of the existing, naturally-occurring information be effective in the roundabout environment? Which intersections need technology solutions to the problem of information access, and can information access be quantified and rigorously evaluated? (The Americans with Disabilities Act requires that public rights of way be accessible to all users. For more information, see the draft of guidelines for accessible public rights-of-way found at http://www.access-board.gov/prowac/draft.htm).

The work of our research team has led to the conclusion that some high-volume one-lane roundabouts and most two-lane roundabouts will require the addition of information to aid the blind traveler in making crossing decisions. We plan to investigate the use of video detection of vehicles and communication of vehicle status to pedestrians as means of lessening risk during roundabout street crossing. Studies like this raise interesting and important human factors questions, including the strategies used to communicate with pedestrians (tones, speech messages) and the need to add information in a way that does not interfere with other information that is available.

Another key issue in intersection access is that of the predictability of information, and the related issue of familiarity with a particular environment. Regarding predictability, individuals learn that some information is available some of the time but not others. For example, a loud truck passing through an intersection will eliminate one's ability to hear other vehicles. Are travelers aware of the need to wait if there is a temporary interruption in information flow? How does general familiarity with environments like the one being negotiated aid in making predictions about the information that will be available and its relative usefulness? If there were more standardization of intersection design, travel would presumably be easier because there would be more ability to predict if features were present and where they were located. Perhaps more standardization would lead to less demand for technology solutions to address the idiosyncratic "information issues" at particular locations. Policymakers have a key role in ensuring that environments are predictable to the extent possible. Standards for placement of accessible pedestrian signal call buttons, for example, call for buttons placed no more than 10 ft from the curb and 5 ft from the outer crosswalk line. It appears that new guidelines will require buttons to be located at the top of curb ramps, which will result in increased use of "stub poles" specifically designed and sited for this purpose.

Specific familiarity should also be explored in relation to street crossing. How does knowledge of a particular intersection affect risk and efficiency (e.g., wait time) in street crossings. Whereas some new intersection types, such as roundabouts, may require the addition of information to ensure relatively low-risk access, other types of intersections may be accessible without modification once travelers learn their characteristics. However, experience with a specific intersection or other feature should not be essential for access. Individuals expect to be able to access intersections even if they have not negotiated them before, and information should be available to permit them to do so. The role of familiarity with the particular environment being negotiated (as compared to general knowledge of the environment being negotiated) on one's ability to solve wayfinding-related problems has not been studied extensively but would be a fruitful line of research that would inform our knowledge base regarding the information acquisition and strategic decision-making aspects of travel without vision.

Little is known about the cognitive "load" imposed by various types and levels of information that pedestrians may attend to at an intersection and how cognitive demands affect one's ability to attend only to relevant information. How does cognitive load relate to strategic decision making and execution? How can information be provided so that decision making is fast and accurate? Can the impact of technology to aid street crossings be evaluated by the reduction it offers in cognitive load? Perhaps with training about the linkage between information content and attentional demands, individuals who are blind may be better able to utilize information about traffic, signals, and layout more efficiently. This issue often is seen in low vision travelers, who attend to visual input when doing so is inefficient and ineffective. When taught to rely on auditory cues for determining when to begin crossing, these individuals often significantly improve their street crossing abilities.

Crossing streets without vision or with impaired vision is an important practical task for many individuals. As this chapter illustrates, there are many sources of information useful for making decisions about the various components of the street crossing task, and there are various strategies to solving travel-related challenges. Much work is needed to determine what information is available to travelers who are blind and what they want and need. We must also learn more about their ability to use information effectively in actual travel situations, recognizing that there is little margin of error for mistakes in judging traffic while crossing streets. The role of training and technology, and the impact of street and signal design policy related to the provision of supplemental information also must be considered.

ACKNOWLEDGMENTS

The project described herein was supported by Grant No. R01 EY12894 from the National Eye Institute, National Institutes of Health, awarded to Western Michigan University's Department of Blindness and Low Vision Studies. Contents of this chapter are solely the responsibility of the author and do not necessarily represent the official views of the National Eye Institute.

REFERENCES

American Foundation for the Blind Statistics and Sources for Professionals. Retrieved July 28, 2006, from http://www.afb.org/Section.asp?SectionID=15&DocumentID=1367/

Ashmead, D. H., Guth, D., Wall, R. S., Long, R., & Ponchillia, P. (2005). Street crossing by sighted and blind pedestrians at a modern roundabout. *Journal of Transportation Engineering, 131*(11), 812–821.

Barlow, J. M., Bentzen, B. L., & Bond, T. (2005). Blind pedestrians and the changing technology and geometry of signalized intersections: Safety, orientation and independence. *Journal of Visual Impairment and Blindness, 99,* 587–598.

Bentzen, B. L., & Barlow, J. M. (1995). Impact of curb ramps on the safety of persons who are blind. *Journal of Visual Impairment and Blindness, 89,* 319–328.

Geruschat, D. R., & Hassan, S. E. (2005). Driver behavior in yielding to sighted and blind pedestrians at roundabouts. *Journal of Visual Impairment and Blindness, 99,* 286–302.

Guth, D. A., Ashmead, D., Long, R. G., Wall, R., & Ponchillia, P. (2005). Blind and sighted pedestrians' judgments of gaps in traffic at roundabouts. *Human Factors, 47,* 314–331.

Guth, D. A., Hill, E. W., & Rieser, J. J. (1989). Tests of blind pedestrians' use of traffic sounds for street-crossing alignment. *Journal of Visual Impairment and Blindness, 83,* 461–468.

Guth, D. A., & Rieser, J. J. (1997). Perception and the control of locomotion by blind and visually impaired persons. In B. Blasch, W. Wiener, & R. Welsh (Eds.), *Foundations of orientation and mobility* (2nd ed., pp. 9–38). New York: American Foundation for the Blind.

Jacobson, W. H. (1993). *The art and science of teaching orientation and mobility to persons with visual impairments.* New York: American Foundation for the Blind

Jansson, G. (1990). Non-visual guidance of walking. In R. Warren & A. H. Wertheim (Eds.), *Perception and control of egomotion* (pp. 507–521). Hillsdale, NJ: Lawrence Erlbaum Associates.

LaGrow, S., & Weessies, M. (1994). *Orientation and mobility: Techniques for independence.* Palmerston North, New Zealand: Dunsmore Press Limited.

Russell J. N., Hendershot, G. E., LeClere, F., Howie, L. J., & Adler, M. (1997). Trends and differential use of assistive technology devices: United States, 1994. *Advance Data, 292,* 1–9.

Whitstock, R. H., Franck, L., & Haneline, R. (1997). Dog guides. In B. Blasch, W. Wiener, & R. Welsh (Eds.), *Foundations of orientation and mobility* (2nd ed., pp. 260–283). New York: American Foundation for the Blind.

18

Why Does Training Reduce Blind Pedestrians' Veering?

David Guth

Defined with respect to straight-line locomotion, to *veer* is to deviate from one's intended straight-line path. In the absence of sources of guidance such as a target to walk toward or a guideline to walk along, veering appears to be nearly unavoidable. This phenomenon has long been a matter of both common and scientific curiosity. Why do sighted people tend to walk in circles when they lack visual guidance? Why do blind people tend to veer when crossing quiet roads?

At a Vanderbilt University conference in 1991, I used the veering of blind pedestrians to illustrate the challenges of measuring spatially directed behavior (Guth, 1992). That conference, organized by the late Everett Hill, also linked basic research to progress in the provision of rehabilitation services to people with visual impairments, and several of the authors in this volume also participated in that conference (see Hill, 1992). In this paper, I revisit the veering problem with an emphasis on what has been learned in the intervening years about the source of the problem and about its remediation. For the former, I lean heavily on recent work by Kallie, Schrater, and Legge (in press), and for the latter, I rely on work carried out in collaboration with my colleagues, LaDuke and Gesink.

WHY DO PEOPLE VEER?

As reviewed by Guth and LaDuke (1994), early studies of veering simply assumed its presence and then sought to explain it. For example, based on studies of human skeletons, *Scientific American* reported in 1893 that "the fact that people lost on a desert or in a forest invariably walk in a circle is due to a slight inequality in the length of the legs" (Why Lost People Walk in Circles, p. 100). Likewise, when the comparative biologist Asa Schaeffer observed similar spiral-shaped paths traveled by organisms ranging from legless spermatozoa to blindfolded humans in 1928, he concluded that this was evidence of an ubiquitous spiraling mechanism, and likely that "the same mechanism is at work in man that operates in the amoeba" (Shaeffer, 1928, p. 349). Studies motivated by the desire to explain veering have occurred regularly from the 1800s to the present, with Kallie et al. (in press) being the most recent in this long line of research.

Thus far such research has not led to practical strategies for avoiding veering or for detecting that it is occurring. Consequently, orientation and mobility (O&M) instructors have emphasized after-the-fact strategies for recovering from the consequences of veering (see LaGrow & Weessies, 1994). That is, whereas the consequences of veering can be identified (e.g., detecting that one has veered into a driveway or a street) and systematic "recovery techniques" employed, persons who are veering typically do not recognize that they are doing so. Fortunately, the pedestrian environment usually includes physical and acoustic features that can be used to limit veering. Physically bounded walking paths such as hallways and sidewalks are particularly useful, as are audible beacons such as those increasingly being installed at signalized intersections as features of accessible pedestrian signal (APS) systems (Barlow & Franck, 2005; Wall, Ashmead, Bentzen, & Barlow, 2004, 2005). Absent such sources of guidance, blind pedestrians can find themselves in undesirable or risky situations such as having walked into a parking lot or an intersection.

As an O&M instructor, I routinely reported to my blind students that they had veered, basing my reports on the consequences of their veering (e.g., "You veered into the parallel street"). As I was to understand later (e.g., Gesink, Guth, & Long, 2003) and as Kallie et al. (in press) point out, this emphasis on the consequences of veering is not very useful for instruction or for research because an infinite number of paths lead from Point A to Point B, and the same path can be created by different walking movements. One possible path is an arced path of constant curvature; a second is an arced path whose radius of curvature varies over the path; a third and fourth are "sidestepping" (translation) by fixed and variable amounts per step while walking forward; and an nth is some combination of these.

In their recent efforts to understand veering, Kallie et al. (in press) conducted a descriptive study of the veering of blind and blindfolded sighted participants and a study of the same participants' thresholds for detecting the curvature of paths they were guided along. The descriptive study followed roughly the same procedures as Guth and LaDuke (1995) and involved walking through obstacle-free open space. Participants established initial alignment by "squaring off" (see LaGrow & Weessies, 1994) to a table placed perpendicular to the intended path, and they then attempted to walk straight away from the table. The paths Kallie et al.'s participants walked were similar to those reported by Guth and LaDuke and were consistent with findings reported by other researchers over the past century. In the curvature detection study, Kallie et al.'s participants were led along various curved pathways via a guidance system designed to minimize rotational torque. The study was similar to work by Cratty (1965), who used a different guiding technique and a different psychophysical method. Both studies yielded threshold radii above which participants could not reliably detect veering.

Kallie et al. (in press) then developed a simple model of veering and tested the model against their data as well as ours (Guth & LaDuke, 1995). The model, which fit those date well, suggests three sources of the so-called *veering tendency*:

- Initial alignment error
- Undetected random errors in step direction
- Undetected systematic errors in step direction

Although the Kallie et al. (in press) model will not be described here, that work is remarkable in several respects. First, a "tendency" by definition comprises variability, and Kallie et al. devised a biomechanically plausible explanation of the variability that has been observed within individuals. That is, descriptive studies of veering have reliably produced trial-to-trial and day-to-day variability, and the Kallie et al. model can account for this. Second, Kallie et al.'s combination of a descriptive experiment and a curvature detection experiment resulted in a strong case that the veering observed resulted from undetected, subthreshold, motor error. That is, veering is likely to result from nonlinear stepping movements that are perceptually indistinguishable from linear movements. LaDuke and I have long suspected this, based on our having asked participants to report whether they had walked straight or veered to the right or left of their intended straight-line path. Our participants almost universally reported that although it felt like they had walked straight, they knew that this was unlikely but had no basis for judging which way they might have veered. Third, Kallie et al. identified the systematic clockwise or counterclockwise rotation of an individual's steps as a likely source of the consistent directional bias observed among many participants in many studies of veering.

The Kallie et al. (in press) findings in support of step direction bias are consistent with the longstanding assumption that veering results in part from the gradual rotation of the body during walking (e.g., Cicinelli, 1989; Cratty, 1971; Schaeffer, 1928). While walking, the path of locomotion is actually a small-amplitude zigzag (Carlsoo, 1972; Chodera & Levell, 1973) that is bio-mechanically useful for maintaining balance. Kallie et al. emphasized that walkers control postural stability in part by varying the lateral placement of the foot and that this generates a rotational torque component that can change the walker's facing direction. However, in addition to such rotation-induced veering, veering would occur if the lateral shifts were asymmetrical (e.g., 5 cm leftward shifts and 8 cm rightward shifts). Such asymmetry could result from the greater sideways mobility of one of the hip, knee, or ankle joints; from "out toeing" that is greater in one foot than the other; and perhaps from many other as yet unidentified biomechanical variables (Engler, 2000; Rosen, 1986). This translation-induced or "sidestepping" form of veering could produce path shapes that are identical to those produced by rotation. Accordingly, veering may result from rotation alone, translation alone, or from some combination of the two—a point I return to later.

DOES TRAINING HELP?

During our descriptive studies, LaDuke and I noticed a subset of blind par-ticipants whose veering was quite severe relative to other participants. These were individuals whose veer consistently averaged about 4–5 m to the left or right of their intended straight-line path after having walked just 10 m for-ward. Two of these individuals as well as three others identified through later screening agreed to participate in a training study that would attempt to reduce this veering.

Once the veering tendency of each of these individuals had been well documented, he or she participated in a series of about fifteen 20-trial train-ing sessions. The training procedure was modeled after bandwidth feedback approaches used in athletic training (Schmidt, 1991). During each training trial, a participant started with his or her back to a portable wall, walked away from the wall, and attempted to stay within a 2-m wide, 20-m long simulated crosswalk defined by two parallel, ankle-level infrared beams. Whenever either beam was broken, the participant immediately heard—through earphones—the direction of the error and the distance that had been traveled before veer-ing out of the "crosswalk." Participants were then guided along a circuitous route back to the starting position. Over a session's 20 training trials, the par-ticipants attempted to increase their distance of travel within the simulated crosswalk. Later in the training they routinely covered the 20 m without break-ing either infrared beam. All participants exhibited marked improvement over the course of this training and, as illustrated in Figure 18–1, the effects were still evident 5 months after the cessation of training. (While I focus here on the overall reduction in veering severity, there also appears to have been a reduc-tion in trial-to-trial variability.)

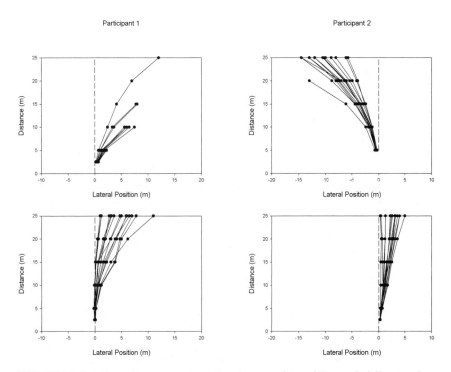

FIGURE 18–1.   Representative pretraining (top panels) and 5-month follow-up data (bottom panels) for two participants. The lines show the paths walked in a test session. Participants were filmed as they walked across a series of lines perpendicular to their intended path at distances of 2.5, 5, 10, 15, 20, and 25 m from Start. The paths that end abruptly are trials on which participants veered out of the measurement grid before the next measurement line was reached.

WHY DID THIS TRAINING HELP PARTICIPANTS
REDUCE THEIR VEERING?

While one participant reported a cognitive strategy that wasn't consistently effective (i.e., "step to the left every few steps"), the others reported that they simply "learned what it felt like to walk straight." They reported that, although they were initially surprised to learn that they veered so much and were frustrated by the early training sessions, they later found themselves having little difficulty staying within the simulated crosswalk's beams for long distances.

It is probably not the case that they became better able to perceive and thereby correct the curvature of their paths. Kallie et al. (in press) guided their participants along arcs of varying radii and reported that their *individual* thresholds (90% correct detection of the direction of the curve) ranged from a radius of 11.5 m to a radius of 36.5 m (see also Cratty, 1965). Had our participants walked smoothly curved paths, their path radii would have ranged from about 11–15 m, suggesting that they were within (albeit at the low end of) the range at which curvature detection is unlikely.

If our participants' improved performance did not result from changes in sensitivity to perceptual input, the alternative explanation must be improved motor output in the absence of feedback. In other words, a new pattern of motor output was learned while the artificially created feedback loop was present during training, and the new pattern was not forgotten after the feedback was removed. Several authors (e.g., Cratty, 1965; Kallie et al., in press) have addressed the difficulty but not the impossibility of creating mechanical systems (wind up toys, robots) that can travel a straight-line path in the absence of a feedback loop. Other authors (e.g., Bruggeman, 2005; Pick, Rieser, Wagner, & Garing, 1999; Rieser, Pick, Ashmead, & Garing, 1995) have demonstrated the recalibration of motor output in the presence of an atypical feedback loop and have shown that this persists, at least for the short run, after the removal of the altered feedback. Is this what our training accomplished? That is, was our feedback atypical in the everyday experience of our participants and useful for recalibrating their "straight line" locomotor output? We believe so.

Our feedback system was unlike anything experienced during the everyday travel of blind pedestrians. It required that well-aligned participants attempt to generate a straight line path and stopped them when they had deviated 1 m to either side of the intended path. On the surface, this may appear to be similar to the everyday experience of walking along a sidewalk and contacting a grassline along the sidewalk with one's long cane. When this occurs, however, the pedestrian cannot be sure whether the contact resulted from a straight line path in the wrong direction (i.e., alignment error) or deviation from a straight line path in the correct direction. The same can be said of the blind pedestrian who finds herself in the middle of an intersection while attempting to cross a wide street: Did this result from alignment error or from veering while walking? If veering is undetectable, as Kallie et al. have argued and as our participants reported, then a blind pedestrian would not be able to answer such questions.

Although blind pedestrians have many opportunities to experience straight-line walking, this experience occurs in the presence of continuous guidance. For example, Ashmead et al. (1998; see also Wiener & Lawson, 1997) documented the well-known ability of blind pedestrians to walk straight-line paths as they travel along walls and explained this ability in terms of the use of variations in the ambient sound field. That such everyday experience does little to affect the veering tendency is suggested by one of the participants in our training study, a teacher working in a large school building. Because he was a friend of ours, we had had many opportunities to observe him travel very straight paths while walking in the hallways of his school. Although he usually walked close to a wall, we cannot remember him ever contacting a wall with either his body or his long cane. Yet under the open field conditions of our veering study, his was among the most severe veering we observed. Other situations in which blind pedestrians commonly have opportunities to experience guided straight-line locomotion are while walking toward sound sources and while walking with human guides and dog guides.

One of the surprising aspects of our training study was that the effects lasted for at least 5 months, the point at which we ceased taking follow-up data. While this was what we hoped for, we had no good reason to expect it. As illustrated in Figure 18–1, however, it is important to note that the training procedure did not eliminate veering. Rather, it served to reduce directional bias such that following the training sessions, the participants appeared to have become "typical veerers" instead of the "severe veerers" they had previously been.

The training study revealed that practice with feedback is useful, but it remains unclear what elements of locomotion were modified during training. In the next section I describe technology development projects that target the underlying geometric characteristics of locomotion: rotation and translation. The first project involved the development of a gyroscope-based training device that provides feedback about the rotation component of an individual's veering. The second project, currently underway, involves the development of an assessment device to determine the relative contributions of rotation and translation to an individual's veering.

TECHNOLOGY FOR ASSESSING
AND REDUCING VEERING

Our first research and development project involved the development of a device that provides feedback about the extent to which an individual rotates while attempting to walk a straight-line path without vision. Our working assumption was that rotation is the primary contributor to veering, and we wanted a training tool that would target only rotation. Our goal was to develop a device that would allow the instructor or student to set parameters such as task difficulty, and whose communication interface would be accessible to blind users. The resulting Anti-Veering Training Device (AVTD) shown in Figure 18–2 is slightly larger than a camera and clips onto a belt. It has a telephone-style keypad for user command and response entry. The device uses spoken messages to present menu options, confirm choices, and provide the user with feedback about performance. The AVTD's primary sensor is a solid state gyroscope that incorporates tilt and temperature compensation hardware and software. The device measures the user's cumulative trunk rotation as he or she walks along a path. An important feature of the AVTD relates to the rhythmic, step-by-step rotation of the body that occurs during normal walking. That is, with every step of the left foot, the body rotates clockwise, and with

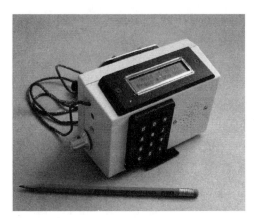

FIGURE 18–2. The Anti-Veering
Training Device.

every step of the right foot, the body rotates counterclockwise (see also Millar, 1999). This results in large variations in the user's facing direction, and the AVTD includes a software filter to remove the irrelevant effects of this variation.

A review of a typical training trial will serve to illustrate how the device is used. The user or O&M instructor first selects an obstacle-free site such as a large gymnasium, parking lot, or athletic field. The user faces the general direction in which he or she will walk and turns on the AVTD. The device then verbally prompts the user for key-pad entries including a maximum trial duration (e.g., 30 s) or distance (e.g., 100 ft) and the maximum amount of body rotation to be allowed during the trial (e.g., 15° to the left and right). These entries are read, checked for validity, and spoken back for confirmation. Re-entry is allowed in case of error. When entries are satisfactory, the device tells the user to "Press # when ready and begin walking at the starting gun." Pressing the # key begins the playing of a 3 s "countdown" tune followed by the sound of a starting gun. If the user has not exceeded the rotation limit as a trial's duration expires, the device plays a short congratulatory tune. If, instead, the user exceeds the selected rotation limit, the device responds with a "stop" tune and informs the user, for example, that "Your veer to the right exceeded 15° at 20 seconds." It then asks the user to "Press # to continue or * to repeat results." The user can thus either replay the performance results or continue to the next trial.

The potential effectiveness of the AVTD, which is about to undergo empirical tests, rests on the assumption that rotation is a primary contributor to veering. This has been the prevalent assumption for over a century; it has been supported by such work as that of Kallie et al. (in press); and it can readily be seen when observing participants walking in studies of veering. However, as I argued above, there may also be a translation (sidestepping) component to veering, and it may be the case that this is an important contributor to some individuals' veer.

To address this concern, Gesink, Buddhadev, and I have been developing a new device, the Veering Analyzer, that will make it possible to disentangle the contributions of rotation and sidestepping to an individual's veering. This tool will make it possible to determine whether the veering results from (a) rotation alone, (b) sidestepping alone, or (c) a combination of these. In order to extract the rotation and sidestepping components of an individual's veer, three parameters must be continuously measured as an individual is walking. These components are the direction the person is facing, the direction the person is moving, and the distance the person has walked. Sidestepping is indicated when there is a difference between facing direction and the direction of movement.

Figure 18–3 illustrates the conceptual basis of how the rotation and sidestepping components of veering can be extracted. At the instant depicted in Figure 18–3, the individual is engaged in a combination of rotation and sidestepping. Vector FD shows the current facing direction of the individual whereas vector MD illustrates the individual's direction of movement. The angles Fa and Ma are the angles of FD and MD relative to the initial direction of travel. Da is the current angle between Fa, the facing direction, and Ma, the motion direction. Geometrically, Da is a measure of the amount of sidestep-

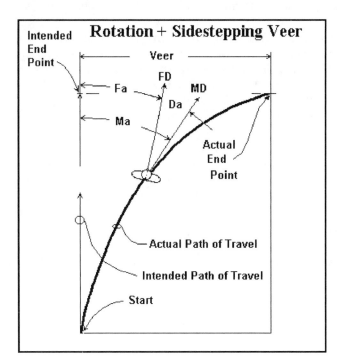

FIGURE 18–3.   Veering Analyzer trajectory geometry showing facing direction (FD) and movement direction (MD).

ping and Ma is a measure of the amount of body rotation. If, unlike the situation shown in Figure 18–3, the individual were always facing in the direction of the path of travel, the angle between the individual's facing direction (FD) and the direction he or she is moving (MD) would be zero, indicating the complete lack of sidestepping. That is, in contrast to what is depicted in Figure 18–3, if the individual had maintained his or her facing direction tangent to the path of travel since the beginning of the trial, he or she would have rotated through angle Ma. The other extreme would be the case if the individual were literally to walk sideways, in which case the angle Da would be 90°.

The Veering Analyzer consists of sensors mounted on a lightweight, 2-wheeled cart. During assessment trials, an individual tows the cart as he or she attempts to travel a straight-line path. The cart is coupled to the user via a belt-mounted, freely rotating, pivot joint. This joint is instrumented with an angular displacement transducer that continuously senses the angle between the direction the cart is pointing and the direction the individual is facing. The shaft connecting the wheeled portion of the cart to the pivot joint uses a shock-isolating mechanism to smooth the cart's tug on the user. The cart is equipped with sensors that measure the distance the cart has traveled and the direction it is facing.

The quantitative information afforded by the Veering Analyzer should be useful in several ways. First, the device will make it possible to conduct studies about the prevalence and severity of the two spatially distinct types of veering and, in turn, point the way for future intervention research. For example, it may be the case that sidestepping is a prevalent but trivial component of veering, in which case the focus should probably be on interventions that target rotation. Or it may be the case that sidestepping is not prevalent but is serious for some individuals, in which case interventions that target sidestepping should be pursued. Second, the device will provide an empirical basis for selecting appropriate instructional interventions for individuals. Interventions that target rotation such as the AVTD may work well when rotation is the primary culprit, only partially when veering results from a combination of rotation and sidestepping, and poorly when sidestepping is the principal culprit. Third, the Veering Analyzer should provide a means of tracking an individual's progress over the course of training. And fourth, with the gradual accumulation of training data for a large number of people, it should be possible to make reasonable predictions for an individual about whether further instruction or practice is likely to make a difference.

A MATTER OF DEFINITION: DOES ALIGNMENT ERROR RESULT IN VEERING?

Following from the widely accepted definition given at the outset of this chapter, *alignment error* is a source of veering because it leads to deviation from one's intended straight-line path. I suggest, however, that O&M instructors and researchers eliminate "alignment error" from their concept of veering and use the concept solely in relation to what happens once walking is underway. Subsuming alignment error in the concept of veering (as many of us have) confuses O&M instructors, blind pedestrians, model-makers, and veering-assessors alike. Consider that alignment error is often studied independent of veering (e.g., Ashmead & Wall, 2003; Chew, 1986; Guth, Hill & Rieser, 1989) and that substantial effort to improve alignment cues at crosswalks has been carried out in the absence of any discussion of veering (e.g., see Stoloff, 2005a, 2005b). An example of the latter is advocacy for the placement of retaining curbs aligned with the crosswalk at the edges of curb ramps (Whipple, 2004). The alignment of these curbs can be accessed with the foot or long cane using techniques developed during the pre-curb-ramp era, when the edge of the sidewalk was typically aligned with the crosswalk (see Hill & Ponder, 1976).

A more common alignment cue at crosswalks is a raised arrow (see Figure 16–2, this volume) that is integrated into the surface or housing of pedestrian push buttons at APS-equipped intersections (Barlow & Franck, 2005; Barlow, Bentzen, & Tabor, 2003). These arrows are intended to identify which crosswalk the button serves and to serve as an alignment cue. Although the usefulness of these arrows for alignment has not been directly studied, there is some indirect evidence that is not encouraging. In a "perceptual pointer" condition, Kallie et al. (in press) used the edge of a table at a participant's side to identify the desired walking direction. Participants felt the edge in order to establish alignment and then walked away from the table. In this condition, they averaged about 6 feet of deviation from their intended endpoint after only 30 feet of forward walking, significantly worse than in other alignment conditions.

CONCLUSION

Veering is a common experience for blind pedestrians although it is not recognized as it is occurring. Its consequences include disorientation, inefficient travel, and risk. The sources of veering are not well understood, but advances are being made toward understanding its underlying biomechanical and geometric properties. These advances, in turn, should promote more effective methods of orientation and mobility instruction. An instructional method described in this chapter was shown to be effective for 5 months following the cessation of training, but the training's longer term effectiveness is not known. New assessment and instructional methods have been devised and need to be evaluated. It may be, however, that even given the best instruction, veering will remain unacceptably risky during such tasks as crossing wide roadways. In such situations, augmenting the travel environment with sources of guidance such as the acoustic guidance provided by some modern APS-systems (Wall et al., 2004, 2005) may be important for helping to equalize the demands of pedestrian travel with and without vision.

REFERENCES

Ashmead, D. H., & Wall, R. S. (2003). Auditory constraints on alignment to traffic sounds. *Proceedings of the 11th annual International Mobility Conference.* Stellenbosch, South Africa: South African Guide-Dogs Association.

Ashmead, D., Wall, R., Eaton, S., Ebinger, K., Snook-Hill, M. M., Guth, D., et al. (1998). Echolocation reconsidered: Using spatial variations in the ambient sound field to guide locomotion. *Journal of Visual Impairment and Blindness, 92,* 615–632.

Barlow, J. M., Bentzen, B. L., & Tabor, L. (2003). *Accessible pedestrian signals: Synthesis and guide to best practice.* Berlin, MA: Accessible Design for the Blind.

Barlow, J. M., & Franck, L. (2005). Crossroads: Modern interactive intersections and accessible pedestrian signals. *Journal of Visual Impairment and Blindness, 99,* 599–610.

Bruggeman, H. (2005). Learning to throw on a rotating carousel. *Dissertation Abstracts International: Section B: The Sciences and Engineering, 65*(8-B), 4325.

Carlsoo, S. (1972). *How man moves.* London: Heinemann.

Chew, S. L. (1986). *The use of traffic sounds by blind pedestrians.* Unpublished doctoral dissertation. University of Minnesota.

Chodera, J., & Levell, R. (1973). Footprint patterns during walking. In R. Kenedi (Ed.), *Perspectives in Biomedical Engineering.* Baltimore, MD: University Park Press.

Cicinelli, J. (1989). *Veer as a function of preview and walking speed.* Unpublished master's thesis, University of California at Santa Barbara.

Cratty, B. (1965). *Perceptual thresholds of nonvisual locomotion (Part 1).* Los Angeles: University of California, Department of Physical Education.

Cratty, B. (1971). *Movement and spatial awareness in blind children and youth.* Springfield, IL: Charles C Thomas.

Engler, B. (2000). *A biomechanical analysis of the walking patterns of blind individuals who consistently veer.* Unpublished master's thesis, Western Michigan University, Kalamazoo, Michigan.

Gesink, J., Guth, D., & Long, R. (2003). A new electronic device for assessing the veering tendency of blind pedestrians. *Proceedings of the 11th International Mobility Conference.* Stellenbosch, South Africa: South African Guide-Dogs Association.

Guth, D. (1992). Space saving statistics: An introduction to constant error, variable error, and absolute error. In E. W. Hill (Ed.), Research and practice in the field of visual impairment: 70 years of vision at Peabody. (Special Issue). *Peabody Journal of Education, 67,* 110–120.

Guth, D., Hill, E., & Rieser, J. (1989). Tests of blind pedestrians' use of traffic sounds for street-crossing alignment. *Journal of Visual Impairment and Blindness, 83,* 461–468.

Guth, D. A., & LaDuke, R. O. (1994). The veering tendency of blind pedestrians: An analysis of the problem and literature review. *Journal of Visual Impairment and Blindness, 88,* 391–400.

Guth, D. A., & LaDuke, R. O. (1995). Veering by blind pedestrians: Individual differences and their implications for instruction. *Journal of Visual Impairment and Blindness, 89,* 28–37.

Hill, E. (Ed., 1992). Research and practice in the field of visual impairment: 70 years of vision at Peabody. (Special Issue). *Peabody Journal of Education, 67.*

Hill, E., & Ponder, P. (1976). *Orientation and mobility techniques: A guide for the practitioner.* New York: American Foundation for the Blind.

Kallie, C., Schrater, P., & Legge, G. (in press). Stepping noise explains veering of blind walkers. *Journal of Experimental Psychology: Human Perception and Performance*.

LaGrow, S., & Weessies, M. (1994). *Orientation and mobility: Techniques for independence*. Palmerston North, New Zealand: Dunmore Press.

Millar, S. (1999). Veering re-visited: Noise and posture cues in walking without sight. *Perception, 28*, 765–780.

Pick, H. L., Rieser, J., Wagner, D., & Garing, A. (1999). The recalibration of rotational locomotion. *Journal of Experimental Psychology: Human Perception and Performance, 25*, 1179–1188.

Rieser, J., Pick, H. L., Ashmead, D., & Garing, A. (1995). Calibration of human locomotion and models of perceptual-motor organization. *Journal of Experimental Psychology: Human Perception and Performance, 21*, 480–497.

Rosen, S. J. (1986). *Assessment of selected spatial gait patterns of congenitally blind children*. Unpublished doctoral dissertation, Vanderbilt University.

Schaeffer, A. (1928). Spiral movement in man. *Journal of Morphology, 45*, 293–398.

Schmidt, R. (1991). *Motor learning and performance: From principles to practice*. Champaign, IL: Human Kinetics.

Stolloff, E. R. (2005a). Developing curb ramp designs based on curb radius. *ITE Journal, April, 26*–32.

Stolloff, E. R. (2005b). Wayfinding at intersections: Efforts toward standardization—A Joint Workshop of the Institute of Transportation Engineers and the U.S. Access Board. *ITE Journal, April*, 20–25.

Wall, R. S., Ashmead, D. H., Bentzen, B., & Barlow, J. (2004). Directional guidance of audible pedestrian signals for street crossing. *Ergonomics, 47*, 1318–1338.

Wall, R. S., Ashmead, D. H., Bentzen, B., & Barlow, J. (2005). Audible pedestrian signals as directional beacons. *International Congress Series, 1282*, 1089–1093. Proceedings of Vision 2005, April 4–7, 2005, London.

Whipple, M. (2004). Curb ramp design by elements and planter strip curb ramp. *Proceedings of the Wayfinding at Intersections Workshop*. Washington DC: Institute of Transportation Engineers/U.S. Access Board.

Why lost people walk in circles. (1893, February 18). *Scientific American*.

Wiener, W. R., & Lawson, G. D. (1997). Audition for the traveler who is visually impaired. In B. Blasch, W. Wiener, & R. Welsh, (Eds.), *Foundations of Orientation and mobility* (2nd ed., pp. 104–169). New York: AFB Press.

19

Visual Experience and the Concept of Compensatory Spatial Hearing Abilities

Robert Wall Emerson
and Daniel H. Ashmead

In this chapter we introduce the idea that the developmental effects of restricted visual experience have often been regarded in terms of a distinction between deficit and compensation models. We attempt to provide a framework for considering those models in terms of different roles of experience in development. Then we consider what circumstances, at the behavioral or neural levels, might lead to compensatory patterns of development. These circumstances or conditions are simply that the compensatory processes be useful for some functionally important activities and that the processes exploit sensory/perceptual abilities that are not typically well developed due to lack of need. It is important not to regard a developmental compensatory process as purposefully driven but rather as something that emerges from functionally driven activities. This overall framework is applied to our research on various aspects of spatial hearing in persons with and without visual impairments.

MODELS OF THE DEVELOPMENTAL EFFECTS OF ATYPICAL VISUAL EXPERIENCE

The effect of restricted visual experience has long been regarded in terms of a distinction between deficit and compensation models (Jones, 1975; Rice, 1970; Zwiers, Van Opstal, & Cruysberg, 2001). In brief, the deficit model holds that a lack of typical visual experience impairs perceptual development

367

and perhaps other aspects of development. The compensation model suggests that atypical visual experience results in enhanced development of nonvisual perceptual abilities. The distinction between these models can be found both in education/rehabilitation literature and in recent psychological and neuroscience literature.

We find it useful to consider this distinction in the context of a typology of roles of early experience in development (Gottlieb, 1976) that distinguishes between induction, facilitation, and maintenance. From this perspective, the deficit model of restricted visual experience poses that vision typically induces or facilitates aspects of development that would not be achieved otherwise. For example, we argue below that perceptual and motor delays reported in infants who are blind could be due to the irreplaceable role of vision in promoting engagement with the surrounding environment. A strong version of the deficit model suggests that late developmental onset of visual disabilities, in childhood or even adulthood, might compromise perceptual abilities that have already developed because vision is no longer available to maintain the abilities. One example of this is the possibility that age-related macular degeneration might compromise sound localization accuracy due to less precise visual feedback about the locations of sound sources. For the most part, the deficit model as applied to visual experience has focused on early development and the lack of visual induction and facilitation of perceptual and related abilities.

The compensation model relates to roles of experience in perhaps a more subtle way than the deficit model. The notion of compensation implies that some aspects of development, nonvisual in makeup, may be induced or facilitated if there is an absence of typical visual experience. For example, there is a long tradition of research on a special hearing ability of persons who are blind, referred to variously as echolocation, facial vision, or the obstacle sense. This hearing ability allows people to sense large surfaces such as walls and to move around smoothly without collisions. Many people believe that this ability develops exclusively or at least most strongly when visual experience is very limited. In terms of Gottlieb's (1976) roles of experience, this would reflect the inductive/facilitative effect of a particular combination of perceptual and motor experience, that is, moving about with good hearing and limited or absent visual ability to detect features such as walls.

Note that the deficit and compensation models are not necessarily mutually exclusive. It seems obvious, for example, that different features of development might be affected quite differently by atypical visual experience. An important issue that has implications for intervention is that there may be alternatives to visual experience that lead to equivalent developmental outcomes. For example, it is reasonable to assume that in persons with typical vision the precision of sound localization is tuned up and maintained, at least in part, by being able to simultaneously see and hear sound sources, such as the mouths of people as they speak. If sound localization by congenitally blind adults is very precise, which it seems to be, then how is such precision achieved and maintained? One possibility is that very subtle head movements result in consistent changes in sound localization cues, providing a way to calibrate the system. Of course we cannot rule out that this helps sighted persons as well, but the point is that it is logically possible that a deficit that might be caused by lack of visual experience is masked by the effect of another kind of experience.

When it comes to considering the effects of restricted early visual experience in humans, there is a marked inconsistency between findings on infants and young children as compared to older children and adults. Infants without discernable useful vision are substantially delayed in motor (e.g., sitting), perceptual-motor (reaching to sound-producing objects), and social (joint attention, dyadic interaction) development, even with what would seem to be optimal caregiving (Adelson & Fraiberg, 1974; Bigelow, 2003; Fraiberg, Siegel, & Gibson, 1966; Troster & Brambring, 1992). In contrast, reports of hearing and other abilities in adults with congenital blindness generally indicate that these abilities are comparable to or better than these abilities in adults with typical vision. There may be some rather uninteresting ways to account for this discrepancy, such as the possibility that different abilities come into play in terms of the research questions at these widely different ages so that there is an "apples and oranges" comparison. Also, there could be greater tendency to include infants and young children with a wide range of abilities as participants in studies, whereas studies of adults tend to focus on persons with a fairly high degree of overall ability and independence. Nonetheless, there is a conundrum here that belies easy explanation. How can it be that total blindness during infancy presents such a challenging set of circumstances, yet presumably many of those individuals go on to productive, independent lives with quite good perceptual, motor, cognitive, and social capabilities?

One part of the answer may be that abilities that are strongly dependent on vision during early development can later be mediated nonvisually, especially when more abstract cognitive processes are engaged. As an example, consider the failure of infants who are blind to respond to sound-producing objects, including people (Fraiberg et al., 1966). By about 4 to 5 months it is typical for sighted infants to turn their eyes and heads toward sound sources and to reach for nearby sources (Clifton, Muir, Ashmead, & Clarkson, 1993), but this is delayed by 2 to 4 months in infants who are blind. One interpretation is that vision plays a privileged role in the engagement of infants' responsiveness to things perceived at a distance. In the terminology of varying roles of early experience, vision plays an inductive role in engaging reaching behavior, and some months later, locomotor behavior. Without this visual "kickstart," auditory information is not acted on until some months later, perhaps when a more abstract ability to represent distant objects has developed. Of course this is a speculative account, and it doesn't explain how the more abstract cognitive abilities emerge. The point is that there must be alternative developmental paths to the use of nonvisual perceptual information.

A teleological explanation is one that conflates the outcome or end product of a process with its inherent design purposes. To some extent, our focus on the deficit/compensation distinction strays into the teleological zone. With the remarkable progress made over the past quarter century in understanding developmental processes in sensory neuroscience, there is a strong biological underpinning to discussions of deficit and compensation. Indeed, the word "compensatory" is frequently used in research articles on the effects of developmental sensory restriction and in articles on the effects of brain injury. It seems unlikely, however, that the processes underlying neural changes have much to do with compensation or deficit in any overall, purposeful sense of those terms. Instead, neuroscience accounts emphasizing concepts such as activity-driven, competitive interactions between neurons are more apt as descriptions of the proximate causes.

There is a larger context in which "purpose" language such as *compensatory effects* makes sense and is desirable. A person (or for that matter any animal) is motivated to carry on a variety of activities, and if visually based performance can be replaced by information from other modalities, then the actor may be motivated to engage the nervous system in patterns of neural events that would otherwise be less likely to occur. According to this view it is the larger, goal-driven activities that set in motion patterns of neural change that may be construed as compensatory. (Alternatively, withdrawal from activities could lead to patterns described as deficits.) This way of thinking is in keeping with active rehabilitation efforts following brain injury.

CIRCUMSTANCES THAT FAVOR COMPENSATION

In the context of a developmental sensory restriction such as congenital blindness, what circumstances tend to promote enhanced utilization of other sensory modalities? We suggest two simple considerations: the functional importance of the information to be gained and the residual capacity of the sensory modality to provide the information. To illustrate, we focus on the ability of many persons who are blind to draw upon auditory spectral analysis of sounds for several kinds of information about surrounding space. Without going into detail, the spectral content of sound is informative about the locations of sound sources, especially their elevation and whether they are in front of or behind the listener (e.g., Lewald, 2002). In addition, the spectral content of the background sound reveals architectural features such as walls, openings, and the size of a room. All of these kinds of spatial information are important for one's situational awareness and are available through vision to those who can see. Thus, the underlying access to information meets the functional impor-

tance criterion. What about the criterion of residual sensory capacity? In studies comparing spatial hearing in persons who are blind with persons who are
sighted, one fairly consistent finding is that sighted persons do worse on measures that depend on spectral analysis, such as perception of elevation. This
suggests that the human auditory system has capabilities for spectral analysis
that are not necessarily developed to their fullest if there is visual access to
the underlying information. In contrast, the literature on spatial hearing generally indicates little if any difference between persons who are blind or sighted
in the perception of the direction of a sound source that is in front and more or
less at ear level. In this case perception is guided mostly by time differences in
the arrival of the sound at the two ears. It appears that many people are about
as sensitive to these interaural time differences as possible, given the geometry of the human head and the temporal resolution of the binaural hearing
system. Therefore, there is not much reserve sensory capacity to draw on for
this aspect of spatial hearing.

Our proposal—that functionally important access to information and the
availability of sensory capacity are considerations dictating the occurrence of
what seem like compensatory developments—provides guidance about domains in which persons who are blind might show especially good perceptual
abilities. However, the ways in which these abilities are acquired are not well
understood. Some clue is perhaps provided by reports of auditory system reorganization based on which aspects of sounds an animal has been trained to
focus upon (Polley, Steinberg, & Merzenich, 2006). The notion is that selective attention to sensory stimulation in the context of a task that is functionally important fosters enhanced neural processing. Research in this area indicates that mere exposure to stimulation is not enough; rather, the stimulation
must be related to ongoing goal-directed behavior. Translating to a situation
related to blindness, a person who cannot see might walk into a new room
and focus on the frequency spectrum and reverberant properties of the
acoustic field in order to "size up" the room, whereas a person who can see
would be exposed to the same acoustics but might not pay much attention
because the spatial layout is visually apparent.

FUNCTIONS OF SPATIAL HEARING

Most research on the effects of visual impairments on hearing emphasizes spatial hearing, especially perception of the locations of discrete sound sources.
In keeping with our discussion of circumstances that might lead to compensatory change, this reflects the enormous contribution of vision to space perception and the possibility that there might be under-utilized auditory capacity
for some features of space perception. Also, the visual and auditory modalities ordinarily combine to provide most of a person's information about objects
and events at a distance, so it is natural to suppose that there are common

neural connections across these modalities that might be especially available to the auditory system when visual input is severely restricted. Examples are from the extensive literature on spatially congruent bimodal stimulation (Gondan, Niederhaus, Rosler, & Roder, 2005). We turn next to review some of the different aspects of spatial hearing, but it should be noted that there is also evidence for substantial reorganization of brain processes with respect to other important functions of hearing, including language (Roder, Stock, Bien, Neville, & Rosler, 2002) and music (Rauschecker, 2001).

Within the domain of spatial hearing research, the single topic that has been investigated most is localization of a stationary sound source by a stationary listener. Different acoustic cues have been identified that specify the horizontal direction, vertical direction, and distance of a sound source (Grantham, 1995). Among the everyday actions that people engage in related to this kind of sound localization are looking, reaching, or walking toward the location. However, in most studies, researchers use response measures in which participants make one of a variety of responses, such as choosing a loudspeaker number or using a pointer (Haber, Haber, Penningroth, Novak, & Radgowski, 1993). A second general area of spatial hearing research is motion perception, which includes both perception of moving sound sources by a stationary listener and perception of self-motion by a listener. The two scenarios that have received the most attention are circular motion of a sound source around a listener, and linear motion of a sound source toward or away from the listener (or vice versa, with the listener rather than the sound source on the move). The study of more complicated motion paths has not been investigated much; however, in the field of orientation and mobility (O&M) there is considerable practical emphasis on teaching pedestrians with visual disabilities to listen to complex patterns of traffic movement (Wiener & Lawson, 1997). A third area of spatial hearing is based on the ambient structure of sound fields, rather than discrete sources of sound. As noted earlier, this includes sensitivity to acoustic variables specifying the presence of walls, openings, and the like. This is possibly another example of a perceptual ability that is at a premium if one functions without vision but that may be undeveloped if vision is available.

DISCRIMINATING LOCATION CHANGES OF SINGLE SOUND SOURCES: AZIMUTH, ELEVATION, DISTANCE

We studied the sound localization abilities of 35 children with visual impairments (average age 14 years), 18 children with typical vision (average age 13 years), and 9 adults with typical vision (Ashmead et al., 1998b). Among the children with visual impairments, 22 had a history of congenital total blindness (light perception or less). The measure was the ability to discriminate the direction of changes in sound source position, with separate tests done in the horizontal, vertical, and distance dimensions. By convention, the horizontal and vertical measures are called minimum audible angles (MAA). An experimenter held a small loudspeaker through which 0.5 s bursts of noise were presented. For the horizontal test, on each trial the sound was presented from 1¾ meters straight ahead at ear level, and then during a 1 s silent period the experimenter moved the loudspeaker to the left or right by a specified angle for the second noise burst. The participant indicated whether the second sound came from left or right of the first sound, either by using direction words or by pointing. Across trials the size of the angular shift was varied by a psychophysical rule so as to find the smallest angle for which the participant could correctly report the direction of change. The vertical and distance tests were identical in structure, with participants reporting whether the sound shifted up/down or near/far.

The children with visual impairments generally performed as well as or better than the sighted children and adults. Within the group of children with visual impairments, the subset with congenital total blindness tended to do somewhat better than those with some visual capacities, but the differences were not significant. The results for the horizontal minimum audible angle can be related to our earlier discussion of circumstances under which compensatory perceptual abilities may emerge. The mean threshold angles were about 1.75° for children with visual disabilities, compared to 1.70° for adults with typical vision and 3.40° for children with typical vision. Typical values for well-practiced adults are about 1 to 2° (Middlebrooks & Green, 1991; Mills, 1972), a level of performance that appears to push against the limits of sensitivity to the underlying sound localization cues. Thus, horizontal sound localization may be a perceptual ability that is used maximally even by sighted persons, leaving little room for compensatory adaptations. It is intriguing, however, that the sighted children in this study had thresholds about twice as high as the children with visual disabilities, suggesting that the rate of development might be enhanced as a result of restricted visual experience.

For the vertical minimum audible angle as well as the minimum audible distance, the children with visual impairments did substantially better than the children or adults with typical vision. Vertical localization of sound sources depends strongly on spectral differences caused by the shape of the pinnae (outer ears) and head. It is reasonable to conjecture that this spectral information might not be used very fully by many persons with typical vision because human activity is focused on events near ground level and much of the needed information is available visually. For persons without vision, vertical sound localization assumes greater importance, for example, in specifying the body height of a conversational partner. Likewise, auditory distance perception depends on a set of cues (such as the ratio of direct to reverberant sound) that may not be well utilized if distances of sound sources can be perceived through vision. In contrast, auditory perception of distance is extremely important when functioning without vision.

Of course when we perceive the location of a sound source in everyday behavior, we have a unified percept of a definite location, not a set of percepts

scattered across three spatial dimensions. What this study of minimum audible
angles and distance suggests (and there is supporting research literature,
though with inconsistencies) is that sound localization is at a premium for
persons without vision. It appears that compensatory changes happen where
there is room, such as with the use of spectral cues. Where the limits to such
changes lie is not well known, but in general the children with visual impairments did not do better than some of the sighted participants. For this reason
we tend to favor an interpretation that restricted visual experience results in
maximal utilization of the ordinary limits of auditory perception. However,
a couple of the children with visual impairments were astonishingly good at
discriminating very small changes in locations of sound sources. It would be
interesting to search for such "super listeners" across a range of persons with
visual impairments and typical vision.

REACHING AND WALKING
TO SINGLE SOUND SOURCES

As noted earlier, most studies of sound localization rely on measures in which
people discriminate between locations (as in our minimum audible angle and
distance work) or make an abstract judgment of location such as selecting
among a set of targets. In everyday listening experiences, however, sound localization often plays out as a spatially coordinated movement, such as shifting
one's gaze toward a sudden sound, facing a conversational partner, reaching
to pick up a telephone, or walking to pick up an object dropped on the floor.
For persons with vision, many of these tasks may be predominantly under visual control after the initial "alerting" function of the sound. When these kinds
of actions are performed without visual support, there may be a greater need
for precise 3-D localization that is coded and remembered long enough to carry
out the action.

In the same study in which minimum audible angles and distances were
measured, the child participants engaged in a task of reaching to nearby sound
sources and a second task of walking to the locations of sound sources between
3 and 7 m straight ahead. In the reaching task, a motion analysis system was
used to monitor the loudspeaker position and the position of the participant's
index finger. On each trial, a 1 s noise burst was presented from the loudspeaker in one of twelve regions within reachable space (left/middle/right;
near/far; ear level/chest level). Immediately after the sound the loudspeaker
was removed and participants reached to position their finger at the perceived
location of the sound. The data consisted of the spatial discrepancy between
the location from which the sound was presented and the finger location. In
the vertical and horizontal dimensions, the errors were similar, and quite small,
for the two groups of children. In the distance dimension, children with typical
vision under-reached by 9.5 cm on average, compared to only 2.7 cm for chil-

dren with visual impairments. This difference was statistically robust, and the undershoot of about 9 to 10 cm would result in a miss in real scenarios of reaching for sounds. It is difficult to relate these findings directly to those on minimum audible angle and distance, partly because the sound sources were much closer in the reaching task (sound localization cues in very nearby space differ from those several meters distant). Also, we cannot say whether the group difference is based on the perception of sound location as opposed to the ability to relate that perception to reaching. It is reasonable to speculate, however, that experience with reaching for nearby objects without visual support would favor development of precise reaching for sound sources.

We also carried out a task in which participants walked to the perceived locations of sound sources. This task was done by the children with visual impairments and a group of adults with typical vision. On each trial, a 1 s noise burst was presented from a loudspeaker placed at ear level straight ahead of the listener at a distance of 3, 4, 5, 6, or 7 m. Holding a guide string to keep on a straight path, the participant walked to where the sound seemed to have been located. Of course the loudspeaker was moved out of the way after the sound was presented. There were actually two versions of the task, one in which participants stood still while listening, and one in which they started walking just before the sound came on. The latter condition provides additional motion-related information about distance (Ashmead, Davis, & Northington, 1995). Although both groups tended to overshoot shorter target distances and undershoot longer distances, the children with visual impairments were more accurate than the adults with typical vision, with errors of about 35–40 cm and 80–90 cm, respectively. The same theoretical considerations apply to this task as to the reaching task in that a history of walking to the location of an acoustic event without visual support would presumably lead to enhanced utilization of distance information and the ability to relate that information to locomotion.

MOVING SOUND SOURCES

Auditory motion perception has received much less research attention than localization of stationary sound sources. However, it is axiomatic in the field of O&M that the motion paths of vehicles provide essential and reliable information about street layout, approaching vehicles, and traffic cycles (e.g., the surge in traffic as a green light comes on). Also, in chapter 15 in this volume, Ponchillia reports on the ability of skilled goalball players to intercept a moving, sounding ball. Perhaps the most systematic work in the domain of moving sound sources and blindness is on the use by a pedestrian of sound from passing traffic to establish correct alignment for crossing a street (Guth, Hill, & Rieser, 1989). The accuracy of alignment based on listening to traffic like this is unfortunately not high, with errors of 10–15° common. These errors are large enough to lead someone into the traffic lane on the street parallel to the one being crossed, so ongoing monitoring during the crossing is essential. In general, the research literature on auditory motion perception indicates that it is rather crude compared to localization of stationary sound sources. This suggests on one hand that there are real limits to the usefulness of auditory motion perception for nonvisual guidance of actions but on the other hand that this could be a domain in which there are opportunities for experience-based enhancement of perception.

Recently we and our colleagues have investigated the use of hearing to identify gaps that allow safe street crossing in freely moving traffic (Guth, Ashmead, Long, Wall, & Ponchillia, 2005). Our purpose was to compare gap detection by experienced blind pedestrians using their hearing and by sighted pedestrians using their vision, so we did not compare the two groups on the hearing version of the task. The general pattern of results was that when traffic was even moderately busy, blind pedestrians missed many crossing opportunities, as well as made unsafe decisions to cross. This work has been taken into account in policy discussions of provisions for pedestrian street crossing. Our conclusion at this point is that in settings with busy, free-running traffic, hearing does not provide sufficient information for making safe crossing decisions. Under quieter conditions with limited traffic, such as many residential streets, hearing may suffice. The complexity of the pedestrian listening task (multiple vehicular sound sources, range of speeds, background sounds) at this point goes beyond what is known about human auditory capacities for perceiving motion.

AUDITORY GUIDANCE OF NAVIGATION

There are suggestions from some of the work summarized earlier, especially on auditory distance perception, as well as from studies reported by other labs, that locomotion through structured settings such as hallways or along streets may be a domain in which a personal history of visual impairment might lead to enhanced auditory guidance. We have worked on two topics related to this. One is the ability to walk parallel to walls by sensing variations in the ambient sound field. The other is the use of acoustic beacons in a pedestrian street crossing situation. In both of these areas we have not focused on differences between people as a function of visual experience but rather on the nature of the underlying auditory information.

The ability of people to use sound to detect a large surface such as a wall was studied in early investigations of *facial vision*, a term based on the feeling that something is impinging on the face (Ammons, Worchel, & Dallenbach, 1953). These studies demonstrated that this ability to perceive surfaces is based on hearing, and there was some indication that the ability was particularly well developed in many persons with visual impairments (Worchel, Mauney, &

Andrew, 1950). During the 1960s there were a number of demonstrations that reflected sound could be used to detect the presence and even the sizes of objects (Rice, 1967). The term echolocation was applied to the general ability to use sound to perceive features of the environment that are not themselves the original sources of sound. Although echolocation is still widely used within the blindness community in this general sense, we think the term is misleading because it implies similarity to the range-finding process used in sonar devices and by some species of bats and marine mammals. Most people can take advantage of subtle reflected sounds to perceive objects. For example, in a typical office setting where there is an air ventilation outlet you can hold up a flat surface such as a book to create an audible reflection of that sound. In street settings the sound from vehicles reflects off signs and poles, providing a way to detect them. This use of reflected sound is not echolocation in the range-finding sense of that term because the listener does not time the sound from its onset to the arrival of its reflection. Nevertheless, the ability is useful for many navigation tasks by persons with visual impairments, such as attending to street architecture during a walk (Strelow & Brabyn, 1982).

Another source of auditory information for guidance of navigation is spatial variations in the structure of the ambient or background sound field. Even in a setting in which there are no discrete sound sources, the background sound level varies in intensity and frequency composition at the boundaries of a space, such as walls and floors. Specifically, low frequency sound (say, below 400 Hz) builds up in intensity within a meter or so of a boundary surface because of interactions with sound reflected from the surface (Ashmead & Wall, 1999). We studied children with visual impairments as they used this ability to walk along artificial hallways created with large cardboard boxes (Ashmead et al., 1998a). The basic task was to walk along a hallway without touching the wall on either side. Children with congenital blindness were quite adept at this task. They could ease toward one side, "find" the wall without touching it, and then walk parallel to it to the end of the hallway. When these children were prevented from using their hearing they did poorly, frequently bumping into the walls. Sighted but unpracticed adults did poorly at this task, but anecdotally, when sighted persons are allowed to practice the task, as several members of our research team did, they can perform quite well. It is interesting that even though the perceptual basis for this navigational ability is auditory, one does not have an impression of hearing the wall. Rather, there is a more direct awareness of the presence of a surface. This is probably the same phenomenology that originally led to the term *facial vision*. The use of hearing to walk parallel to walls is considered a skill that persons with visual impairments are expected to have in their repertoire. However, there has been little if any systematic research on variations in this ability or on the role of visual experience in its acquisition.

Another navigational situation in which spatial hearing plays a key role is in the use of a beaconing sound to guide one's walking path. This works in many indoor situations such as walking for a ringing telephone. We investigated this ability in an outdoor pedestrian situation, using audible crossing signals to guide street crossing within the established crosswalk (Wall, Ashmead, Bentzen, & Barlow, 2004). The primary purpose of the study was to determine effective properties for signal presentation. Although both blind and sighted participants were included, performance was equivalent for the two groups. We found that the standard practice of providing audible signals from both ends of the crosswalk was not very helpful for staying in the crosswalk during the crossing because the far side signal is not very detectable as the crossing begins and both signals typically stop when the pedestrian is about halfway across (to prevent someone from initiating a crossing at that time). Presenting a signal from the far (destination) end of the crosswalk only was helpful, but what helped most was presenting a subsidiary signal from the far end during the late stage of the crossing. There are logistical problems with incorporating these signal scenarios into street settings in which there are multiple pedestrians with different travel goals, but this study suggests that acoustic beaconing is an underutilized design feature. The fact that blind and sighted participants performed equivalently in this task is consistent with the idea that the benefit comes from localization of a single sound source that is presented intermittently, which is quite similar to a minimum audible angle task.

SUMMARY

In this chapter we have attempted to provide a framework for thinking about the developmental effects of restricted early visual experience with an emphasis on ways in which spatial hearing might be expected to be especially good. The idea is simply that in the absence of visual support for certain kinds of spatially coordinated behavior, there is a premium on using auditory information. When this information is helpful for functionally important activities such as safe locomotion, and when auditory sensitivity is utilized to a greater extent than is typical in persons with vision, we are inclined to refer to the ability as *compensatory*. Although this term has limited usefulness as an account of the proximate processes underlying development, it appropriately draws attention to the desirability of encouraging full utilization of remaining sensory abilities by persons who have sensory restrictions.

REFERENCES

Adelson, E., & Fraiberg, S. (1974). Gross motor development in infants blind from birth. *Child Development, 45*(1), 114–126.

Ammons, C. H., Worchel, P., & Dallenbach, K. (1953). Facial vision: The perception of obstacles out of doors by blind-folded and blind-folded deafened subjects. *American Journal of Psychology, 66*, 519–553.

379

Ashmead, D. H., Davis, D. L., & Northington, A. (1995). Contribution of listeners' approaching motion to auditory distance perception. *Journal of Experimental Psychology: Human Perception & Performance, 21*(2), 239–256.

Ashmead, D. H., & Wall, R. S. (1999). Auditory perception of walls via spectral variations in the ambient sound field. *Journal of Rehabilitation Research and Development, 36*(4), 313–322.

Ashmead, D. H., Wall, R. S., Eaton, S. B., Ebinger, K. A., Snook-Hill, M.-M., Guth, D. A., & Yang, X. (1998a). Echolocation revisited: Using spatial variations in the ambient sound field to guide locomotion. *Journal of Visual Impairment and Blindness, 92*, 615–632.

Ashmead, D. H., Wall, R. S., Ebinger, K. A., Eaton, S. B., Snook-Hill, M. M., & Yang, X. (1998b). Spatial hearing in children with visual disabilities. *Perception, 27*(1), 105–122.

Bigelow, A. E. (2003). The development of joint attention in blind infants. *Developmental Psychopathology, 15*(2), 259–275.

Clifton, R. K., Muir, D. W., Ashmead, D. H., & Clarkson, M. G. (1993). Is visually guided reaching in early infancy a myth? *Child Development, 64*(4), 1099–1110.

Fraiberg, S., Siegel, B. L., & Gibson, R. (1966). The role of sound in the search behavior of a blind infant. *Psychoanalytic Study of the Child, 21*, 327–357.

Gondan, M., Niederhaus, B., Rosler, F., & Roder, B. (2005). Multisensory processing in the redundant-target effect: A behavioral and event-related potential study. *Perception & Psychophysics, 67*(4), 713–726.

Gottlieb, G. (1976). Conceptions of prenatal development: Behavioral embryology. *Psychological Review, 83*(3), 215–234.

Grantham, D. W. (1995). Spatial hearing and related phenomena. In B. C. J. Moore (Ed.), *Handbook of Perception and Cognition: Hearing* (pp. 297–345). San Diego, CA: Academic.

Guth, D., Ashmead, D., Long, R., Wall, R., & Ponchillia, P. (2005). Blind and sighted pedestrians' judgments of gaps in traffic at roundabouts. *Human Factors, 47*(2), 314–331.

Guth, D. A., Hill, E. W., & Rieser, J. J. (1989). Tests of blind pedestrians' use of traffic sounds for street-crossing alignment. *Journal of Visual Impairment and Blindness, 83*(9), 461–468.

Haber, L., Haber, R. N., Penningroth, S., Novak, K., & Radgowski, H. (1993). Comparison of nine methods of indicating the direction to objects: Data from blind adults. *Perception, 22*(1), 35–47.

Jones, B. (1975). Spatial perception in the blind. *British Jouranl of Psychology, 66*(4), 461–472.

Lewald, J. (2002). Vertical sound localization in blind humans. *Neuropsychologia, 40*(12), 1868–1872.

Middlebrooks, J. C., & Green, D. M. (1991). Sound localization by human listeners. *Annual Review of Psychology, 42*, 135–159.

Mills, A. W. (1972). Auditory localization. In J. W. Tobias (Ed.), *Foundations of Modern Auditory Theory* (Vol. 2, pp. 301–348). New York: Academic Press.

Polley, D. B., Steinberg, E. E., & Merzenich, M. M. (2006). Perceptual learning directs auditory cortical map reorganization through top-down influences. *Journal of Neuroscience, 26*(18), 4970–4982.

Rauschecker, J. P. (2001). Cortical plasticity and music. *Annals of the New York Academy of Sciences, 930*, 330–336.

Rice, C. E. (1967). Human echo perception. *Science, 155*, 656–664.

Rice, C. E. (1970). Early blindness, early experience and perceptual enhancement. *American Foundation for the Blind: Research Bulletin, 22*, 1–22.

Roder, B., Stock, O., Bien, S., Neville, H., & Rosler, F. (2002). Speech processing activates visual cortex in congenitally blind humans. *European Journal of Neuroscience, 16*(5), 930–936.

Strelow, E. R., & Brabyn, J. A. (1982). Locomotion of the blind controlled by natural sound cues. *Perception, 11*(6), 635–640.

Troster, H., & Brambring, M. (1992). Early social-emotional development in blind infants. *Child Care Health and Development, 18*(4), 207–227.

Wall, R. S., Ashmead, D. H., Bentzen, B. L., & Barlow, J. (2004). Directional guidance from audible pedestrian signals for street crossing. *Ergonomics, 47*(12), 1318–1338.

Wiener, W. R., & Lawson, G. D. (1997). Audition for the traveler who is visually impaired. In Blasch, B. B., Wiener, W. R., & Welsh, R. L. (Eds.), *Foundations of orientation and mobility* (2nd ed., pp. 104–169). New York: American Foundation for the Blind.

Worchel, P., Mauney, J., & Andrew, J. G. (1950). The perception of obstacles by the blind. *Journal of Experimental Psychology, 40*, 746–751.

Zwiers, M. P., Van Opstal, A. J., & Cruysberg, J. R. (2001). A spatial hearing deficit in early-blind humans. *Journal of Neuroscience, 21*(9), RC142: 141–145.

20

Rehabilitation Strategies in Individuals With Age-Related Macular Degeneration

François Vital-Durand

Epidemiological data stress the dramatic increase of age-related macular degeneration (AMD) in developed countries. In a country like France (62 million habitants) 80,000 individuals are legally blind as a consequence of this single pathology, and an estimated 1.5 million are classified as low vision patients. Similar figures are reported in North America (Bressler, Bressler, West, Fine, & Taylor, 1989), and it is expected that the numbers will keep growing (Brown & Mellish, 2001; Vingerling, Hofman, Grobbe, & de Jong, 1996).

AMD patients suffer major visual disabilities when the second eye becomes affected. Central vision loss implies loss of fixation control. The patient cannot identify faces or fine details, and localization is inaccurate when manipulating tools or pouring drinks. More dramatically, reading becomes impossible (Stevenson, Hart, Montgomery, McCulloch, & Chakravarthy, 2004; Tejeria, Harper, Artes, & Dickinson, 2002). Daily life is technically and psychologically impaired. The patients are often judged harshly by others who do not understand that they can see some elements of the scene and not others. They might, for example, be accused of cheating. The common attitude toward providing help is to offer optical equipment, magnifying glasses, magnifiers, closed-circuit television, telescopes, lighting advice, and in some cases, orientation and mobility training. The goal is to improve visibility and preserve autonomy. It has been observed, though, that this technical help is often not very beneficial and is quickly disregarded (Harper, Doorduyn, Reeves, & Slater, 1999; Watson, De l'Aune, Long, Maino, & Stelmack, 1997).

In the best cases, the patients are offered various programs of rehabilitation designed to train in the use of optical tools (Nilsson, Frennesson, & Nilsson, 2003; Nilsson & Nilsson, 1986; Reeves, Harper, & Russell, 2004) and establish a new retinal locus suitable for reading (Nilsson, Frennesson, & Nilsson, 1998). Some of these programs have been properly evaluated in terms of number of sessions but not really in terms of content or benefit (Goodrich et al., 2004).

I focus in this chapter on the rationale of a rehabilitation procedure based on a thorough assessment of a patient's visual behavior, one postulate, and three main objectives determined by patient expectations. The postulate is that functional vision can be improved by training, at least to some extent, as it has been repeatedly shown in amblyopic cases (Polat, Ma-Naim, Belkin, & Sagi, 2004; Simmers & Gray, 1999). Aging individuals are gifted with enough brain functional plasticity and learning capacities that they can develop new visual strategies to foster the use of their residual capacities (Cheung & Legge, 2005; Nilsson et al., 2003).

The first objective is to determine which retinal area is best fitted with the optimal visual capacity. The second objective is to train the patient to use one, sometimes two of these preferred retinal loci, then called trained retinal loci (Nilsson et al., 1998). The third objective is to systematically use these trained retinal loci to restore an improved performance in reading ability. Assessment includes an estimation of visual acuity, contrast sensitivity, binocularity, and determination of the retinal areas used by the patient. It also includes a questionnaire on the patient's expectations and lifestyle. It has been observed that these patients spontaneously develop several preferred retinal loci, which allows them to see some details although they have no access to spatial coordinates of the target and cannot intentionally return to the same spot, losing the object they had just seen. As a result, perception is unstable. The object disappears when the patient tends to fixate with the damaged fovea (Deruaz, Whatham, Mermoud, & Safran, 2002; Duret, Issenhuth, & Safran, 1999).

In the case of patients with relative scotomas, often a consequence of verteporfin treatment, or in case of rather small absolute scotomas (less than 10° in diameter), adaptive strategies are more difficult to adopt because the patient tends to maintain a central fixation strategy that may be efficient only if the object is particularly large or high contrast. But in most cases, he will use several preferred retinal loci located within relative scotomatous locations, although he has no clue as to the relative spatial location; thereby his gaze efforts bring more confusion than help, and functional performance remains very limited. (Nguyen et al., 2004a, 2004b). Some patients spontaneously develop the use of a single preferred retinal locus and do not require special intervention. However, most patients require the benefit of a rehabilitation program to regain reading capacities.

When optical aids, closed-circuit television, magnifying glasses, and telescopes are provided, some patients will spontaneously make the best possible use of them. For those who do not profit from optical equipment, early attempts are often made to promote visual rehabilitation focused on training visual function, adapting the patient to visual aids, and stressing psychological support (Krischer, Stein-Arsic, Meissen, & Zihl, 1985) so as to provide a basic program of care (Massof, 1995, 1998). Several researchers support the idea that training can foster a plasticity phenomenon to improve the use of residual visual or substitutive capacities. Some propose a global rehabilitation of sensorimotor functions, for instance with aerobic training. An effect has been shown on cortical activation interpreted as an efficient control of biological and cognitive senescence (Colcombe et al., 2003). A more specific study demonstrated the benefit of visual training of an amblyopic eye (Polat et al., 2004), in line with results obtained in low vision patients (Beard, Levi, & Reich, 1995). Several teams have proposed rehabilitation programs for low vision patients, largely based on training in the use of low vision aids (Nilsson & Nilsson, 1994).

We tested the hypothesis that a thorough assessment of retinal sensitivity and training of the various sensorimotor loops involved in visual behavior would foster control of eye position and the use of a single trained retinal locus. Assessment of retinal sensitivity can be performed using the scanning laser ophthalmoscope, which provides the location of the preferred retinal loci (Guez, Le Gargasson, Rigaudiere, & O'Regan, 1993), or the less costly wagon wheel test (MacKeben & Colenbrander, 1999), but the most sensitive tool is the Goldmann dynamic perimetry, a fairly long and tiring test.

Our study was performed at the Institution Nationale des Invalides (Paris, France). It was aimed at fostering the use of a single preferred retinal locus, under the control of the orthoptist checking the retinal area used by looking at the corneal reflex of the fixating eye (Hirschberg, 1885), and by training the patient on visuomotor coordination tasks with the hope that better spatial control of hand position will transfer to the control of eye position and gaze (MacKeben, 2002). The criterion we used as the ultimate output of the rehabilitation procedure was reading speed.

METHOD

Patients were referred by their ophthalmologists when they presented with a disabling condition that prevented reading and that had been stable over the previous 6 months. We recruited 44 patients with advanced AMD who wanted to improve their daily living condition. Inclusion criteria included bilateral atrophic or exudative AMD, logMAR acuity ≤0.4 logMAR (Early Treatment Diabetic Retinopathy Scale, sometimes called ETDRS). Mean age was 76.78 ± 7. 85 years (range, 49–89). The 49-year-old patient was the only one under 60. Exclusion criteria included any comorbidity affecting gross motor and/or mental abilities. The initial session included a detailed assessment of each individual's visual capacities, availability and motivation, needs and expectations, and comorbidity. Visual capacity assessment includes Goldmann dynamic perimetry; optical needs; distance and near acuity; contrast sensitivity; form perception; visually guided hand control on barring, crossing, and circling tests; ocular motility; and reading performance. Each session was programmed to fit the capacities of the patients in terms of resolution and fatigue. Practice was recommended at home in between sessions. The patients were presented with a notebook of exercises including various sorts of drawing, writing, circling, crossing, and tracing. Several of these tasks are shown in Figure 20–1. When a patient reached a stable level of performance, optical aids were provided that boosted reading ability. When the patient reached a plateau in reading capacity, a final assessment was performed, similar to the initial assessment.

RESULTS

Compliance

Three patients abandoned the protocol, one who suffered an occurrence of a comorbidity requiring hospitalization, one who moved out of the area, and one who lost motivation. Thus these preliminary data are based upon 41 patients, 59% women, 41% men, 95% right-handed.

Choice of a Trained Retinal Locus

We use the results of the Goldmann dynamic perimetry shown in Figure 20–2 to choose the best possible location to train a stable fixation. This zone may

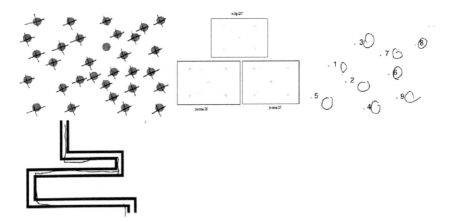

FIGURE 20–1.   Examples of tasks used to assess and improve eye–hand coordination: crossing, pointing, circling, tracing. Notice that in these examples taken from the initial assessment, the patient is fairly inaccurate in all tasks.

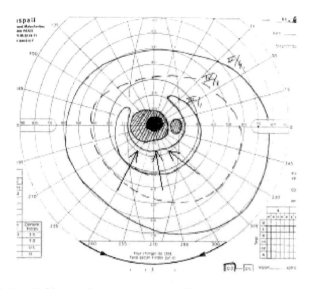

FIGURE 20–2. Goldmann dynamic perimetry. Three levels of sensitivity were tested. Arrows indicate the location where a trained retinal locus will be trained for systematic use.

not be the one with the highest acuity because it is often located between the scotoma and the optic disk. It needs to be sufficiently extended to allow reading a complete word. In the example of Figure 20–1, we choose a zone below the scotoma.

It is possible to determine the type of fixation used by the patient: stable central (nonapplicable here), unstable central, nystagmic, stable eccentric, unstable eccentric, and lack of fixation. Then the patient is trained to recognize shapes, contours, letters, numbers, and, progressively, groups of letters and numbers. Only when a fair amount of success is obtained is the patient introduced to optical aids.

Patient Expectations

A majority of patients expect to be able to read again. Some also quote daily task and mobility, as shown in Figure 20–3. Most patients recovered some reading abilities, some of them up to near 100 words per min, as shown in Figure 20–4.

Number of Sessions

The number of rehabilitation sessions with the orthoptist in order to reach a stable level of performance varied with individual capacities, as can be seen

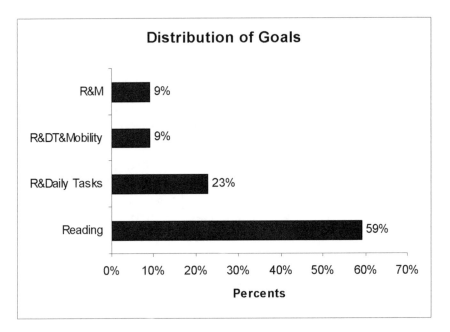

FIGURE 20–3.   Distribution of goals as expressed by the patients: Reading (R), Mobility (M), Daily Tasks (DT). Percentages indicate distribution of outcomes across participants.

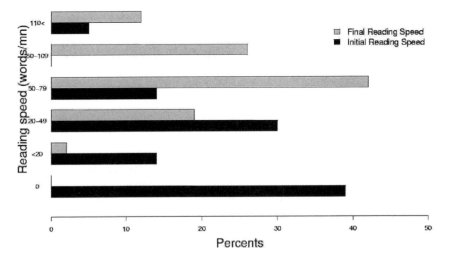

FIGURE 20–4.   Distribution of reading speed expressed in words per minute before (black) and after (shaded) rehabilitation. Percentages indicate distribution of outcomes across participants.

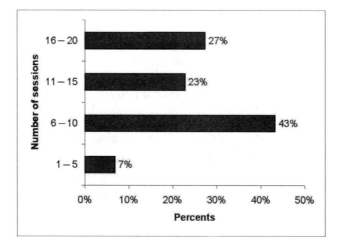

FIGURE 20–5.   Number of sessions needed to reach a stable level of performance in reading. Percentages indicate distribution of outcomes across participants.

in Figure 20–5. A majority of patients required six to ten sessions. Some needed more as their condition was hampered by a larger scotoma, older age, or additional impairments.

DISCUSSION

This study was designed to test the reliability of training a patient to use a single or a limited number of trained retinal loci to recover reading abilities. We emphasized the choice of a location in the spared retina that could encompass at least a complete word. Each patient was trained under control of his fixation by the orthoptist who constantly observed the corneal reflex. During the training sessions, the patient was encouraged to perform shape discrimination and visuomotor tasks in order to help the stabilization of the gaze by all possible means. This last element is based upon the close relationship between the sensory and motor functions that contribute to spatial behavior— i.e., visual, vestibular, kinesthetic, and motor (Borel, Harlay, Magnan, & Lacour, 2001; Sober & Sabes, 2005). This is the rationale for training visually guided hand movement with tasks involving barring, crossing, circling letters or spots, and drawing between borders.

It is clear that the level of motivation, often impaired by depressive conditions, is a prerequisite for a successful rehabilitation. A mini mental state–questionnaire is administered to check this point. Depending upon age and individual level of cognitive abilities, some patients would certainly benefit from cognitive remediation. This point is not considered here. Globally, patients invest a lot of energy to regain visual capacities, and dropping out is infrequent. On the contrary, it is common that a patient will ask for more homework. It is clear from our data that the benefits of the program keep the patient going, up to a level where access to reading material is restored. Only at this point are visual aids provided that could improve the performance. They are not provided initially because we want to encourage patients to boost their perceptual and cognitive abilities to decipher the shapes of the letters and pictures.

Additional research is underway in my laboratory to investigate to what extent stimulation of other sensory functions, including vestibular and motion sensitivity, would improve control of all spatial functions, including voluntary gaze control.

ACKNOWLEDGEMENTS

This work was supported by European project AMD-READ QLK6-CT-2002-2014, a grant from Fédération des Aveugles et Handicapés Visuels de France, and Inserm-ATC Vieillissement 2002 AMGo2003CSA

We gratefuly acknowledge our collaborators, Catherine Dauxerre, orthoptist; Françoise Koenig-Supiot, ophthalmologist; Eugen Ionescu, ENT; Kenneth Knoblauch, PhD; and Xavier Radvay, Damien Dupré, Delphine Thibault, Caroline Tournebize, Stéphanie Duhoux, Cécile Bordier, students.

REFERENCES

Beard, B. L., Levi, D. M., & Reich, L. N. (1995). Perceptual learning in parafoveal vision. *Vision Research, 35*(12), 1679–1690.

Borel, L., Harlay, F., Magnan, J., & Lacour, M. (2001). How changes in vestibular and visual reference frames combine to modify body orientation in space. *Neuroreport, 12*(14), 3137–3141.

Bressler, N. M., Bressler, S. B., West, S. K., Fine, S. L., & Taylor, H. R. (1989). The grading and prevalence of macular degeneration in Chesapeake Bay watermen. *Archives of Ophthalmology, 107*(6), 847–852.

Brown, S. B., & Mellish, K. J. (2001). Verteporfin: a milestone in ophthalmology and photodynamic therapy. *Expert Opinion on Pharmacotherapy, 2*(2), 351–361.

Cheung, S. H., & Legge, G. E. (2005). Functional and cortical adaptations to central vision loss. *Visual Neuroscience, 22*(2), 187–201.

Colcombe, S. J., Erickson, K. I., Raz, N., Webb, A. G., Cohen, N. J., McCauley, E., et al. (2003). Aerobic fitness reduces brain tissue loss in aging humans. *The Journals of Gerontology. Series A: Biological Sciences and Medical Sciences, 58*(2), 176–180.

Deruaz, A., Whatham, A. R., Mermoud, C., & Safran, A. B. (2002). Reading with multiple preferred retinal loci: Implications for training a more efficient reading strategy. *Vision Research, 42*(27), 2947–2957.

Duret, F., Issenhuth, M., & Safran, A. B. (1999). Combined use of several preferred retinal loci in patients with macular disorders when reading single words. *Vision Research, 39*(4), 873–879.

Goodrich, G. L., Kirby, J., Oros, T., Wagstaff, P., McDevitt, B., Hazen, J., et al. (2004). Goldilocks and the three training models: A comparison of three models of low vision reading training on reading efficiency. *Visual Impairment Research, 6,* 135–152.

Guez, J. E., Le Gargasson, J. F., Rigaudiere, F., & O'Regan, J. K. (1993). Is there a systematic location for the pseudo-fovea in patients with central scotoma? *Vision Research, 33*(9), 1271–1279.

Harper, R., Doorduyn, K., Reeves, B., & Slater, L. (1999). Evaluating the outcomes of low vision rehabilitation. *Ophthalmic and Physiological Optics, 19*(1), 3–11.

Hirschberg, J. (1885) Uber die messung, des schieldgrades und die Dosierung des schieloperation, zentrabl. *Prakt. Augenheilkd, 8,* 325

Krischer, C. C., Stein-Arsic, M., Meissen, R., & Zihl, J. (1985). Visual performance and reading capacity of partially sighted persons in a rehabilitation center. *American Journal of Optometry and Physiological Optics, 62*(1), 52–58.

MacKeben, M. (2002). Kinesthetic feedback enhances self-exploration of the visual field while learning eccentric viewing. Paper presented at *Vision,* July 23, Goteborg, Sweden. International Society for Low Vision Research and Rehabilitation,

MacKeben, M., & Colenbrander, A. (1999). Topographic measurement of low contrast letter recognition as a tool for diagnosis and visual rehabilitation. Paper presented at *Vision,* 1999, New York. International Society for Low Vision Research and Rehabilitation.

Massof, R. W. (1995). A systems model for low vision rehabilitation. I. Basic concepts. *Optometry and Vision Science: Official publication of the American Academy of Optometry, 72*(10), 725–736.

Massof, R. W. (1998). A systems model for low vision rehabilitation. II. Measurement of vision disabilities. *Optometry and Vision Science: Official publication of the American Academy of Optometry, 75*(5), 349–373.

Nguyen, T. H., Stievenart, J. L., Saucet, J. C., Le Gargasson, J. F., Cohen, Y. S., Pelegrini-Issac, M., et al. (2004a). Cortical response in age-related macular degeneration. Part I. Methodology and subject specificities. *Journal Français d'Ophtalmologie, 27*(9,Pt 2), 3S65–71.

Nguyen, T. H., Stievenart, J. L., Saucet, J. C., Le Gargasson, J. F., Cohen, Y. S., Pelegrini-Issac, M., et al. (2004b). Cortical response in age-related macular degeneration. Part II. Methodology and subject specificities. *Journal Français d'Ophtalmologie, 27*(9,Pt 2), 3S72–86.

Nilsson, S. E., & Nilsson, U. L. (1994). Educational training in the use of aids and residual vision is essential in rehabilitation of patients with severe age-related macular degeneration. I. Principles and methods. *Conference on Low Vision: Research and New Developments in Rehabilitation.* e. a. A.C. Kooijman. Groningen, The Netherlands, IOS Press: 147–150.

Nilsson, U. L., Frennesson, C., & Nilsson, S. E. (1998). Location and stability of a newly established eccentric retinal locus suitable for reading, achieved through training of patients with a dense central scotoma. *Optometry and Vision Science: Official publication of the American Academy of Optometry, 75*(12), 873–878.

Nilsson, U. L., Frennesson, C., & Nilsson, S. E. (2003). Patients with AMD and a large absolute central scotoma can be trained successfully to use eccentric viewing, as demonstrated in a scanning laser ophthalmoscope. *Vision Research, 43*(16), 1777–1787.

Nilsson, U. L., & Nilsson, S. E. (1986). Rehabilitation of the visually handicapped with advanced macular degeneration. A follow-up study at the Low Vision Clinic, Department of Ophthalmology, University of Linkoping. *Documenta Ophthalmologica. Advances in Ophthalmology, 62*(4), 345–367.

Polat, U., Ma-Naim, T., Belkin, M., & Sagi, D. (2004). Improving vision in adult amblyopia by perceptual learning. *Proceedings of the National Academy of Sciences, 101*(17), 6692–6697.

Reeves, B. C., Harper, R. A., & Russell, W. B. (2004). Enhanced low vision rehabilitation for people with age related macular degeneration: a randomised controlled trial. *The British Journal of Ophthalmology, 88*(11), 1443–1449.

Simmers, A. J., & Gray, L. S. (1999). Improvement of visual function in an adult amblyope. *Optometry and Vision Science: Official publication of the American Academy of Optometry, 76*(2), 82–87.

Sober, S. J., & Sabes, P. N. (2005). Flexible strategies for sensory integration during motor planning. *Nature Neuroscience, 8*(4), 490–497.

Stevenson, M. R., Hart, P. M., Montomery, A. M., McCulloch, D. W., & Chakravarthy, U. (2004). Reduced vision in older adults with age related macular degeneration interferes with ability to care for self and impairs role as carer. *The British Journal of Ophthalmology, 88*(9), 1125–1130.

Tejeria, L., Harper, R. A., Artes, P. H., & Dickinson, C. M. (2002). Face recognition in age related macular degeneration: perceived disability, measured disability, and performance with a bioptic device. *The British Journal of Ophthalmology, 86*(9), 1019–1026.

Vingerling, J. R., Hofman, A., Grobbe, D. E., & de Jong, P. T. (1996). Age-related macular degeneration and smoking: The Rotterdam study. *Archives of Ophthalmology, 114*(10), 1193–1196.

Watson, G. R., De l'Aune, W., Long, S., Maino, J., & Stelmack, J. (1997). Veterans' use of low vision devices for reading. *Optometry and Vision Science: Official publication of the American Academy of Optometry, 74*(5), 260–265.

Author Index

Page numbers in roman refer to citations in the text. Numbers in *italics* refer to the reference lists at the end of each chapter.

Subject Index

Posterior STG, 50, 52, 53
Posterior superior parietal cortex, mental
    rotation process and, 249
Precuneus, 74
Preferred retinal locus, 211
Prefrontal cortex, auditory belt projections
    to, 50
Pressure, 191, 192
Primary V1 area, 57, 73
Print size, 212, 213, 218
Project ACTION, 316
Prosthesis that substitutes vision with audition
    (PSVA), 70–73
Prosthetic devices, 34–35, 70–73
    neural plasticity and, 145–146
    visual, 34, 57
    visual illusions using, 78–79
Pseudophone, 18
PSVA. *See* Prosthesis that substitutes vision
    with audition
Psychomotor skills, Braille reading and, 295
Psychophysics, 160
Pulvinar, 59

R

Raised line pictures/drawings, 303
Reaching, auditory information and, 369–370,
    374–375
Reading
    difficulty of using peripheral vision for,
        210–214
    training peripheral vision for, 209–224, 382,
        384–387
Reality, touch as harbinger of, 259–261,
    276–277
Redundancy gain, in haptic object recognition,
    195–196
Redundancy withdrawal, 196
Redundant information, 204
Regional brain glucose metabolism, 68–69
Rehabilitation
    for individuals with age-related macular
        degeneration, 381–388
    motivation and, 387–388
    patient age and, 145
    plasticity and, 34–36, 128–129, 144–146
Rehabilitation Act (1973), Section 502, 314
Relative scotomas, 382
Research, use-oriented, 4–5

Restorative surgery, 14–19
    neural plasticity and, 145–146
    perceptual experiences following,
        139–143
Retinal image, functional significance of
    inversion of, 16–17
Retinal lesions, filling in, 133
Retinal locus, training, 382, 383, 384–385
Return curbs, 344
Reverse-occlusion studies, 44
*Revised Draft Guidelines for Accessible Rights-of-
    Way*, 329–330
Rotations, spatial orientation and, 229–230,
    235, 247, 248–250
Rote learning, 159
Roundabout intersections, 339–349

S

SC. *See* Superior colliculus
Scale, touch and, 267
Scotomas
    adopting preferred retinal locus, 211
    reading and, 209–214
    relative, 382
Sculpting, nonvisual, 304–307
Semantic word processing, 93
Senses
    compensating for missing, 128–135
    dominance relations between, 260,
        264–265, 276
    intermodal transfer between, 14–15
    intersensory conflict between, 263–268
    neural basis of compensating for missing,
        131–135
    perceptual judgment making and, 260
Sensory bandwidth, 157
Sensory deprivation, 127–146
    age of deprivation, 127
    compensating for missing sense, 128–135
    cross-modal plasticity and, 136–138
    rehabilitation and age of, 144
    rehabilitation implications of, 144–146
    role of experience in maintaining sensory
        function, 139–144
Sensory integration, 9
Sensory pathways
    plasticity between, 102–103
    plasticity within, 101–102
Sensory processing, multimodal, 37